Orlan boy

SUPPORTING SAINTS:

Life Stories of Nineteenth-Century Mormons

PUBLICATIONS IN THE COMPANION
RELIGIOUS STUDIES CENTER MONOGRAPH SERIES

SUPPORTING SAINTS:

Life Stories of Nineteenth-Century Mormons

Edited with an Introduction by
Donald Q. Cannon and David J. Whittaker

With a Foreword by
Larry C. Porter

Volume One
in the Religious Studies Center
Specialized Monograph Series

Religious Studies Center
Brigham Young University
Provo, Utah

Library of Congress Catalog Card Number: 84-71425
ISBN 0-88494-565-0

First Printing, 1985

Produced and Distributed by
BOOKCRAFT, INC.
Salt Lake City, Utah

Printed in the United States of America

To our supporting saints:

JoAnne M. Cannon

Linda S. Whittaker

Contents

Foreword

This volume constitutes the inaugural work of a second series of publications from the Brigham Young University Religious Studies Center. Heretofore, most of the volumes produced by the Center were generated as a direct result of special symposia sponsored by the directors. Papers from future symposia will continue to be published in the original series; however, there has been a recognized need for a more versatile publication which would allow the presentation of a greater diversity of materials in the respective areas of study embraced by the Center. It is felt that this first volume in the second series typifies the expressed need for such an outlet and is representative of the excellence of scholarship which is the trademark of the Religious Studies Center.

In their masterful work, *Supporting Saints: Life Stories of Nineteenth-Century Mormons,* Donald Q. Cannon and David J. Whittaker have amassed not only a corps of uniquely capable historians and writers, but they have also been particularly careful in their selection of those individuals possessing an expertise on the lives of Saints whose biographies represented the primary theme "Supporting Saints." The Saints so categorized in this volume were, for the most part, in the second echelon. This stylization has placed them in the position of those Latter-day Saints who gave of their energies at a Church level once removed from certain of their contemporaries who, because of their assigned stations, have often received the greater recognition through the years. The figures identified as "Supporting Saints" are drawn from the sometimes nameless ranks of those individuals who were very literally the spokes which made the greater wheel of Zion go around. Though capable leaders themselves, they followed the direction of their leaders and in the process distinguished themselves within their particular spheres of influence.

A study of the intricacies of the combined lives of the individuals named herein will provide an invaluable index to many historical elements of the past and at the same time introduce the reader to an important dimension of the faith exhibited by these Saints as they helped facilitate the building of the kingdom.

LARRY C. PORTER

Introduction

This volume had its genesis in a discussion between the editors in May 1978. Many subsequent conversations with our colleagues convinced us that this project was worth pursuing.

Through the essays in this volume we hope to accomplish several purposes. Above all, the essays testify of the rich heritage that Latter-day Saints have in the diverse and insightful lives of their forefathers and foremothers. In this sense, each of the essays tells us of the service, devotion, talent, sacrifice, and love that permeated the lives of early members of The Church of Jesus Christ of Latter-day Saints.

A second objective has been to show writers of Latter-day Saint biography the valuable insights that can be gained by taking as subjects for biographies individuals who were not directly in the limelight of Church history. We have come to believe that Mormon biography suffers from the same focus that has plagued the writing of American history: the presidential synthesis. Too often our biographical efforts have concentrated on those who have held center stage in our history—those who were Presidents, prophets, and Apostles. While we do not wish to suggest that the lives of such key Church leaders are any less important, we do believe that those of the "middle wagon," in J. Reuben Clark's words, played important roles in the drama of the Latter-day Saints. Hence, our title, *Supporting Saints*.

We have attempted to select authors and subjects that would give a broad view of the nineteenth-century Latter-day Saint experience. It is our hope that these essays will enlarge the window through which our heritage can be seen. We hope these sketches will help us "remember" our past.

In the first essay, coeditor David J. Whittaker provides an introduction to the subject of biography, giving particular attention to the historical context of Mormon biography. The essay is descriptive as well as prescriptive.

Then follow the thirteen biographical essays. As indicated previously, care has been taken to select men and women of the nineteenth century who were generally behind-the-scenes figures, supporting Saints in both their allegiance to the leaders of the Church and in their secondary roles. While they share these features, each is distinctive in his or her own way. Among these four women and nine men are architects, business people, miners, farmers, schoolteachers, boardinghouse proprietors, politicians, and writers. There are also polygamists (men and women), missionaries, a General Authority, stake presidents, bishops, and Relief Society presidents.

Ronald W. Walker's essay on the mother of Heber J. Grant is the first essay. Written for this volume but previously published in *Dialogue: A Journal of Mormon Thought,* this essay tells us of the different, even tragic, life of Rachel Ivins Grant. Her life is evidence that many nineteenth-century women indeed had a hard life. Her courage and dignity in the face of such hardship are certainly worthy of our admiration. Her legacy, through her son, Heber J. Grant, continues to influence the Church.

William Howells, the first LDS missionary to France, is the subject of the second essay. Ronald D. Dennis, with his skills in William Howells's native Welsh language, has been able to interpret the feelings and experiences of this interesting man. The trials and problems of early missionary work are graphically portrayed here. We catch a glimpse of what it was really like to open a mission in Europe in the nineteenth century.

The third essay treats Andrew Jenson. In this essay Keith W. Perkins writes about the dedicated historical career of this Scandinavian immigrant. Having learned by hard experience that farming was not his natural vocation, Andrew Jenson turned to collecting sources on and writing about Church history. In 1889 he began visiting the stakes of the Church, collecting local history and journals. At first his work was done entirely on his own, but eventually the Church helped when he became Assistant Church Historian. His work on the Journal History, *Church Chronology, Encyclopedic History of the*

Church, and *LDS Biographical Encyclopedia* produced a treasure trove of historical information still widely used by students of Church history.

Lavina Fielding Anderson in the fourth essay explains the life and times of Martha Cragun Cox. Martha Cox left behind a three-hundred-page autobiography which skillfully tells the story of her life and her struggle. Her journal and, in turn, this essay tell of her polygamous marriage and of her sixty-year career as a schoolteacher in Utah, Arizona, Nevada, and Mexico.

The fifth biographical essay explains the career of Mormon architect Truman Angell, who left an enduring monument in the Salt Lake Temple. Paul Anderson, himself an architect associated with the Arts and Sites Division of the LDS Historical Department, examines the conversion, Church career, personal life, and architectural work of this fascinating but relatively unknown figure from nineteenth-century LDS history.

In the sixth essay, coeditor David Whittaker deals with an obscure but significant aspect of the life of Richard Ballantyne. While many Latter-day Saints recognize Ballantyne as the founder of the Church's Sunday School, few are familiar with his work as a missionary in India. In this detailed article, the author presents the work of Ballantyne as a "publishing missionary," an aspect of missionary work which has yet to be fully studied and understood.

The seventh essay, by Thomas E. (Ted) Lyon, presents a portrait of John Lyon, a Scottish convert and prolific poet. By presenting a biographical sketch interwoven with the poetry born of a fruitful life of service, Ted Lyon shows how one man tried to capture the meaning of the restored gospel in aesthetic form. Ted Lyon is currently at work on a full-scale biography of John Lyon, and, no doubt, his appreciation for his work is enhanced by the fact that the subject of his study is his great-grandfather.

In the eighth essay, Chad J. Flake describes the frontier life of his ancestor Lucy Hannah White Flake. Her diaries reveal the story of a woman who experienced heartache and problems as she lived the life of a polygamous wife struggling to colonize the Arizona frontier. Her accounts of the death of several of her children forcefully display the harsh life many pioneers faced.

The ninth essay is D. Gene Pace's study of Elijah Sheets. Serving the longest tenure of any bishop in the history of the Church, Elijah Sheets was bishop of the Salt Lake Eighth Ward for almost fifty years. In this interesting essay, Pace considers Sheets's attempt to promote unity in his ward, his use of teachers to visit ward members, and his attitudes regarding social welfare. Through this study we can gain considerable insight into the office of ward bishop in the late nineteenth century.

William G. Hartley's study of Edward Hunter constitutes the tenth essay. Although he was a General Authority, Bishop Hunter is relatively unknown. Hartley's treatment of Bishop Hunter tells us much about this man's life as well as the relatively new office of Presiding Bishop. Under Hunter's direction, the office grew in importance and influence and assumed greater responsibility for temporal affairs in the kingdom.

The eleventh essay concerns the life of Emmeline B. Wells. This study by Carol C. Madsen skillfully and gracefully describes the challenging life of this nineteenth-century LDS woman. Emmeline's life included, in the words of the author, "disappointment, disillusionment, and even despair." In examining the career of this female writer and editor, the essay helps us understand the nature of Mormon women's concerns. Emmeline Wells served for thirty-seven years as editor of the *Woman's Exponent,* one of the great literary efforts of the Restoration.

James R. Christianson's essay on Jacob Spori is the twelfth subject in this book on "Supporting Saints." Jacob Spori was a convert to the Church in Switzerland. After some years of Church service in Europe, he immigrated to Utah. Five years later Jacob returned to his native Switzerland whence he served a very difficult mission to Constantinople. In later years Spori and his family moved to Idaho, where he was influential in Church education.

Angus M. Cannon is the subject of the final essay, written by Donald Q. Cannon. Emphasis in this study is on Angus's Church career, especially his role as stake president of the Salt Lake Stake for twenty-eight years, from 1876–1904. His experience as stake president tells us much about the nature of the Church and, particularly, the role of stake presidents in the last quarter of the nineteenth century. The author, a great-grandson of Angus M. Cannon, draws heavily upon the subject's large collection of letters, diaries, and business papers.

We are grateful to many people. In reality, as editors, we have only provided a forum for each of those who contributed to this volume. In this sense, this volume is really theirs. We express thanks to them for working with us during the months and years it took to assemble this volume.

We express thanks to Larry C. Porter for his continued support and encouragement for this project. His enthusiasm, together with the approval of those who direct the Religious Studies Center at Brigham Young University, has made this task an easy burden to bear.

For expert editorial help, we are grateful for the services of Linda Hunter Adams and Don E. Norton. We acknowledge the editorial assistance of numerous students in the BYU Humanities Publication Center. We also appreciate the fine work done by the secretaries in Religious Education at Brigham Young University, who typed several drafts of each of the essays in this volume.

Finally, we are grateful to our families, who lived with this project and with the subjects of the essays for these past years. They too are supporting saints.

DONALD Q. CANNON

DAVID J. WHITTAKER

David J. Whittaker

The Heritage and Tasks
of Mormon Biography

A native of California, David J. Whittaker now resides with
his wife and four children in Provo, Utah. His current
position is University Archivist and Archivist of the Mormon
Experience at Brigham Young University. He received his
B.A. from Brigham Young University and his M.A. from
California State University at Northridge. He received his
Ph.D. from Brigham Young University. He has published
widely in Church periodicals and professional journals.

The historian," wrote Eugen Rosenstock-Huessy of Columbia
University, "is the physician of memory."[1] Yosef Hayim
Yerushalmi, also of Columbia University, has suggested that it
would be more accurate to call the historian a pathologist of
memory, pointing out that the collective memory of any group
does not depend entirely on the work of historians.[2] But we
cannot ignore the potential that written history and biography
have for helping us all to claim and relate to a common heritage, a claim that seems to be directly related to the establishment of our individual and group identities.

The Hebrew word for memory is *zakhor,* and its use in
ancient Israel implied that not everything is worth remember-

ing. But it also implied that to forget that which is worth remembering is a dangerous thing. Moses commanded the Israelites to "remember" what great things the Lord had done in delivering them from the captivity of Egypt (e.g., Deuteronomy 32:7–47). Alma, a record keeper in the Book of Mormon, justified his efforts at record keeping by saying that "it has hitherto been wisdom in God that these things should be preserved; for behold, they have enlarged the memory of this people, yea, and convinced many of the error of their ways, and brought them to the knowledge of their God unto the salvation of their souls" (Alma 37:8). Thus, the prophets and record keepers in ancient Israel and in the Book of Mormon taught that "to remember" was a critically important part of the religious life of both the group and of the individuals composing the group.

As was ancient Israel's theology, Mormonism is grounded in specific historical events. Joseph Smith's first vision and the visits of such individuals as Moroni, Peter, James and John, and Elijah to early leaders are for Mormons what the events leading to the Exodus were for Israel. And, like ancient Israel, Mormons have not been entirely dependent upon historians to help them relate to or become part of this heritage. For it is primarily through recital and ritual that both groups relate to a common heritage of sacred events.[3] Thus, it was in covenant-making experiences that each person was tied into the larger scheme of things and given a set of values to assist in the task of deciding what was worth "remembering." For both groups, the keeping of records and the remembering of the past is a central part of their religious life. For both, to forget is a form of apostasy, and to be removed from the records of the group is true banishment because it means one is literally cut off from the source of one's identity.

On 6 April 1830, the day The Church of Jesus Christ of Latter-day Saints was organized, Joseph Smith received a revelation for those gathered for the occasion. It commanded that a record be kept of the activities of the group (see D&C 21:1). In time a specific individual was assigned to oversee this task. By

1831 the assignment had transferred to John Whitmer who was specifically told to "write and keep a regular history" (D&C 47:1). Later that same year, John Whitmer was told that he should continue "writing and making a history of all the important things which he shall observe and know concerning my church" and further that he should travel among the various branches of the Church "that he may the more easily obtain knowledge—Preaching and expounding, writing, copying, selecting, and obtaining all things which shall be for the good of the church, and for the rising generations that shall grow up on the land of Zion" (D&C 69:3, 7–8). About one year later, Joseph Smith wrote to William W. Phelps in Missouri, specifically counseling that the duty of the clerk in the Church was "to keep a history, and a general church record of all things that transpire in Zion, and of all those who consecrate properties, . . . their manner of life, their faith, and works" (D&C 85:1–2).

Thus, from the beginning in 1830, a variety of records, both institutional and personal, have been kept—works that both encouraged and edified members.[4] In fact, the major historical record-keeping project during the Prophet's lifetime, the "History of Joseph Smith," was a blend of both biography and institutional history. In many ways, it became a model for other similar works in Mormonism. While not constituting Joseph Smith's personal diary, the "History" did gain its focus by placing Joseph at the center, occasionally citing from his personal diaries and then surrounding these quotes with various documents generated by the Church over which he presided. Throughout the work, there was a marriage of history and biography, although the institutional history of the group was the major focus.[5]

Mormon biography has continued to be a blend of biography and institutional history. Emphasis on the latter has generally forced the former into a secondary role. The reasons for this lie, in part, in the emphasis on group memory wherein the interests and experiences of the community are primary and those of the individual are secondary. Thus, with the exception of a few individuals (usually the prophets and Apostles of the Church), most of Mormon biography has not focused on the common members. But at least one other reason can account for this emphasis—the influence that biography in western culture in general has exerted on Mormon writing. Much of what we expect of biography comes from both sacred and secular traditions. Biography in western culture has looked to both the scriptures and to secular sources as models for writing the lives of its heroes and villains, its saints, and its devils.

The model for secular biography was firmly established by Plutarch, a man whom many consider to be the father of classical biography.[6] In his *Paralleled Lives of Noble Greeks and Romans,* he provided the biographies of forty-six statesmen, rulers, and heroes. They were men of action who held important positions within their communities. Plutarch, as one scholar has noted, emphasized their positions rather than their personalities.[7] Biographies written by Tacitus and Suetonius continued this tradition by looking at the leaders of Roman society.

Plutarch's influence declined after his own time (until the Renaissance), but his biographical model was felt. However, as the leaders of society were more and more religious personalities, biography tended to move more from secular to religious models and subjects. Thus, biographies of bishops, saints, and martyrs became the main fare for writers. Here, too, the facts became less important than the moral lessons that the life of a given person could teach. In the extreme, the stories sounded the same as the biographies became standardized. There was apparently only one way a writer could portray a saint! By the fifteenth century, because the moral emphasis of the Middle Ages was firmly established, most biographies "sought by eloquence to teach men virtue and to stimulate them to right conduct."[8] Throughout these developments, the *position* of a given individual was more important than the various real dimensions of his life. From this emphasis on position developed the "gesta," a work which described the lives of certain officeholders.[9] The product was an institutional biography, not the biography of a distinct individual.

It was not until the Renaissance, with its rediscovery of classical literature, that biographers began to emphasize individuals as the proper subjects for biography.[10] The earlier models did not disappear, however, and biography has been a mix of classical, medieval, and more modern approaches ever since.

In addition to classical biography, another important influence on our understanding of biography has been English biography and its Puritan derivatives. English biography reached its greatest heights in the publication of James Boswell's *Life of Samuel Johnson* (1791), a height that some argue has never been equaled. Johnson, himself, was an ideal subject, keeping a good account of his life and thinking about the craft of biography in ways that sound very modern. Consider his comments published in 1750:

> But biography has often been allotted to writers who seem very little acquainted with the nature of their task, or very negligent about the performance. They rarely afford any other account than might be collected from public papers, but imagine themselves writing a life when they exhibit a chronological series of actions or preferments; and so little regard the manners or behavior of their heroes, that more knowledge may be gained of a man's real character, by a short conversation with one of his servants, than from a formal and studied narrative, begun with his pedigree and ended with his funeral.[11]

Most scholars agree that Boswell's biography reveals all the major ingredients of modern biography. Boswell himself read widely, and his subject (Johnson) taught him to be truthful and to approach his task with sympathy and understanding. His larger awareness of the world of learning seems to have given him a passion for accuracy and completeness. To all of this, Boswell added his own genius.[12]

Boswell's biography was an exception, however, and most of the products of English authors fell way short of this masterpiece. Generations before Johnson, the Reformation had triggered in England a broad-based movement to reform and purify the Church of England. These Puritans looked outward at the problems of their society and inward for evidence that their lives were worthy of God's saving grace. The first Puritan biographies were a type of autobiographical explanation to themselves. American Puritans continued this approach in their histories, in which they sought to provide religious justification for their "cities upon the hill." Borrowing the concept of a "chosen people" from the Old Testament, they viewed their colonization of America in biblical terms. As God's chosen people, their histories provided modern extensions of their scripture. They saw in their institutions and personal lives the unfolding of God's intentions and designs. In a very real sense, their histories were a form of promotional literature for the folks back home in England. Works such as William Bradford's *Of Plymouth Plantation* and Cotton Mather's *Magnalia Christi Americana* explained to themselves and to others why they came to America. Thus, their histories told of personal experiences not so much to discover but to protect their identity and to justify their quest for a new Zion. Their purposes were mainly didactic, primarily to provide spiritual guides for wayward souls and to invite others to join their movement.[13]

In the hands of writers like Bradford and Mather, history became a biography in which the critical moments in Puritan society were portrayed as personal crises and social conflicts in the struggle of individual Christians with Satan.[14] Such biography tended toward *hagiography,* or the biography of saints. In this sense, these biographies had much in common with the medieval "Lives of Saints,"[15] but Puritan histories broadened their scope to include biographies of individuals other than the leaders. The existence of large numbers of Puritan autobiographies testifies to the fact that each man was his own biographer, that each person had a responsibility and accountability before God to record the workings of God in his or her life.

In time, due primarily to the influence of the Enlightenment, the Christian emphasis on supernatural causes of historical events gave way to a more secular interpretation of history based upon the concepts of human progress, reason, and material well-being. Enlightenment thinkers taught men to believe that man, by the use of his reason, could control his destiny and determine his own material and intellectual progress in this world. Newton's discovery of "natural law" did not dispense with God, but in time it seemed to make God and accompanying supernatural explanations less necessary.[16]

The implications for biographers were obvious; the Christian theory of history was gradually abandoned and replaced by a quest for natural laws as the motivating forces in human history. The major historians of the American Revolution seldom brought God into the picture, and the historians and biographers of the new American nation continued this pattern. Biographies that appeared in the early years of the new nation were patterned after Puritan models; however, the religious sense of mission was gradually replaced with a more secular view that substituted patriotism for religiosity. Biography thus told of the rise of liberty and human rights rather than the quest for the city of God, even though a Christian nation was assumed.[17]

It was into this setting that Mormonism was born. Like ancient Israel and early Christianity, Mormonism partook of a concrete existence in time and space by its claims of visitations of God and angels at specific times and specific places. These claims gave the movement a historical substance that encouraged followers to record their own place in the unfolding of the Restoration.

As in Puritanism, the first records of Mormonism were journals and autobiographies—records, on the whole, of private experiences and divine happenings.[18] Most early members were too busy to be very introspective, and thus the first attempts at biography were mostly tied into the early events of their institutional history. Thus, the first efforts at biography combined both history and autobiography. This can be seen in the first letters from missionaries in the field, many of which were published in early Mormon newspapers, as well as in the defensive histories of the Missouri persecutions. Almost unconsciously, however, these reports contained as much about themselves as about the Church they were representing.[19]

This combination of history and autobiography is also evident in the first real biography to appear in the Church: Lucy Mack Smith's *Biographical Sketches of Joseph Smith the Prophet and His Progenitors for Many Generations* (1853). Like the Book of Mormon, this work was the history of an extended family. It told of the faith, dreams, and experiences of the Macks and the Smiths on the New England frontier. Its narrative depended on family records and personal observation, given focus by a strong sense of calling which came to rest on the experiences and visions of Joseph Smith, Jr. In this volume, too, the family's story is eventually subordinated to the emerging institution of the church Joseph founded. Throughout the pages of this volume, Lucy weaves the threads of her own experience with those of the Smith and the Mack families and of Joseph Smith, Jr., into a richly textured cloth that traces the emergence of the institution her family anticipated and played such a prominent role in establishing. To read this family history is to share the pride of the first Mormon matriarch.[20]

This pride in history and family permeates other early attempts at Mormon biography. For example, the overriding principle of the numerous biographical sketches that were published by Andrew Jenson, Orson F. Whitney, and Frank Esshom is a strong veneration of forebears.[21] But all of these biographical collections also shared the traits of the "mug book" type of biography that was being produced in America during and after the centennial celebration of 1876.[22] While the collections of biographies contain the "essentials" of numerous lives, they also show the flaws of other similar works of the late nineteenth century. For one thing, they read more like eulogies than biographies. Seldom do the sketches move beyond chronological summary; almost all the portraits are flat, one-dimensional views; seldom are women included; and, for the most part, the decision to include anyone was based almost entirely on administrative considerations. Thus, most of the sketches emphasize career rather than character.

Because the focus was ecclesiastical and bureaucratic, individuality was almost always subordinated to hierarchic considerations. For the most part, Mormon biography has maintained this emphasis to the present day.

However, there were signs of an emerging, more mature, biography in Mormonism by the 1870s. Edward Tullidge's biographies—*Joseph Smith* (1878) and *Brigham Young* (1876)—show strong evidence of an emerging craft. While these works could combine hero worship and hatred, their contents reveal an immigrant convert's attempt to understand his new religion as well as his new homeland. His biographical sketches in other more topical histories are also worth reading, even though his emphasis was institutional and political.[23] Much of the same could be said about T. B. H. Stenhouse, whose *Rocky Mountain Saints* (1873), in spite of its critical stance against Brigham Young, did try to let his subjects speak for themselves.[24]

At another extreme was George Q. Cannon's biography of Joseph Smith (1888), parts of which were actually written by his son, Frank Cannon.[25] Its intended audience was the youth of the Church; thus, the tone and content of the volume were very laudatory and the authors made little attempt to probe beneath the surface of the Prophet's life.

Even B. H. Roberts's *Life of John Taylor* (1892) bordered on eulogistic biography.[26] Roberts's research and access to Taylor's journals and family papers remind us that he did his homework. But the final product, appearing as it did in an age of active anti-Mormonism, was much less of an accomplishment than would have been possible in a less defensive atmosphere.

Early twentieth-century Mormon biographers were generally unable to surpass the limitations of earlier works. But works by authors like Matthias F. Cowley, John Henry Evans, Edward Anderson, and Bryant S. Hinckley do suggest several things.[27] First, there was a growing market, hence a larger audience, within Mormonism for biographical works. Second, they show that even the non-Mormon publishing houses could be convinced that Mormon subjects were salable. Finally, they reveal that biography is a viable channel for historical study.

The appearance in 1945 of Fawn Brodie's biography of Joseph Smith was something of a watershed in Mormon biography. For many it represented the biographical craft at its worst: a secular portrait of a religious man. While some continue to praise this study as a valid explanation of the Prophet in naturalistic terms, Mormon scholars have suggested that, while students of early Mormonism do not have to believe Joseph's claims to revelations, they do have to believe that *Joseph* believed they were real.[28] Thus, Brodie's biography, whatever its historical and literary merits, has served to raise important questions in Mormon scholarship. In addition to setting an agenda for a new generation of studies on Mormons, it revealed the extremes of secular scholarship growing incapable of treating religious experience in any other than naturalistic terms.[29]

Juanita Brooks was the first to demonstrate how both accurate historical research and a keen sense of the spiritual dimension of an individual could be combined to create a great biography. Her study of John Doyle Lee, with its honesty, its pathos, and its vividness, shows what can be done, and continues to serve as a model for the craft of LDS biography.[30]

Unfortunately, few biographies since Brooks's have ventured beyond the limiting format of chronology and systematic moralizing. Those biographies which have tried to transcend these more cardboard-type portraits have been noted in recent essays.[31] A sampling would include Truman G. Madsen's *Defender of the Faith: The B. H. Roberts Story* (1980), Leonard J. Arrington's *Charles C. Rich* (1974) and *Edwin D. Woolley* (1976), Edward and Andrew Kimball's *Spencer W. Kimball* (1977), Andrew Karl Larson's *Erastus Snow* (1971), D. Michael Quinn's *J. Reuben Clark: The Church Years* (1983), and Stanley B. Kimball's *Heber C. Kimball* (1981).[32]

All of these works constitute good biography because their authors tried to get at the truth by conquering the documents and milieu of their subjects' lives. Each author knew there was no substitute for hard work, much time, and deep thought. They portray the careers *and* character of their subjects in their own way. Each author seems to have caught the spirit of the counsel that Marion G. Romney, First Counselor in the First Presidency of the Church, gave to the biographers of J. Reuben Clark.

> Any biographer of President Clark must write the truth about him. To tell more or less than the truth would violate a governing principle in his life. When I first met with those who are writing his biography, I explained that I did not want them to produce a mere collection of uplifting experiences about President Clark . . . nor did I want a detailed defense of his beliefs. I wanted a biography of the man himself, as he was, written with the same kind of courage, honesty, and frankness that J. Reuben Clark himself would have shown. An account of his life should tell of his decisions and indecisions, sorrows and joys, regrets and aspirations, reverses, and accomplishments, and, above all, his constant striving.[33]

André Maurois, one of the successful writers of biography in the twentieth century, observed years ago that the responsibilities of the biographer include being both a historian and a portrait painter. "An honest biographer," he wrote, "should sit in front of his documents as an honest painter sits in front of his model, thinking only: 'What do I see, and which is the best way to convey my vision to others?' " As historian, the biographer seeks for truth; as portrait painter, he seeks for beauty, or at least an artistic rendition of the subject being represented by his work.[34]

Mormon biography has suffered from an imbalance of these two main ingredients. While good biography is a craft, much of Mormon biography has not yet attained the delicate balance between life as history and life as art. We lack what Virginia Woolf calls the "creative facts" which the biographer must use *after* he has conquered the known documents.[35] Unlike the novelist who can ignore the facts, the biographer must not ignore the historical truth about his subject. But the biographer must do more than simply give us more "facts" about an individual; he must give us an increased sense of recognition of our own life and the world in which we live. It is in this ability that the biographer can combine the facts of history and the truths of life.[36]

Throughout our history, biography has served to enlighten, enrich, and encourage us. A good biography always leaves us edified and educated. It also is a celebration of individuality—of the freedom of choice—which reminds each of us that the choices we make reaffirm our own uniqueness, our eternal self-worth, that which makes us truly sons and daughters of God.

Notes

1. Yosef Hayim Yerushalmi, *Zakhor, Jewish History and Jewish Memory* (Seattle: University of Washington Press, 1982), pp. 93, 94.

2. Ibid. The distinction here is between one who cures or heals and one who diagnoses.

3. See David J. Whittaker, "A Covenant People," *The Seventh Annual Sidney B. Sperry Symposium Papers,* 27 January 1979 (Provo: BYU Press for the Church Educational System, 1979), pp. 196–216.

4. For an overview of Mormon historical writing, see David J. Whittaker, "Historians and the Mormon Experience: A Sesquicentennial Perspective," *The Eighth Annual Sidney B. Sperry Symposium Papers,* 26 January 1980 (Provo: BYU Press for the Church Educational System, 1980), pp. 293–327.

5. On this history, see Dean C. Jessee, "The Writing of Joseph Smith's History," *Brigham Young University Studies* 11 (Summer 1971): 439–73; Dean C. Jessee, "The Reliability of Joseph Smith's History," *Journal of Mormon History* 3 (1976): 23–46; and Howard C. Searle, "Early Mormon Historiography: Writing the History of the Mormons, 1830–1858" (Ph.D. diss., UCLA, 1979), pp. 200–336.

6. See the short discussion in John A. Garraty, *The Nature of Biography* (New York: Alfred A. Knopf, 1957), pp. 45–49.

7. Ibid., p. 46.

8. D. J. Wilcox, *The Development of Florentine Humanist Historiography in the Fifteenth Century* (Cambridge, Mass.: Harvard University Press, 1969), p. 29, as cited in Maurice Kenn, "Chivalry, Heralds, and

History," in *The Writing of History in the Middle Ages,* ed. R. H. C. Davis and J. M. Wallace-Hadrill (Oxford: Clarendon Press, 1981), p. 393.

9. Ernst Breisach, *Historiography, Ancient, Medieval and Modern* (Chicago: University of Chicago Press, 1983), p. 100.

10. See Garraty, *Nature of Biography,* p. 63f; Richard Daniel Altick, *Lives and Letters: A History of Literary Biography in England and America* (New York: Alfred A. Knopf, 1966), pp. 9–45; and Myron P. Gilmore, *The World of Humanism, 1453–1517* (New York: Harper and Brothers Publishers, 1952), pp. 201–3.

11. Samuel Johnson, "The Usefulness of Biography" (1750), in *Biography and Truth,* ed. Stanley Weintraub (Indianapolis: Bobbs-Merrill Co., 1967), p. 16.

12. This is Garraty's evaluation (Garraty, *Nature of Biography,* p. 94). See also the Introductory Essay by Pat Rogers in the World's Classic edition of the *Life of Johnson* (Oxford: Oxford University Press, 1980).

13. There has been a great amount written on the Puritans; good introductions to their historical attitudes and biographies are found in Peter Gay, *A Loss of Mastery, Puritan Historians in Colonial America* (New York: Random House, Vintage Books, 1968); Kenneth Murdock, "Clio in the Wilderness: History and Biography in Puritan New England," *Church History* 24 (Sept. 1955): 221–38; Peter A. Smith, "Politics and Sainthood: Biography by Cotton Mather," *William and Mary Quarterly,* ser. 3d, 20 (Apr. 1963): 186–206; and Cecelia Tichi, "Spiritual Biography and the 'Lords Remembrancers,' " *William and Mary Quarterly,* ser. 3d, 28 (Jan. 1971): 64–85. I have drawn on all these works.

14. Peter Gay, *Loss of Mastery,* p. 62.

15. On the medieval *Lives* of Saints, see Altick, *Lives and Letters,* pp. 5–7; Donald A. Stauffer, *English Biography before 1700* (Cambridge, England: University Press, 1930), pp. 4–22; and Waldo H. Dunn, *English Biography* (New York: E. P. Dutton & Co., 1916), pp. 1–45.

16. A good summary of the transition to Enlightenment thought is found in Ronald N. Stromberg, *An Intellectual History of Modern Europe,* 2d ed. (Englewood Cliffs, N. J.: Prentice-Hall, 1975), pp. 1–195. See also John E. Van De Weterung, "God, Science, and the Puritan Dilemma," *New England Quarterly* 38 (Dec. 1965): 494–507; Joseph J. Ellis, *The New England Mind in Transition: Samuel Johnson of Connecticut, 1696–1772* (New Haven, Conn.: Yale University Press, 1973); and Henry F. May, *The Enlightenment in America* (New York: Oxford University Press, 1976).

17. This is shown in Bert James Loewenberg, *American History in American Thought: Christopher Columbus to Henry Adams* (New York: Simon and Schuster, Touchstone Book, 1973), pp. 184–308; Lester H. Cohen, *The Revolutionary Histories: Contemporary Narratives of the American Revolution* (Ithaca, N. Y.: Cornell University Press, 1980), pp. 86–106; and in George H. Callcott, *History in the United States,*

1800–1860: Its Practice and Purpose (Baltimore: Johns Hopkins Press, 1970), pp. 151–73.

18. See, for example, Lucy Mack Smith, *Biographical Sketches of Joseph Smith, the Prophet, and His Progenitors for Many Generations* (Liverpool: Published by S. W. Richards, 1853); and *The Autobiography of Parley Parker Pratt,* ed. Parley P. Pratt, Jr. (New York: Russell Brothers, 1874).

19. See, for example, *Journal of Heber C. Kimball* (Nauvoo, Ill.: Printed by Robinson and Smith, 1840). This was also true of the histories of the Missouri persecutions issued after 1838. See particularly Parley P. Pratt, *History of the Late Persecution* (Detroit: Dawson & Bates, Printers, 1839); John P. Greene, *Facts Relative to the Expulsion of the Mormons or Latter-day Saints, from the State of Missouri* (Cincinnati: Printed by R. P. Brooks, 1839); and Sidney Rigdon, *Appeal to the American People: Being an Account of the Persecutions* (Cincinnati: Shepard and Stearns, 1840).

20. Regarding Lucy Mack Smith's history, see Searle, "Early Mormon Historiography," pp. 358–428; Richard L. Anderson, "His Mother's Manuscript: An Intimate View of Joseph Smith" (Forum address, Brigham Young University, 27 January 1976); and Jan Shipps, "The Prophet, His Mother and Early Mormonism: Mother Smith's History as a Passageway to Understanding" (MS, 1972).

21. Andrew Jenson, *Latter-day Saint Biographical Encyclopedia,* 4 vols. (Salt Lake City: Jenson History Company, 1901–1936). Jenson first published a "Biographical Encyclopedia" as an 1888 supplement to his *Historical Record.* Orson F. Whitney, *History of Utah* (Salt Lake City: George Q. Cannon & Sons Co., 1904); volume 4 was a biographical volume. Frank E. Esshom, *Pioneers and Prominent Men of Utah* (Salt Lake City: Utah Pioneers Book Publishing Co., 1913).

22. See the comments of John Walton Caughey, *Hubert Howe Bancroft, Historian of the West* (Berkeley: University of California Press, 1946), pp. 314–29. It should be remembered that Andrew Jenson's *Historical Record* was a subscription historical/biographical periodical.

23. Edward W. Tullidge, *Life of Brigham Young or Utah and Her Founders* (New York: n.p., 1876); Edward W. Tullidge, *Life of Joseph the Prophet* (New York: n.p., 1878). See Ronald W. Walker, "Edward Tullidge: Historian of the Mormon Commonwealth," *Journal of Mormon History* 3 (1976): 55–72.

24. Thomas B. H. Stenhouse, *The Rocky Mountain Saints* (New York: D. Appleton and Co., 1873). See Ronald W. Walker, "The Stenhouses and the Making of a Mormon Image," *Journal of Mormon History* 1 (1974): 51–72.

25. George Q. Cannon, *The Life of Joseph Smith, the Prophet* (Salt Lake City: Juvenile Instructor Office, 1888).

26. B. H. Roberts, *The Life of John Taylor, Third President of The Church of Jesus Christ of Latter-day Saints* (Salt Lake City: George Q. Cannon & Sons Co., 1892).

27. Matthias F. Cowley, *Wilford Woodruff . . . History of His Life and Labors* (Salt Lake City: Deseret News, 1909); John Henry Evans, *Joseph Smith the American Prophet* (New York: Macmillan Co., 1933); John Henry Evans, *Charles Coulson Rich: Pioneer Builder of the West* (New York: Macmillan Co., 1936); John Henry Evans and Minnie Egan Anderson, *Ezra T. Benson: Pioneer-Statesman-Saint* (Salt Lake City: Deseret News Press, 1947); Edward H. Anderson, *The Life of Brigham Young* (Salt Lake City: George Q. Cannon & Sons Co., 1893); Bryant S. Hinckley, *Daniel Hamner Wells and Events of His Times* (Salt Lake City: Deseret News Press, 1942); and Bryant S. Hinckley, *Heber J. Grant: Highlights in the Life of a Great Leader* (Salt Lake City: Stevens and Wallis, 1949).

28. Fawn M. Brodie, *No Man Knows My History: The Life of Joseph Smith, the American Prophet,* 2d ed. (New York: Alfred A. Knopf, 1971). See, most recently, Marvin S. Hill, "Secular or Sectarian History? A Critique of *No Man Knows My History,*" *Church History* 43 (Mar. 1974): 78–96; and "Brodie Revisited: A Reappraisal," *Dialogue: A Journal of Mormon Thought* 7 (Winter 1972): 72–85.

29. Especially revealing are the comments of Dale Morgan in his 7 January 1946 letter to Fawn Brodie: "I don't think you fully recognize the extent to which your book was written out of an emotional compulsion, and the extent to which your compulsion persists. You are looking for something that will occupy and satisfy your emotions as Mormonism has done, and it is hardly likely that you will find such a topic or subject. Because writing Joseph's biography was your act of liberation and of exorcism" (MS in Brodie Papers, Special Collections, Marriott Library, University of Utah, Salt Lake City, Utah).

30. Juanita Brooks, *John Doyle Lee, Zealot-Pioneer Builder-Scapegoat* (Glendale: The Arthur H. Clark Co., 1962).

31. Davis Bitton, "Mormon Biography," *Biography: An Interdisciplinary Quarterly* 4 (Winter 1981): 1–16; and Ronald W. Walker, "The Challenge and Craft of Mormon Biography," *BYU Studies* 22 (Spring 1982): 179–92.

32. Truman G. Madsen, *Defender of the Faith: The B. H. Roberts Story* (Salt Lake City: Bookcraft, 1980); Leonard J. Arrington, *Charles C. Rich: Mormon General and Western Frontiersman* (Provo: BYU Press, 1974); Leonard J. Arrington, *From Quaker to Latter-day Saint: Bishop Edwin D. Woolley* (Salt Lake City: Deseret Book Co., 1976); Edward L. Kimball and Andrew E. Kimball, Jr., *Spencer W. Kimball* (Salt Lake City: Bookcraft, 1977); Andrew Karl Larson, *Erastus Snow: The Life of a Missionary and Pioneer for the Early Mormon Church* (Salt Lake City: University of Utah Press, 1971); D. Michael Quinn, *J. Reuben Clark: The Church Years* (Provo: BYU Press, 1983); Stanley B. Kimball, *Heber C. Kimball: Mormon Patriarch and Pioneer* (Urbana: University of Illinois Press, 1981).

33. See Foreword by Marion G. Romney to Frank W. Fox, *J. Reuben Clark, the Public Years* (Salt Lake City and Provo: Deseret Book Co. and BYU Press, 1980), p. xi.

34. André Maurois, "The Ethics of Biography," ed. and comp. Rudolf Kirk, et al., *English Institute of Annals, 1942* (New York: Columbia University Press, 1943), pp. 6–28. Also in Weintraub, *Biography and Truth,* pp. 44–50.

35. Virginia Woolf, "The Art of Biography," *Atlantic Monthly* 163 (1939): 506–10. See also Lewis Mumford, "The Task of Modern Biography," *English Journal* 23 (Jan. 1934): 1–9.

36. Insightful essays on biography by Mormon authors, in addition to those cited in note 31 include James B. Allen, "Writing Mormon Biographies," *World Conference on Records: Preserving Our Heritage* (Salt Lake City, 12–15 August 1980), series 116, 2:1–15; and Davis Bitton, "Family History: Therapy or Scholarship[?]," *World Conference on Records: Preserving Our Heritage,* series 109, 2:1–6. Other recommended studies for students of biography, in addition to the excellent Garraty and Altick volumes cited above, are Catherine Drinker Bowen, *Biography: The Craft and the Calling* (Boston: Little, Brown, and Co., 1968); Robert Gittings, *The Nature of Biography* (Seattle: University of Washington Press, 1978); Alan Shelston, *Biography* (London: Methuen and Co., 1977); Daniel Aaron, ed., *Studies in Biography,* Harvard English Studies, 8 (Cambridge, Mass.: Harvard University Press, 1978); Leon Edel, et al., *Telling Lives: The Biographer's Art,* ed. Marc Pachter (Washington, D.C.: New Republic Books for the Smithsonian Institution, 1979); and Edel, *Writing Lives, Principia Biographica* (New York: W. W. Norton, 1984).

Ronald W. Walker

2

Rachel R. Grant:
The Continuing Legacy
of the Feminine Ideal

Ronald W. Walker, a native of Montana, resides in Salt Lake
City with his wife and their six children. He is currently
Associate Professor in the Joseph Fielding Smith Institute for
Church History. He received his B.S. and M.A. from
Brigham Young University and his Ph.D. from the
University of Utah. Early in his career he taught in LDS
seminaries and institutes. Later, he served as a senior
historical associate with the LDS Church Historical
Department. His publications include several book reviews
and scholarly articles. For several years he has been at work
on a major biographical study of Heber J. Grant. In this
essay Walker introduces the mother of Heber J. Grant. He
skillfully and sympathetically describes the dignity and
courage which Rachel Ridgway Ivins Grant displayed in the
face of adversity.

We can imagine ourselves visiting Aunt Rachel Grant, long-
time president of the Thirteenth Ward Relief Society and one
of The Church of Jesus Christ of Latter-day Saint's "leading
ladies," at her home on Salt Lake City's Second East Street. In

This essay was written for this volume, but was previously published in
Dialogue: A Journal of Mormon Thought, 15 (Autumn 1982): 105 – 21.

the year of our visit, 1890, her two-story, plastered adobe home partakes of the prevailing feminine ideal which stresses homemaking and handicraft. The stove is highly burnished, while the arms of each chair are covered with homemade lace crocheting. A corner "whatnot" meticulously displays pictures, small framed mottoes, wax and hair flowers, and other curios. Rachel's person also reflects her times. Despite her sixty-nine years, her skin remains supple and clear. She credits her preservation to a lifetime devotion to skin hygiene—no cosmetics, no sunlight without a protecting bonnet, no dusting or sweeping without gloves.[1]

We visit Rachel Grant not wishing to find fault with her domesticity and primness nor with the other Victorian values she so fully embodies. Rather, we seek to understand her and her age—and in a sense ourselves. Aunt Rachel may not be as celebrated a feminist as her contemporaries Eliza R. Snow, Bathsheba W. Smith, or Emmeline B. Wells. But she has influenced later generations certainly as much and perhaps a great deal more. In our age which often overlooks the obvious, we forget the power which a nineteenth-century woman often wielded from her home. Rachel's only child, Heber J. Grant, with whom she enjoyed a particularly close relationship, led the Church for twenty-seven years of the twentieth century, preaching and practicing the values he had learned from her.

When we understand Rachel Grant, we will also learn something about the personality of present-day Mormonism.

II

Rachel Ridgway Ivins was born at Hornerstown, New Jersey, 7 March 1821, the sixth of eight children. She would have few memories of her parents. Caleb, her father, evidently involved himself in the family's expansive business concerns which included Hornerstown's distillery, country store, and grist and saw mills. Due to apparent sunstroke exposure, he died when Rachel was six. To compound the tragedy, Edith Ridgway Ivins, her mother, described by her contemporaries as a "lovely, spirited woman, liked by all," died just four years later.[2]

The orphan was subsequently raised by a succession of her close-knit relatives. For several years she remained at Hornerstown with Caleb, Sr., her indulgent grandfather. However, she found the stringent household of her married cousins Joshua and Theodosia Wright at Trenton more to her liking. The Wrights' home, which was set off by gardens complete with statuary and wildlife, represented no diminution in her lifestyle. Moreover, much to Rachel's delight, the house was run by cousin Theodosia with precision, industry and regularity. Under the older woman's demanding, six-year tutelage, teenage Rachel learned both personal discipline and the domestic arts. An able student, she returned to Monmouth County when she was about eighteen as a housekeeper for Richard Ridgway, her widower uncle.[3]

She must have marveled at the religious changes in her neighborhood. Like upstate New York's earlier and more famous "Burned-Over" district, central New Jersey experienced wave after wave of religious excitement during the first half of the nineteenth century, with the newfangled and despised Mormons competing with the more established Methodists, Baptists, and Presbyterians. By the late 1830s, a cadre of some of Mormonism's ablest missionaries, including Jedediah Grant, Erastus Snow, Benjamin Winchester, Wilford Woodruff, and Orson and Parley Pratt had founded a half-dozen Latter-day Saint congregations in central New Jersey, several with their own unpretentious chapels.[4]

Rachel's kin played a major role in this activity. Young Israel Ivins was the first LDS convert from Monmouth County. Merchants Charles and James Ivins soon followed. Parley Pratt described the latter as a "very wealthy man" and enrolled him, along with himself, as a committee of two to reissue the Book of Mormon in the East. But no conversion was as telling upon Rachel as that of her older sister, Anna Lowrie Ivins. Optimistic and stoical, Anna was her alter ego and would remain so to the end of her life.[5]

Little is known of the sociology of conversion and less of its psychology, but Rachel, despite her initial belief that the Mormon preachers were "the false prophets the Bible speaks of," seemed ideally prepared to accept the new religion. She always had been "religiously inclined, but not of the long-faced variety" and had enjoyed reading the Bible. Yet in a century which cultivated such things, she was a young lady without strong ties to a visible religious establishment. For generations her progenitors had been practicing Quakers, but by the nineteenth century this commitment had begun to wane; Rachel herself bridled at the Friends' prohibition against song. While at the straitlaced Wrights', who banned music from their home, she would retreat to a small grove of trees where she would sing as she sewed for her dolls. This penchant for music may have contributed to her conversion at sixteen to the more musically inclined Baptists, though her commitment failed to go very deep. She later claimed to have "never learned anything from them."[6]

When Anna and a friend from Trenton told her that Erastus Snow and Joseph Smith, the Mormon Prophet, would preach at the "Ridge" above Hornerstown, she concluded after some hesitation to go. Though she found Joseph to be a "fine, noble looking man . . . so neat," she was by her own account "prejudiced" and thus paid little heed to his message. Only politeness to her Trenton friend persuaded her to return the following day, Sunday, to hear Joseph Smith once more. Thereupon she returned to her room and pled for the Lord's forgiveness for deliberately listening to false doctrine on the Sabbath. But Joseph Smith's preaching planted a seed which continued to grow. "I attended some more meetings," she recalled, "and commenced reading the Book of Mormon [so enthralled she began reading one evening and did not stop until almost daybreak], *Voice of Warning,* and other works," and was soon convinced that they were true. "A new light seemed to break in upon me, the scriptures were plainer to my mind, and the light of the everlasting Gospel began to illumine my soul." When a Baptist minister's funeral sermon consigned an unbaptized youth to hell she noted with favor the contrast of Orson Hyde's discourse on the innocence and salvation of young children.[7]

Rachel's interest was neither isolated nor unique. "Hundreds attended the [Mormon] meetings," a local historian wrote of Joseph Smith's preaching foray, and he "sealed [in baptism] a large number." The drama of the moment was heightened when the Prophet anointed a lame and opiated boy, promised him freedom from both his pain and crutches, and saw the results as promised. Alarmed at the rising Mormon tide, the old-line clergy used stern methods to put down the new faith. Rachel's Baptist minister admonished her that if she continued attending the Mormon meetings, she could retain neither her pew nor her fellowship in the congregation. "This seemed to settle the question with me," Rachel remembered "I soon handed in my name [to the Mormons] for baptism and rendered willing obedience."[8]

"Oh, what joy filled my being!" she exclaimed. Her conversion opened a floodgate of suppressed emotions which brought her Quaker relatives to the point of despair: ("When she was a Baptist, she was better, but now she is full of levity—singing all the time.") She delighted in the words of Joseph Smith and those of another young dynamic preacher, Jedediah Grant, and became completely enmeshed in the Saints' close-knit society. In addition to the Ivinses, of whom probably a dozen joined the new faith, many of her neighbors also were baptized. "What good times we had then," she proclaimed years later.[9]

Nevertheless, Rachel wanted to settle in Nauvoo, Illinois, the hub of Mormon activity during the early 1840s. Already Charles and James Ivins had reconnoitered the area and returned with plans to move their families there. Driven by "the spirit of gathering," Rachel along with several of her Ivins relatives ventured to the Mormon capital in the spring of 1842.[10]

"The first year of my stay was a very happy one," she remembered. Her cousins Charles and James Ivins rose to immediate prominence. As two of the richest capitalists in the young city, they resumed their merchandising, met in council with Church leaders, and eventually operated the Nauvoo ferry. Their imposing, Federal-style, three-building complex on the corner of Kimball and Main streets was used for retailing and small community gatherings and served as a home as well. Here Rachel lived with James and his family in comfort and relative high style.[11]

Well bred and in her early twenties, Rachel must have turned the head of more than one admirer. While she herself denied having been a belle, she possessed charm and quiet refinement. A friend remembered her Nauvoo appearance: "She was dressed in silk with a handsome lace collar, or fichu, and an elegant shawl over her shoulder, and a long white lace veil thrown back over the simple straw bonnet. She carried an elaborate feather fan . . . , I recall the fascination of that fan. One could easily discern the subdued Quaker pride in her method of using it, for Sister Rachel had the air, the tone, and mannerisms of the Quakers."[12]

There was more than a subdued and attractive facade. While little is known of her daily Nauvoo activity and interests, her bosom companion was Sarah Kimball, which suggests a great deal. Several years Rachel's senior, this young and affluent matron entertained Mormon leaders with memorable elegance. Significantly, she was a thorough-going feminist who sought stimulation beyond the thimble and needle and who helped to initiate the Nauvoo Female Relief Society. The intimate friendship of Sarah and Rachel would continue the rest of their lives.[13]

During these Nauvoo days Rachel came to see the Church and its leaders at close view. Her understanding and acceptance of LDS teachings deepened. Because of her love of family and tradition, she especially found the newly declared doctrine promising salvation to the worthy dead "very precious to my soul." Yet, Joseph Smith proved to be an enigma. When he preached, his power deeply affected her. But in private and informal moments, he seemed distressingly "unProphet-like."

Outgoing and playful, his personality was the polar opposite of Rachel's—and contradicted her view of what a prophet should be.[14]

There were interludes when Joseph whittled away at her sectarian seriousness, and she came to admire him, along with his brother Hyrum, more than any men she had ever known. She was often at the Prophet's home for parties, although he was present only occasionally. "He would play with the people, and he was always cheerful and happy," she remembered of these occasions. Once while visiting the Ivinses on the Sabbath, he requested the family girls sing the popular "In the Gloaming." Rachel believed singing and newspaper reading breached the Sabbath and responded with a mortified, "Why Joseph, it's Sunday!" Smith swept her objections aside with a smile and the comment, "The better the day, the better the deed."[15]

These pleasant moments were not long lasting. Smith's opponents, some of whom were in Rachel's own household, were gathering force. Charles and apparently James Ivins joined the Law, Foster, and Higbee brothers in resisting the growing economic and doctrinal complexity of Mormonism. Charles, who despite his original capital worth, had not prospered in Nauvoo, reacted with particular outrage to rumors that some Church leaders were teaching and practicing plural marriage.[16]

Rachel also knew of these rumors in a very personal way. When Joseph sought an interview with her, she believed he wished to ask for her hand in plural marriage. Her personal turmoil over this prospect must have been excruciating. On one hand, there was the weight of outraged tradition, her cautious and puritanical instincts, and her family's clamor that she withdraw from the Church with them. (Charles Ivins's name appeared on the anti-Smith *Nauvoo Expositor* masthead as one of its publishers.) Her initial response was offended outrage, and she vowed with untypical shrillness that she would "sooner go to hell as a virtuous woman than to heaven as a whore." Yet in other moments she must have considered her still strong feelings for Mormonism and her respect for Joseph. In her emotional distress, Rachel found it impossible to throw off a persistent fever which eventually threatened her life.[17]

The record during these difficult times is inconsistent, perhaps reflecting her own ambivalence. She refused to meet with Joseph Smith, yet years later she insisted that her faith in Mormonism never wavered. In fact, she repeatedly requested that the elders rebuke her illness; each time she felt strengthened. When Sidney Rigdon sought to lead the Church after the Prophet's assassination, she saw Joseph's mantle fall instead upon Brigham Young. "If you had had your eyes shut," she later testified of President Young's remarkable speech, "you would have thought it was the Prophet [Joseph]. In fact he looked like him, his very countenance seemed to change, and he spoke like him."[18]

Notwithstanding these remarkable experiences, Rachel left Nauvoo in late 1844 bewildered and emotionally scarred. As her son later revealed, "When plural marriage was first taught, my mother left the church on account of it." She returned to New Jersey, ailing physically as well as spiritually and planning never to mingle with the Saints again. She would be gone almost ten years.[19]

III

In Victorian symbolism, a dried white rose had an unmistakable meaning: better be ravaged by time and death than to lose one's virtue. While Mormon leaders insisted that their plural marriage was heaven-sent and honorable, Rachel, like most women of her generation, initially rejected the practice. She was, in fact, the quintessence of the nineteenth century's prevailing feminine ideal. Where and how she absorbed these values can only be suggested. Her first school was an eighteen-by-twenty-four-foot affair with a ceiling hardly high enough for an adult to stand, but nothing is known about what really counts—her teachers, primers, and curricula. She continued her formal studies while living in Trenton. Schools for young women in the area, like the Young Ladies' Seminary at Bordertown, emphasized as their most important duty "the forming of a sound and virtuous character." Rachel was schooled in the heart, not necessarily the mind. She also assimilated the ideal image of womanhood by reading popular religious literature and almost certainly women's magazines and gift annuals—the common purveyors of the reigning feminine ideal.[20]

Following her Nauvoo experience and her return to the East, Rachel first ran the old Hornerstown household. When her brother Augustus married, she transferred her talents successively to the homes of her sisters Anna, Edith Ann, and particularly Sarah. Very much in her natural element, Rachel became a devoted spinster-aunt. She sang to her nieces and nephews the melodies of her own youth, sewed their clothing, and did more for them, according to their hard-pressed mothers, than they themselves could do. There were also times of inspiration. When consumptive Sarah lay discouraged because of her daily fevers and chills, she asked Rachel to pray and sing several Mormon hymns. When Rachel rendered, "Oh, Then Arise and Be Baptized," Sarah found the unexpected strength to sing with her and, remembering the hymn's message, requested LDS baptism. Thereupon Sarah's fainting spells ended.[21]

The New Jersey branches which previously had yielded LDS converts so bounteously still had some members. Sam Brannan recruited some of the New Jersey Saints to join the *Brooklyn*'s 1846 voyage to California. Two years later Elder William Appleby returned from the West to revive the local flocks and, incidentally, to administer to Rachel for her periodic bronchitis. But this activity was a pale imitation of the excitement which had once burned through the region. Seeking to integrate Mormonism more fully with their daily lives, Anna Ivins, her husband-cousin Israel, and several other members of the Ivins family still loyal to the new faith decided in 1853 to join a large company of New Jersey Saints gathering to Utah.[22]

The request forced Rachel into a final weighing of Mormonism and plural marriage. For a time after Nauvoo she had compartmentalized the two. Even in her early distress about polygamy, she had refused to listen to William Smith, Joseph's schismatic brother, when he had come to the Ivinses' Horners-town home preaching "another Gospel." When possible she continued her outward LDS activity. But for at least several years she struggled with plural marriage, until at some point through prayerful self-searching she found she could accept the doctrine. Although anti-Mormon family members warned that the westward journey would endanger her health and offered a lifetime annuity if she would stay, Rachel turned her face once again to the Mormon promised land, and this time she did not look back.[23]

She prepared carefully. Anticipating frontier scarcity, she filled a chest with bedding, wool and calico piece goods, and a practical wardrobe of bonnets, gloves, and dresses. Other members of the emigrating party, all relatively prosperous, were equally well stocked. By their preparations they were in fact saying good-by to their life in the East.[24]

The emigrants traveled comfortably. Rachel had the familiar society of several of her Ivins relations, including her cousins Theodore McKean and Anthony Ivins as well as Anna and Israel. Leaving Toms River on 5 April 1853, the party—comprising "a large number of persons from Toms River and other places in the state"—made its way to Philadelphia, boarded the train to Pittsburgh, and then floated on river steamers via Saint Louis to Kansas City. After visiting sites of interest in Jackson County, they purchased mule and wagon outfits (remembered as "one of the best equipments that ever came to Utah in the early fifties") and began the trek west.[25]

The two-and-a-half months on the plains passed equally pleasantly. Anna and Israel traveled with a milk cow and two heavily provisioned wagons. One of these was furnished as a portable room, complete with chairs, a folding bed, and stairs descending from its tailgate. Rachel walked, spent much of her time knitting, and when tired mounted the stairs and the bed for a rest. Rachel believed the arid Great Plains air permanently thinned and dried her hair, but it also cured her long-standing bronchitis. After about a 130-day journey from New Jersey the

Ivins pioneers arrived in Salt Lake City on 11 August and turned up Main Street. There they found temporary lodging with their preacher-friend from years before, Jedediah Grant.[26]

Rachel was now a mature thirty-two. The bloom of youth had passed, but her statuesque charm remained. In polygamous Utah, where sex ratios were perhaps slightly in her favor, she must have had her admirers. But the Ivinses seemed unhurried and cautious about such things. Three of her four brothers never married, and the fourth waited until he was in his thirties. Two of her sisters married cousins. For Rachel's part, she discounted romance or physical attraction. "One could be happy in the marriage relations without love," she reportedly advised, "but could never be happy without respect."[27]

Whether seeking respect or more likely hoping to find a spouse worthy of her own esteem, Rachel's hopes were fulfilled by Jedediah Morgan Grant. She had known him from her late teens when "Jeddy," as he was familiarly known, barnstormed through the New Jersey camp meeting circuit as a Mormon missionary. His wit and eloquence won scores of Mormon converts and his preaching reputation became a local legend. A biographer has aptly labelled him "Mormon Thunder," but he was more than a religious enthusiast. As a teenager he ambitiously read from Wesley, Locke, Rousseau, Watts, Abercrombie, and Mather. In Salt Lake City his charity was open-handed and widely heralded. Brigham Young chose him as his counselor and as mayor of Salt Lake City. Already much married, Jeddy sought out Rachel's hand as his seventh wife two years after her Utah arrival.[28]

Given Grant's church, civic, and connubial duties and Rachel's practicality, their courtship was probably unceremonious and perfunctory. Brigham Young insisted that she first be "eternally sealed" by proxy to his predecessor, apparently to satisfy any obligation owing Joseph. Then on 29 November 1855, Rachel left the home of Anna and Israel, where she had lived for the last two years, and married Grant "for time [in mortality] only" in the Endowment House.[29]

Life at the Grant adobe home on Main Street (the site now occupied by downtown ZCMI) must have been challenging to a woman so private and self-controlled. In turn, her ways and presence unsettled others. When little Belle Whitney was once sent to the Grant home for silk thread, she was startled. "I saw this strange, beautiful woman sitting there," she recalled. "She looked to me like a queen, and I really thought she was one. I did not dare ask her for the silk . . . I turned and ran [away]." Initially the other Grant wives were also caught off guard. Instead of exchanging close confidences as women of the century were prone to do, Rachel was restrained. "She writes frequently [to you]," complained one of Jeddy's wives with some edge, "but does not see fit to read them to us."[30]

Rachel was not altogether happy at the Grant household. "Remember the trials your dead grandma had and that she was only a wife for a year," wrote her son many years later to one of his own children. The fault did not lie with Jeddy. Though he was often absent on church assignment, the two evidently enjoyed a satisfactory relationship. She remembered her tendency to "lean" upon him—perhaps too much she later wondered—and in after years she never expressed a hint of criticism of her husband. In turn, one of Grant's few surviving letters expresses concern, cautioning her "not to work to[o] hard." On 22 November 1856, she bore him a son, Heber Jeddy Grant, nine days before "lung disease," a combination of typhoid and pneumonia, took his life at the early age of forty.[31]

For a time attendants also feared for the new mother's life. Rachel's labor had been difficult, and the shock of her husband's sudden death weakened her further. Without him she had no tangible source of security. Her cache of New Jersey "store goods" had long since been personally used or distributed to those around her, while Grant's small estate would have to be divided with her sister-wives. Her eastern relatives had promised that the latch-string would always be out for her return—if she would renounce her religion. But she rejected this; in matters of faith Rachel had made her decision.[32]

Rachel eventually recovered, and because of the two dominant forces which now shaped her life—her religion and her son—she remarried. President Young promised the Grant wives that if they would remain as a unit and accept George Grant, Jeddy's brother, as their new husband, they would successfully raise their children to be faithful Mormons. Rachel and several of the Grant wives complied, although her preference was to return to Anna's Salt Lake household. She married George on 17 February 1858, resolute in her religious obedience and hopeful for the future of her son.[33]

The union was a disaster. George, once a faithful churchman, Indian fighter, and hero of the 1856 handcart tragedy was, unbeknown to Church leaders, on a downward course. His erratic and immoderate behavior, apparently due to alcoholism, soon became public. Six months after his marriage to Rachel, George "committed an unprovoked attack on Thos. S. Williams with [the] attempt to kill." The fracas ended in a street brawl. With such incidents and George's drinking becoming more common, President Young dissolved the two-year-old marriage, but Rachel's hurt never entirely healed. "It was the one frightful ordeal of my mother's life, and the one thing she never wishes to refer to," Heber remarked in later years.[34]

Rachel thereafter rejected every opportunity for remarriage. Although prizing her independence, her overriding concern was Heber. Nothing—not a new father nor any other uncontrollable circumstance—must inhibit his promise. For several years she and her son remained at the Grant home on Main Street with a couple of the other widowed and now divorced wives. But the lack of money forced the sale of that property and the break-up of their extended family. With President Young's permission, Rachel took her $500 share of the transaction and purchased a cottage on Second East Street.[35]

The change in living standards was wrenching. The disappointed and disoriented six-year-old Heber wandered back to the Main Street home and vowed that some day he would live there again. Certainly the new home had no luxuries.

Rachel at first had only six dining plates, two of which were cracked, an occasional cup and saucer, her bed and bedding, and several chairs. There were blustery nights with no fire and a meager diet which allowed only several pounds of butter and sugar for an entire year. One Christmas Rachel wept because she lacked a dime to buy a stick of candy for her boy's holiday.[36]

Poverty, or at least scarcity, was a part of pioneer living, and Rachel's situation differed from many others only in degree. Yet being accustomed to relative affluence and to giving rather than receiving, she must have found these trials poignant. Once while visiting Anna, who had moved to St. George in southern Utah, she firmly declined an offer from President Young of Church aid. Instead, she supported herself and Heber by sewing, at first by hand in the homes of others and later with a Wheeler and Wilcox sewing machine in her own house. "I sat on the floor at night until midnight," Heber remembered many evenings, "and pumped the sewing machine to relieve her tired limbs." The machine's constantly moving treadles became a symbol of the Grant family's stubborn independence.[37]

Despite her financial distress, she retained her personal style and preferences. A willing hostess, she often subjected Heber and herself to a diet of "fried bread" (slices of bread warmed in a greased frying pan) so she could "splurge" on entertaining her friends. And she continued her fastidious habits. "She could wear a dress longer than anyone I have seen and have it look fresh and nice," a relative recalled. "She always changed her dress in the afternoon and washed herself and combed her hair, and if at home put on a nice white apron. . . . It would not look soiled [for several days]." Only her providence allowed this. She often cannibalized several threadbare garments to produce something "new" and usable.[38]

About five years after moving to Second East Street, Rachel began serving meals to boarders out of her small basement kitchen. Alex Hawes, a non-Mormon New York Life insurance man, helped make her venture successful. Attracted by her intelligence, charm, and culinary skill, Hawes first boarded and then at his own expense outfitted a small room at the Grants for his use. His rent and warm testimonials to Rachel's cooking provided her, as the boarding business increased, with a growing margin of financial security.[39]

Conversation at the Grants' boarding table was interesting and at times lively. "How I used to chaff her on matters religious or otherwise," Hawes recalled, "& how with her quiet sense of humor she would humor my sallies! We even made bets on certain events then in the future." The intelligent, detached, and agnostic Hawes enjoyed the iconoclast's role. "I know I respected [Hawes]," remembered Miss Joanna Van Rensselaer, a Methodist boarder, "notwithstanding his belief or want of belief—and recall vividly an argument between him and Miss Hayden—as to whether there was a real Devil."[40]

Rachel was Hawes's antithesis. She permitted no smoking in her home; gentlemen were told to indulge their habit on a tree stump in the yard. She was equally firm in defending Mormonism before her gentile boarders, never neglecting, as she remembered, "any opportunity to introduce Mormonism to them." W. H. Harrington, an editor of the Salt Lake *Herald*, recalled her kindly and repeated assurances of his forthcoming but never realized conversion ("at which I would smile quietly"). Her boarders came to call her "Aunt Rachel, following the lead of her two nieces who served the table.[41]

Shortly after starting her boardinghouse business, Rachel was "blessed and set apart" as the Thirteenth Ward Relief Society "presidentess." Relief Societies had been organized briefly in Nauvoo and later in Utah during the middle 1850s, but not until a decade later did the movement gain momentum. When it reached Rachel's Thirteenth Ward, she fit Bishop Edwin D. Woolley's bill of particulars for the job. "It was not his habit to be in a hurry in his movements," Woolley told the women at their organizing session, and he wished the Relief Society sisters to be likewise "cool and deliberate" and their leaders obedient in carrying out "such measures as he should suggest from time to time." His eye naturally rested upon Rachel.[42]

The burden of leadership was often heavy. She trembled to overcome her diffidence when speaking or conducting meetings. The kind Scandinavian sisters unknowingly repelled her as they grasped and kissed her hand. She "scarcely knew what to do" with some women who behaved irrationally and then demanded the Society's charity. Rachel repeatedly gave herself solace by saying "it was not the numbers that constituted a good meeting." And there was Bishop Woolley, whose bark was as legendary as his toothless bite. He scolded them for having "left undone some things that he told us to do, and we done some things that we ought not to." But his comments apparently were nothing more serious than passing irritation, for he and his two successors retained Rachel in her position for thirty-five years.[43]

The detailed minutes of the Thirteenth Ward Relief Society suggest she closely resembled the nineteenth-century Mormon ideal woman. On occasion she prophesied. She experienced uncommon faith and expression while praying. Following priesthood counsel, she used when possible articles manufactured in Utah, and when Brigham Young requested women to abandon their cumbersome eastern styles, she wore, despite ridicule from many women, the simplified and home-designed "Deseret Costume." Her name appeared with those of a half-dozen other prominent LDS women protesting the passage of the anti-Mormon Cullom Bill. Likewise, she was a member of a committee of leaders representing the "large and highly respectable assemblage of ladies" thanking Acting Governor S. A. Mann for his approval of the Utah Women's Suffrage Act.[44]

However, as her Relief Society sermons show, Rachel was more a moralist than an activist. "We all have trials to pass through," she spoke from personal experience, "but if living up to our duty they are sanctified to our best good." Her tendency was to see only the good in life. She called for obedience to authority and the avoidance of faultfinding. God's hand and his rewards were omnipresent. "I am a firm believer in our being rewarded for all the good we do," she insisted, "& everything will come out right with those who do right." She had long since made her peace with plural marriage. While its practice might be a woman's "greatest trial," she rejoiced that she herself had experienced the "Principle." Propounding duty, goodness, obedience, toil, and sacrifice, her Quaker-Mormon attitudes blended comfortably with the era's prevailing Victorianism.[45]

Rachel and her Thirteenth Ward sisters did more than sermonize. Notwithstanding "often having to endure insults," the Relief Society block teachers canvassed the congregation to discover the needy and to secure for their relief an occasional cash donation. The sisters were usually more successful in procuring yarn, thread, calico pieces, rugs, and discarded clothing which they transformed into stockings, quilts, and rag rugs. The Relief Society women also braided straw, fashioned hats and bonnets, stored grain, and sewed underwear, buckskin gloves, and burial and temple garments. On these items the poor had first claim; the remainder were sold with most of the proceeds going to charity. During Rachel's three-and-a-half-decade ministry, a time of scarcity and deflated dollars, the Thirteenth Ward Relief Society's liberality in cash and goods exceeded $7,750. The little money left she invested for her sisters in securities which appreciated spectacularly after her death. By 1925 the Thirteenth Ward Relief Society had assets worth $20,000.[46]

Rachel Grant's "greatest trial" during her years as Relief Society president was her worsening hearing. She had noticed a hearing loss in late adolescence, but when she was almost fifty, an attack of quinsy left her virtually deaf with what she described as a "steam engine going night and day" in her head. No longer hearing melody, much conversation, nor the proceedings of her church meetings—among the things she valued most—she nevertheless attempted to carry on. In her Relief Society meetings she compensated for her disability with what her friends felt to be an extra sense. "She often picked up the thread of thought and conversation," commented one of her Relief Society coworkers "and voiced her own conclusions so appropriately and so ably that her associates marveled afresh at the keenness of her spiritual comprehension.[47]

Because she led the women of the prominent Thirteenth Ward, and in part because of her able manner, her influence in later years spread. She became recognized as one of Mormondom's "leading sisters" who in lieu of a centralized Relief Society staff, traveled throughout the territory speaking and advising on distaff questions, becoming "Aunt Rachel," an honored pioneer title, to more than her boarders. While never rivaling Eliza R. Snow, Bathsheba W. Smith, or Emmeline Wells as women's exponents (the latter two served under her presidency during the Thirteenth Ward Relief Society's early years), she was nonetheless esteemed as a model of proper behavior. Stately, serene, fastidious, and proper, Rachel came to be compared with Victoria herself.[48]

Rachel might travel and preach in the outlying settlements, but she was always uneasy at center stage—restrained not only by her natural hesitancy and lack of hearing but also by her preoccupation with Heber. She never doubted that the boy's destiny would at least equal his father's, and her urgent anticipations coupled with her light discipline did much to forge his character. If the youthful Heber took advantage of her leniency and proved to be very much a boy, in later years his attitude toward her became reverential. "There are many things about her that I could wish were different," he candidly declared in adulthood, apparently with reference to her firmly programmed ways and mannerisms, "but mother is one of the sweetest and kindest of women and as loveable as can be."[49]

In many ways, and especially in the ways most pleasing to her, Heber proved a facsimile of herself. Neither prim nor systematic, he accepted the Ivinses' business-mindedness and Rachel's Victorian values. Above all, she bequeathed to him her towering commitment to Mormonism along with her feelings of LDS embattlement and persecution. As Heber J. Grant rose to commercial and Church prominence, becoming during the last twenty-five years of her life a member of the Quorum of the Twelve Apostles, his career was the fulfillment of her own.

Her last years were again dominated by family concerns. Due to the long illness and eventual death of Lucy Stringham Grant, the first of Heber's three plural wives, Rachel's grandmotherly duties were heavy. For a time, the seventy-year-old woman personally tended Lucy's six children. Later she moved to an upstairs room and surrendered much of this role to her son's second wife, Augusta Winters Grant. Yet she still darned, mended, and sewed for the family and invited her grandchildren to her room for school study and silent companionship—though they learned that Rachel's displeasure might easily be aroused if they wandered too close to her immaculate and painstakingly made bed. Her deafness insulated her from the family's quarrels and prompted occasional humor. The children "had no idea," she told them, "how funny it was to see their angry faces and hear none of their words."[50]

Such a statement reveals a characteristic attempt to see the bright side of her tormenting disability. To the end she refused to accept its finality. She was repeatedly anointed and blessed. As a measure of their regard, congregations from Idaho to Arizona in 1900 fasted and prayed for her hearing. She repeatedly repaired to the temple, hoping that baptism in a holy place might bring a cure. "I watched in breathless silence to see the miracle performed," Susa Young Gates recalled of one such temple experience. "I saw my miracle . . . eight long agonizing times [she was baptized with no effect] . . . the vision of Aunt Rachel's beaming smile at God's refusal to hear her prayer gripped my soul with power to bear." The miracle, of course, lay within Rachel herself.[51]

Rachel Grant was equanimity personified. The financial panics of the 1890s crushed her son's ascendency for several decades; to aid him, she transferred to him the stocks and properties which he had previously given her. She reacted with similar stoicism to the death of little Heber, her semi-invalid grandson upon whom she had lavished so much love and attention. In 1903 at the age of eighty-two, she retired from the Thirteenth Ward Relief Society. "I am not one," her resignation read, "who wishes to hold on to an office when I can not do as I wish." She thus conceded to old age what she had steadfastly refused to grant to her deafness.[52]

During her final five or six years Rachel retired from most pursuits—with the exception of her reading, meditating, and letter-writing. She was annually honored by a "surprise" birthday party. After one such fete, a reporter from the *Woman's Exponent* found her "the picture of health and happiness. . . . It can truly be said of Sister Rachel, that she has grown old gracefully." Yet her lifetime of physical and psychological toil had its effect. Rheumatism, nerves, and the constant cacaphony within her head would often not allow sleep until 3:00 or 4:00 A.M. Accordingly, she would take a hymnal from under her pillow and sing the silent sounds of the past. "I was awake early this morning & thinking of my past life," she wrote revealingly to Heber on such an occasion. "When you were young I thought & prayed that I might live to see you grown then I would be satisfied, if you wer[e] a faithful L[.]D[.] Saint . . . when thinking of the many things I had passed through hard & unpleasant how happy it makes me now that I never complained . . . not even to my sister. I knew she would feel bad. I can talk about them now without cairing." Clearly her outward serenity had often been a mask.[53]

After fighting for a week with pneumonia which brought little actual suffering, Rachel died on 27 January 1909 at 1:10 A.M.—with "absolute and perfect confidence" in what lay ahead. She was almost eighty-eight. Heber, who would justify his mother's faith by becoming the president of The Church of Jesus Christ of Latter-day Saints, was at her bedside. Through him and his administration of almost three decades, her personality would touch yet another generation of Saints.[54]

Ronald W. Walker

Notes

1. Lucy Grant Cannon, "A Few Memories of Grandma Grant," undated manuscript, Heber J. Grant (herafter cited as HJG), Letterpress Copybook, vol. 65, pp. 182, 185 (hereafter cited as LC by volume and page), Heber J. Grant Papers, Library-Archives, Historical Department, The Church of Jesus Christ of Latter-day Saints, Salt Lake City, Utah; hereafter respectively cited HJG, LC, and LDS Church Archives. Annie Wells Cannon, "Rachel Ivins Grant," *Improvement Era* 37 (Nov. 1934): 643. I am indebted to Marlena Ahanin and Peggy Fletcher for their assistance in researching this paper.

2. Luther Prentice Allen, *The Genealogy and History of the Shreve Family,* p. 210, as quoted in Frances Bennett Jeppson, "With Joy Wend Your Way: The Life of Rachel Ivins Grant, My Great-Grandmother," p. 1, typescript, 1952, LDS Church Archives.

3. Jeppson, "With Joy Wend Your Way," p. 2; Rachel Ridgway Grant [hereafter RRG] to HJG, 18 December 1904, Box 176, fd. 22, HJG Papers; and Lucy Grant Cannon, "Recollections of Rachel Ivins Grant," *Relief Society Magazine* 25 (May 1938): 295–96.

4. The Mormon invasion and success in central New Jersey is an important but untold story of early LDS proselyting. The Mormon chapels must have been among the earliest built by Church members anywhere. William Sharp, "The Latter-day Saints or 'Mormons' in New Jersey," typescript of a memorandum prepared in 1897, LDS Church Archives, p. 3; Edwin Salter, *History of Monmouth and Ocean Counties* (Bayonne, N.J.: E. Gardner and Son, 1890), p. 253; and Franklin Ellis, *The History of Monmouth County, New Jersey* (Cottonport, La.: Polyanthos Publishing Company, 1974), p. 633. Later in the 1840s, LDS converts apparently founded a small fishing village on the New Jersey coast which they named "Nauvoo," Stanley B. Kimball, " 'Nauvoo' Found in Seven States," *Ensign,* Apr. 1973, p. 23.

5. Anthony W. Ivins, Diary, vol. 1, p. 3, Utah State Historical Society, Salt Lake City, Utah; Kimball S. Erdman, *Israel Ivins: A Biography* (n.p., 1969), p. 3, LDS Church Archives; Parley P. Pratt to Joseph Smith, Jr., 22 November 1839, Joseph Smith papers, LDS Church Archives. At the Mormon Church conference held in Philadelphia, 13 January 1840, Ivins suggested and Joseph Smith agreed that the Book of Mormon should be printed instead in the West, Philadelphia Church Records, 1840–1854, microfilm, LDS Church Archives.

6. RRG, "How I Became a 'Mormon,' " unpublished memorandum, HJG Papers, Box 177, fd 19; RRG, "Minutes of a Meeting of the General Boards of the Young Men and Young Women MIA," 11 June 1902, in LC 35:324; *Woman's Exponent* 31 (1 and 15 Dec. 1902): 53. For women and nineteenth-century religion see Barbara Welter, "The Feminization of American Religion: 1800–1860," in *Clio's Consciousness Raised: New*

Perspectives on the History of Women, eds. Mary S. Hartman and Lois Banner (New York: Harper & Row/Harper Colophon Books, 1974), pp. 137–57; and Mary P. Ryan, "A Woman's Awakening: Evangelical Religion and the Families of Utica, New York, 1800–1840," *American Quarterly* 30 (Winter 1978): 602–23.

7. RRG, "How I Became a 'Mormon,' " p. 1; and RRG, "Joseph Smith, the Prophet," *Young Woman's Journal* 16 (Dec. 1905): 550–51.

8. Sharp, "The Latter-day Saints or 'Mormons' in New Jersey," pp. 1–2; Salter, *History of Monmouth and Ocean Counties,* p. 253; RRG, "How I Became a 'Mormon,' " pp. 1–2.

9. RRG, "How I Became a 'Mormon,' " pp. 1–2; RRG, "Minutes of a Meeting of the General Boards"; and Relief Society Minute Book 1875, Thirteenth Ward, 1 April 1875, p. 10, LDS Church Archives. In addition to the Ivinses, the Appleby, Applegate, Brown, Bennett, Curtis, Doremus, Horner, Implay, McKean, Robbins, Sill, Stoddard, Woodward, Wright, and Wychoff families mixed together without social distinction in their central New Jersey branches.

10. Erastus Snow, Journal, typescript, vol. 2, p. 25, LDS Church Archives; and RRG, "How I Became a 'Mormon,' " p. 2. Snow, who visited his New Jersey flock in late 1841, declared, "I found them strong in the faith, many having of late been added to them and several families, I found about ready to move to Nauvoo," Journal 2:28.

11. RRG, "How I Became a 'Mormon,' " p. 2; Journal History of the Church, 30 April, 27 June, and 14 August 1842, LDS Church Archives. Nauvoo Trustees Land Book, Part B (p. 29), LDS Church Archives; Nauvoo City Tax Assessments Books, Wards 1–4, 1841–1844, LDS Church Archives; and Nauvoo Restoration, *The James Ivins-Elias Smith Printing Complex* (Nauvoo, Ill.: Nauvoo Restoration, Inc., n.d.), pp. 1–4. Visitors in present-day Nauvoo identify the Ivins buildings as belonging to John Taylor and used for the printing of the *Times and Seasons,* an early Church periodical.

12. Emmeline B. Wells as quoted by Mary Grant Judd, "Rachel Ridgway Ivins Grant," *Relief Society Magazine* 30 (Apr. 1943): 229.

13. Their intimate friendship is repeatedly mentioned in the HJG Papers; see for instance HJG to Harold A. Lafount, 24 April 1924, LC 61:839; Sarah Kimball's life is sketched by Jill C. Mulvay, "The Liberal Shall Be Blessed: Sarah M. Kimball," *Utah Historical Quarterly* 44 (Summer 1976): 205–21.

14. RRG, "How I Became a 'Mormon,' " p. 2; and RRG, "Joseph Smith, the Prophet," p. 551.

15. RRG, "Joseph Smith, the Prophet," p. 551; HJG, "Remarks Made at a Sunday School Union Board Meeting," 7 Jan. 1919, draft in LC 54:348; RRG to Edith [Grant], 17 September 1904, Family Correspondence, HJG papers; and Thirteenth Ward Relief Society Minutes, Book B: 1898–1906, 17 March 1902, pp. 100–101, LDS Church Archives.

16. Thirteenth Ward Relief Society Minutes, Book A: 1868–1898, 11 February 1897, p. 611, LDS Church Archives. In several letters to Brigham Young, Ivins steadfastly maintained his innocence. "I can say that I never to the best of my recollection persuaded the first person to join either Law or Sidney [Rigdon]—all I have bin guilty of is believing the doctrine of Mormonism as it was taught me in the beginning," Charles Ivins to Brigham Young, July 1845, Brigham Young Papers, LDS Church Archives.

17. Lucy Grant Cannon to Truman G. Madsen [?], 15 April 1960, quoted in Truman G. Madsen, *The Heritage of Heber J. Grant* (Salt Lake City: privately published, 1969), pp. 12, 30; RRG, "How I Became a 'Mormon,' " p. 2; and HJG to Ray O. Wyland, 12 December 1936, LC 74:530–31. Erdman, *Israel Ivins,* pp. 5–6, claims that Joseph Smith actually proposed to her.

18. RRG, "How I Became a 'Mormon,' " p. 2; and RRG, "Joseph Smith, the Prophet," p. 551.

19. HJG to Heber M. Wells, 28 April 1904, and HJG to E. S. Tainter, 25 August 1926, LC 38:590 and 64:611; and HJG and Anthony W. Ivins, "Remarks at a Birthday Dinner for Heber J. Grant," transcript in HJG Typed Diary, 22 November 1924, pp. 314–15, HJG Papers.

20. Barbara Welter, "The Cult of True Womanhood," pp. 151, 153; and Ellis, *History of Monmouth County,* p. 639. The school described here was probably Rachel's, for John Horner, as cited in Ellis, recalled attending his early grammar studies with her.

21. Cannon, "A Few Memories of Grandma Grant," p. 181; and RRG, untitled and undated memorandum, HJG Papers, Box 147, fd. 9.

22. William Appleby Journal, 17 November 1845, 26 October and 1 November 1848, LDS Church Archives.

23. RRG, untitled and undated memorandum, HJG Papers, Box 147, fd. 9; and Jeppson, "With Joy Wend Your Way," p. 8.

24. Jeppson, "With Joy Wend Your Way," p. 9; and [Toms River] *New Jersey Courier,* 9 November 1934.

25. Sharp, "The Latter-day Saints or 'Mormons' in New Jersey," pp. 2–3; Theodore McKean, "Autobiography," unpublished draft, p. 2, LDS Church Archives; and [Toms River] *New Jersey Courier,* 9 November 1934.

26. Jeppson, "With Joy Wend Your Way," pp. 9–10.

27. Cannon, "A Few Memories of Grandma Grant," p. 181; and Wayne L. Wahlquist, "Population Growth in the Mormon Core Area: 1847–90," *The Mormon Role in the Settlement of the West,* ed. Richard H. Jackson, Charles Redd Monographs in Western History, no. 9 (Provo, Ut.: Brigham Young University, 1978), pp. 116–24. Wahlquist found the female imbalance to be most significant during the years of marriageability—a tendency which plural marriage must have heightened.

28. Gene A. Sessions, *Mormon Thunder: A Documentary History of Jedediah Morgan Grant* (Urbana: University of Illinois Press, 1982), p. 265.

29. Caleb Ivins, Jr., Group Sheet, Archives, The Genealogical Society of The Church of Jesus Christ of Latter-day Saints, Salt Lake City, Utah; and HJG, "Remarks at a Birthday Dinner for Heber J. Grant."

30. Israel Whitney Sears to HJG, 20 February 1919, General Correspondence, HJG Papers; and Susan and Rosetta Grant to Jedediah M. Grant, 7 January 1855 [1856?] photocopy of holograph, Grant Family Correspondence, LDS Church Archives. Another wife complained that the frequently writing Rachel monopolized all the news, ibid.

31. HJG to Florence [Grant], 8 June 1905, LC 39:832; RRG, Thirteenth Ward Relief Society Minutes, Book A, 7 July 1870, p. 70; and Jedediah M. Grant to Susan Grant, 14 October 1856, photocopy of holograph, Grant Family Correspondence.

32. HJG to Claus [?] H. Karlson, 28 October 1885, LC 6:203–4; Jeppson, "With Joy Wend Your Way," p. 9. Eventually only four of the Grant wives participated in the distribution of their husband's property— those who left the Grant homestead and remarried elsewhere were excluded.

33. Cannon, "A Few Memories of Grandma Grant," pp. 182–83.

34. George Goddard Journal, 27 August 1858, LDS Church Archives; HJG to Junius F. Wells, 30 March 1905, LC 39:502; and Cannon, "A Few Memories of Grandma Grant," p. 183.

35. Jeppson, "With Joy Wend Your Way," p. 12.

36. "Two Octogenarians," *Improvement Era* 39 (Nov. 1936): 667; HJG, "Faith-Promoting Experiences," *Millennial Star* 93 (19 Nov. 1931): 760; Cannon, "A Few Memories of Grandma Grant," p. 183; and RRG, Thirteenth Ward Relief Society Minutes, Book B, 13 February 1903, p. 95.

37. [Toms River] *New Jersey Courier,* 9 November 1934; HJG, "Faith-Promoting Experiences," p. 760. Her refusal of aid was categorical. "I . . . told him [Brigham Young] that persons had said to me I was a fool for working as I did when your father [Jedediah] killed himself working in the kingdom. I told him I did not wish to be supported by the church. I was too independent for that." RRG to HJG, 19 October 1901, Family Correspondence, HJG papers.

38. Cannon, "A Few Memories of Grandma Grant," p. 183.

39. HJG, *An Address Delivered by Invitation Before the Chamber of Commerce, Kansas City, Missouri* (Independence, Mo.; Zion's Printing and Publishing Co., 1924?), p. 15; HJG, Press Copy Diary, 20 August 1887, HJG Papers; HJG, Remarks, "President Grant's Seventy-first Birthday Party," memo in Box 177, fd. 23, HJG Papers. Heber was explicit on Hawes's effect upon the Grant household: "I may say the turning point in my mother's life came when Colonel Hawes entered our home as a boarder," HJG to Elizabeth L. Peltret, 19 March 1914, LC 49:363.

40. Alexander W. Hawes to HJG, 28 December 1912, LC 48:151–52; and Joanna H. Van Rensselaer to HJG, 21 January 1925, General Correspondence, HJG Papers.

41. Cannon, "A Few Memories of Grandma Grant," p. 184; RRG, Thirteenth Ward Relief Society Minutes, Book A, 7 March 1872, pp. 106–7; and W. H. Harrington to HJG, 1 December 1897, HJG Papers.

42. Thirteenth Ward Relief Society Minutes, Book A, 18 April 1868, pp. 1–2.

43. RRG, Thirteenth Ward Relief Society Minutes, Book B, 17 March 1902, pp. 100–101; Cannon, "A Few Memories of Grandma Grant," p. 184. Thirteenth Ward Relief Society Minutes, Book A, 7 August 1873, 29 June 1876, and 26 October 1887, pp. 154, 260, and 466. Sister Emma Goddard, the secretary, discreetly crossed out Woolley's remarks and replaced them with a more grammatical sentence, see Relief Society Minute Book 1875, Thirteenth Ward, 3 June 1875, pp. 25–26.

44. RRG to HJG, 8 January 1891, 12 October 1901, and HJG to RRG, 12 October 1907, Family Correspondence, HJG Papers; Hannah C. Wells to HJG, 28 February 1907, General Correspondence, HJG Papers; Cannon, "A Few Memories of Grandma Grant," p. 187; *Woman's Exponent* 37 (Apr. 1909): 52; HJG, "Address at BYU Centennial," 16 October 1925, in LC 63:553–54; Thirteenth Ward Relief Society Minutes, Book A, 15 April 1875, p. 227; Relief Society Minute Book 1875, Thirteenth Ward, 1 April 1875, pp. 9–10; Thomas G. Alexander, "An Experiment in Progressive Legislation: The Granting of Woman Suffrage in Utah in 1870," *Utah Historical Quarterly* 38 (Winter 1970): 20–30.

45. RRG, Thirteenth Ward Relief Society Minutes, Book A, 5 March 1874, 4 June 1874, 2 September 1875, and 13 January 1898, pp. 175, 188–89, 244, and 633; RRG, Thirteenth Ward Relief Society Minutes, Book B, 13 March 1902, pp. 97–98; Lucy Grant Cannon, "Recollections of Rachel Ivins Grant," *Relief Society Magazine,* 25 (May 1938): 293–98; RRG to HJG, 7 May 1905, Family Correspondence, HJG Papers.

46. RRG, Thirteenth Ward Relief Society Minutes, Book A, 4 December 1873, p. 164; "Rachel Ridgway Grant," memorandum dated 28 March 1903, Box 176, fd. 22, HJG Papers; *Woman's Exponent* 4 (1 Dec. 1875): 98, 5 (1 June 1876): 5, and 14 (15 June 1885): 13–14; and Cannon, "A Few Memories of Grandma Grant," p. 184.

47. Cannon, "A Few Memories of Grandma Grant," p. 187; Jeppson, "With Joy Wend Your Way," p. 13; Susa Young Gates, "Relief Society Beginnings in Utah," *Relief Society Magazine* 9 (Apr. 1922): 189; and *Woman's Exponent* 31 (1 and 15 Dec. 1902): 53.

48. Mary Grant Judd, "Rachel Ridgway Ivins Grant," *Relief Society Magazine* 30 (May 1943): 316; and May Booth Talmage, "Coronets of Age: Rachel R. Grant," *Young Woman's Journal* 19 (Apr. 1908): 182–85. The *Woman's Exponent* occasionally recorded Rachel's visits among the outlying areas, see 9 (15 June 1880): 13; 12 (1 and 15 Sept. 1883): 55, 60; 14 (1 Oct. 1885): 70; and 15 (1 Apr. 1887): 164.

49. HJG to Lucy Grant, 17 April 1892, Lucy Grant Papers, LDS Church Archives. Her parenting provided the classic conditions which often pro-

duced an entrepreneurial type of personality, see Everett E. Hagan, *On the Theory of Social Change* (Homewood, Ill.: Dorsey Press, 1962), p. 93; and David C. McClelland, *The Achieving Society* (Princeton, N.J.: D. Van Nostrand Co., 1961), especially pp. 353–76.

50. Jeppson, "With Joy Wend Your Way," p. 17; Cannon, "A Few Memories of Grandma Grant," p. 188.

51. Susa Young Gates, "A Tribute to Rachel Ivins Grant," *Young Woman's Journal* 21 (Jan. 1910): 30.

52. Jeppson, "With Joy Wend Your Way," pp. 17–18; RRG to HJG, 28 June 1903, Family Correspondence, HJG Papers.

53. *Woman's Exponent* 31 (Mar. 1903): 77; Cannon, "A Few Memories of Grandma Grant," p. 181; and RRG to HJG, 27 November 1904, Family Correspondence, HJG Papers.

54. HJG Manuscript Diary, 27 January 1909, HJG Papers; and HJG to Mrs. S. A. Collins, 12 February 1909, Family Correspondence, HJG Papers.

Ronald D. Dennis

3

William Howells:
First Missionary to France

Ronald D. Dennis was born in Myton, Utah, and now
resides in Provo with his wife and six children. He is
currently Associate Professor of Spanish and Portuguese at
Brigham Young University. He received his B.A. from
Brigham Young University and his M.A. and Ph.D. from the
University of Wisconsin. He has published in language
journals and has done research in LDS history, particularly
in Wales. His interest in William Howells relates to his skill
in the Welsh language, as well as his forthcoming study of
the history of the Church in Wales.

I sincerely beseech everyone not to give the name of 'Saints'
to this foul mob; rather let them be given their proper names,
that is, 'Nineteenth-century Satanists.' " This exhortation appeared in March 1846 in the preface of a twenty-page Welsh
pamphlet aimed at bringing the "deceit of the creatures who
call themselves 'Latter-day Saints' " to the attention of the
public.[1]

This epithet, coined by W. R. Davies, was immediately
adopted by other Mormon-haters throughout the principality
of Wales. W. R. Davies, a well-known Baptist minister in the

Dowlais-Merthyr Tydfil area of south Wales, ranked as Mormonism's greatest antagonist in Wales from about 1844 to his death in 1849. He was joined in his lecturing and writing campaign against the Mormons by many of his fellow nonconformist ministers.[2]

William Howells, a fellow Baptist in a neighboring parish, took great interest in the raging controversy surrounding the Latter-day Saints. He was a draper and operated a dry goods store in Aberdare.[3] Characterizing himself as "too bashful" to approach any of the Mormons directly for information concerning their sect, he later wrote: "But a poor widow, supported with her family by the poor fare of the parish, found means to get a tract, which she gave me; which, like the little captive maid of Israel, in the house of Naaman the leper, convinced me of the poverty of my religion."[4] To certain ministers the tract Williams Howells referred to was "an odious patchwork," "dull and idiotic," "blasphemous to the common sense of the Welsh," and "presumptious rubbish" which had been printed on a "prostitute press" at Rhydybont.[5] But to Howells the pamphlet was the catalyst which prompted him to seek out its author, Dan Jones, and request baptism at his hands.

A year and a half after casting his lot with the unpopular Mormons, William Howells, by writing a 2,100-word letter in his eloquent and flawless Welsh, answered a question posed by John Davis, editor of *Udgorn Seion (Zion's Trumpet),* as to how much good the Reverend W. R. Davies and others had done in speaking against the Saints. Stating that he had known very little about the Saints until the Reverend W. R. Davies came to Aberdare to expose their deceit, Howells wrote:

> And to my surprise the more he shouted while pounding his Bible on the pulpit, "Great fraud, devilish hypocrisy, and miserable darkness of the Satanists of the Latter Days" all the more the principles of the Saints, like rays of divine truth were shining to the point of making me begin to believe that if these men were Satanic, that his "Satanic Majesty" had more of the divine truth of the Bible than did the religion which I professed.[6]

Howells revealed that his love for the ministers had cooled over the years as he observed their lust for money and their swollen, boastful spirits, so full of self-love. He had tolerated these imperfections, blaming them on human weakness, because of his love for the Baptist religion, but upon reading a forty-page pamphlet written by Dan Jones in defense of Mormonism, Howells was completely won over.

Elder Dan Jones was understandably excited at the conversion of William Howells:

> Last evening, I baptized a gentleman who is now, and has been, a Baptist minister for the last eighteen years: he preached to his flock last Sunday, and has an appointment for the successive Sunday. He came four miles purposely to be baptized, though he had never heard a sermon, only reading my publications; especially my last reply . . . finished him entirely, and he came in as good a spirit as any one that I ever saw, and has just returned on his way rejoicing. He is a wealthy man of great influence, and, as he said, he feared that he was not a servant of God, because he heard every person universally praising him, whereas the scripture says, "Wo unto you when all men shall speak well of you."[7]

Since Howells was only thirty-one years old at the time of his conversion to Mormonism, it is rather doubtful that he had been a Baptist minister "for the last eighteen years." Furthermore, there is no evidence whatsoever that he had ever been ordained a minister.[8] But he had spent nearly twenty years with the Baptists[9] and was a "wealthy man of great influence," wealthy, at least, according to the prevailing standards of the day in Wales.

Prior to Howells's Conversion to Mormonism

Because his journals apparently have not survived and because much of what he wrote is in Welsh, the short life of William Howells is not widely known; nevertheless, it is one that deserves greater attention and one that furnishes the historian with insightful information concerning the early days of Mormonism in Wales and of the taking of the gospel into France.

William Howells was christened 18 September 1816 at St. Donat's, Glamorganshire. St. Donat's, in the extreme southern portion of Wales, was at one time of considerable importance as the site where the Normans staged their conquest of the county of Glamorgan. The ancient castle which they erected overlooks the Bristol Channel. In 1816 there were fewer than two hundred inhabitants. Although at the time of William's birth his parents resided at Penmark, about six miles east of St. Donat's, both Lewis Howells and Anne Priest had been born at St. Donat's and would later rear their family there.

Because Lewis Howells's occupation was a carpenter, one would expect his son, William, to become something similar. Normally the children of Welsh laborers did not go very far from home and became laborers themselves. In William's case, however, either there was some money in the family or perhaps a relative resided in London, because as a young man he went to London and worked in a dry goods store.[10] Whether this was an official apprenticeship is not clear from family records, but it was in London that he learned the trade of keeping shop. Later he would have his own shop at Aberdare. In Aberdare he met Martha Williams, three years his senior and the daughter of the well-to-do Reese Williams. They were married 26 September 1839.

Mid-Nineteenth-Century Wales

At this time the industrial revolution in Britain was in full swing, and the massive migratory movement from the rural area to the mining centers in the Rhondda Valley was gaining momentum. Tenant farmers learned that they could earn four or five times as much money in mining as they did on their farms. The rocky soil of Wales had never been very productive, and this factor combined with the attraction of providing a better living for themselves and their families, tempting the country folk to break with tradition and cast their fortunes with the underground operations in the growing population centers. Wales would never be the same; gaping holes were made in her once luxuriant, green surface, and the mining refuse was piled in large, unsightly, cone-shaped heaps or "tips."

After making their first break with tradition by moving to an urban setting, the newcomers were prepared to make a second and equally momentous break—changing their religious preference. In 1800 only about 10 percent of the population of Wales practiced nonconformity. The religious census of 1851 reveals, however, that Merthyr Tydfil's population was composed of 60 percent religious worshippers of which 90 percent were nonconformists.[11]

Between 1801 and 1851 Great Britain almost doubled in population,[12] and in Merthyr Tydfil the growth rate was even more spectacular as the population of 7,705 in 1801 increased to 46,378 by 1851.[13] Such rapid growth was not without its problems. Crowded conditions were made worse by lack of proper drainage, sanitation, and lighting. One of the biggest problems, however, according to the nonconformist ministers during the second half of the 1840s, was the menace of Mormonism.

The Mormon missionary effort began in south Wales in late 1840. The first missionaries spoke no Welsh; nevertheless, there were converts from both the English- and the Welsh-speaking Welshmen. By January 1846 there were about five hundred members of the Church, most of them in south Wales. As five hundred more were converted during the year of 1846, the ministers became increasingly annoyed. And many of them became nearly frantic as they witnessed almost one thousand more Welshmen join ranks with the Mormons during 1847.[14] Their impassioned lectures and publications failed to keep many of their most stalwart parishioners from abandoning their pews in favor of the hated "Latter-day Satanists."

The Mormons proselyted more aggressively as their numbers grew. A monthly publication, *Prophwyd y Jubili (Prophet of the Jubilee),* was begun in July of 1846; numerous pamphlets appeared in large editions from the press in Rhydybont, owned by Dan Jones's brother, John, who at the time was a nonconformist minister himself.[15] Lectures were given and polemics were engaged in. The most significant polemic as far as William Howells was concerned was the one between Dan Jones and Edward Roberts, a Baptist minister at Rhymni, which began in September 1847. After a couple of lectures by each, Dan Jones produced a forty-page pamphlet entitled "A review of the lectures of the Rev. E. Roberts (a Baptist minister in Rhymni, against Mormonism which were delivered in Caersalem, September the 2nd, and in Bethania (a chapel of the Independents), September the 3rd, in Dowlais." In it he treated the numerous objections and accusations made by Reverend Roberts and used over one-third of the text to shed light on the Spaulding manuscript story, a story which Roberts had used to discount the validity of the Book of Mormon. Dan Jones concluded the pamphlet by stating that he would much rather argue principles than "answer the fool according to his foolishness."[16]

Conversion to Mormonism

It was a copy of this pamphlet that William Howells obtained from the poor widow of his congregation. After reading it with intense interest, he threw his allegiance to Dan Jones, sought him, and received baptism at his hands. The two immediately became the truest of friends. Even though Jones was but seven years older than Howells, the latter often referred to the former as his "adored father," no doubt because through Jones he was figuratively born into the truth of the restored gospel.

Membership in The Church of Jesus Christ of Latter-day Saints for William Howells was not without its price. Many of his customers took their business to other shops. No longer could the Howellses afford to send their seven-year-old daughter, Ann, to boarding school in Swansea. William's father-in-law became so irate at their conversion to Mormonism that he

threatened to cut off the monthly allowance he had been giving them since their marriage.

Although his wealth and prestige were dwindling rapidly,
Howells apparently still wielded some influence; he immediately began proselyting friends, family, and former parishioners. On 19 March 1849 he reported to Orson Spencer[17] his
success in bringing others into the Church, writing, "I have in
the course of the last twelve months, baptized about one
hundred, which I consider a fair commencement."[18] It was
typical for all new converts to set about warning their friends
and neighbors of the urgency of becoming affiliated with the
restored gospel, but for one individual to bring in over one
hundred converts in only a year was truly extraordinary.

One of Howells's great tools in convincing others of the
truth which he fervently believed he now possessed in Mormonism was undoubtedly his power of articulation in English
as well as in Welsh. His flowery style and skillful use of imagery
are typical of the nineteenth century, and his letters to the *Millennial Star* and to the *Udgorn Seion* were woven from the
same cloth as those of his brethren. His description of his
reaction to first hearing Mormon doctrine serves as a brief
example:

> But what astonished me, was, that the armour I then wore, was
> nought but the traditional perplexing doctrines of the learned,
> which were blown like chaff before the Euroclydon of truth, that
> proceeded from the Mormon missionary [Dan Jones].[19]

Dan Jones became a center of controversy not only among
his foes from among the nonconformists but among Church
members and former members as well. Statistics printed in the
Udgorn Seion and the *Millennial Star* reveal that there were
many excommunications during this period. And occasionally,
as in the days of Joseph Smith, these disaffected persons would
turn on those who had caused (as they supposed) their troubles.
As the mission president (his actual title was President of
the Church of Wales), Dan Jones was often the target of scorn
and threats of personal injury. These threats became so heated

just prior to his departure with the first Welsh Mormon emigrants in February 1849 that President Jones required round-the-clock protection for his safety. His residence had to be guarded for weeks before he left. And finally he had to flee in secret before the scheduled time without being able to bid farewell to his wife and baby.[20]

Amidst all these difficulties one of Jones's most ardent defenders was William Howells. Evidence of this loyalty is a two-thousand-word letter to Orson Spencer dated 19 March 1849. Because of the calumny which had been heaped on Dan Jones, Howells proceeded "to describe the impression his holy conduct has made upon my heart; and . . . thousands in Wales, besides." The words of praise and the superlatives which follow would cause the most flowery of funeral eulogies to pale by comparison:

> In truth, it can be said of him, that he was a man of observation and reflection; with soberness, righteousness, and godliness, continually assimilating his mind with ardent love and ambitious zeal to fulfil the solemn duties of his exalted station, so that he might be approved by his master, as a good and faithful servant. His sublime, generous, diligent spirit, applied itself with new exertion continually, as circumstances and experience opened an enlarged field for duty.[21]

One further example:

> Our beloved brother's affection and humility on one hand, his resolution and courage on the other; bearing the contempt of the world with dignity and appulse with decency; had gained the affection of the members of the church of Jesus Christ; particularly those holding the priesthood, to such a degree, that the thought of parting for a short time, would cause a sensation, not to be described by words.[22]

Such was the expression of fierce allegiance William Howells held toward the messenger who had brought him into Mormonism.

At Dan Jones's last conference prior to departing for Utah with the first group of Welsh emigrants, Howells stated:

> The Welsh Saints wish to bear sincere witness to the faithful ful-
> fillment of their dear brother, Capt. D. Jones, by laboring day and
> night in their midst; and they are unable to express in words the
> reverence they have toward him and his priceless service in the
> kingdom of our Lord Jesus Christ in Wales.[23]

He then proposed that a suit of clothes be presented to Dan
Jones and Brigham Young and that Welsh woolen dresses be
presented to their wives. His proposal received unanimous
support, and the clothes were made and given as suggested.

First Journey to France (Le Havre)

The fervor for gathering to Zion was so great among the
Welsh during the late 1840s that it was no doubt painful for
William Howells to have to defer emigrating. Certainly he
could have made arrangements to be among the 350 who constituted the first group of Welsh Mormons to leave Wales for
their new "homeland." His faith was not shaken by the prediction that the emigrants would be sold into slavery as they
passed Cuba,[24] nor was he deterred at the prospect of having
to engage in physical labor upon arriving in Utah, even though
he had a frail constitution. But a mission call to France caused
him to sail east instead of west.

Prior to his conversion to Mormonism, Howells had served
for the Baptists as a missionary in Brittany, that part of France
which had been settled centuries earlier by fugitive Britons.[25]
Details of his first experience in Brittany are not known;
however, it was no doubt a sizable challenge, inasmuch as he
did not speak Breton, and his French was very limited. Nevertheless, the fact that he had had this experience and his great
missionary zeal resulted in a call to return to Brittany, this time
as a Mormon missionary. Within six months following his conversion, the thirty-two-year-old Howells was asked to prepare
to serve, the call made official on 14 August 1848.[26] Earlier,
however, Howells had made mention of rejoicing "in the
honour of being sent as an ambassador of the gospel to France

and Brittany.''[27] The necessary preparations for such an under-taking must have posed considerable difficulty to him, for it was nearly a year before he crossed the Channel.

Although the distance to his assigned field of labor was but two hundred miles, bidding farewell to his wife, Martha, his nine-year-old daughter, Ann, his six-year-old son, William, and his ten-month-old son, Reese, was a most difficult task for William Howells. In a report to Brother Davis, Howells in-serted his journal entry for 2 July 1849:

> Last day before starting on a mission to France; oh, how hard to part with a beloved wife and little children, and leave them in the midst of persecuting enemies—leave her and her young family to be provided for from a business that calls for the presence of a person who understands the nature of such an occupation— leave them in the midst of the plague that is reigning with deadly arrows next door on the right and left, etc. . . . . But God com-mands me to go! his servants command me to![28]

The "plague" Howells mentioned was cholera morbus, and his fears were well founded, because, as he reported to Dan Jones, in Aberdare alone in the space of just one month there were nearly one hundred deaths.[29] Not much was known about the disease then except that it struck fast and was highly contagious. Within a matter of days its victims were either improved or dead. Clothes were systematically burned to prevent further spread, and those who had not contracted the disease were terrified to be around those who had. It is little wonder, then, that William Howells was reluctant to leave his wife and children in the midst of such an epidemic, not knowing whether or not he would see them alive again.[30]

Howells's travels took him first to Swansea, where he slept in the same house in which his "dear father in the gospel," Dan Jones, had slept just five months earlier on his way to Zion.[31] Howells's deep desire was to follow him; duty, however, called him the opposite way. On the morning of 4 July 1849 he boarded the same steamer (the *Troubador*) that the first Welsh Mormon emigrants had used under the leadership of Captain Jones to make their way to Liverpool prior to sailing west.

Howells's purpose for going to Liverpool was to confer with President Orson Pratt, recently called as president of the Church in England. Orson Pratt, in size and appearance, was very similar to William Phillips, successor to Captain Dan Jones in Wales. Howells's excitement ran high: "My heart is leaping with joy now, upon thinking that such a pair who are younger than Jesus, are leading the brave hosts which are in Wales and England."[32] Upon conferring with Orson Pratt, William Howells was ordained a high priest in the High Priesthood, an honor reserved for only a select few in the early days of the Church. The ordination was deemed necessary, in all likelihood, because he was to be the sole representative of the Church in France.

As William Howells made his way from Liverpool to Le Havre, his first city in France, a drama was unfolding in Aberdare. Reese Williams, his seventy-four-year-old father-in-law, was becoming more and more antagonistic toward the Church and especially toward the involvement of his daughter, Martha, and her family. The call for his son-in-law, William Howells, to leave Wales to serve a mission in France was more than he could stand. On 9 July 1849, just a few days after Howells had left Wales on his mission, Reese Williams sent his son on a mission of his own—to convince Martha Howells to come to her senses and leave the Church. His express command was that she not only sever all connections with the Mormons but also that she refrain from sending any money to her husband in France. Noncompliance with his wishes would mean disinheritance for Martha and a discontinuance of the monthly allowance she had been receiving for years. When his son returned with the message that Martha felt safer in complying with the will of her Heavenly Father than with that of her earthly father, Reese Williams went into a rage. He struck the table with his cane and vowed that the following day he would send for his lawyer and cut Martha off without a penny.

Following her brother's visit, Martha attended the Monday night prayer meeting scheduled for the Aberdare Branch and received not only the solace of the meeting but an additional benefit as well. One brother arose and spoke in tongues, and the interpretation was that the sister who was troubled about her financial affairs should take comfort, as all things would work to her good. Later that night Martha's brother came by once again, this time in great haste to get her back to their father's home where he lay dying. Old Reese Williams had been taken severely ill after supper and did not recognize his daughter when she arrived sometime around midnight. He died shortly thereafter without having had time to alter his will; consequently, Martha continued to receive the monthly allowance and received her share of her father's land and his coal mine. Williams's death on 9 July 1849 ironically coincided with the date his son-in-law first set foot on French soil as Mormonism's first missionary to that country.[33]

Had anyone checked Howells's baggage when he landed at Le Havre on that July day of 1849, they would have found it filled with pamphlets in both English and French. Actually, the French publication could be better described as a flier printed on both sides. Entitled "L'Evangile" ("The Gospel"), it contained a series of scriptures in support of the first principles, the necessity for proper authority to act in God's name, the angel bringing the everlasting gospel prophesied of in Revelation 14:6, and the spiritual gifts mentioned in Mark 16:17–20. Nowhere in the two-page flier is "Mormonism" mentioned; however, the full name of the Church, "L'Eglise de Jesus Christ, aux Saints des Derniers Jours," is given once. Then an appeal is made to the reader to search the scriptures carefully to determine whether their church has the proper characteristics and then to come and embrace the true gospel. No author is mentioned, although William Howells must have had a hand in producing this small tract, which was printed by John Davis in Merthyr Tydfil.

The established procedure for proselyting at that time was to loan out tracts to whoever would accept them and then to call back for them in a few days. A person could purchase the publications if he or she wished or simply exchange one on loan for another. This was what William Howells did, with one exception—the tract in French he simply gave away. Since he was laboring in a port city and had very little knowledge of the French language, he adopted the custom of visiting the American ships in port and encouraged other missionaries to do likewise where possible. His visits in the city were to English families. His efforts during the first three weeks of his mission produced very few positive results and a sizable amount of discouragement.

His journal entry for 28 July 1849 is indicative of how the work was progressing:[34]

> Rather idle in the morning, so low spirited. Had a long conversation again with a fine young Dutchman, whom I hoped to baptize. He refused to obey, and was taken very ill and constrained to go home to Holland immediately. I took him to lodge with me, believing that I should be successful in getting him into the kingdom. He was a zealous professor of the Dutch religion, but after all my kindness to him he left me minus of a shirit [sic], which he took away in mistake perhaps. Distributed about fifty tracts in Rue de Paris. They are desirous of having tracts, but will not give a *sou* for a dozen.[35]

But 30 July was a much more successful day—Howells performed his first baptism as a missionary to France. The new member was Augustus Saint d'Anna, thirty years old, single, and a foreigner by birth.[36] He was fluent in English, French, Italian, Spanish, and Creole languages and agreed to meet Howells in St. Malo at the end of August after the latter had made a brief trip back to Wales to check on his family. Whatever happened to Augustus Saint d'Anna is not recorded in any further writings of William Howells.[37]

Two days later Howells's spirits got another lift as he conversed with Monsieur Piclard, a French Protestant minister who questioned Howells through an interpreter minutely for eleven hours. Piclard sought out the missionary the next day and took him by the arm to the interpreter where he questioned him further about mesmerism, a topic of great interest throughout Great Britain and on the Continent in those days. He was apparently very happy with the responses he was receiving, for he bought a copy of all the tracts Howells had with him and even put his hand in his pocket and offered a handful of money, an offer declined by the missionary, as he was not then in want. Howells later referred to Piclard as the person "who first believed the gospel in France."[38] Belief, however, was never translated into action as far as the records show. Curtis Bolton recorded in his journal that Piclard had committed to be baptized on one occasion but backed out at the last minute.[39] Certain members of Piclard's congregation in Le Havre, however, did join ranks with the Mormons.[40]

On 3 August 1849, exactly one month from the time Howells had left Aberdare on his way to France, and just under four weeks from the time he had first begun his labors at Le Havre, he left for Wales to visit his family.

Back in Wales

A tragedy that served to strengthen the faith of the Saints and to frighten their enemies took place during Howells's sixteen-day stay in Aberdare. An explosion of foul air in the coal pit at Cwembach, three miles from Aberdare, killed several people and brought grief to the widows, children, and friends of the victims. Knowing there were many Latter-day Saints living in that branch, Howells accompanied some of his brother officers down into the mine. There "in the midst of the slaughter [they] found that the only Saint that worked in the pit had escaped without losing a hair off his head." Surrounding him were fifty-five corpses who "to a man" had been persecutors of the Saints.[41]

Another experience Howells had in connection with a mining accident was related in his daughter Ann's biography decades later:

> One day Ann saw a multitude of people surrounding the house of a collier, who had just been carried home on a stretcher, apparently dying. A great lump of coal had fallen on his back and broken his spine. . . . He had lately joined the Church but his wife had not. Great sympathy was felt for the man, and several

doctors were sent for by various people. They held a consultation and came to the conclusion that the man would only be able
to live a couple of hours at the most. But the injured man whispered to his wife to send for the "Mormon" elders. Brother
Howell, who was President of the branch, came with his
counselors and they administered to the sick man and Brother
Howell commanded him in the name of Jesus Christ to arise from
his bed. And those who stood around the bed heard the bones of
the sick man's body crack as they slid back into their places and
the man arose from his bed and gave thanks to God for his
mercy.[42]

Martha's brother, who had been sent to persuade Martha to
abandon the Mormons, was in a real quandary as William
Howells returned from his first journey to France. A few days
after Reese Williams's death the wife of Martha's brother had
accepted baptism. Then her family almost caused her to withdraw from Mormonism and return to the Baptists. Her father
had nearly convinced her that all the Mormons wanted from
people was their money. William Howells arrived back in
Aberdare just in time to steady her before she fell, and to give
her added strength, he baptized her husband, Martha's
brother, who no doubt had given much thought to what Mormonism was doing to his life. The baptism took place on the
property which had belonged to Reese Williams. Set for 5:00
A.M. Sunday, 19 August 1849, it represented the last item of
business that Howells had to take care of before departing a
second time for France.[43]

William Howells had been in the Church by this time just
under two years. One of his biggest disappointments had been
his failure to bring his parents and his brothers and sisters into
the gospel also. During this brief interim in Wales, he visited all
of them and extracted a promise from each that he or she
would be baptized on William's next visit to Wales.[44] His father
he described as "a worthy man, a millennarian, having many
interesting ideas in conneion [sic] with the restoration of the
Jews, the millennial reign of Jesus, the restoration of all things,
etc."[45]

Second Journey to France (St. Malo)

Soon after baptizing his brother-in-law, Howells departed once again to continue his mission in France, this time accompanied by a junior companion, his nine-year-old daughter, Ann. Thinking perhaps that she would be able to learn the French language more readily than he and also hoping that she might soften some hearts because of her age, William Howells had Ann by his side for the next three months.[46]

Their first stop was at Cardiff, the largest city in Wales, where Howells preached at the 11:00 A.M. meeting and then again at 6:00 P.M. They left the following morning headed for the Channel Islands, where they arrived on Tuesday morning, 21 August. There they were met by Brother William C. Dunbar, one of the very early converts in England and a member of the Church for nine years, who was then serving a mission on these out-of-the-way islands. Elder Dunbar was having a great deal of success in baptizing the English as well as the French on the Isle of Jersey. Howells offers a possible answer for such astounding success: "Brother Dunbar seems to suit the place exceedingly well; both himself, brother officers, and the cholera, are exerting themselves, bringing in a fine harvest of souls to the kingdom."[47] Also a factor was the tracts and pamphlets. Howells had given Dunbar four hundred of his French tracts and proudly reported of one of the converts that "she was convinced, and converted to the truth by reading my little tract."[48] Memories of Howells's days as a Baptist missionary came to him during his brief stay at Jersey: "Thursday afternoon I preached to a group of Jerseyites in English. It was very strange to me, for two years ago I preached for the Baptist Church here at the request of the minister, who, I was sorry to hear, has just got out of jail!"[49]

On Friday morning, 24 August, father and daughter left Jersey for St. Malo, three hours distant. Elder Dunbar promised that a French brother officer should follow Howells there in about a month's time. It would certainly have been a boost to the effort had someone fluent in the French language been assigned to work side-by-side with Howells. But there is no indication that he ever received such assistance; furthermore, his first convert in France, Augustus Saint d'Anna, apparently did not keep his commitment to meet Howells in St. Malo at the end of August.

In St. Malo the newly arrived Mormon missionaries visited a few English families. On Sunday, two days after their arrival, they attended services at an Episcopalian chapel, which was small but "well filled with pride and lukewarm religionists, without even the form of godliness."[50] Follow-up visits to the clergymen and flocks triggered from them insulting abuse and accusations of blasphemy. One man who was particularly upset was a Mr. Huddlestone, an American. On the morning of 29 August he called at the lodgings of Howells and asked that the Mormon missionary be sent for. Howells describes the ensuing encounter thus:

> Trembling with passion, grinding his teeth, and shaking his clenched fist in my face, he said, "You villain. If you bring any more of these accursed tracts to my house . . ." and a volley of threatenings which I do not remember. When he heard that I was going to open a place for preaching not far from his house, he vowed that he should attend, and if I attempted to do so that he would break every bone in my body (he had never tried I suppose, the toughness of a Welshman's bones).[51]

Howells was then negotiating for the rental of Ebenezer Chapel[52] in St. Servan. The first meeting of the Mormons in France was held there less than one month later on 23 September 1849. Huddlestone, however, was not in attendance. Howells received information which he was unable to substantiate that two of Huddlestone's children had died in the interim.

Many years later Ann recalled some of their experiences in St. Malo and St. Servan, a very short distance away. She said that many times while distributing tracts they were driven away with threats and that she had to run as fast as she could to escape trouble. On one occasion, had it not been for the intervention of friends, Howells would have been thrown into a pond of water. Their first night at St. Servan mob violence forced them into a grove where they succeeded in eluding the mob until towards morning. Then Ann's father told her to stay where she was while he went into the city to ascertain how matters stood at their lodgings. He said he would return soon with some breakfast. Shortly after his departure some of the mob returned and found the little girl. They took her with them as they continued their search for her father, but a lady who lived near the entrance to the grove convinced the mob to let her take the girl and care for her. Fortunately, they agreed. Ann kept a close watch for her father to return and had a joyous reunion a short time later.[53]

Howells reported that his landlady and all in the house except the servant joined together in calling him a "false prophet." But the intrepid father-and-daughter team continued their distribution of French and English tracts in spite of any and all opposition. Said Howells: "Welsh blood is not to be daunted easily, as the devil shall well know before the end comes; he is daily kicking me here, and also taking my half-pence away, but I expect to master him shortly."[54] The "half-pence" reference has to do with the expense to Howells each time someone returned his tracts by post; to retrieve them he had to pay postage due. Instead of paying the postage due, however, he would use the situation as an excuse to return to the sender to ask them for money to get his tracts from the post! He does not state, however, whether such attempts were successful.

The Howellses did succeed in making a few friends despite all the hostility, and these friends informed them that their enemies were going to arrange for the mayor to prosecute Howells for distributing tracts in St. Servan. Howells went to St. Malo to the English consul for advice, and the advice was to refrain from distributing tracts, even though it was not illegal. Howells seized the opportunity and preached the gospel to the consul, "but he actually refused to be baptized for the remission of his sins."[55] One sees these occasional specks of humor in Howells's writings, evidence that the persecution and discouragement were not totally overwhelming.

Having completed all necessary arrangements for the rental of Ebenezer Chapel, Howells scheduled the first meeting for 23 September 1849. The two meetings held there represent the first official meetings of the Mormons in France. The attendance was slight in the morning, but more came for the 6:00 P.M. service, and Howells was elated. Attendance at both meetings was no doubt affected by such things as one brewery master who threatened his workers with immediate dismissal should they venture forth to the Mormon meeting.[56]

Several who went to the meetings were touched by the spirit of conversion. The first one to request baptism was Mademoiselle Ann Browse, "a Lady of Fortune and great learning, member with Mr. Penlee's Church of England for the last 20 years with great influence with all the great folks of the place, Protestants and Catholics."[57] After her confirmation, she rose and presented William Howells with a "small cassette" containing a precious gold ring. He was greatly flattered and commented to his friend Dan Jones in a letter, "Really when I put it on my finger I looked like a gentleman, and no mistake."[58] The Sunday of Ann Browse's baptism was very cold, and because of a lingering illness she had had for years, her friends warned her that her baptism would cost her her life. Undaunted, she went down into the water of a bay near St. Malo. Howells was ecstatic at the result:

> The disease that had preyed upon her constitution for years, and baffled the power of the physician, was completely eradicated. The pallid cheek from that moment showed the healthy bloom of youth, so much so that all congratulated her, and the report circulated that a ducking in the sea on such a cold morning was a sure cure.[59]

While in Wales, Howells had been able to observe the conflict between the established religion and the various nonconformist sects. In France he was able to see yet another dimension of this conflict between the nonconformists and the Catholics. Catholicism was not something he was very familiar with, since it was rare among the Welsh. He noted with some amusement the rivalry between the Catholic and Protestant professors of Christianity in France and was unable to say which hated the other more. The way the Catholics shunned the Bible particularly interested him. After conversing with a learned Catholic priest for some hours, Howells was astonished to hear his views of the Bible: " 'I believe the Bible to be true, because the church gave it me as such, otherwise I should think no more of it than Punch [a humorous British periodical].' "[60] Howells learned of a member of a missionary society who had visited families which he was then visiting. The society was distributing tracts and copies of the Bible. Although received with great politeness, the publications were promptly burned at the departure of the donor according to the general plan the Catholics had adopted. As for Mormon tracts, both Protestants and Catholics took delight in using them to light their fires.

After two months in St. Servan, Howells reported that the persecution was not diminishing. Rather, because of the opening of a place for preaching and the baptism of a Brother William Peddle, the opposition increased to the point of causing Howells and daughter to continue their proselyting elsewhere for a time. So he ordained Brother Peddle to the priesthood, presented him with a number of French tracts, and made his way to Dinan, about twenty miles distant.[61]

At 7:00 P.M. on 23 October 1849 on the steamer for Dinan he met an English clergyman who informed him that should he fail to locate lodgings for himself and daughter that they would have to return to the packet (boat). Howells replied that he had been refused permission to remain on deck. The clergyman made no further comment. Unsuccessful in finding a place to stay, Howells spent the dark, cold night of 23 October with his daughter in his arms at the base of a monument erected in honor of a celebrated person who had conquered the English on the spot five hundred years before. Howells pointed out: "Had the gentleman-clergyman taken us as his guests, 'forgetting not to entertain strangers,' we could not have spent the night more happy."[62]

During the month Howells spent with his daughter in Dinan, apparently no one chose to join the Church. At least no one is mentioned in his lengthy letter about this period of time which was printed in the *Millennial Star.* In addition to the regular tract distributing, William and Ann also visited a Roman Catholic seminary which contained eleven tutors and one hundred and thirty students. They were received with patience and politeness as Howells presented the "plain truths and hard sayings" of his sermons. The visit must have made a great impression on Howells, for he promised President Orson Pratt a more complete account of a "Latter-day Saint's visit to a Catholic college" when they both settled in "Zion's happy land."[63] This he intended to take from his journal, an item that lamentably has yet to surface.

An Irish gentleman who was then in prison in Dinan for debt began circulating anti-Mormon reports as soon as he received word that a Mormon missionary had come to Dinan. French law at that time authorized the creditor to take the body of a debtor without any previous notice; consequently, this Irishman had been put in jail although his coach and horses would have been sufficient to pay his whole debt. Howells spent some time with him and explained the gospel to him and the next day sent him some tracts to convince him to cease from spreading the negative reports.[64]

After having spent one month by himself in Le Havre and three months with his daughter in St. Servan, St. Malo, and Dinan, Howells summed up his efforts: "I have not as yet reaped a rich harvest, but the few that have entered the kingdom by being 'born of water and of the Spirt' [sic] have received glorious testimonies of the power of the truth as it is in Jesus."[65]

Back in Wales Again

After completing the three months of missionary activity with his daughter in St. Malo, St. Servan, and Dinan, William Howells returned to Wales to visit his family, stopping briefly at Jersey Island to visit Brother William C. Dunbar and the Saints, and also at Southampton and Bristol. Father and daughter reached Wales on 27 November 1849 and found that all was well with Martha and the other two children. There is little doubt that Howells rejoiced in being in familiar and somewhat less hostile territory once again. In his 21 December 1849 letter to Orson Pratt, Howells reported having baptized since his arrival in Wales "an intelligent Baptist minister, upwards of 60 years old."[66]

Just prior to Howells's departure for France, William Phillips replaced Dan Jones as Church leader in Wales. Upon Howells's return to Wales, he did not hesitate to throw his allegiance to this new leader. In his 25 January 1850 letter to Orson Pratt, Howells expressed great confidence in William Phillips, and in his two counselors, Abel Evans and John Davis. He referred to President Phillips as "another Samson brought up amongst his brethren, flesh of their flesh, bone of their bone, who would fight the Philistines and cause their dagon to fall more perplexed than ever." President Phillips carried out his new responsibilities with such energy and courage, according to Howells, that "the Saints shouted aloud for joy, for truly the vacuum left by the absence of Brother Captain Dan Jones is amply filled by our young president Brother W. Phillips, in the Church, the families, and the hearts of the Saints of God in Wales."[67]

From all outward appearances the work of the kingdom seemed to be progressing reasonably well in Wales. Thus, one year after Phillips began his tenure, the appointment of Elder Levi Richards, an American, to be representative of the Church in Wales must have come as somewhat of a surprise. It was not intended that Elder Richards replace Phillips, but rather that he work with him in a supervisory capacity, something to which Dan Jones had not been subjected. Furthermore, the Welsh were requested to offer support, both moral and financial, to Elder Richards and his wife during their time in Wales. Although there may well have been some murmuring among the Welsh at this kind of treatment, Howells wished for the Church leaders in Liverpool to know of his loyalty and undeviating support:

The officers present in council, with few exceptions, were all Welsh, yet they received the intelligence about Brother Richards, with as much pleasure as the English officers themselves; they saw that the appointment was pleasing to Brother Phillips, therefore to themselves also, so Brother Levi Richards will be received, not by the English only, but also with open bosom by the Welsh, and by none more than by Brother Phillips and Davis, and also by your humble servant and Brother.[68]

Third Journey to France (Boulogne-sur-mer)

After ten weeks in Wales over the Christmas of 1849, William Howells once again returned to France. This time he went to Boulogne-sur-mer, another seaside city, and it appears that he went without his daughter, Ann. After meeting with and addressing the brethren in London on 11 February 1850, Howells started toward the steamboat which would take him to a "strange country bound with more snares of the devil than any country under the sun." His task was "to undo the knots, in spite of the teeth of the roaring lion and all the fiery spears of his faithful servants."[69]

Upon arriving in Boulogne, he took lodging on the Grande Rue with a Wesleyan family by the name of Gregory. For some reason Howells did not inform the Gregorys concerning his religious persuasion or his purpose for being in France. A couple of days after his arrival, however, Mr. Gregory asked some questions about religion and determined that his lodger was a Mormon missionary. At this point Mrs. Gregory revealed that she had a sister and brother-in-law who had lived at Nauvoo and had gone to Great Salt Lake City. The Gregorys had received letters from their Mormon relatives persuading them to accept baptism; however, there is no indication that they ever did.[70]

On 17 February 1850, a Sunday, just five days after Howells landed at Boulogne, all the Wesleyan churches were called together to hear a sermon concerning the "false prophet" who had just come into their midst and the false doctrine he was distributing throughout the town in the form of scurrilous pamphlets. Howells was there in attendance and called the sermon "one of the most clever and cunning" he had ever heard. Earlier Howells had been to the minister's home and had offered him tracts and conversation about the gospel. The minister refused him with the answer "that he knew sufficient concerning the matter."[71]

Upon returning to his lodgings, Howells encountered a group of individuals awaiting him, among them "one of the leading gentlemen of the place, the expert of Boulogne in debate, a perfect enemy of Mormonism."[72] And although the spirit of this powerful individual influenced Howells "like mesmerism," the Mormon missionary judged himself to come out victorious on every topic during three evenings of debate. At last his opponent "had a fit of temper, clenched his fist, and shouted with others to see miracles."[73] At that Howells arose and left them. Having kept with the first principles, he believed that all present had been able to see how easily he had confused his adversary. Undaunted by it all, Howells continued his proselyting activities and soon had copies of "The Kingdom of God" in the hands of fifty families in Boulogne.

On 28 February 1850 a newspaper of Boulogne, the *Interpreter,* gave in English and French an assessment of Howells's efforts to that point and a prediction concerning his chances for the future:

> It seems we have been lately favoured with the visit of a Mormon prophet here, who has taken up his abode in Grande rue. We fear that the poor fellow's chance of success is very faint indeed, as, although he has been now resident nearly a fortnight, during the course of which he has had several controversies (in all of which it is needless to say, he has been worsted;) he has not yet succeeded in making a single convert.[74]

Naturally, Howells did not see it that way and reported to Orson Pratt that "Mormon doctrines *cannot be worsted*" and that there were already families in Boulogne who had believed the gospel.[75]

About this time Howells received the welcome news that other missionaries had been called to France. John Taylor, Curtis E. Bolton, and John Pack were then on their way from Utah to officially open up the proselyting effort among the French. Howells was ecstatic at the knowledge that soon it would no longer be a one-man effort.

Howells secured a room in Capicure, just in the center of the lower town, for the holding of Sunday services. At the first sermon which he preached at Boulogne on 3 March 1850 there were seven persons present from five different places: France, England, Scotland, Germany, and Wales. Some of the English residents warned the owners of the rented room that various curses would follow should they continue to cooperate with the Mormon missionary and that the family would surely be struck blind. Their response to the ominous warning was to accept payment from Howells for five more weeks of use.[76]

In attendance at the first service held in Boulogne was George Viett, a teacher of languages in the public school. Before the month was out Viett, his wife, and son received baptism. He then proceeded to write the first principles in the German tongue. Mrs. Viett's baptism was held in a river two miles from home, and she had to walk the distance afterwards in wet clothes in cold weather, yet she testified the next day that she had never felt as healthy and happy as she did then.[77]

Some in attendance at Mrs. Viett's baptism expressed their desire to receive baptism soon. And by 6 April 1850 Howells was able to commemorate the twentieth anniversary of the organization of the Church with a branch organized at Boulogne.[78]

Just before the organization of the small branch in Boulogne, Howells was cheered with letters from Sister Anne Browse in St. Malo, Brother William Peddle in St. Servan, and Mr. Piclard in Le Havre. Sister Browse announced that one gentleman by the name of Mr. de Pau, who had been present when Howells was arguing the principles of Mormonism with the learned Catholic priests, was now ready to accept baptism.

Brother Peddle informed Howells that some of their chief enemies in St. Servan were then willing to give nearly everything they had to be baptized and accepted into the Church.[79] Mr. Piclard stated that he still believed in Mormonism. Although it had been seven months since he first met Howells in Le Havre, he had not yet requested baptism.

Fourth and Final Journey to France

Sometime during April or May, William Howells returned to Wales in order to make preparations to return with John Taylor and his party. On 9 June 1850 Howells attended a special general conference held in Merthyr Tydfil to receive the Apostle on his visit to Wales. John Taylor had visited Wales on one previous occasion in January 1847, and he had received an enthusiastic welcome at that time as the first Apostle to be in Wales. There were fewer than one thousand members of the Church then.[80] By the time of his June 1850 visit there were four times that number to hail his presence.[81]

Addressing an audience in which a majority could not understand English was a new experience for John Taylor. There is no evidence that simultaneous interpreting was furnished for the Welsh monoglots. Apparently they were left to rely on understanding by the Spirit. Others, however, were called on to speak in Welsh so that all would be considered. Among those to address the conference in Welsh was William Howells, greatly beloved by his compatriots, who took pride in his being the first missionary to France. John Davis was elated as he reported the proceedings of the conference to Orson Pratt in Liverpool: "We shall never forget such a conference. . . . It makes our hearts to burn within us; our first love is kindled anew."[82]

After the conference sessions on Monday, a group accompanied Brother Taylor to Cardiff, about an hour's train ride from Merthyr Tydfil, where a large congregation had gathered to hear him. The following evening William Phillips, president of the Welsh Mission, went with Elder Taylor to Bristol. Two days later William Howells met John Taylor in Bristol; together they traveled to London to meet with Curtis Bolton and John Pack prior to crossing the Channel to France. William Howells was thrilled to serve as escort to this little group and filled with awe to spend so much time in the presence of an Apostle.

The three days in London prior to their journey to France were days of meetings, mingling together, and rejoicing. Almost constantly at their side was Monsieur Piclard. Still unbaptized and still unable to understand English, Piclard was fascinated by this strange group of people who called themselves Mormons. He stayed at their side in London and joined with them a few days after their arrival in Boulogne, where he spent time with them every day for about two weeks. Howells was no doubt pleased to have living proof of his initial success in France to show to his colleagues.

The procedures used by John Taylor to get established in new circumstances varied somewhat from those which William Howells had used. It was an advantage to come from America, a credential which carried far more weight than merely coming from across the Channel. Elder Taylor brought with him official letters and papers from the governor of Deseret. When these were presented to the mayor of Boulogne with a request to be allowed to preach the gospel in his city, permission was "granted nobly with the greatest amiability."[83] A visit to a gentleman by the name of Monsieur Tatar resulted in permission to preach in his Sale de Concerts located at 21 Rue Montseigny. Monsieur Pater, editor of the newspaper *Interpreter,* gave the group a favorable reception as well as permission to write about Mormonism in his paper. The earlier taunting which had appeared in this same paper concerning the supposed lack of success of William Howells apparently did not constitute an obstacle to the editor's cooperation.

One week following the missionaries' arrival in Boulogne they all gathered at the seashore where a prayer was offered by Elder Taylor. Present were John Taylor, Curtis Bolton, and John Pack from America; William Howells from Wales; and Elders Piercy and Stayner from England. Howells was so moved by the prayer that he translated it and sent it to be published in the *Udgorn Seion.*[84] Among other things, Elder Taylor prayed for "wisdom to lay before this people the principles of eternal truth," and further to ". . . help us to fulfill the callings that devolve upon us, in a manner that shall bring glory to thy name, do honor to ourselves, and lead many to a knowledge of the truth; that thousands in this land may rejoice in the fulness of the blessings of the Gospel of peace."[85] He also asked that no legal obstruction would be in their way.

Thirteen years before this the gospel had been introduced to England and a short time after that to Wales. The converts came in large numbers in both places. There was no reason to believe that France's outcome would be any different. But a century would pass before the number of converts would reach into the thousands. Initially, a more modest counting system would have to be used. There were no legal obstructions; the missionaries were experienced and had known great success in other settings, and the French people were no more apathetic than the English. Why, then, had Howells's success been so small and why were the seats empty at the sermons and the debates?

Certainly the lack of effective communication constituted a major barrier. Curtis Bolton had been to France years before as a student and knew something of the language, but he was far from fluent. William Howells's knowledge of French was severely limited. Furthermore, the only thing in print for Frenchmen to read about the restored gospel was still the two-page leaflet which Howells had written a year before.

Another factor was the stifling effect which Catholicism had on its members in France. The various Protestant sects were allowed to exist in that country but had experienced only a modicum of success. In America, England, and Wales, the converts came from Protestantism and were consequently accustomed to change. With centuries of tradition in their background, the French Catholics were less inclined to accept any radical changes in their lives.

Before any of this became apparent to the hopeful half-dozen, it was decided to stage a "public discussion" in accepting the challenge thrown out to the Mormons by three Protestant ministers. Placards were posted all over town in the full expectation that scores of people would crowd the hall which had a seating capacity of four to five hundred. But the number on the stage exceeded that in the audience. John Taylor published the proceedings of the "Three Nights' Public Discussion" in hopes that more people would be reached by the printed than by the spoken word. But because the publication was written in English, it would have little impact on the French.

During the debate William Howells was called on to relate his experience with gifts of the Spirit. He gave the following instance:

> A person of the name of John M'Manmouth, from Hindostan, intimately acquainted with Dr. Cary, a Baptist Missionary at Calcutta, and a member in his church, understanding seventeen oriental languages, came to reside in the neighborhood of Merthyr Tydvil. He was induced to attend a Saints' meeting; in the meeting, he understood seven languages, spoken in by the gift of tongues by the brethren and sisters present. He testified that the young servant girl I had, prayed in the Malabar tongue. The said girl, on another occasion, prayed in the Hebrew tongue. A Jew present stating he understood what she said, but not the whole, she having spoken in the ancient Hebrew and not the modern.[86]

William Howells stayed with Elder Taylor and the others for about two more months. He went with them to Paris and continued to proselyte. John Taylor made the following statement concerning William Howells:

> Brother Howell who has been labouring here, is a faithful good man, and has laboured with indefatigable zeal, yet, from want of books, and being but imperfectly acquainted with the language, he has, like ourselves, had many difficulties to contend with.[87]

On 25 September 1850 Howells received a release from his mission to return to Wales and prepare to journey to Zion.[88]

Final Four Months in Wales

Once again in Wales, Howells divided his time between assisting in the proselyting effort there and preparing for the journey to Zion. In December he accompanied William Phillips and a couple of other brethren to a conference held in Brecon, about twenty miles north of Merthyr Tydfil. Missionaries had been sent to Brecon a few months before and had encountered much resistance. The mayor of the town sprang to defend the townspeople against the Mormons. Howells, in a letter to Orson Pratt and F. D. Richards, describes the situation:

> On the right he was well supported by the great folks, and also the Protestant parties, with their clergymen, learned tutors, students, and a host of local preachers; and for the left in such emergency, the alliance and help of the Roman Catholic church, *"the old Mother,"* was not to be despised; besides they had barracks filled with soldiers, and noble officers in reserve in case of necessity; so the mayor with great confidence informed the two little Mormon officers, that they should not preach within the confines of the town![89]

Then the battle commenced, and the victory went to the Mormon underdogs. Soon they had their headquarters established in the Bull Inn, and a branch was organized. By the time the December conference was held Brecon had a new mayor. He along with the superintendent of police and other distinguished citizens of the town were "acting with Christian kindness and benevolence to the brethren."[90]

Toward the end of December John Taylor paid his third and final visit to Wales. He honored his predecessor in the French Mission with a visit to his home in Aberdare. While there, Elder Taylor took ten-year-old Ann Howells aside with her parents and gave her a special blessing. At a Sunday meeting Ann was requested to sing, "Home, Sweet Home." Elder Taylor was so delighted with her singing that he had the song printed on pink silk and gave it to her as a keepsake. Many decades later Ann, who at age nine had also served in France as a missionary, still treasured the blessing and the keepsake.[91]

From Wales to Liverpool to America

Just a few weeks later William Howells, his wife, Martha, then four months pregnant, their daughter, Ann, their seven-year-old son, William, and their two-year-old son, Reese, plus two servant girls, began their journey to Liverpool on their way to Zion. In spite of his longing to join the main body of Saints in Salt Lake City, William Howells waxed poetic at the prospect of turning his back on his beloved Wales:

> The mountains and vallies [sic], towns and villages, of his [the Welshman's] native land, enchanted as it were by the various romantic elegies of the Welsh Bards, cause his heart to cleave to the home of his fathers, shuddering at the thought of having his death bed surrounded by strangers, and his grave in a foreign land.[92]

But he received encouragement from a song which had become very popular among the emigrating Saints:

> The Upper California, Oh! that's the land for me;
> It lays between the mountains, and great Pacific Sea;
> The Saints can be supported there, and taste the sweets of
> liberty;
> In Upper California, Oh! that's the land for me.[93]

Martha Howells did not record her feelings as she left Wales, but they were doubtless mixed. With her family members begging her to stay, her share of her father's estate having to be put in court of Chancery, and the awesome uncertainty of several weeks on the sea followed by several months of journeying to some remote spot in a foreign country during which time she would be required to give birth to the child then growing in her womb, she faced enough to give pause to even the most stalwart of women. Had she known of some other hardships that would be required of her—the loss of her husband before the year was out followed by the loss of her eight-year-old son—one can only conjecture what her response would have been.

William Howells was appointed president of the emigrating company on the *Olympus.* On board were two hundred fifty Saints, and fifty-two non-Mormons and members of the crew. On board also was a large supply of books—Howells's personal library, which he intended to contribute to the library in Zion. They set sail from Liverpool on 4 March 1851.

In his account of the crossing, Howells paints a blissful picture: religious services on Sunday, daily prayer meetings morning and evening, daily school classes for the study of English and French and other topics, evening lectures, and the like. All these involvements, according to Howells, left no time for faultfinding, backbiting or quarrelling. Certainly, there must have been some moments when total harmony did not prevail, but they were apparently rare, for nearly every one of the fifty-two non-Mormons were impressed with their strange fellow passengers, especially with the Saints' singing songs of joy, praise, and thanksgiving during rough weather.[94] Their admiration, combined with the proselyting efforts of William Howells and others, was such that twenty-one of them accepted baptism during the crossing. These baptisms were performed on a platform thrown overboard and lowered to the water. The captain was kind enough to devise this unique way of baptizing on the high seas. As they reached New Orleans, twenty-nine more received the ordinance and joined forces with their new brothers and sisters.[95]

And the success did not end once the emigrants reached their new land. It was reported in the *Millennial Star:*

> And no less singular [than the fifty baptisms on board the *Olympus*] is a circumstance that occurred on the "Statesman" after her arrival here [at Kanesville]; her cooks and deck hands left her, preferring rather to be teamsters across the plains for the Mormons, and have their society in fair Utah, than remain any longer cooks and deck hands on the muddy waters of the Missouri.[96]

William Howells and Orson Pratt were both on board the *Statesman* and most likely had something to do with the decision of the cooks and deckhands.

In Council Bluffs

After such a pleasant crossing, there was no reason to expect anything other than continued good fortune. Once in Council Bluffs William Howells set up a store. Martha gave birth to a son, Lewis, on 20 June 1851. Plans and preparations were being made for the trek across the plains the following year. A few short months later, however, William Howells was stricken with sickness. His frail constitution was not able to throw off the illness, and he died 21 November 1851, just barely thirty-five years of age.[97]

Those Left Behind

Howells's untimely demise left Martha with the enormous challenge of getting herself, her babe-in-arms, and her three other children 1,500 miles across the plains to Salt Lake City. She was forced to sell the large supply of books at a sacrifice. The money was needed, and the books constituted too heavy a cargo to transport such a great distance. During the wagon journey toward Utah, Martha suffered yet another personal tragedy—the death of nine-year-old William. He had fallen asleep beneath a wagon wheel and did not hear anything when the wagon started in motion.[98]

Martha, a true stalwart in every sense of the word, continued faithful to her conviction of the truthfulness of Mormonism right up to her death nearly thirty years later in 1879. After ten years of a harsh existence in Utah she made a one-year visit to Wales, where she finally received her share of her father's estate.[99]

Martha and William's son Reese later became a wealthy merchant in Ogden. Their daughter, Ann Howells, also continued faithful until her death in 1916. Her life was filled with the many hardships of a pioneer existence. And, in addition to her brief mission to France as a nine-year-old in 1849, she later served two years in the Sandwich Islands as a missionary with her husband.[100]

In the four years from his conversion to Mormonism to his death, William Howells brought in nearly two hundred other converts, opened up the missionary effort in France, had miracles performed through him, and presided over a company of Mormon emigrants across the ocean. What other accomplishments he might have been responsible for had he been permitted to live another two or three decades one can only imagine. One would suppose that the name of William Howells would have become well known in Mormondom if an early death had not claimed him first.

Notes

I wish to thank the Religious Studies Center for their assistance in making it possible for me to do research in Wales in person.

1. W. R. Davies, *Y Sentiau Diweddaf. Sylwedd Pregeth a Drad-dodwyd ar y Gwyrthiau, er mwyn Goleuo y Cyffredin, a Dangos Twyll y Creaduriaid a Alwant eu Hunain yn "Seintiau y Dyddiau Diweddaf"* (Merthyr Tydfil: David Jones, 1846), p. iv. Translated title: "The Latter Saints [*sic*]: Substance of a Sermon Which Was Delivered on the Miracles, in order to Enlighten the Public and Show the Deceit of the Creatures Who Call Themselves 'Latter-day Saints.' " All translations from Welsh into English are mine.

2. The term *nonconformist* has reference to any of the Protestant sects which did not conform to the practice of being members of the Church of England.

3. Aberdare is about seven miles from Merthyr Tydfil. According to his marriage certificate, William Howells resided at "Penpound," that part of Aberdare town where the Baptist chapel "Carmel" stood. In all likelihood Howells frequented this chapel. I am indebted and grateful to Mr. D. L. Davies of Aberdare for this information.

4. "Extract from a Work by Elder John Taylor about to be Published in France," 15 March 1851, *Millennial Star* 13:80.

5. *Seren Gomer* 30:374–75. Translated title: *Star of Gomer*. This was a periodical published by the Baptists at the town of Carmarthen.

6. William Howells to John Davis, *Udgorn Seion* 1 (May 1849): 94. Translated title: *Zion's Trumpet*. This periodical was the sequel to *Prophwyd y Jubili (Prophet of the Jubilee)* and was published by several editors from January 1849 to April 1862.

7. "Extracts from Elder Dan Jones's Letters to Orson Spencer," 3 November 1847, *Millennial Star* 9:364.

8. Neither the denominational journals nor the chapel histories of the period contain any reference to a "Reverend William Howells, of Aberdare." It is far more likely that Howells became, as many others did, a recognized Baptist lay preacher. Furthermore, in the 1841 census for Aberdare, he gives as his "condition" (i.e., occupation) that of "Draper." Had he trained for the ministry or been ordained, Howells would no doubt have stated his theological role. Thanks again to D. L. Davies for this clarification.

9. William Howells to the Editor, 11 May 1848, *Millennial Star* 10:175.

10. William Louis Howell, "Life of William Howell," p. 1. An eighteen-page typewritten nonpublished manuscript. A copy is in Special Collections, Harold B. Lee Library, Brigham Young University, Provo, Utah. William Howells's name appears frequently without the final *s,* a form currently used by his descendants. I have chosen to spell his name with the final *s,* however, inasmuch as he himself signed it that way in his 27 September 1849 letter to Dan Jones, the original of which is housed in Salt Lake City at the Library-Archives, Historical Department, The Church of Jesus Christ of Latter-day Saints (hereafter cited as LDS Church Archives).

11. E. T. Davies, *Religion in the Industrial Revolution of South Wales* (Cardiff: University of Wales Press, 1965), pp. 33–38.

12. *Report of the Population Panel* (London: Her Majesty's Stationery Office, March 1973), p. 29.

13. E. T. Davies, *Religion in the Industrial Revolution of South Wales,* p. 8.

14. *Millennial Star* 9:107; 10:121, 253.

15. Rhydybont is located about fifty miles to the northwest of Merthyr Tydfil. There is evidence that John Jones joined The Church of Jesus Christ of Latter-day Saints, but not until several years later in 1854.

16. Capt. D. Jones, *Adolygiad ar Ddarlithoedd y Parch. E. Roberts* (Merthyr Tydfil: D. Jones, 1847), p. 40. Translated title: "A Review of the Lectures of the Rev. E. Roberts."

17. Orson Spencer's title was then "President of the Church in the British Isles."

18. W. Howells to Editor, 19 March 1849, *Millennial Star* 11:121.

19. Ibid.

20. Dan Jones to John Davis, 18 April 1849, printed in *Hanes Ymfudiad y Saint i Galifornia* (Merthyr Tydfil: J. Davis, 1849), p. 8. Translated title: "An Account of the Saints' Emigration to California."

21. Howells to Editor, 19 March 1849, *Millennial Star* 11:119.

22. Ibid., p. 120. The word *applause* is misspelled *appulse* in the *Millennial Star*.

23. "Glamorganshire Conference," Merthyr-Tydfil, *Udgorn Seion* 1:21.

24. "A Review of Mormonism and the Reverend T. Williams," signed "Anti Humbug," *Seren Gomer* 31:305.

25. Dan Jones to the Editor of the *Deseret News*, 22 October 1850. Original is at LDS Church Archives. No details of Howells's mission for the Baptists to Brittany have survived among his descendants.

26. "Conference Minutes," Manchester, England, 13 August 1848, *Millennial Star* 10:254.

27. Howells to Editor, 11 May 1848, ibid., p. 175.

28. Howells to Davis, 10 September 1849, *Udgorn Seion* 1:171–72.

29. William Howells to Dan Jones, 27 September 1849. The original is at LDS Church Archives.

30. One of the fatalities which caused very little sorrow among the Mormons was the death of the infamous W. R. Davies, who fell ill at 9:00 on the morning of 1 September 1849. By 7:00 the same evening the cholera had claimed another victim (see J. Ronald Williams and Gwyneth Williams, *History of Caersalem, Dowlais, Welsh Baptist Church* [Llandysul: Gomerian Press, 1967], p. 35).

31. Howells to Davis, 10 September 1849, *Udgorn Seion* 1:172.

32. Ibid.

33. Howell, "Life of William Howell," p. 13.

34. The "journal entry" is actually part of his 9 August 1849 letter to Orson Pratt. It has the appearance of a journal entry and was probably transcribed from his journal.

35. Howells to Editor, 9 August 1849, *Millennial Star* 11:263.

36. Howells does not specify his nationality.

37. Curtis E. Bolton does not make mention of Augustus Saint d'Anna in his journals either.

38. William Howells to William Phillips and John Davis, 8 August 1850, *Udgorn Seion* 2:235.

39. *Curtis Edwin Bolton, Pioneer, Missionary: History, Descendants and Ancestors,* comp. Cleo H. Evans (Fairfax, Va.: n.p., 1968), p. 45. Entry for 1 December 1850.

40. Ibid., pp. 68–70. Entries for 27 October and 1 November 1851.

41. Howells to Editor, 11 August 1849, *Millennial Star* 11:267.

42. Howell, "Life of William Howell," pp. 13, 14.

43. Howells to Editor, 26 August 1849, *Millennial Star* 11:295.

44. Ibid.

45. Ibid.

46. Howells made two subsequent journeys to France of three months each. There is no indication that Ann accompanied him on either of these.

47. Howells to Editor, 26 August 1849, *Millennial Star* 11:296.

48. Ibid.

49. Howells to Davis, 10 September 1849, *Udgorn Seion* 1:174.

50. Howells to Editor, 26 August 1849, *Millennial Star* 11:296.

51. Howells to Jones, 27 September 1849.

52. It is not clear from Howells's letter, but this appears to be a Protestant chapel.

53. Sophy Valentine, *Biography of Ann Howell Burt* (Brigham City, Utah: n.p. 1916), p. 10. The only time William Howells mentions in his writings about spending a night out-of-doors was their first night in Dinan where they arrived late and were unable to find lodging. Perhaps Ann confused her experience there with the one which she attributed to St. Servan.

54. Howells to Editor, 26 August 1849, *Millennial Star* 11:296.

55. Ibid.

56. William Howells to William Phillips and John Davis, 23 September 1849, *Udgorn Seion* 1:217.

57. Howells to Jones, 27 September 1849.

58. Ibid.

59. William Howells to Orson Pratt, 21 December 1849, *Millennial Star* 12:12.

60. Ibid., p. 11.

61. Ibid., pp. 11–12.

62. Ibid., p. 12. The monument is most likely the equestrian statue of the fourteenth-century hero, Bertrand Du Guesclein. Unlike many statues in France which were melted down for ammunition by the Germans during World War II, this one still stands. It was allowed to remain because it symbolized supremacy over the British.

63. Ibid., p. 13.

64. Ibid.

65. Ibid., p. 14.

66. Ibid.

67. Howells to Editor, 25 January 1850, ibid., p. 90.

68. Ibid., p. 91.

69. Howells to Phillips and Davis, 23 February 1850, *Udgorn Seion* 2:83.

70. Howells to Orson Pratt, 7 April 1850, *Millennial Star* 12:158.

71. Howells to Phillips and Davis, 23 February 1850, *Udgorn Seion* 2:83.

72. Ibid.

73. Ibid., p. 84.

74. *Interpreter,* 28 February 1850, cited in *Millennial Star* 12:158.

75. Howells to Orson Pratt, 7 April 1850, ibid.

76. Ibid.

77. William Howells to William Phillips and John Davis, 11 April 1850, *Udgorn Seion* 2:94.

78. Ibid.

79. The number, if any, of these "chief enemies" to actually receive baptism is not a matter of record.

80. "Merthyr Tydfil Conference," 3 January 1847, *Prophwyd y Jubili* 2:16, 17.

81. *Udgorn Seion* 2:202.

82. John Davis to Orson Pratt, 13 June 1850, *Millennial Star* 12:219–20.

83. Howells to Phillips and Davis, 8 August 1850, *Udgorn Seion* 2:233.

84. Ibid., pp. 233–35.

85. John Taylor to the Editor, 21 July 1850, *Millennial Star* 12:269.

86. "Three Nights' Public Discussion between the Revds., C. W. Cleeve, James Robertson, and Philip Cater, and Elder John Taylor of The Church of Jesus Christ of Latter-day Saints at Boulogne-sur-mer, France" (Liverpool: Published by John Taylor, 1850), p. 32.

87. Taylor to the Editor, 21 July 1850, *Millennial Star* 12:270.

88. *Curtis Edwin Bolton,* p. 43. Entry for 25 September 1850.

89. William Howells to Orson Pratt and F. D. Richards, 11 December 1850, *Millennial Star* 13:11.

90. Ibid.

91. Valentine, *Biography of Ann Howell Burt,* p. 9.

92. William Howells to F. D. Richards, 15 February 1851, *Millennial Star* 13:78.

93. Ibid. Incidentally, "The Upper California, Oh! That's the Land for Me" was written by John Taylor.

94. Letter of William Howells, 27 April 1851, ibid., p. 189.

95. Ibid., pp. 190–91.

96. "Arrivals" quoted from *Frontier Guardian,* ibid., p. 255.

97. Howell, "Life of William Howell," p. 18.

98. Valentine, *Biography of Ann Howell Burt,* pp. 16–17.

99. Ibid., p. 19.

100. Ibid., p. 27.

Keith W. Perkins

4

Andrew Jenson:
Zealous Chronologist

Keith W. Perkins was born in Phoenix, Arizona. He is married to Vella Crowther of Malad, Idaho; they have four children and one grandchild. He received his B.A. degree from Arizona State University in Secondary Education (history) and his M.A. and Ph.D. degrees from Brigham Young University in Church History and Doctrine. For three years he served as principal of Granite Seminary in Salt Lake City and for four years as an instructor at Tempe (Arizona) Institute of Religion. For the past ten years he has been at Brigham Young University and is currently Chairman of the Department of Church History and Doctrine. He has published widely in LDS periodicals, with emphasis on the Kirtland, Ohio, period of Church history.

The time was 3:00 P.M. on 4 July 1935. The place—Rebild Park, Denmark. Andrew Jenson stepped to the microphone. Sitting behind him on the stand was a distinguished group, consisting of Dagmar, the sister of the king of Denmark; Prime Minister Stauning; Dr. P. Munch, minister of Foreign Affairs; and Mrs. Ruth Owens, ambassador from the United States. Andrew Jenson had been selected by Governor Henry H.

Blood of Utah as his personal representative to present to Denmark a covered wagon typical of the ones used by Danish emigrants in the year 1853 as they crossed the plains of western United States. As Jenson spoke, his voice was broadcast not only throughout Denmark but also to the United States.

That evening Andrew Jenson sat by Prime Minister Stauning at a banquet given in Jenson's honor. Eleven days later he was standing in the Christiansborg Castle in Copenhagen waiting to be ushered into the presence of King Christian X. When the door was opened, Andrew bowed graciously before the king; the king arose and greeted him warmly. King Christian indicated he had listened with interest to Jenson's speech over the radio. Jenson remarked that he had always held the land of his birth in dear remembrance and that he was immensely enjoying this special visit. The king listened as Jenson traced the journey of the first Mormon emigrants from Denmark to the United States and then explained to the king some of the doctrines of his church. In connection with the Word of Wisdom, Jenson said that he enjoyed Danish *Smorrebrod* but did not use strong drinks. After a fifteen-minute interview, King Christian grasped Jenson's hand "as though he had been an intimate friend of years standing," and the Mormon historian departed.[1] Jenson expressed great pleasure at his visit to Denmark, stating that these were days never to be forgotten—a royal welcome, indeed, to one who eighty-five years before had been born in a humble cottage, a descendant of the Danish peasantry.

Andrew Jenson[2] was born 11 December 1850 on a small farm called Damgren (branch of a pond), Torslev parish, Hjørring amt (county), Jutland, Denmark, the son of Christian Jenson and Kirsten Andersen. His people had lived in the same general region for about two hundred years. The family was almost penniless, and it was necessary for the children to support themselves at a very early age.

In 1850 the first missionaries of The Church of Jesus Christ of Latter-day Saints arrived in Denmark. By 1854 the elders had traveled to Damgren. After a short investigative period Christian and Kirsten Jensen were converted to the Church and were baptized 8 December 1854. Andrew was baptized in 1859 at age eight.

Andrew spent his early school years studying under the tutelage of his mother since the local schoolteacher was bitterly anti-Mormon. The main literary diet of young Andrew was the Bible, the Book of Mormon, and a few Church publications, including *Skandinaviens Stjerne (Scandinavia's Star),* the Latter-day Saint semi-monthly periodical printed in the Danish-Norwegian language.

While Andrew was living in Denmark, *Skandinaviens Stjerne* published a series of articles on the Prophet Joseph Smith, from which Andrew first acquired his interest in Church history. These articles probably helped determine his later style of writing, as he memorized the dates of the important events about which he read,[3] which led to a factual rather than an interpretive emphasis.

At the suggestion of the missionaries, he began at the age of thirteen to keep a journal. This was the beginning of a life of record keeping—for himself and for the Church. Of this chronicle he later wrote: "History has been my major interest since . . . a missionary's journal inspired me to record my personal history. . . . In keeping this journal, which has been uninterrupted since that day, I have learned that a person can't be a natural historian until he commences with his own life."[4]

Andrew immigrated with his family to the United States in 1866. His journey by ship and across the plains is one of the unique recordings of such an experience by a teenage boy. One of the most poignant experiences he recalled years later was the hunger that he faced in the journey. He was reminiscing with a Mr. William H. Jackson, who as a young boy had traveled east from Salt Lake City. Jackson followed behind a wagon load of apples and ate apples until he couldn't lift another one. Andrew replied, "Yes, I know. . . . Here it is in my journal, the record of coming along the next day. I was a hungry youth of 15, and I saw those peelings. You mayn't believe it, but I collected all the peelings I could find, and ate them. They were pretty thin, but they tasted mighty good to me then."[5]

The Jensons settled in Pleasant Grove, Utah, where young Andrew took up many occupations to sustain himself and assist in supporting his family. Although he preferred study to hard manual labor, he was forced to work as a farmhand, a railroad construction crew laborer, and a cowboy. His journal provides an excellent description of a nineteenth-century cattle drover.[6]

At age twenty-two Elder Andrew Jenson was called on his first of ten missions for the Church. The call was to his native Denmark. While on this mission his interest in producing historical works was further intensified. He began by writing a history of the Aalborg Conference. "And so that is how I came to myself, and found myself walking in the Aalborg Conference, preaching and commencing my historical career."[7]

After his return home, he married and began his family. To support his new family he continued to perform manual labor, which proved very unsatisfactory. He had learned from experience that farming was not his natural vocation and that he was not gifted in doing mechanical work as was his father. From his youth he "had been of a studious nature," particularly fascinated by the reading and writing of history. As he meditated and prayed about his future, the thought came to him "as if by direct inspiration from heaven" to continue the work that he had contemplated, to translate certain portions of the history of Joseph Smith into Danish. He called his new work *Joseph Smith Levnetsløb*.[8]

Thus began a new and lifetime career of translating and writing the history of the Church. Because of the limited funds of the Danish Saints, Jenson was forced to publish his literary venture in serialized form, selling the weekly series to his subscribers. Only after the entire series was completed would he then have the series bound into a single volume. This pattern of publishing his history would continue throughout his life, since he financed almost all of his historical works himself. Only near the end of his life did the Church assist in financing his works.

From this modest beginning his historical works started to increase greatly. His next work was to assist in the publication of the Danish-Norwegian paper *Bikuben (Beehive).* This work was interrupted by another call to a mission in Denmark. While there, following the death of the mission president, Andrew served as president for a brief period of time. Following his return, Jenson continued his work in providing Scandinavian Latter-day Saints with the history of the Church by publishing *Morgenstjernen (Morning Star).* As was his first venture, this work was possible because he sold subscriptions in advance of publication. Although sales of *Morgenstjernen* grew steadily, it was not enthusiastically received by all the Scandinavian Saints. Jenson notes of a visit to one of these settlements:

> I here met some peculiar cold and indifferent members of the Church who appeared to be as ignorant and careless concerning anything of an intellectual nature as any I have ever seen. It seemed as easy to make them fly to heaven as sustain anything of a literary nature. If people are to be saved according to the knowledge they gain in this life however will such people ever get into heaven?[9]

However, this discouraging experience did not alter the enthusiasm Andrew had for producing historical works for Latter-day Saints. His next work was the translation of the Pearl of Great Price into Danish. Although it began as a private venture, it later became a Church publication. He also served as editor of *Utah Posten,* a Danish language newspaper, in 1855.

In May 1889 Andrew Jenson began many years of travel to the various stakes of the Church, beginning with a visit to a conference of the Wasatch (Utah) Stake. To obtain some local Church history, he perused several private journals written by older settlers. This set the pattern he later followed. He would travel to an area, glean information from private journals and original records, then bring the information home and arrange it into a history of the area.[10]

One of these visits to another stake demonstrates his method of travel and gives us a fair sample of the diligence he exercised in gathering the history of the Church. He rode the Rio Grande Western Railroad to the Thistle station. After a long wait of several days, he caught a ride from Thistle on a flatcar loaded with rails. His chair was a keg of railroad spikes. All during the seventeen-mile trip a terrible wind and hailstorm raged. He arrived in Indianola alive, "although cold and chilled through," and then walked a mile to a member's home. After a short time, he rode a lumber wagon part of the way to Milburn, walking the last two or three miles into town. He walked from Milburn to Fairview and then on to Mt. Pleasant. The bishop at Mt. Pleasant gave him a ride to Ephraim.[11] His success in his research was ample reward for the rigors of travel.

> [I] Found in the house of the late H. F. Peterson the documents, on loose scraps of paper and small note books, which would make a fair history of Ephraim, if properly compiled. They were papers concerning the existence of which the authorities of Ephraim were entirely ignorant. I find that the ward clerks . . . are and have always been very slow in keeping their records. . . . After visiting several parties in Ephraim in order to obtain historical information, I rode by chance to the house of widow Olsen north of Manti, where I found some valuable records kept by the late Rasmus Olsen of Ephraim, deposited in the loft of an old house where they served as feed for mice. I spent most of the afternoon sorting the Records.[12]

With the excellent work he had done with the stakes of the Church, the Brethren decided to send him on a tour of the missions of the world in order to gather material for Church history.[13] This work enabled him to write the history of the missions of the Church and also assisted in the preparation of two of his major works—the four-volume *Biographical Encyclopedia* and *Encyclopedic History of The Church of Jesus Christ of Latter-day Saints.*

Biographical Encyclopedia is unique from many standpoints. It is Jenson's only major work that has been reprinted in its entirety (by Western Epics in 1971). It is the first and most extensive compilation of its kind ever published in the Church. *Biographical Encyclopedia* is impressive in the variety and types of people represented. Although all General Authorities are delineated, most of the names listed are unknown to us today. Few Church books have given such extensive coverage to the average, commonplace variety of Latter-day Saints. Women, who are generally neglected in Latter-day Saint history, are given frequent coverage in these volumes. Another group of Latter-day Saints who receive extensive coverage in *Biographical Encyclopedia* are the Scandinavians. This is well demonstrated by his reaction to the treatment that Frederik Samuelsen, a member of the Danish Rigdag (Parliament) and a convert who had labored diligently to help the cause of the Church in Denmark, had received because of the difficulty he had with the English language. Jenson comments that it was the general opinion that Samuelsen died "broken-hearted as the quiet life he had been forced to lead in Utah was such a contrast to his public activities in his native country."[14]

With the work Jenson was doing on the histories of the stakes and missions, he saw the need of a detailed history of the Church from its organization to the present time. Thus the work of compiling a journal history of the Church was begun. Charles W. Penrose began such a work, but he was unable to finish it. Elder Penrose must have been delighted that Andrew Jenson continued on and expanded the work he had just started. This resulted in one of Jenson's most ambitious works, over seven hundred legal-size manuscript volumes.

This was also a period of intense spiritual striving for Andrew Jenson. On a number of occasions Jenson describes going alone to pray about something which only the Lord knew. Later he reveals that the prayer concerned a dream he had where he was sustained as one of the seven presidents of the Seventy. He also began to hear reports that one of the leaders of the Church had been inquiring concerning his faithfulness, character, and family affairs. Later he reveals that because of a vacancy in the First Council of Seventy his name had been brought before the First Presidency and the Twelve, along with other names of Scandinavian descent, to determine who should fill the vacancy. "I have in the past tried *not* to seek for office or position, but I can not deny that I would consider myself much favored by the Lord if he accepts me as His servant in this respect."[15] Although he was considered, Andrew Jenson was not chosen.

After the completion of *Morgenstjernen,* he was asked by many of the English-speaking Saints if he could not do for them what he had done for the Scandinavian Saints. With this encouragement, he launched another of his major accomplishments, the *Historical Record.* This work was briefly interrupted but greatly benefited by a special mission for the Church to the "waste places of Zion" in company with Edward Stevenson and Joseph Smith Black. This mission took him back to the early scenes of Church history. Historical information gained from this trip proved invaluable not only in his publication of *Historical Record* but also in all his future historical works. Besides the many important insights gained, Jenson was able to look at the past persecution of the Church in Missouri with some humor. In the valley of Adam-ondi-Ahman they found "a fine watermelon patch," of which Jenson wrote:

> In consideration of this being the land of the Saints, and that the occupants had not paid any rent for many years, we consecrated two of the melons to our own use; they tasted very good; in fact they were the best melons we had on our intire [*sic*] journey.[16]

They were surprised to find that the infamous Thomas C. Sharp, "the once notorious editor of the Warsaw 'Signal' (who did, perhaps, as much as any other man to incite the populace to murder the Prophet Joseph and his brother Hyrum)," was now editing the *Carthage Gazette.* They found the elder Sharp very uncommunicative, but his son William treated them kindly and asked them a very interesting question. "Do you think . . . that the Mormons would kill my father if he were to visit Utah?" Surprised by the question, they responded that

Latter-day Saints were not a bloodthirsty people and "did not seek satisfaction in retaliation."[17]

His next work, *Church Chronology,* along with the monumental work he had done already, led to his appointment as an assistant Church Historian. Concerned that his work was not properly being recognized by the leaders of the Church, he took the matter directly to the First Presidency. During the course of the interview, President George Q. Cannon moved that Andrew Jenson be appointed Assistant Church Historian. The motion was seconded by President Wilford Woodruff and was unanimously sustained by all present. Andrew Jenson's name was presented at general conference on 10 April 1898 where he was sustained by the general membership of the Church.[18]

However, although his work on *Church Chronology* may have helped gain him the office of Assistant Church Historian, two years later it seemed to stand in the way of further recognition. Many of the presiding officers in the wards and stakes urged the Saints to purchase the book with the disconcerting result that in some instances Jenson was criticized because he "pushed too hard" for the sale of the work.[19]

Events at this time seemed to turn against Andrew. At the October 1900 conference he was not sustained as Assistant Church Historian. He was also informed that the new Historian's Office would probably not be built for some time. All that he had worked for during the last several years now seemed to be fading away. He became more and more depressed at the situation. What would he do? Where could he go? If the Brethren would not recognize him in the position he felt he deserved, he would take his problems to the Lord. On 11 August 1901, Andrew took a "lonely" walk into the mountains behind Ensign Peak. There he stopped and engaged in secret prayer and meditations for some time. He recorded the manifestation that came to him following his heartfelt prayer:

> My Son, be of good cheer, thy prayers are heard and shall be answered upon thy head with the blessing thou so earnestly desire. The Lord has not rejected thee, but he has permitted thee

to pass through trials and affliction in order to try thy faith and thy integrity. . . . Thou has not lost thy position in the Church as a Historian; thy zeal and integrity in that capacity is known to God and is pleasing in his sight; and it is God who has inspired thee to do the work which thou has done. But thou hast been too ambitious and has cared too much for the opinion of men; and this is the main cause of thy present disappointment.[20]

Lifted by this revelation, he made his way home "fully determined to take a new stand" and obey the words that had been given to him. He continued his work and started new projects. It appears, though, that he began to contemplate leaving the Church Historian's Office, for he started making plans to organize the Andrew Jenson History Company.[21] In the April 1902 conference, however, he was again sustained as Assistant Church Historian.

Nevertheless, his troubles were not over. Andrew Jenson had watched three fellow Assistant Church Historians move to greater prominence in the Church: Charles W. Penrose to the First Presidency, Orson F. Whitney to the Quorum of the Twelve, and Brigham H. Roberts to the First Council of Seventy. Had his time finally arrived? Were the years of frustration at seeing others appointed to higher position in the Church, while he remained behind, finally coming to an end? He had been disappointed before, but he knew that these past experiences had been for his good and that they helped develop his will power and stability of character, "as I have so far been able to bear up under it." He realized he would be rewarded for his diligent efforts some time:

> If I am not rewarded for my integrity before God and my energy in the interest of God's work on the earth in this life I have great faith in that which in the life to come will come to them that persevere and remain steadfast and faithful to the end. And by the help of the Almighty I shall indeavor [sic] to act as becometh an Elder of Israel and servant of God the remainder of my life.[22]

But now, at last, it appeared he might receive some of his reward in this life. With the death of President Anthon H. Lund there was a vacancy in the presiding councils of the Church and in the office of Church Historian. In addition, previous to his being selected as a member of the First Presidency, President Lund had been the "Scandinavian Apostle." Once more Jenson began to construct "air castles" only to have them shattered to the ground.

While doing research in the St. Louis Public Library, he read in the *Deseret News* that the new Apostle selected was a Scandinavian, but a Norwegian, not a Dane—John A. Widtsoe —and that the new Church Historian was Joseph Fielding Smith, Jenson's former assistant. This bitter pill was almost impossible for Jenson to swallow. In the privacy of his journal he revealed his innermost feelings and emotions over this experience:

> Why have I been sidetracked so repeatedly? Why this slight in the face of my known ability and activity in the historical field? . . . Way back in 1884 when my name was canvassed in connection with filling a vacancy in the First Council of Seventy, and I was sidetracked, the late Erastus Snow told me not to feel bad about it for the Lord had a better position reserved for me. I now query, as I have often done before, if I have done anything wrong whereby the Lord should be displeased with me, or why with my increased ability and diligence I should lose out instead of gaining with my brethren in the Priesthood. Yet, here I am, sidetracked once more, after a life-long struggle, during which I have given my best to Church work and have reserved nothing so far as I understand myself for selfish motives. Is it wrong in the sight of the Lord for a man to expect reward or recognizance for real merit. Is there no such thing as appreciation when a man puts his whole soul into a work which is aimed at doing good and to benefit the cause of God and mankind generally? I left the library in a solemn mood.[23]

Unfortunately Andrew had not yet learned the lesson that Anthon H. Lund had tried to teach him nine years before. He had similar feelings then which had resulted in his going to his good friend President Lund and confiding in him his concerns. President Lund had told him "he must not harbor such feelings. He was honored in the Church and it is not position but works that will count."[24] Nor had he taken seriously the counsel of Apostle George Albert Smith:

> Some wondered why Andrew Jenson was not promoted to a position among the Twelve or chief quorum of Seventies; but where there were hundreds of men in the Church who could be chosen for Apostles there were only a few indeed who could fill the position that I held or do the work I did.[25]

But still he continued to brood. "I am driving no stakes, laying no plans and having no expectations, so I look for no disappointments."[26]

Jenson need not have worried that his work did not receive the recognition he thought it should. It was during the later years of his life that he received his greatest acclaim. President Grant personally told him how pleased he was with his work.[27] The Church periodical *The Improvement Era* was also laudatory, "No man has done more—if any has done so much —in the cause of abundant and correct data for the Church records."[28] In addition, editors of many newspapers outside Utah lauded the "Mormon historian." Andrew Jenson probably did as much to spread goodwill among non-Mormons as any other person in the Church. Typical of their response is the following:

> Professor Jenson has devoted his life to the study of Mormon history, and in his exhaustive research work through a period of more than forty years has come to be regarded as one of the foremost living authorities on that era of mid-century expansion that preceded and coincided with the Civil War period. Although he has devoted himself assiduously to the perpetuation of the vivid history of his particular faith, his work has gained him wide recognition beyond church circles.[29]

Jenson's work was becoming so well known and accepted that even the once vociferously anti-Mormon newspaper, the *Salt Lake Tribune,* asked him to write a series of historical articles. Not to be outdone, the *Deseret News* asked him to write two historical articles for them on a regular basis, one daily and one weekly.

It was during these climactic years that the Church agreed in 1941 to publish the *Encyclopedic History of The Church of Jesus Christ of Latter-day Saints.* His own story, *Autobiography of Andrew Jenson,* was sent to the 1,245 ward and branch libraries of the Church.

On 15 November 1941, at nearly ninety-one, after a lifetime of service to the Church, Andrew Jenson suffered a heart attack and died three days later.

What evaluation can we make of the contribution of this Danish-born peasant who later dined and conversed with some of the great dignitaries of the world? The sheer magnitude of his works is unbelievable. Jenson was an author, compiler, translator, and preserver of Church history. He authored twenty-seven books, fifteen volumes of diaries (1863 to 1941), some two thousand historical articles for the *Deseret News,* a long series of articles in the *Salt Lake Tribune,* and twenty-two articles for the *Improvement Era.* He collected fifteen thousand biographical sketches. He compiled eight hundred and fifty manuscript volumes of Journal History and histories of stakes and missions, twenty-six scrapbooks primarily with articles written about or by himself, and ten major indexes. He translated the scriptures and Church history into Danish.

In addition he was a world traveler, covering nearly a million miles. He circumvented the globe twice, visiting every continent but Antarctica, crossing the Pacific Ocean four times and the Atlantic thirteen. He visited every stake of the Church and every mission but one. He was actively involved in the civic affairs of Utah as a city commissioner, judge, school trustee, delegate to the constitutional convention of 1887, a founder and lifelong member of the board of the Genealogical Society of Utah, member of the Old Folks Central Committee for fifty-eight years, president of the Utah State Historical Society for four years, a member of the executive committee of the Utah Trails and Landmarks Association, and a copious political and Church speaker, delivering more than six thousand addresses in his lifetime. He fulfilled ten missions for the Church, one as mission president.

Many wondered why Andrew Jenson was not given a more prominent position in the Church. He had served as Assistant Church Historian for forty-two years, and his historical work had received considerable praise. Why then was he not ever made Church Historian? Jenson had two characteristics that seemed to stand in his way: his personality and his personal drive and ambition. Many commented on how difficult a man he was to work for.[30] He expected others to work as hard, as long, and as dedicated as he did. His determination was not understood or appreciated by most people. The feeling that he was not accepted and given credit for all the work he had accomplished drove him to constantly push himself to the front. He seemed to lack that basic humility needed by most leaders. The leaders over him and the revelations he reported receiving all stressed his need for more humility. He apparently never fully understood nor appreciated Anthon H. Lund's comment to him that works rather than position mattered in this life. He was always building air castles and seeking higher positions.

But his personal ambition and need to be accepted drove him to produce that which he did. In 1934, when he received considerable praise for his work, he produced more than he had ever produced before, even though he was eighty-four years old. Therefore, looking back over his career, we find that perhaps his personality, which seemed to stand in the way of his progression in this life, was really an asset. Without this need to be accepted he probably would never have produced the fantastic amount of material that he did, and the Church would have been the loser. He laid a historical foundation that many historians have built on. His prodigious works have enabled modern historians to produce their historical works in greater abundance.

What did Andrew Jenson accomplish that had not been done before and some of it perhaps never again? First, he gathered original records from all over the world. Much of this material would have been lost or destroyed. These records enable historians to write a much more complete history of the Church.

Second, he gathered biographical sketches of over fifteen thousand people. Most of these people are dead and have left no other record of their lives. But their biographies have been recorded and preserved, thanks to Andrew Jenson.

Third, he encouraged and directed the clerks of the Church throughout the world in their record keeping by visiting most of them in his worldwide tours. As a result of these visits, he initiated a new method of keeping records in the Church, a method which was later adopted Churchwide. The fact that so many records have been preserved in the Church is probably largely due to the efforts of Andrew Jenson.

Fourth, he organized and systematized materials at the Historian's Office in a useable form for research. Before Jenson arrived at the Historian's Office, the records were in a deplorable state.[31]

Fifth, he prepared eleven indexes to some major works. A few of them are indexes to the *Deseret News,* Journal History, the history of Joseph Smith in the *Millennial Star,* Latter-day Saint periodicals, missionaries, obituaries, and similar records. These are a great boon to the modern researcher. Without them, historians would have to spend considerably more time culling information from voluminous records.

Sixth, he filled a void in the written history of the Church. After 1880 there was no comprehensive record of the Church being kept; he therefore commenced the histories of the stakes and missions and the Journal History of the Church.

Seventh, he had a conception of the worldwide nature of the Church which he had gained from visits to almost all of the wards, branches, stakes, and missions. He had traveled nearly one million miles in his lifetime. Probably no other man in his day had the same perspective of Church history, because few men had traveled as extensively as he had.

Eighth, not many writers have given such broad exposure in their writings to the ordinary Latter-day Saint. He was one of the first to give wide coverage to women and to so many different races and nationalities. He was also the first to publish the history of the Church into foreign languages.

Finally, his personal journals are a vast storehouse of historical information. These journals fill fifteen large volumes. And he personally knew all the Presidents of the Church from Brigham Young to Heber J. Grant. Undoubtedly, not many journals have the scope or depth of Andrew Jenson's. He had encircled the world twice, recording in his journals the events he witnessed. His intimate insight, many times recorded in great detail, into the Church and its leaders with whom he had labored for sixty-five years is invaluable.

Truly, Andrew Jenson was one of the great Latter-day Saint historians.

Notes

1. Andrew Jenson Journal, Book N, p. 375, Library-Archives, Historical Department, The Church of Jesus Christ of Latter-day Saints, Salt Lake City, Utah; hereafter cited as LDS Church Archives.

2. "In regard to spelling my name Jenson instead of Jensen. When I came here at 15 years of age not having done much as a boy I was influenced to change my Danish name Andreas to its equivalent in English, namely Andrew. And in making this change I thought I might as well introduce the o in Jensen instead of the e as the Icelanders, the English and Scotch spell it Jenson to this day." (Andrew Jenson to Richard R. Lyman, 11 February 1938, Andrew Jenson Papers, LDS Church Archives.)

3. Jenson Journal, Book A, p. 18.

4. *Deseret News,* 11 December 1936, p. 17.

5. Ibid., 13 June 1934, p. 11.

6. Jenson Journal, Book A, pp. 246–83.

7. Andrew Jenson, Excerpts of a sacrament meeting held 27 December 1936, honoring Andrew Jenson, Jenson Papers, LDS Church Archives.

8. Jenson Journal, Book B, pp. 296, 298.

9. Ibid., Book C, pp. 339–40.

10. Ibid., Book E, pp. 172–74.

11. Ibid., pp. 281–82.

12. Ibid., p. 283.

13. Ibid., p. 751.

14. Andrew Jenson, *Autobiography of Andrew Jenson* (Salt Lake City: Deseret News Press, 1938), pp. 603–4.

15. Jenson Journal, Book D, p. 20.

16. Ibid., Book E, p. 110.

17. Jenson, *Autobiography,* p. 180.

18. Jenson Journal, Book G, p. 24.

19. Jenson, *Autobiography,* p. 394.

20. Jenson Journal, Book H, pp. 54–55.

21. Ibid., pp. 75, 78, 79.

22. Ibid., Book K, p. 262.

23. Ibid., Book L, pp. 49–50.

24. Anthon Hendrik Lund Journal, 22 October 1912, pp. 110–11, LDS Church Archives.

25. Jenson Journal, Book I, p. 548.

26. Ibid., Book L, p. 427.

27. Keith W. Perkins, "Andrew Jenson: Zealous Chronologist" (Ph.D. diss., Brigham Young University, 1974), p. 200.

28. James H. Anderson, "One Andrew Jenson," *Improvement Era,* July 1921, p. 787.

29. *Fremont Evening Tribune,* Jenson Scrapbook, Book M, 1925, p. 95.

30. Martin S. Lindsay to President Lorenzo Snow and Counselors, 29 June 1900, Lorenzo Snow Papers; Anthon Henrik Lund Journal, 25 July 1900, LDS Church Archives.

31. Charles P. Adams and Gustive O. Larson, "A Study of the LDS Church Historian's Office, 1830–1900," *Utah Historical Quarterly* 40 (Fall 1972): 381–88.

Lavina Fielding Anderson

5

A "Salt of the Earth" Lady: Martha Cragun Cox

A native of Idaho, Lavina Fielding Anderson now resides
with her husband, Paul L. Anderson, and their son in Salt
Lake City. Currently she works as president of Editing,
Incorporated. She received her B.A. and M.A. from Brigham
Young University and her Ph.D. from the University of
Washington. She has published in the *Ensign, Dialogue,
Exponent II, Sunstone,* and *Utah Holiday.* Her interest in
Martha Cox stems from her long-term interest in LDS
women's history.

Martha James Cragun Cox was born into a Salt Lake family
on 3 March 1852, married into a polygamous St. George family
on 3 December 1869, had eight children, buried three, and
died 30 November 1932. To support her family she taught
school all over the southern end of the Mormon corridor in the
small towns of Utah, Arizona, Nevada, and Mexico. She went
to Mexico in time to be expelled by the Revolution. She loved
history, and her narrative gift found expression in Church
periodicals. She spent her last years in temple work in St.
George, Manti, and Salt Lake City.

Why is she important? Because she left a handwritten auto-biographical record just over three hundred pages long, written in 1928. It is because of this autobiography that she is more than a name on the family group records of her hundreds of Latter-day Saint descendants. She claims neither unusual beauty, power, intellect, wealth, nor influence, though she seems to have been above average in her hunger for knowledge, her energy, and her loyalty. But her autobiography, by its very existence, transcends the limitations of her time and place to show her struggling towards a sense of self, struggling to make sense of the world, and struggling to make sense of her life. In her autobiography, she performs the labor which is the distinctive work of that genre; and by so doing, she has stocked the toolshelf and provided cheerful companionship for scholars of first-generation Utah, of second-generation Mormonism, and of future generations. It is a record, quite simply, of a strong, uncomplicated woman, a lady who was the salt of the earth. Like salt, she both seasoned and preserved what she touched. And like salt, her influence was subtle, not compelling or dominating.

Her autobiography sets one goal for itself in the first two sentences: "There are few lives so uneventful that a true record of them would not be of some worth, in which there are no happenings that can serve as guide or warning to those that follow. It is to be hoped that in the pages that follow there will be some things found that may be taken as good lessons to those who read."[1] Because she has perceived shape and direction in her own life, she is a reliable guide.

Martha's record reveals three traits that were with her from her earliest memories and that shaped her last years: an insatiable curiosity, a spunky sense of independence, and a loyalty that, once given, did not waver. Her arena for the development of these traits was small and restricted by poverty: her family, her schoolroom, and, above all, her religion. Mormonism gave her the history of a people beyond her own family, a people who were yet her; it also gave her the very reason for her driving curiosity to know the generations behind her parents. Mormonism gave her a cosmology; it provided both the ground of her faith and the field in which that faith was exercised. It provided informal beliefs where doctrine was lacking. Its philosophy and prophecies were the rocks around which the current events of her time eddied. It gave her its temples with their doctrine of vicarious ordinances of salvation for the dead—both the reason for and the opportunity of binding herself to the past generations and an anchor from which she could cast securely and serenely into her own future after death.

Despite her undeniable commitment to the Church, her love of the gospel, and her willingness to serve, she never records holding an executive position. No doubt one reason was the demands school placed on her time. Another may have been the family's poverty, limiting her availability. And certainly part of it must have been her mobility in a period when callings tended to be given for extremely long periods. Once she left St. George, she never taught in the same school longer than three years. In addition, Martha seems to have placed relatively little importance on callings herself. Apparently the only reason she mentions she was secretary of St. George's Third Ward Relief Society is that the blessing in setting her apart to that calling contained a phrase she found prophetic. She taught children in Sunday School frequently from the time she was sixteen, and it seems to have been a natural extension of her school teaching. At the age of seventy-seven, for instance, she answered the plea of her Salt Lake ward's Sunday School superintendent and taught the Old Testament class, commenting, "I cannot refuse to go to the aid of the children in our own ward" (p. 209).

Still, it would be difficult to understand Martha's autobiography without understanding her Mormonism. Even the shape of the document reflects her core beliefs. Because her history, her religion, and her family are all intertwined, the autobiography begins with an apparently discursive prologue about her ancestors, seemingly recording every story she can recall hearing her parents tell about themselves and their home states. As she begins to tell the story of her own life, the autobiography steadies into a fairly straightforward narrative designed to tell the reader the events of her life, particularly her spiritual growth and the story of the Church's conflicts with the world as she observed them. But as she nears 1928, the year in which she is writing, her record becomes a list of quotations from the newspaper with her disapproving comments on the state of the nation, scraps of family news, and the weather reports suitable to a daily journal. Again, her framework is religious: these are the evils of her generation and God's judgments on them.

Throughout, she was guided in her writing by family papers and her daily journals; but they were only a guide. She sometimes tells the same story twice, not always with the same details. Into her own narrative, she heaps the stories of others, sometimes commenting that their own families do not know these experiences. She records accounts of miraculous healings, prophetic experiences, and answered prayers—both her own and others'. Sometimes she makes no claims for their truth; at other times she meticulously records the source of her information. She sometimes records tales that we would question today—Jacob Hamblin, for instance, saying that Joseph Smith taught him the earth was convex at the north pole to receive a new planet, the impact of which will cause the mountains to melt, the seas to change positions, and the earth to reel to and fro, obviously prophecies of the last days (p. 100). Because Martha has included such information, her autobiography becomes a valuable index to the ordinary member's understanding of the gospel during the late nineteenth and early twentieth centuries.

One senses in her pages both the pleasure in recollection that is one of the joys of reminiscence and also an urgency to record, to make an island of permanence in an ocean of evanescence. Thus it is also a vivid and little-mined scrapbook of small-town life along the Mormon southern corridor—dances, courting, Indian relations, diet, and doctrinal understanding are all there. But in other ways, it is frustratingly sparse.

Although she taught school for almost sixty years, she never describes her courses, her pedagogical philosophy, nor any of her teaching equipment, except for the kitchen breadboard that, painted, served as her blackboard. She is not deeply introspective, but her record is candid and honest, and the reader trusts her. And even though her overt purpose is to instruct, she never tells a story didactically. She has a narrative gift for highlighting drama, making the events of her physical autobiography mirror the meaning that was gradually taking shape and form beneath the surface of events. "All the dead are mine," she once told an old man in the temple (p. 213). Now she is dead, and she is ours.

Martha was born 3 March 1852 in Mill Creek Ward, then a settlement a little south and east of Salt Lake City. Though she never uses her middle name in her record, it was James, presumably after her father. He was second-generation American, his grandfather an Irish sailor who had left ship in Virginia at age thirteen. James's father, Elisha, took his family to Indiana where "the gospel found them in 1843" (p. 4). James had, by that time, married Eleanor Lane, the daughter of a well-to-do family that had moved before her birth from Susquehanna to Indiana; and several members of both families who accepted baptism from the Mormon missionaries moved to Nauvoo, arriving during the height of the confusion following the assassinations of the leader, Joseph Smith, and his brother Hyrum in June 1844. As the Church moved on—to Winter Quarters in 1845–46 and then to Utah—not all the brothers and sisters went with James and Eleanor. This weeding-out in her own family gave Martha a sense of selection but also fed her interest about her relatives back East.

Martha devotes about thirty pages of her record to narratives of her relatives in the East. An avid though vicarious participant in the trek across the plains for another twenty pages or so, she not only records the hardships faced by her parents but also the tales of others. She tells, for instance, of a woman who for fifteen years wore faded ribbons on her bonnet that her daughter had sewed there as she lay dying, and of a thirty-six-hour blizzard sent expressly to punish those who wished to go at a more leisurely pace than the captain wished.

Throughout she emphasizes her mother's courage and her father's obedience, traits she reemphasizes with dramatic vignettes about their settling, first in the Old Fort, then in Mill Creek. One such example came apparently in 1855–56 when a plague of crickets coupled with late-season drought and more than four thousand newly arrived emigrants strained the pioneers' meager resources. Martha would have been four at most during this "starving time" when a brother came to their door, asking for a little flour for his children who had been without bread for three days. Eleanor replied truthfully that there was only enough flour left for "one small baking" and that they were already sharing with a widow and her four children. Martha remembers how sadly the man turned away. However, James called him back, commenting, "My children can suffer no more than yours, my brother, if starvation comes. If it comes we'll starve together. You may have half of the flour we have."

Their own half was soon gone. Breakfastless, her father went to plow and her mother to search for greens. When she returned, the empty sack behind the door was full. Excitedly she interrogated first the children, then her husband. Writes Martha, "I recall my father's answer when she had run out of breath and questions. 'I know of no one but God who could provide us with bread at this time' " (pp. 51–53).

Possibly a four-year-old, even witnessing these events, may not have remembered them in such vivid detail. However, less important than the factual accuracy is the fact of the story itself, ritualized through many retellings and embedded in her narrative as in her memory to anchor her belief in God's benevolent watchcare.

In the fall of 1862, James Cragun was called to Utah's Dixie where St. George had been settled just the year before. They left the following May 1863. Martha, now eleven, enjoyed the trip, noting landscape features with relish and retelling the version of the Mountain Meadows Massacre that she had heard.

They spent the first summer in Pine Valley and, by November 1863, the family was installed in St. George in "a board shanty" with their three wagon boxes "opening into one side of it" for bedrooms (p. 79).

Martha's quick mind had seized upon reading with delight. She had learned her letters in a few days at a Salt Lake school with her sister, and she followed her mother around, spelling words she did not know so that her mother could pronounce them for her. At the age of eight, she had read Lucy Mack Smith's biography of Joseph Smith, the Book of Mormon, the Bible, and a single volume of the *Journal of Discourses,* with two histories too advanced for her to follow —all the books in her home—but "I am grateful to my heavenly father that those were the only books thrown in my way during those years" (p. 69). "Now," she writes of herself at age twelve, "I had . . . reached the period of romance," and describes herself as "fascinated" by *Jane Eyre* and the stories of Henry Ward Beecher. She also read biographies of Daniel Boone, Lady Jane Grey, and George Washington, the *New York Tribune, Fowler's Phrenological Journal,* and *Uncle Tom's Cabin,* thanks to the interest her brother-in-law, James McCarty, took in her education. She borrowed serials and story papers for herself and read voraciously (p. 80).

She may have turned all the more eagerly to reading because of her need to escape. She remembers her teenage years as a continual conflict with her older brothers and sisters. When Martha was thirteen, an older sister, Mary Ellen, married, and Martha recalls that it "was a great relief to me. I was glad to have her go." She is characteristically candid but also fair in her perception of their differences: "I looked upon her as a hard task master." Mary Ellen dissolved into tears if her will were crossed; rather than see her weep, her parents would give in. Mary Ellen was meticulous in dress while Martha admits to "slovenly habits." Worse, Mary Ellen considered Martha's reading to be "idleness" (p. 83).

Martha's conflicts with her brother James, whom she describes as a "surly domineering old bachelor" were even worse (p. 84). In the fall of 1865, when Martha was thirteen, her parents went to Salt Lake City, leaving twenty-five-year-old James in charge. Martha had only one dress, "an old purple calico whose straight skirt had done good service right side and had now been inverted and brought to the required length by a row of pink around the bottom." Humiliated by this violent color scheme below her "red face," she planned to weave herself a new dress length. Furthermore, "there was to be school and books for the winter. . . . It dwelt as a halo around my day and night visions" (p. 85). But James, apparently to be contrary, forbade any weaving, then carried her off to cook for him and another brother in Pine Valley until her parents returned in February. It was an embittering experience. Martha had nothing to do but clean house, the only neighbor family was unfriendly, her brothers were frequently gone, and she was terrified by the very real threat of Indian attack. "It was years before I ceased hating Jim," she says simply (p. 86).

The one benefit was her first recorded experience with answered prayer. She never prayed "as long as I could help myself," but one night, angry, alone, in actual fear for her life, "I begun in earnest to tell my Father my troubles and my request that He help me was answered and His peace fell over me" (pp. 91–92). Her prayer's sturdy independence, directness, and unmistakable answer seem characteristic of the experiences she would have later as well.

She was fourteen the summer after her parents returned, and her longing for school was even more intense—yet the family's poverty was still acute. By now she was doing most of the family weaving and "complained bitterly," saying that her work should earn her more privileges. Her father informed her curtly that "if I had to earn my own living I would go naked and starve compared with what I was getting at home." Surprised rather than wounded, Martha thought it over carefully and wrote a private injunction on the web beam of her loom: "Now Marth Cragun [earn] your own food and clothes or starve" (pp. 94–95).

She did not tell her parents of her resolve but bargained with her mother to share "the labor and profits" of the weaving. Adding cooking to her regular chores of washing and cleaning would, she figured, pay for her board and lodging. It was a discouraging first year. She had only two dresses by its end and worked barefoot and ragged at her loom. But she learned housekeeping. She learned discipline. She learned to appreciate her parents' hard work. And she learned independence. No longer available to "promenade down town with the girls," she learned to rely on her own resources; and when the teaching of her Sunday School class was given without warning to a "richly clad" newcomer, she was "hurt" but spent her Sundays reading undisturbed in an unfinished wardhouse nearby (p. 96).

At age fifteen when her brother-in-law, James McCarty, offered her a chance to attend his school in nearby Santa Clara—at least partially to separate her from her brother— she accepted with delight but soon found "that meeting with friends three nights out of every week to read novels aloud had not made me acquainted with literature." Her brother-in-law taught her more important lessons, too. "I was brought face to face with my own nature and saw much there that was bad. . . . I had a hard unyielding spirit . . . that . . . brooked no restraint. I had a fearful temper and my anger found free vent on every occasion. I never held words back for a second thought. These lessons were not easily learned and several times I contemplated leaving school and going home so great was the ordeal" (p. 98). But she stuck to her school as she had stuck to her loom and returned "with a crown of Jewels on my head" (p. 98).

She learned another important lesson from a customer. Finishing a rough length, she apologized for its "nappy" yarn, and he responded with unexpected soberness: " 'Twill soon be worn out and then my nappy cloth and the weaver's work will be forgotten—and the weaver too, though she becomes round shouldered over the loom in trying to serve people with good cloth." Struck by a sense of futility, Martha wept. "If I could only do some undying thing I felt it would move my arm to action. But to write my name on nothing except that that bore the device 'Passing Away,' was not intended in my creation I was sure of that" (p. 115). McCarty advised her, " 'Every wholesome thought you succeed in planting in the mind of a little child, even, will grow and bear eternal fruit that will give you such joy that you will not ask to be remembered.' His words, though they enlightened brought to me an awful sadness of soul. I was so ignorant" (pp. 114–15).

It was her conviction of her own ignorance and compassion for those in a similar condition that triggered a final decision. She saw a group of boys playing truant. When they asked her to teach them, Martha lamented, " 'I wish I knew enough to teach you.' . . . One bright little fellow spoke up and said, 'I should think you'd teach us that that you *do* know' " (p. 116). Surprised, Martha thought, "Why not give the little I had, if I could not give much. The bantering words of these rude boys on the street aroused a feeling hard to resist, and . . . I decided to become a teacher" (p. 116).

She does not say when she wove with her nappy yarn or talked to the boys. These events may have been separated by months, then telescoped for dramatic effect. But apparently they occurred when she was sixteen or seventeen, for she became an assistant teacher in late December 1869 at age seventeen and opened her first school in the fall of 1871 when she was eighteen.

And before she launched on this new career, she made another decisive choice. She married Isaiah Cox, "one of the poorest men in Washington Co., and one who had already two wives and a family of seven children" (p. 117). Her decision was not a popular one. A former friend sneered that she "had no need to lower herself" to marry a married man (p. 122). Her family's reaction was initially so negative that Martha calls it "hatred" (p. 118).

But Martha herself "had studied out the matter. . . . If the Lord would have manifested . . . that the principle of plural marriage was wrong . . . I felt I should be happy. But it only made me miserable beyond endurance when I tried to recede from the decision I had made to enter it. My only relief was in prayer, and prayer only strengthened my resolve to leave father, mother and all for—I scarcely knew what. I was sorry sometimes that I had taken up the question at all," she adds wryly, "but having assumed it I could not recede. . . . I had asked the Lord to lead me in the right way . . . and I must follow in the pathe He dictated and that was all there was to it" (pp. 117–18).

Martha and Isaiah were sealed in the Endowment House in Salt Lake City on 6 December 1869. She was seventeen. Isaiah was thirty. The son of Jehu and Sarah Cox, Isaiah had accompanied them to settle Union, where he met and married his first wife, Henrietta Janes, served in Lot Smith's company during the campaign against Johnston's Army in 1857, moved to Mount Pleasant and then to North Bend, then was called to the Dixie Mission in the first group of settlers. His profession is given as carpenter and wheelwright; and he reportedly worked on the St. George Temple from its beginning in 1871 until its completion in 1877.[2]

The shrewdest blow Martha's family dealt her in their attempts to dissuade her from the marriage was the observation that "it was not a marriage of love." She admits that it was not, "though I loved his wives and the spirit of their home" (p. 118). Even though she is writing this reminiscence almost sixty years after that wedding and more than thirty after Isaiah's death, there is a determined honesty in her account. There is no evidence that she ever loved Isaiah Cox "as lovers love" (p. 118). She never refers to him by his full name (not unusual in the nineteenth century), only rarely calls him "my husband," sometimes "Brother Cox," and more frequently, "the father of the house" or "our husband." Although she had eight children, it is virtually impossible to tell from her record when Isaiah lived in the same house. She never seems to have relied on him financially—wisely, since he seems to have had no luck with money even though he was a "good workman" and faithfully worked long days (p. 131). The only direct interaction she records between them was in telling of the anger she felt when, in about 1892, he returned from three years in Mexico with a fourth wife and decided to sell the family farm in the Muddy Valley settlement of Nevada that Martha had schemed and scraped to purchase for the children. In recording the event, almost thirty years after it happened, she gives her only direct opinion of her husband:

> It is strange how woman, though the weaker sex, often in time of trouble, calamity, or persecution prove stronger, more courageous, more able to bear up under difficulties than does man. Here was Lizzie dragged two or three times with her children to the Beaver [federal] court to testify [in polygamy trials]. . . . Auntie had to give up her home and live with her children, while she saw her daughters exiled yet all were calm in spirit and finding happiness every day. While here the husband who had not borne half the trial they had endured, was so rattled under the situation he was literally giving away . . . *good land.*

Even though it was, for all practical purposes, her property, Martha does not dispute Isaiah's legal right to dispose of it. "I had used the best of my reasoning power with Bro Cox to withhold a consumation of the bargain . . . to let his sons have a chance" (pp. 196–97). In that single sentence is the only record of any conversation she ever held with her husband on any subject—Martha, who recorded in loving and lavish detail conversations with total strangers. (She persuaded the son of another wife to buy the property, incidentally.) When Isaiah died in 1896 of a heart attack, she mentions it only to explain why the bishop had felt reluctant to let her son go on a mission the next year (p. 199).

However, though Isaiah Cox may have been neither companion nor provider as might have been desirable, by their marriage Martha wedded herself to his first two wives, Henrietta Janes ("Auntie") and Elizabeth Ann Stout ("Lizzie"). As she admits from the beginning that she loved his wives, though not Isaiah, so the rewards she found in marriage came, after an initially difficult adjustment, from her association with those two women. Though she had grown up in a poor home, she was now in a poorer and learned "to eat a dinner without meat and salt-rising bread without salt." Until she adjusted to her new schedule, she rose exhausted at 5:00 A.M. and dutifully retired at 9:00 P.M. "to toss sleeplessly there until the middle of the night" (p. 123). Relentlessly, she schooled her "hot Irish temper" (p. 122). She does not say what made her angry, but there is no indication that it was ever her sister wives, for she describes that relationship lovingly and happily, giving one of the most harmonious portraits we have of plural marriage.

Henrietta Janes, the first wife, was born in Mansfield, Connecticut, to Josiah and Asenath Slafter Janes. She accompanied them to Nauvoo and then, after her father died, came with her widowed mother to Utah where they settled in Union. She was twenty when she and the sixteen-year-old Isaiah were married and thirty-four when he married Martha. She had already borne him five children and was pregnant with a sixth; she would give birth to three more, two of whom would die in childhood. The second wife, Elizabeth Ann Stout, was just twenty-one when the seventeen-year-old Martha joined the household. Like Martha, she had married Isaiah at seventeen. She had borne him two children, was pregnant with a third, and would eventually give birth to an additional five. The daughter of Hosea and Louisa Taylor Stout, she and Auntie had already established a close relationship. According to family sources, Auntie had greeted Lizzie and Isaiah after their return from the Endowment House "with open arms" and "a very affectionate hug and a kiss" for each.[3]

Apparently the household work was managed by Auntie; and during the decade that the three women lived together, they were a smoothly functioning economic unit. They grew their own apples and grapes, preserving much of their own food. Martha leaves a warm and memorable picture:

> We had our work so systematized and so well ordered that we could with ease do a great deal. One would for a period superintend the cooking and kitchen work with the help of the girls. Another make beds and sweep. Another comb and wash all the children At 7.30 all would be ready to sit down to breakfast.

Lizzie was the dress maker for the house and she was always ready to go to her work at eight or nine o'clock. She was also the best sales woman of the house. She generally did most of the buying, especially the shoes. She was a good judge of leather. Auntie did darning and repairing. I seldom patched anything. She did it all for me. She never ironed the clothes. I did most of that. When wash day [came] all hands were employed except the cook. On that day we liked the boiled pudding. Noon saw our family wash on the line.

We usually bought cloth by the bolt and whoever needed most was served first. In fact we had in our home an almost perfect United Order. No one can tell the advantages of that system until he has lived it. We enjoyed many privileges that single wiferey never knew. We did not often all go out together. One always stayed at home and took care of the children and the house. In that way we generally came home with a correct idea of what was given in the sermon.

Whenever one was indisposed she was not obliged to tie up her head and keep serving about the house but she could go to her room and lie down knowing that her children and all her share of the work would be attended to. No one was obliged to bend over the wash tub when she was delicate in health or condition. All stepped into the breach and helped each other.

We acted as nurses for each other during confinement. We were too poor to hire nurses. One suit or outfit for new babies and confined mothers did for us all, and when one piece wore out it was supplied by another. For many years we lived thus working together cooking over the same large stove with the same great kettles, eating at the same long table without a word of unpleasantness or a jar in our feeling portrayed. The children we bore while we lived together in that poor home love each other more than those that came to us after the raid on polyga- mists came on and we were obliged to separate and flee in differ- ent directions.

To me it is a joy to know that we laid the foundation of a life to come while we lived in that plural marriage, that we three who loved each other more than sisters, children of one mother, love, will go hand in hand together down through all eternity. That knowledge is worth more to me than gold and more than com- pensates for all the sorrow I have ever known (pp. 128–29).

Martha reiterates that feeling a few pages later in a paragraph that pays tribute to the first wife. After describing how tenderly Auntie loved her children and Lizzie's, Martha records:

> One day I ventured to say to her that I was sure that many times she had been grieved and even felt heart broken under her trials of plural marriage and poverty, though she had never shown to us by tear or word that she felt so. She looked me squarely in the face and said these words that I shall never forget. "Whenever my heart comes between me and my Father's work it will have to break. And if you have not learned that lesson the sooner you learn it the better for you." Glorious woman! No better ever lived. Israel never produced a better Latter Day Saint. She honored the Priesthood her husband held and preserved a perfect peace in his house. One of my sweetest thoughts on eternity has been that I shall be privileged through all eternity to go hand in hand with those two dear women with whom I served through hard work and poverty through so many years. They are more beloved by me than is any of my natural sisters: I mean the daughters of my mother. The Lord was good to leave us in our poverty that we might learn to cleave together (p. 132).

Throughout the rest of her record, Martha speaks as often of the other wives' children as of her own. Many of them lived with her as she moved from place to place. And finally, six months after Isaiah's death, these three wives would take yet another step in concert and receive a cancellation of their sealings to Isaiah. Martha does not mention this event in her record. President Wilford Woodruff's letter, addressed to Lorenzo Snow as president of the Salt Lake Temple, merely directs him to record the cancellation, without giving any reason. His correspondence file for that year contains no letter from any of the three women requesting such an action, and it thus remains puzzling. Although the first wife was sealed to Joseph Smith ten years later, not an uncommon practice, none of the three remarried.[4]

But this was far in the future for Martha, just back from her wedding trip. She began teaching within days, first as an assistant for a year and a half. Her first child, a daughter, was born 11 January 1871. The baby's death, two days later, "was my first real sorrow and the bitterest disappointment I had ever known," she recalls (p. 124). She spent the spring of 1871 going to school at Richard Horne's "at an expense and great sacrafice but I felt that I must get some training as a teacher if I ever succeeded in giving my 'street boys' instruction. I had those idle marble players ever on my mind" (p. 124).

They had not forgotten, either; and one of them reminded her of her promise to teach them that summer. In September 1871, she began her teaching career with a humiliating series of rebuffs and failures. First, the trustees of the Third Ward School refused it to her on the grounds that her "rude boys" would destroy the property. When she began recruiting students, some refused politely, but one woman sneered that she was giving herself airs and another did not want " 'to trust my children in a class built up for the teacher's test.' " Martha persisted anyway, began small, and within a month had overflowed her borrowed classroom. With the help of the children and her sister wives, she patched a floor into an unfinished room of her own house and kept teaching until her success prompted the ward school trustees to offer her a position. Her first full year of the ten she would teach in St. George closed in triumph in March 1872 and on 29 May a daughter, Rosannah, was born. "It was hard to secure teachers in St. Geo.," she observes. "The pay was too poor— generally the produce of the country had to be collected by the teacher. . . . Yet still I know the idle boy obliged to be out of school held my sympathy. I felt obliged to stay with it because there was so few that would" (p. 129).

We see what she means by that when she volunteered to take widows' children free and ended up with "few on the pay roll . . . But I was game" (p. 130).

Her third child, Edward Isaiah, was born 9 June 1874 followed by Franklin Lane on 4 September 1876. Family finances took a turn for the worse when Isaiah cosigned a note to back the opening of a mine and was left holding one-third of the debts when the manager absconded with the funds. It took the combined efforts of the whole family more than a year to raise the seven hundred dollars he was liable for.

In 1877 Isaiah was on the school board and approved the principal's plan to use all the experienced teachers in his school in the basement of the St. George Tabernacle. Martha resisted bitterly, feeling that experienced teachers were needed most in the ward schools; but since "the one to whom I was supposed to render obedience was then a trustee of the school," she "could see no way but to yeild." Her children, cooped up in a narrow room between two others without fresh air, "turned savage," and Martha's sympathies were with them (p. 134).

She did not teach in 1878–79. Amelia was born 24 October and Martha taught the family's children for a few months, helped with the housework, and launched a loving labor that would claim increasing amounts of her time and attention for the next fifty years. Her patriarchal blessing would, in 1880, promise her that in "the Temple of the Lord . . . you will accomplish a great and mighty work for your dead for they are crying for help to day to redeem them out of their prison" (p. 144). But Martha had already begun. She had attended the St. George Temple dedication in 1877. The doctrine of temple work at the time permitted only the oldest member of the family to perform such vicarious ordinances as baptisms, washings, anointings, endowments, and sealings of spouses to each other and parents and children on behalf of the dead. Martha shared a concern that she "would never have the privilege again of experiencing the Temple ordinance"; but Wilford Woodruff, then an Apostle, felt inspired to call as proxies "his friends who had their hearts set on the work" for his own enormous file of names. Martha was in the first company of proxies in the St. George Temple, and afterwards "every spare day I had I spent there" (pp. 144–46).

She also began research efforts by contacting her mother's relatives. One responded favorably, but the "saucy note" of another taught her "to not try to cram my religion down any body's neck unless they asked for it or it was my mission to do so" (p. 147).

Looking back on her life, Martha would call that summer of 1881 the close of a chapter. She was twenty-nine, had been a teacher for eleven years, borne six children, and buried two. Isaiah went to Arizona to look for work but also to avoid the harassment of federal deputies in search of polygamists. Auntie went to nearby Rockville to live with a married daughter. This separation was the beginning of Martha's wanderings as a migratory schoolteacher on the Mormon frontier. Though she would return "home" to St. George periodically, she would not have a permanent residence until the last few years of her life in Salt Lake City.

The new chapter began with an invitation from two or three families who had moved from St. George to the Muddy Valley in southeastern Nevada. Brigham Young had sent colonists there in the 1860s, but conditions were so severe that he cancelled the mission in 1870. Most left, but others came to try again. As usual, the family finances were an important factor in Martha's decision. The three wives had, through a son, borrowed enough money to purchase the lot next to theirs in St. George and had jointly decided that Martha's teachings would help them "raise our debt" (p. 141).

The story of her certification is one of the most dramatic in her narrative. She had resumed teaching in 1879; a daughter, Amy, had been born 28 October 1880 and died the next summer. The day after the funeral, she received the letter setting the date of the examination in Pioche, a town which was two days away in eastern Nevada—too far to reach in time. Furthermore, she could expect no concessions since "the very name of 'Mormon' was hated in Nev[ada]." Still, she went. The superintendent received her coldly, would not call the examining board together, refused to certify her on the strength of her Utah certificate, and indeed refused to look at it. But "as I turned to leave his office a spirit rose within me that I could hardly understand, a spirit of strength and peace." She told him that she had had no control over the date, that the people of the Muddy Valley had appealed to her and that she had promised to do her best, which she had now done, and "furthermore I told him that I exonerated him from all blame in the matter" (pp. 141–42). His manner changed markedly. He offered her a seat, fetched another member of the examining committee, and refused to let him test Martha with such esoteric subjects as Latin grammar. She received her certificate.

She made the four days' journey to the Muddy alone, leaving all of her children with her sister wives, and arrived to find the schoolhouse unfinished. She opened school "under the beautiful cottonwood trees by the side of the lovely clear stream" by stringing up her black-painted breadboard. "A good thing I brought it," she observes (pp. 148–49).

She does not mention classroom activities, but there was activity enough outside it. One non-Mormon objected to the location of the schoolhouse and to having his children taught by a Mormon. Pluckily, Martha called on him, and he, in her presence, objected only to the location. She, for her part, was disgusted by "his tobacco drulling [drooling] from his mouth and his otherwise stinking person" (p. 149). At a public meeting, each citizen was asked to vote on her, and only this non-Mormon withheld his support.

She was boarding with a previous resident of St. George, doing housework to pay for her room, milking for a share of the milk, and finally, after she ran out of supplies, picking cotton and cutting sunflowers to pay for her meals. Labor was one thing but propriety was another; and she moved out when the woman left for Salt Lake, expecting her to cook for the men. Her lodging thereafter was a bedroll in a cotton storage room while she cooked outside and either sat in the dark or visited a neighbor in the evenings (see p. 151). In November, she records a graphic picture of her poverty: "I cannot now take my crust in my hand and eat my supper as I walk on the hills a half mile distant—which I had formed the habit of doing to conquer the loneliness and yarning to be with the children. I had sold my shawl for six dollars which I used to keep up my necessities for a month and I could not withstand the rigor of the wind. The evenings without light or fire began to be unbearably long" (pp. 155–56). Still, it is a tribute to her generous spirit that, in such straitened circumstances, she sold an Indian one of her three dresses so that his wife could work in a family. She took what he offered her in exchange—one dollar (see p. 156).

Martha does not say whether this was her first experience with Indians after her fear of them as a teenager, but her admiration and respect are refreshing notes. She does not see them primarily as Book of Mormon peoples, a convenient stereotype for many Latter-day Saints. Instead she recalls her experience with individuals. Joe Mason, for instance, "worked hard all day and carried home the greater share of what was given him for meals to his little children" (p. 156). Sent to the store for some change, another did not return until after a three-day spree in which he drank and gambled everything he owned down to his shoes—except for that money (see p. 170). Martha repaid them in her own coin years later by submitting their names for temple work so "they have all been endowed" (p. 177).

Obviously, Martha was living on scanty resources; but when a good 160-acre farm came on the market in Overton, she consulted with her sister wives and decided to buy. Isaiah Cox brought down the wagon that was part of the bargain and "closed the deal," but it was Martha who "promised to repay the borrowed money" (p. 158).

But now she needed money more desperately than ever, and her school would close the last of February. The Pioche superintendent offered her the school in Panaca, a mining town only a few miles from Pioche from which the teacher had "fled . . . to save his life." He warned her that she would succeed only if she taught "with a book in one hand and a blackwhip in the other" (p. 158). Painfully Martha records driving away, leaving Rosannah standing in the doorway reminding her, " 'Mother you promised you would never leave us your children again,' " She adds, "Oh! The horrid phantom of debt. . . . Money loses its luster when you consider the sacrifice made to get it" (p. 163).

That spring school in Panaca in 1882 was the scene of Martha's greatest recorded triumph. "I don't think a teacher ever met a more rebellious looking group of children than I greeted," she recalls. Cannily, she began by complimenting them on the size and beauty of their town, then noticing "six or seven sticks, thick as clubs standing in the corner," had the boys chop them up for kindling. By the time she let school out, the news was all over town. One woman said, "I hear you let John take those clubs Martin used to beat him with and chop them up." Deliberately missing the point, Martha replied, "I think [it] was John who did it." When a "sober-faced trustee" warned her the next morning, " 'You may need them before school is out,' " she deliberately misunderstood him as well: " 'Panaca is a rich little place. You may get here anything you need, from a tooth-pick to a wagon tongue' " (pp. 160–61).

Needless to say, she never needed the clubs, and "the people gave me more praise than was my due" (p. 162).

The trustees, recognizing a good thing when they saw it, offered her the school for the next year. Interestingly enough, she refused, not only because "I could not leave my little children again" but because she also felt apprehensive: "I had stepped on too high a step in Panaca. I had let myself rise too high in the estimation of the people. I could not maintain my standard, I fear, so backed right out" (pp. 164–65). In another place, she refers to her Panaca experience again and terms her success "sailing under false colors" (p. 195). But why should she mistrust her ability to maintain that success? Toward the end of her life, she quoted from her patriarchal blessing that she should "be a counsellor in Zion" and concluded, "I am not meant, I believe, to be the leader" (p. 295). Clearly, she had the natural ability required. She thought fast, talked persuasively, was able to make decisions, and was willing to take risks. But in Panaca, where she was so indubitably a success, she retreated from her popularity. Certainly the opportunities for a woman—even one with Martha's abilities—were limited on the Mormon frontier. But almost as certainly, Martha's image of herself did not include a public role outside her classroom, and she seems not to have had the kinds of friends and supporters who could persuade her to change that image.

The next few months were plagued with illness and worry about her debts. Rachel Evelyn was born in St. George 23 November 1884. Martha did not teach that year, only the second year she had not stood before a class since her marriage fifteen years earlier. Back in Overton, Isaiah was made the newly organized ward's first bishop but "felt his position as a great burden to him" and was released a year later (p. 173). Martha's eighth and last child, Geneva, was born on 15 July 1886. Her father died, she became ill again, and her depression over debt increased as the months passed.

Isaiah had now removed himself effectually by marrying Mary Jane Millett on 22 September 1888, and "to save himself from the law he had gone into Mexico." Martha is fair: "We all had approved the action but it brought hardship upon us all. . . . I did not know how sad I was nor what effect my gloomy feelings were having upon me, until one day I happened to open my hymn book. I sat down with my baby on my lap and began to sing her to sleep. At the first notes she raised her head and gave me a frightened look. At this I laughed which frightened her the more. I then knew I was not used to singing or laughing" (p. 178).

About this time, she had a dream which she considered to be divine intervention to free her from her "bitter hatred" of the federal marshals and her own depression. Rather like Dickens's figure of Marley's ghost, she saw herself with a chain around her neck so laden with heavy bundles that she could not lift her head to see the sky. Advised by an unnamed person to hang the bundles on the rod over her fireplace, she did so. Among them was a "large bundle" of "wicked words I had said about the Utah Marshalls," another was debts she had not been able to collect, and another was baby clothes that she used to spread on her bed "on lonely stormy nights when there [was] no one . . . to see or hear me weep over them." Each parcel became miraculously light as she lifted it to the rod, and when the last was gone, "lo, the chain was gone and I was free." She woke, resolved to be free indeed. When an Indian mother begged clothes for her child, Martha took out her box of baby clothes and dressed the child, feeling "shame for the tears I had shed over [them]" (pp. 178–79).

Freed of her depression, she looked to the future again and, after the years of scraping by at Overton, accepted an 1889 offer from Bunkerville, Nevada, a tiny hamlet originally founded as a Mormon communal order in 1877 by Edward Bunker, whom she had known in Santa Clara and for whom she had named her first son. "I rejoiced to be among my own people again," she writes (p. 186).

In 1890, her daughter Amelia, who was suffering from diabetes, gradually weakened and, in October, died just a few weeks short of her twelfth birthday. That fall, Martha again opened her Bunkerville school with the only comment she ever makes on her curriculum: "history, astronomy and English laid out for the classes." Edward, now sixteen, reluctantly came to her school—"afraid of his mother," she dryly notes. "But he soon adjusted himself to the situation" (p. 192).

By 1891 she began thinking of buying a home in Bunkerville, but when a midyear vacancy came up in the school at Beaver Dam in Arizona, Martha promptly took eighteen-year-old Rose to Kingman, Arizona, several days away on the other side of the Grand Canyon, for certification. She records, scandalized, the tipsy women in the boardinghouse parlor, another who was celebrating a successful abortion, and the open coal-stealing from the railroad. As the final proof of gentile wickedness, Rose passed the examination with 90 percent but received a certificate marked 80 percent, the superintendent ingenuously explaining that the highest Arizona applicant had only made 85 percent "and they couldn't let a Mormon girl from Nevada come and put it over on them that way" (p. 194).

Martha and Rose had spent the summer of 1891 in Provo at Brigham Young Academy's summer school. The experience awakened not only her own unfed hunger for more education but a strong desire to see her children educated there. Both the bishop and a son-in-law counseled her so strongly against it, though, that she changed her mind.

> The bp [Edward Bunker] was an old fashioned man and not afraid to put his hand into the collar of a boy and draw him into line. That fact had a great bearing and that I might not have influence to keep my boys at work while out of school was another thought. When I considered the whole situation I concluded to stay in Bunkerville. This blessing came from my later decision. My children married well there. [Three married into the Bunker family.] My sons both married . . . good housekeepers, good cooks, good mothers to as many children as our Father has been pleased to send them, therefore good Latter Day Saints (p. 196).

Of her own needs and desires, she says nothing and apparently resolved to spend the rest of her life in the Mormon southern corridor. It was about that time that Isaiah reemerged from Mexico and sold the farm she had painfully acquired and kept in Overton. With that loss, she seems to have cut a tie. "We" —apparently meaning her and the children—"bought a home in Bunkerville in 1893, a lot," and her teenage sons put together a "shanty" (p. 198). Bunkerville was building its first chapel, and the overextended people resisted the bishop's house-to-house appeal for enough money to put in windows and buy nails. Recalls Martha:

> When he called upon me, I could not see at first that I could advance anything, but his tired face touched my finer feelings, and I said, "I'll give this month's wages on it." My own words lightened my soul. He seemed to doubt my words. And asked me to repeat them. I said again "I'll put in my month's pay check all except the tithing on it. . . ." I had no thought of making sacrafice or offering. I felt it my duty to help lift the burden. The result was wonderful, and the Lord blessed the whole people through that gift made to Him. One man rather miserly, said, when found out what I had given "Well, if that poor widow with all those children can give her month's wages I'll give some work and a little money" and so the spirit spread.

Proud of their building, the ward members made it the center of other projects, and "the little town soon became known as a town of thrift, culture, education etc. As I look at [it] now, though I had no such thought then, my gift was a pure offering before the Lord and the fact that so much good came from it shows to me that our Father accepted it as such" (p. 278).

In this passage, possibly as much as anywhere, we see the savor in Martha's salt. The details of the bishop's "tired face" and her own forthright offer, even the reinforcing detail of the "miserly" man, demonstrate her ability to tell a good story. That the story involved sacrifice for her church is utterly characteristic of Martha. And as she reflects on the event, drawing from it meanings that she did not give it then, she finds it to be surrounded by a halo of blessedness, a goodly impulse that set off ripples of further goodness. And because both the deed and her retelling of it are an offering, freely and lovingly made to her Heavenly Father, there is a sweetness and purity about its telling that carries its own spirit to the reader.

Isaiah died in 1896. Her twenty-three-year-old son Edward was called on a mission in 1897, and "I was rejoiced that he had been honored by this call." Although the bishop wanted to have him wait to earn more money, Martha spunkily replied, " 'While I have a roof to cover my head I can send my boy on a mission when he is called,' and I felt strengthened by my answer" (p. 199).

In 1900 Martha, teaching school in Mesquite close to Bunkerville, began to think about Mexico where the Mormon colonies had been established in 1885. She was forty-eight and after leaving St. George had never lived more than three years in the same place. Perhaps her curiosity was aroused. Perhaps she hoped that the family fortunes would improve. Certainly she was anxious to be in a place where polygamy was not against the law. Although the 1890 Manifesto had greatly curtailed United States plural marriages, it would not be until 1904 that Latter-day Saints stopped forming such marriages, rather openly in Canada and especially in Mexico. When Francis M. Lyman of the Quorum of the Twelve "gave full permission" in conference for migration to Mexico (p. 201), Martha's last question was answered, and she left in May 1901 with a large family caravan by team and wagon.

That abortive Mexican venture took ten years of Martha's life and it repaid her ill, but she does not complain. Her record comes alive with pleasure as they began the trek across Arizona. She rambled after wildflowers, gained a new appreciation for the "bitter waters of the Virgin river" in this utterly dry desert, was an eager sightseer among the "Nephite" ruins en route, and inquisitively interviewed inhabitants of Phoenix (pp. 220–21).

At Naco, on the border, they bogged down completely, first in paper work, then in inspections. Members of the party sought work. Geneva began a Sunday School class. Fellow Saints from the Mormon colonies brought the discouraging word that there was no work to be had there that season. Storms were followed by hoof-and-mouth disease among the stock and violent fevers among the party. When a resident of Diaz offered to take them there, Martha seized upon it (pp. 224–25). They arrived 24 August 1901 and a week later she was teaching one class in its academy and another in Sunday School. The rest of the family straggled in slowly. Five of the children among the family had either died en route or in the first few months. A prophetic dream on Christmas Eve, later confirmed, warned Martha of her mother's death.

In 1902 Martha taught in Morelos. Her children were scattered throughout the colonies, and she lengthened the distance by returning to Arizona in 1904 to teach at Beaver Dam, then at Cane Springs. Her curiosity burned as bright as ever; and on her way out of Mexico, she spent on a Spanish-English dictionary the four dollars earmarked for a shawl, warming herself with thoughts of "the treasured book" as she shivered through the mountains near Prescott, Arizona (p. 232). Her interest in learning made her unusually open-minded, and she found "the faces of Hidalgo and Benito Juarez . . . just as beautiful to me as that of George Washington" (p. 233). In Salt Lake City at the age of seventy-seven, she would briefly teach English in the Pioneer Stake's Mexican branch, pleased she could still manage the Spanish language after twelve years and observing, "I find them, the Mexicans, a splendid people" (p. 295).

Worried about her children and the political situation in Mexico, she returned to Mexico in the summer of 1906. Martha, teaching in Juarez in 1907 when the first skirmishes began, found "the smell of wounded horses and wounded men . . . unbearably obnoxious" by summer (p. 239) and tells the story of the battle of Casas Grandes as though it happened the same year even though Raoul Madero's forces did not fight over the town until 6 March 1911. Her twelve-year-old grandson was given a gun and went eagerly off to the battle lines. Martha "asked him if he realized that he might be shot and killed before noon," and he responded bloodthirstily, " 'If I'm killed I'll bet I get a few Mexicans first.' I could not try to describe my feelings as I looked upon that accoutred boy and heard the guns of that battle" (p. 243). Her sorrow and fear did not quench her curiosity, however, and she found a large window in a top story from which to watch the battle (pp. 243–44).

In 1911 she left Mexico and joined her daughter Geneva, then teaching school in Richfield, Utah. There Martha helped her with her papers, taught her history class (and Sunday School again), and watched as the Saints in Mexico wavered between trying to defend their property and obeying instructions from both political and religious leaders to leave the dangerous zone. Among those who escaped in the summer of 1912 was her daughter Evelyn. Seven months pregnant, Evelyn sat on a bench in a coal car for a day and most of a night, holding her other two children on her lap, because there was no room on the floor (p. 248). She took temporary refuge with Martha and Geneva who had married George M. Cope on 29 May 1912. He was also sealed to Amelia on the same day (p. 248).

Martha took up teaching again, first in Richfield in 1912–13, then in Burrville in the nearby mountains, where she adapted easily to six-foot snowdrifts as "a kind of novelty" (p.

255). Her spare time went to collecting genealogical information, and her summers were partially spent in the Manti Temple.

For two years she taught at Aurora, about fifteen miles from Richfield, but she didn't care for the principal ("a man of little or no faith") and further resisted the superintendent's demands for Saturday work (p. 256). Her contract was not renewed, but she was not sorry to leave. The genealogical promise of her patriarchal blessing was much on her mind. Frustrated at not having ancestral records, she made it a matter of prayer: "one day as I was walking home to dinner . . . I saw in a vacant lot on my right a piece of newspaper. A thought came into my mind, 'Perhaps there is something on that paper you'd like to read.' " She tore her dress on the barbed wire fence and walked over the muddy furrows to discover on "the old sunburnt scrap" a notice that a Boston genealogist had passed through Salt Lake City. She wrote to him and heard in return that she could get four volumes of family names for thirteen dollars. "I felt that the Lord had heard my prayers, and had answered them in wonderful way" (p. 257).

Then World War I struck, bringing changes that horrified Martha. One grandson enlisted, then he added "another . . . sorrow" by marrying a non-Mormon Californian (p. 262). The influenza pandemic of 1918 prostrated them. Martha herself was spared but agonized over her children and grandchildren, "too helpless to lift a cup of water to their lips" (p. 261). Even though scientists had rejected the idea that the disease was born by prevailing winds, Martha's description reflects the older belief, now embedded in the folk mind: "The currents of air that sweep the earth in its revolutions now had the time required to bring the miasma from the slightly buried dead, mingled with the poison gas used in life's destruction to the shores of our country" (p. 260). Amazingly, none of her family died of the disease that killed an estimated twenty million worldwide.

Even though she was sixty-five in 1917, "all who had ever taught were requested to again occupy the pedagogical chair"

(p. 260). She taught in Enterprise, Utah; St. Thomas, Nevada; and Gunlock, Utah, which, in 1920, marked the end of her formal teaching.

A visit to Salt Lake City and a conference with another ardent genealogist launched her, at the age of sixty-nine, on another "career"—that of temple work. She spent the summer of 1920 and parts of 1921–22 in the Salt Lake Temple, diligently performing three proxy endowments a day —a full day's work with each session lasting three or four hours. She refused two offers to become an assigned temple worker because she felt so responsible for her own dead. But when a woman who frequented the temple told her of a vision in which she had seen Martha performing those very duties, Martha reconsidered and thus saw that her prayers had been answered, for names from her file were given out to other proxies—sometimes ten or twenty of both sexes in a day compared to her maximum of three women. And, ever practical, she noted that she would receive her lunch every day, "which is not a small item," although she refused the modest stipend which was also offered.

An unusual spiritual experience confirmed her decision. During that same summer of 1922, her mother, who had been dead since 1901, appeared in a dream to Geneva and showed her a list containing about a hundred names. Martha interpreted the dream to mean that she should find the names in Genealogical Library records. As she worked, a man overheard her mention Lane, her mother's maiden name, and gave her a letter from her mother's nephew that had been written almost exactly a year earlier and forwarded through four hands. "Circumstances like [this] strengthens my belief . . . that those who have gone to the other side are active in behalf of their own work and often have permission to aid their friends on this side who are earnestly working for their redemption" (pp. 270–71).

This conclusion touches a chord of memory, and Martha records an outpouring of similar experiences. One involved her dead daughter, Amelia. Martha's sister wife, Lizzie, told her she had dreamed of seeing Amelia standing by her bed, requesting her to "give her a white dress that she might join a company that were going to a place higher up" and explaining that she was asking Aunt Lizzie because " 'I can't make [mother] understand.' " Both women interpreted the dream to mean that the child was requesting a proxy endowment. This must have occurred when Martha was teaching away from St. George, for she asked Lizzie to see that Amelia's work was done (pp. 271–72). There is a singular earnestness and a ringing sincerity about Martha's recital of this and other experiences. No one can read them and question whether Martha believed they had actually happened.

In 1924, Martha's health took a turn for the worse. The next year, Geneva, after giving birth to her eighth child, died. Her husband, remarrying both to provide "a mother to his brood" and to release Martha to return to the temple, died suddenly of typhoid fever in 1926. That same month, a granddaughter died of complications resulting from premature childbirth.

This spate of family disasters brought Martha's record up to the time of writing; and she continues a journal, recording family events—visits, births, missions, deaths, marriages—and some of her most outspoken longings for money to help Geneva's children and George's posthumous daughter then being gallantly reared by his second wife. Twice Martha wonders helplessly, "Is it wrong to wish for money?" (pp. 276, 283). Her sense of helplessness finds vent in recording and denouncing current conditions: the narcotics industry, the scanty dress of the women, the droughts of Europe, the judgments of God in the forms of floods and wars, and the desire for luxuries among the Saints. One chastisement is worth mentioning: her disgust at "young women" who "love to fill offices and prefer to earn money rather [than] keep house and raise a family" (p. 289). This may sound odd from Martha who taught every year but two between age seventeen and age sixty-nine; but despite her independence and financial self-reliance, she was not a feminist ahead of her time. Nothing she says about teaching indicates that she saw it as a "career" as we would understand the term today.

This section of her episodic and largely unreflective record continues up to the last paragraph in the book, where she sums up hastily, "This volume now closed. I wish I had written it better. I could have made a better record. I have tried to tell the truth but it was awkwardly done. May my second book be clearer and better" (p. 305). Characteristically, she was forward-looking, though not much time remained. On 30 November 1932 she died. Anthony W. Ivins of the First Presidency and a friend from Mexican days spoke at her funeral, and she was buried in Salt Lake City Cemetery.[5]

She left thirty-six grandchildren, seventeen great-grandchildren—and her autobiography. As a consequence, she left a vital breath of her own personality. She was the salt of the earth, and she seasoned it.

Notes

1. Martha James Cragun Cox, "Biographical Record of Martha Cox: Written for My Children and My Children's Children, and All Who May Care to Read It." Library-Archives, Historical Department, The Church of Jesus Christ of Latter-day Saints, Salt Lake City, Utah, (hereafter cited as LDS Church Archives) p. 1. Grateful thanks are due to Leonard J. Arrington, director of the Joseph Fielding Smith Institute for Church History, for encouraging this project, not only with his enthusiasm but also with the very material aid of making time available for his secretary, Kathy Stephens, who completed a definitive typescript July 1979. A second typescript is available in the LDS Church Archives, but it is an edited version of this volume, as are typescripts in the Utah Historical Society and the Harold B. Lee Library at Brigham Young University. All citations are from the Stephens typescript and will be cited hereafter parenthetically in the text. Terminal punctuation and initial capitals have been added where necessary. The author's frequent use of the short dash has been regularized into commas or semicolons as appropriate, and inadvertent repetitions have been silently omitted. When she has added material in the margins without indicating where it should be inserted, I have included it in what seems to be the most logical place. In May 1985, the Francis N. Bunker family organization and the Isaiah Cox family organization, Martha Cragun branch, published this reminiscence as *Face Toward Zion: Pioneer Reminiscences and Journal of Martha Cragun Cox*. No editor is identified. Standardizing

of spelling, punctuation, and grammar has been done silently. There is no index, although a useful chart of Isaiah Cox's wives and children has been included. Martha's second volume, which brings her life up to date and then becomes a daily journal, has not been published and is in the possession of a granddaughter.

2. Journal History of The Church of Jesus Christ of Latter-day Saints, 19 October 1862, p. 6, LDS Church Archives; and Wayne D. Stout, *Our Pioneer Ancestors: Genealogical and Biographical Histories of the Cox-Stout Families* (privately printed, 1944), pp. 72–77, 82.

3. Family group sheet of Isaiah Cox and Henrietta Janes submitted by Brent Foutz, family group sheet of Isaiah Cox and Elizabeth Ann Stout submitted by H. Reed Black, and family group sheet of Isaiah Cox and Martha James Cragun submitted by Martha M. Judkins in the Genealogical Library, The Church of Jesus Christ of Latter-day Saints, Salt Lake City, Utah; and Stout, *Our Pioneer Ancestors,* p. 77.

4. Wilford Woodruff to President Lorenzo Snow, 13 October 1896, First Presidency Letterpress Copybooks, 1877–1949, LDS Church Archives; family group sheet of Isaiah Cox and Henrietta Janes, and family group sheet of Isaiah Cox and Elizabeth Ann Stout. The unanimity of cancellation followed by divergence of action afterwards is particularly mystifying. According to one interpretation of the sealing doctrine at the time, women sealed to an "unworthy" man could not inherit celestial glory. The fact that only one wife had herself sealed to an indubitably "worthy" personage, Joseph Smith, seems to rule out any question of Isaiah's moral standing. The fact that the wives did not remarry other men also seems to rule out suppressed dissatisfaction with the marriage that surfaced only after Isaiah was dead. Wayne Stout, after recording Isaiah's brief marriage on 29 November 1888 to Sophie Annie Morris and its subsequent annulment on 10 January 1892, observes: "This unfortunate incident did not cause Isaiah's first three wives to ask for an annulment as some people believe"; but he does not elaborate further (Stout, *Our Pioneer Ancestors,* pp. 83–84). A granddaughter in the early 1980s who pursued the matter with officials of the Genealogical Department of The Church of Jesus Christ of Latter-day Saints waited while someone checked the records, which are not available to the public, and was reassured that the sealing was in force.

5. "Martha Cragun Cox," *Salt Lake Tribune,* 4 December 1932, B-9.

Paul L. Anderson

6

Truman O. Angell: Architect and Saint

Paul L. Anderson was born in Pasadena, California. He now
lives with his wife and son in Salt Lake City. Paul is
currently Curator of Historic Sites and Exhibitions with the
Museum of Church History and Art in Salt Lake City. He
received his B.A. from Stanford University and his Master of
Architecture from Princeton University. He has published
widely in Latter-day Saint periodicals and professional
journals. His interest in Truman Angell relates to his training
and interest in architectural history.

I was called to be and act as Architect," wrote Truman
Osborne Angell in 1868, nearly twenty years after receiving
that call from his brother-in-law Brigham Young. "In this," he
added, "I labored as hard as enny man could."[1] The statement
is an apt summary of his life.[2]

Like many others of his generation who embraced the Mormon faith, Truman Angell found that his religious commitment
swept him along in a wave of history and carried him to places
and tasks he would never have chosen for himself. A carpenter
who preferred working with his hands to working with his

head, he became, almost by default, the most important architect in pioneer Utah. His unwavering devotion to the Church and its leaders pushed him to accomplish things beyond his aspirations: his designs included some of early Utah's major public buildings and the homes of many of its leading citizens, as well as Mormondom's most important monument, the Salt Lake Temple. And like many of his contemporaries, Angell discovered that such achievements were purchased at an enormous physical and emotional price. In his fifty-five years as a Latter-day Saint, through persecution, sickness, poverty, disappointment, and frustration, he truly "labored as hard as enny man could."

Truman was born on 5 June 1810 in North Providence, Rhode Island, the fifth child and third son of James W. and Phoebe Morton Angell, a working-class couple.[3] Both parents were descended from old New England families. The father's ancestry included Thomas Angell, who came to America with Roger Williams and assisted in founding Rhode Island. His mother's American genealogy went back farther still to the Mayflower.

Truman's life was hard almost from the start. His parents' marriage was not a happy one. After prolonged "family difficulties," James left the family when Truman was five or six years old. Phoebe struggled alone to support the seven children. Consequently, what schooling Truman got was in "winter schools," which he apparently attended for only brief periods of time. James returned to the family when Truman was nine, but the boy was sent to live elsewhere shortly thereafter. Truman's autobiography gives little detail about the next eight years, telling only that he continued to live in North Providence, visiting his parents' home infrequently. Remembering his youth, he commented, "Having no father to restrain me, I pleased myself; and did many things I ought not."[4]

At seventeen, Truman began to learn the trade of carpenter and joiner from a man in his family's neighborhood. He continued working there until 1830 when he was twenty. The Providence area provided a stimulating environment for an ambitious young man in the building trade. Founded as a refuge for religious dissenters from the Puritan colonies, the city had grown to be New England's second largest, an important center of international shipping and industry. Truman had ample opportunity to see fine examples of architecture and craftmanship while learning his trade in this prosperous, bustling city.

As Truman was completing his training as a carpenter, his thoughts turned to religion. This interest may have been encouraged by his older sister, Mary Ann, who was an enthusiastic Free-will Baptist. By his own account, his decision to become a Free-will Baptist was accompanied by a permanent change of heart. "From then on my mischievous life and shortcomings were laid aside; and I have ever since tried to do what was right; feeling that God required it."[5]

His parents' marital difficulties had persisted during the years Truman was growing up away from home. When Truman was twenty-one, he brought his mother to live with him "in consequence of the conduct of my Father towards her."[6] They lived together in North Providence until the next fall when they decided to move to China, Genessee County, New York, to be near her father and brothers and sisters. One factor in their decision to move may have been a visit from Truman's cousin, Joseph Holbrook, whose family had moved to upstate New York a few years earlier. Joseph gave the Angells a glowing report of opportunities in that booming area along the Erie Canal. The Angell family's move was completed in September 1832. Apparently, all the unmarried children and the father Joseph moved together. On 7 October of the same year Truman married Polly Johnson, a native of Genessee County.

Joseph Holbrook recorded that during the summer of 1832, before the Angells' arrival in New York State, "many vague reports were circulated about a certain set of people who were called Mormonites."[7] Not long after the Angells' arrival, Mormon missionaries held a meeting in the China schoolhouse which Joseph Holbrook and Mary Ann Angell attended. Mary Ann had previously acquired a copy of the

Book of Mormon and had circulated it among her family and friends. Another missionary visited the Angells a few weeks later. Both Phoebe's father and her brother were alarmed at the family's interest in this new religion and tried to discourage them from investigating further. However, Mary Ann joined the Mormons in December 1832. The next month Joseph and Phoebe accompanied her to a Mormon meeting in Warsaw, about twelve miles away, and both were baptized by the missionaries before returning home. Truman and Polly Angell met the same missionaries later that month and were also baptized. Five weeks later, Truman was ordained an elder.

In April 1833, Truman and Joseph Holbrook, still enthusiastic about their new faith, left on a mission of their own. Holbrook's detailed account describes their travels in which they visited relatives and friends across New York and Massachusetts.[8] According to Holbrook's account, he and Truman traveled twelve hundred miles in seven weeks, "held fourteen meetings, baptized three besides bearing testimony to hundreds in family."[9]

In July, just a few weeks after Truman's arrival home, he and Polly moved about forty-five miles east to Lima in Livingston County, New York. Truman's mother remained behind in China with the rest of the family. That winter news of the expulsion of the Saints from Jackson County, Missouri, reached the Angells. In March 1834 Orson Pratt and others passed through recruiting volunteers to go to Missouri as part of Zion's Camp. Truman's brother Solomon and cousin Joseph Holbrook volunteered. Truman considered going, but he was preparing for his first full season on his new farm and Polly was expecting their first child in May. Truman recalled,

> My heart burned with anguish. I sent them a stand of arms, but my extremely low circumstances, and the council of Elder Orson Pratt and others, who were made acquainted with my situation, prevented me from joining the "company" and going up myself to the rescue of the brethren.[10]

Truman remained on his farm where his daughter, Sarah Jane, was born on 28 May 1834. He worked the farm two full seasons, and then, in the fall of 1835, took his family to gather with the Saints in Kirtland, Ohio.

As a carpenter, Truman Angell could hardly have come to Kirtland at a better time. He arrived on Saturday and attended a meeting in the unfinished temple the next morning. Most of the exterior masonry work was finished, but the inside carpentry was just beginning. The meeting was held "on a loose floor which had been arranged for carpenters benches, etc., the house was partly (perhaps two-thirds) filled, the people being seated on work benches and other things."[11] He went to work with the team of carpenters and continued working through the temple dedication in 1836. Although Truman was a late arrival, his skills were recognized and he was placed in charge of finishing "the second, or middle wall of the Temple; including the stands."[12] Since the middle wall of the building extended through the two major floors, this statement suggests that Angell had charge of building the elaborate pulpits and woodwork on the east end of both major meeting rooms where the presidency of the Aaronic Priesthood would sit. Like all the woodwork in the building, the east pulpits were crafted with great skill and precision, making use of a variety of Federal and Greek Revival style patterns. Interestingly, the carving on the window frame at the east end of the upper room is different from the other major windows, with graceful and delicate flowering vines weaving their way up both sides of the arch to a keystone carved with an urn holding another flower. It is possible that this window, sometimes called the Window Beautiful, represents an original contribution from Truman Angell's imagination.

For Angell, however, the Kirtland Temple was more than an architectural achievement. His autobiography records several spiritual events that made a deep impression on the young carpenter. One of his descriptions of the building mixes the architectural with the spiritual: "The roof was supported by four trusses, which left us five rooms [in the attic]. In these same rooms the power of God was manifest to encourage us wonderfully."[13] Angell received his "first Endowments" in these attic rooms prior to the dedication of the rest of the structure.[14] He was also present when Joseph Smith entered the building to discuss the seating arrangement with the "leading mechanic" or foreman, John Carl, a carriage builder. He recorded that the mechanic suggested a different arrangement than that proposed by Joseph. The Prophet insisted that his own plans be carried out and added that "he had seen the inside of every building that had been built unto the Lord upon this earth and he hated to have to say so."[15]

Angell also reported an interview that took place between a carpenter named Rolph and Frederick G. Williams, one of the counselors to President Smith. The carpenter asked President Williams what he thought of the building. Frederick G. Williams answered, "It looks to me like the pattern precisely" and then related a vision he had shared with the other members of the Presidency:

> Joseph received the word of the Lord for him to take his two counsellors Williams and Rigdon and come before the Lord, and He would show them the plan or model of the House to be built. We went upon our knees, called on the Lord, and the Building appeared within viewing distance: I being the first to discover it. Then all of us viewed it together. After we had taken a good look at the exterior, the building seemed to come right over us, and the Makeup of this Hall seemed to coincide with what I there saw to a minutia.[16]

Truman Angell's conviction of the sacredness of the place and the inspiration of its design was further confirmed by experiences during and following the dedication of the structure. During the prayer of dedication, he shared "a sensation very elevation to the soul"[17] with other members of the congregation. Frederick G. Williams rose following the prayer to testify that an angel had seated himself on the stand during the prayer; later that day the Prophet Joseph identified the angel as Peter who had come to accept the dedication. Some time after this occurrence, Truman himself saw two personages marching back and forth in the air in front of two attic windows like guards on sentry duty. Angell's memory of this vision was vivid late in his life when he recalled that one of the angels "turned his face to me for an instant; but while they walked too and fro, but a side view was visable."[18] Truman was not a man much given to visions and dreams. He records no other comparable spiritual manifestations in his journals and reminiscences, but these experiences confirmed a commitment to the Church and its leaders that would last a lifetime. In 1884 he added these experiences to his autobiography, "thinking it may do someone good as it has me."[19]

Working on this important construction project had given Angell the opportunity to become well acquainted with most of the leaders of the young Church, including Joseph and Hyrum Smith. When Truman's own father, now a member of the Church, declined to give him a father's blessing, the young man approached the Patriarch to the Church, Joseph Smith, Sr., instead. The patriarchal blessing warned Angell of coming trials, promised divine protection, revelations, visions, and missionary success. In light of his role in building Salt Lake City, one sentence in the blessing seems particularly appropriate: "Yea thou shalt be mighty as Enoch who built a city unto God."[20]

Angell's most important connection with the presiding quorums of the Church was through Brigham Young, the brother of one of the missionaries who had first brought the new religion to the Angell family. In February 1834, the Angells had moved to Ohio, the widowed Brigham Young married Truman's older sister, Mary Ann, who reportedly had remained single until she was nearly thirty because she had resolved "never to marry until she should meet a 'man of God.' "[21] The marriage was a long and happy one, and Truman came to regard Brigham more as a father than as a brother-in-law.

In the same year as the temple dedication, Truman was ordained a seventy and became a member of the Second Quorum of Seventy. Since this position involved special responsibility for missionary work, he began preparations for a mission while remaining busy with construction work. When the Prophet Joseph approached him about building a store, Truman replied that he "was about to go out into the vineyard to preach." The Prophet told him to go ahead but apparently reconsidered his need for the skilled carpenter and returned with his counselors the next day to renew the request. Truman records the conversation in his autobiography:

> The next day I looked up and saw the Presidency of the church together. I dropped my head and continued to work, at this time a voice seemed to whisper to me, "It is your duty to build that house for President Smith," and while I was meditating upon it I looked up and Brother Joseph Smith was close to me, he said "It is your duty to build that house." I answered, I know it. Accordingly, I changed my determination and yielded obedience.[22]

This encounter pointed the direction for most of the rest of Truman's life: he "yielded obedience" and went to work.

The year of the temple dedication had been a marvelous one for Truman and the Church—a year of spiritual ecstasy and material success. But the next two years were disastrous. The national financial panic of 1837 swept the Kirtland Bank away, and many of the disappointed investors blamed the leaders of the Church. Characteristically, Angell remained loyal to the leaders, blaming the crisis on a dishonest clerk, defaulting Gentiles, and "false brethren."

Despite personal financial ruin, Truman, as did other faithful Saints, made preparations to follow the Church leaders to Missouri. In the spring of 1838 he loaded his family into a one-horse wagon and started on the thousand-mile journey. In addition to horse and wagon, his assets were the family's clothing and a fifty-cent piece with which he paid for repairs on the wagon the first day out. It was a discouraging moment: "A rickety wagon, a balky horse, not a penny in my pocket, a family to feed and a thousand miles to go."[23] Providentially, a Brother James Hallman lent the Angells five dollars, which they used to exchange their horse for a better one. By selling some clothing, including the children's Sunday suits, the family raised enough money to go two hundred miles farther. They stopped while Angell worked for three weeks and then proceeded by stops and starts until they reached Missouri, trading their horse for land in an outlying area.

If Truman Angell had come to Kirtland at the best possible time, he arrived in Missouri at the worst. Just three days after his arrival he was driven from his land. "I was forced on the march and remained so until the exterminating proclamation . . . [when I was] forced to fly for my life; and no means of doing so, my land not being available."[24] Like many other Latter-day Saint men whose lives were threatened, Angell fled to Illinois during the winter of 1838–39, leaving his family, who were in less immediate danger, to make the trip as best they could. About five miles west of Quincy, Angell found work framing a barn for a Mormon farmer named Hail Travis. He agreed to receive his pay in provisions so that he would have food for his family when they arrived.

After seven anxious weeks without a word, a late-night visit from Joseph Holbrook reassured him that both of their families had arrived on the other side of the river but that Polly, who was pregnant, was seriously ill. The two men set off early the next morning to find their families. They walked to Quincy and crossed the river without a boat, wading "about half-knee deep in mud, about five miles." Altogether they traveled eleven miles over difficult terrain before finding the camp where a hundred Latter-day Saints were waiting for the completion of a new ferry to replace the old one that had been washed away. Truman found his wife and two children under a makeshift tent composed of several blankets. The pitiful scene was one he remembered vividly the rest of his life:

> There lay my poor sick wife; her bed upon the melting snow, very ill; my two little ones—the last was born in Ohio, were by her side, their clothes almost burned off, from standing by log camp-fires; no one to care for them; all the Brethren and sisters having cares enough for their own; though they were kind beyond what could be expected.[25]

The next day the ferry was completed, and the family crossed to Illinois. Truman took his wife and children to the farm, where the owner treated them kindly. Even with good care, Polly Angell's recovery was slow. Six years later Truman writes that her health was not fully restored and that "she has never been able to work much since."[26] The Angells remained on the Travis farm for two years before gathering with the Saints in Nauvoo in 1841.

Truman and his family arrived in Nauvoo not long after Joseph Smith had announced a revelation commanding the Saints to begin work once again on a temple. Angell writes in his biography, "I was chosen the first foreman on the Temple (Nauvoo) and gave general satisfaction to all."[27] Although he records no further details of his life during this period, contemporary records show that he was a member of the Nauvoo Legion and was a partner in the construction business in late 1843 and early 1844 with Joseph Coolidge, the builder of Joseph Smith's Mansion House. They had offices on the same block as Jonathan Browning's home and gun shop.[28]

However, most of Truman's time and energy must have been devoted to building the temple. In this work, he labored under the direction of the Prophet Joseph Smith and architect William Weeks.[29] Truman's other associates on the project included many craftsmen who would be his lifelong professional associates in Utah, including Miles Romney, William Folsom, and Elijah Fordham. Truman and Polly Angell added to their family shortly after arriving in Nauvoo—a daughter, Mariah, born 23 March 1841.

As envisioned by the Prophet and drawn by the architect, the temple was to be a magnificent structure many times larger than the Kirtland Temple and more monumental in its form and details. Constructed of limestone quarried nearby, the temple walls were ornamented with pilasters all around in a variation of the Greek Revival style, popular for churches, public buildings, and houses since the late 1820s. The Prophet apparently had considerable influence on the design despite the fact that his architect seems to have been well trained and skillful in his trade. Joseph's history records an 1844 disagreement with his architect where the Prophet clearly prevailed:

In the afternoon, Elder William Weeks (whom I had employed as architect of the Temple), came in for instruction. I instructed him in relation to the circular windows designed to light the offices in the dead work of the arch between stories. He said that round windows in the broad side of a building were a violation of all the known rules of architecture, and contended that they would be semi-circular—that the building was too low for round windows. I told him I would have the circles, if he had to make the Temple ten feet higher than it was originally calculated; that one light at the center of each circular window would be sufficient to light the whole room; that when the whole building was thus illuminated, the effect would be remarkably grand. "I wish you to carry out *my* designs. I have seen in vision the splendid appearance of that building illuminated, and will have it built according to the pattern shown me."[30]

Joseph's direction over the design of the structure probably set the pattern for Truman's later relationship to Brigham Young, when he planned other structures for the Church. Truman sought Brigham's counsel often and usually deferred to him in cases of disagreement.

Not only did Truman Angell neglect to record much about his personal and professional life during this period, but he also wrote little of the larger historical events occurring around him. He mentions only that he "suffered much—in common with the rest of my Brethren—during the persecutions in which the Prophet and Patriarch lost their lives."[31] Angell's loyalty lay with the Apostles in the aftermath of this tragedy. "Although the Prophet Joseph and Hyrum Smith had lost their lives by mob violence," he writes, "the Twelve Apostles came forward, with Brigham Young at their head, and the mantle of Joseph was upon them in all that was done."[32]

The year after Joseph's martyrdom, 1845, was an eventful one for the Angell family. A son, Truman Carlos, was born in January. Work on the temple was pushed ahead very rapidly. "We are here [at the temple] all of our time and make but few acquaintances elsewhere," Truman writes.[33] In May, Angell and the other temple laborers were invited to receive a patriarchal blessing from John Smith, the Prophet's uncle. Truman's blessing includes the statement "You are more called to assist the Saints to build cities and temples, and teach the principles of architecture as they have been in the church from the beginning, and then to preach the gospel."[34]

By the end of the summer, the building was enclosed. In the completed attic, Truman and Polly, among others, "received our Endowments and afterward our Sealing and second annointings, which far excelled any previous enjoyments of my life up to that time."[35] While the attic was in use throughout the fall and winter, construction continued on the lower rooms and basement. Two days after Christmas, Angell wrote to President Brigham Young on behalf of the workers on the temple, requesting the President's assistance in getting firewood for them. "There is a great deal of suffering among us at this time for the want of fuel." Angell suggested a general "Church Bee" to haul wood to the temple.[36]

During the winter, Truman's family ties to the new leader of the Church also increased. In January, Truman's mother and his sister Jemima were sealed to Brigham Young as plural wives, joining his sister Mary Ann.

When Brigham Young and other Church leaders crossed the Mississippi to begin the westward trek in February 1846, temple architect William Weeks went with them, leaving Angell in charge of completing the design and finishing the first floor assembly room. In a few months, Orson Hyde returned from the encampment of the Twelve to dedicate that portion of the building. With his work completed, Angell left the finishing of the remainder of the building to others while he began his preparations for going West with his family. A Church committee was instructed to help him get an outfit but was unable to do so until well into the summer. Angell eventually got two wagons which were in bad condition. After repairing them, he loaded his family and possessions and crossed the river where he was supplied with "young and unbroke" oxen and money to buy provisions. With the summer nearly gone and his wife expecting another child shortly, Truman and his family set off for Winter Quarters. Partway across

Iowa, Truman's health failed and he had to hire two black teamsters to drive his wagons to Winter Quarters.

The Angell family had already shared much of the persecution and suffering of the Saints, and their experience in Winter Quarters was no different. Truman remained sick with fever and chills all winter. In late October Polly gave birth to a daughter, Almirah, who died soon after. On 2 December Martha Ann, their ten-year-old daughter, also died.

By spring, Truman's health had improved and he was called to join the first company of pioneers. Besides his brother-in-law Brigham Young, other family members on the trek included his brother Solomon and cousin Joseph Holbrook. Like many others of the company, Angell stayed in the Great Salt Lake Valley only long enough to get the settlement organized and then made the return trip to Winter Quarters, arriving in the fall after a seven months' absence. On 29 October 1847, probably a few weeks before Truman's arrival in Winter Quarters, his only son, Truman Carlos, died at the age of two.

During the second winter, Angell made preparations to move his family to the West. They left early the next year with Brigham Young's company of about one hundred and fifty families. Truman's description of his third crossing of the plains is brief and poignant: "I made a fitout, and took my family in the Spring and started for our new home; arriving in Utah in the Fall with an Ox team, a distance of over 1000 miles; moving my sick wife on her back every rod of the way; having two children with us; having buried three in Winter Quarters."[37]

Shortly after his arrival in the Salt Lake Valley, Truman sought President Young's counsel about the work he should undertake. Brigham put him to work enclosing and finishing a house purchased for the President's own family, including Truman's sister Mary Ann. In the months that followed, Angell placed himself completely at the service of President Young. "I paid strict attention to all his calls, went and came at his bidding—for this I rejoice."[38]

William Weeks, the architect of the Nauvoo Temple, had come West with the first company in 1847, but the personal tragedy of losing two children in Winter Quarters and his distaste for the discipline of pioneer life soured his feelings toward the Church. After spending a winter in Utah, he left the Saints and returned to the East. President Young, who had planned for Weeks to continue as Church Architect, was left with the problem of finding someone to take his place. For the first public building to be planned, the Council House, a Brother Major (probably William Major, an artist from England) prepared and presented a design. President Young consulted his brother-in-law about the plan. "Being asked how I liked it," Angell later wrote, "I said that it did not please me, considering the newness of the country and our material."[39] President Young apparently concurred and asked Angell to prepare an alternate design. With the acceptance of the scheme, Truman Angell found himself the Architect of Public Works for the new city. At President Young's request, he devoted all of his energies to making designs and plans and supervising construction, rather than trying to become established on his own farm.

Truman Angell had always before earned his living by working with his hands. He found that the transition to his new duties was not easy. "It is a trifle to labour with one's own hands [compared] to the labour of the mind," he writes. "While one tires the extremities, the other wearies the man in his whole system."[40] Despite his personal difficulties and inexperience, the first six or seven years of his career as architect were probably his most successful and productive. As the most prominent architect in the Valley, he designed many of the best homes and nearly all of the important public buildings. Drawings and photographs of his buildings that remain from this period illustrate Angell's progress, both in his increasing skill as a draftsman and his growing sophistication as a designer.

The Council House, Angell's first design, was a simple square building with walls made of stone on the first story and adobe on the second. The building's overall form was a severely simplified version of the common Midwestern court-house topped with a cupola. In projects that followed, Angell apparently tried to improve his designs by studying the building pattern books that were available in the Valley. An 1852 inventory of the Territorial Library listed ten such volumes, including older books featuring Federal and Greek Revival style details and several recently published works advocating picturesque designs using Romanesque and Gothic elements.[41] Angell made specific reference to only one of these books, but his drawings contain many details that appear to be taken from others as well.[42]

Many of the houses Angell designed in his first few years as architect were plain rectangular structures similar to those built in Nauvoo with decorations that hinted vaguely of Federal or Greek Revival styles, but they were constructed of adobe instead of brick. Some of the houses, like Brigham Young's White House of 1849, had simple but graceful cornices and arched ceilings inside. Most included porches, an element that was popular in warmer parts of the country but had not been common in Nauvoo. Many of these early Utah homes, such as those for E. T. Benson, Horace Eldridge, Edwin D. Woolley, and Willard Richards, looked remarkably substantial and handsome for a struggling pioneer community.

In his design for a Seventies Hall prepared in 1851 and 1852, Angell tried his hand at more pretentious and fashionable architecture. His drawings envisioned a building with a dome-shaped roof over a large meeting room and octagonal turrets on the corners. Borrowing details from Greek and Gothic examples in his books, Angell decorated his proposal with castlelike battlements on the parapets, Greek pediments on the walls, and Gothic details on the windows. The scheme was quite ambitious, and Angell was proud enough of it to make a perspective drawing. Its extravagance may have been the reason it was never built.

Another important public building he planned in 1851 and 1852 was the city's first large assembly structure, the Old Tabernacle, located on the southwest corner of Temple

Square. Like many of the roughest pioneer shelters, it was a dugout, with a floor below ground level, adobe walls, and a simple gabled roof. It was surprisingly large, however, seating twenty-five hundred people. Angell designed the unconventional sixty-foot ceiling trusses with the aid of a model which he tested for strength. Both gable ends of the building were ornamented with triangular panels containing carved rising suns reminiscent of the sunstones on the Nauvoo Temple, and the ends of the roof were decorated with large barge boards cut out in a Gothic trefoil pattern apparently copied directly from a builders' book.[43]

By the end of 1851, Angell was growing accustomed to his new life. He had become a prominent man in the community, planning and directing many projects, and enjoying his success and prestige. His family life had also changed with the addition of a plural wife, Susan Eliza Savage, who would ultimately bear six children. Perhaps sensing the importance of his position in the Church, Truman started keeping a journal of his work that December. In the first few pages he lists with evident satisfaction the many buildings "progressing smartly" under his direction, describing his style of supervision as "the care of a kind father over his household" and referring to himself as "an architect and a master."[44] He also acknowledges the constant pressure of his job, which causes him "to dog around more than many might think," and records the first of many complaints about the nervous strain he feels working at his drawing board. "I find my spirit more willing," he writes, "than my body strong."[45]

As 1852 began, Angell had twenty-two projects underway or about to be started, the most elaborate being the state house or capitol to be constructed at Fillmore in central Utah. Because this structure was to be built without Angell's constant supervision, the architect prepared more detailed drawings and specifications than on previous projects. His design for the large stone building included four two-story wings projecting from a central domed rotunda. The dome towered above the wings and terminated with a statue of an eagle standing on a beehive. The entire building was surrounded by a two-story porch decorated with lattice panels and Gothic pinnacles. The strange proportions and mixture of styles made the design somewhat ungainly. Only the south wing was constructed, however, and standing alone without the elaborate porch, its sandstone walls, arched windows, and pilasters have a dignity reminiscent of the Nauvoo Temple.

Other important projects begun in 1852 included the Social Hall (a simple two-story adobe and stone building), a new residence for the governor, and a meetinghouse for Provo. For Brigham Young's impressive three-story official residence, Angell experimented with a grand symmetrical plan including a semicircular staircase. The details for this house, developed over the next two years, included carved mantle-pieces and a handsome observatory topped with a beehive. The Provo meetinghouse gave Angell the opportunity to design a rather large church. Although local tradition has ascribed its design to "English Presbyterian" influence, the building was actually a fine example of the American meeting-house tradition executed in adobe. The exterior was simple and well proportioned with a substantial domed tower. The interior included a large meeting room with a gallery on three sides. Angell also designed an outdoor baptismal font, walls, and elaborate gates for Temple Square, and worked on some scenery for the Social Hall.

Angell continued to enjoy his job through most of the year: "My heart is glad to see the order as I now have it."[46] After feeling a bit discouraged because he was not properly recognized, he was very pleased to be sustained in his position along with other Church leaders by vote at April conference. Increasingly secure in his abilities, Angell writes of the committee's purchasing building materials, "how perplexing it is to be ruled by inexperienced men."[47] Angell's prestige was further enhanced by his position as an officer in the militia.

Early in 1853 Angell began work on the most important project of his career, the Salt Lake Temple. Brigham Young had selected the temple site within days of the arrival of the first pioneers, but construction of the building had been deferred while the community overcame the basic problems of survival. But with a large number of faithful Saints gathered in numerous settlements, with many homes and a few public buildings completed, and with an architect who had demonstrated some talent and ability, Brigham was ready to begin.

Angell helped the First Presidency lay the southwest cornerstone on 6 April 1853.[48] According to a statement by William Ward, a talented young stonecutter who worked as Angell's draftsman in 1855 and 1856, the basic elements of the temple design were dictated to Angell by the President:

> Brigham Young drew upon a slate in the architect's office a sketch, and said to Truman O. Angell: "There will be three towers on the east, representing the President and his two counselors; also three similar towers on the west representing the Presiding Bishop and his two Counselors; the towers on east the Melchisedek priesthood, those on the west the Aaronic priesthood. The center towers will be higher than those on the sides, and the west towers a little lower than those on the east end. The body of the building will be between these and pillars will be necessary to support the floors." Angell then asked about the height, and drew the following vertical section according to Brigham's instructions. . . .[49]

The plan of the building was familiar to Angell since it followed the pattern of the Nauvoo Temple with large meeting rooms on the two main floors, rows of offices on mezzanines above the sides of the large rooms, and a baptismal font surrounded by smaller rooms in the basement. The most distinctive new elements were the six towers on the ends of the building. These towers externalized the priesthood symbols of the triple pulpits that had been the main features inside the meeting rooms of the earlier temples. It seems likely that the multiple spires were intended to give the building a dramatic silhouette reminiscent of the Gothic cathedrals Brigham had so admired in England, although their number and placement on the temple followed no European precedent.

Although the President had dictated the main elements of the building and followed its progress closely, the design details and styles of the structure appear to have been left to the architect. William Ward recalls,

> On several occasions the foundation and thickness of the walls was the subject of conversations. But I do not recollect any talk between Brigham and Angell in regard to the style of the building. Angell's idea and aim was to make it different to any other known building, and I think he succeeded as to the general combination.[50]

As he had done before in the Old Tabernacle, the Seventies Hall, and the state house designs, Angell experimented with medieval details from his most up-to-date pattern books. One of his early drawings shows a window with a pointed arch, giving evidence that Angell considered using correct Gothic details on the building. However, he discarded this idea in favor of round-arched windows which more closely resembled those on the Nauvoo Temple. The decision to use round arches in combination with medieval details like parapets, pinnacles, and buttresses may have reflected Angell's familiarity with the Norman or English Romanesque style which enjoyed a brief vogue in the 1840s and 1850s in America. Some of the pattern books available to Angell discuss the style and show examples of picturesque villas combining these very elements. Angell's design for the temple towers is particularly interesting in comparison with illustrations from two contemporary pattern books available in the Territorial Library. *The New Practical Builder,* by Nicholson, whose writings are mentioned elsewhere in Angell's journal, includes a castellated Gothic mansion with a tower combining corner pinnacles, battlements, and other ornaments strikingly similar to the upper portion of the temple towers.[51] A facade of a church in Shaw's *Rural Architecture,* available in the Territorial Library, also resembles the temple in its general proportions, window details, and the unusual double buttresses and pinnacles at each side of its tower.[52]

In assembling the details gleaned and adapted from various sources, however, Angell showed a degree of originality and a grasp of architectural principles. He took particular pride in the triple-tiered spires. "The finishing touches are quite original," he writes, adding with obvious enthusiasm, "I have a large field to launch forth into."[53]

While working on the preliminary temple plans, Angell also labored on an equally challenging but ultimately less successful project. The machinery for a sugar factory had been brought to Utah the previous year from England. In the spring of 1853 Angell was assigned to build a factory on the Church farm four miles south of the city in the area now called Sugar House. Unfortunately, the plans delivered with the machinery did not give sufficient detail about how the parts should be fitted together. In addition to planning the building to house the equipment, Angell spent much time over the next two years trying to put the machinery into working order. His drawings for the factory are among the most complicated and careful he ever made. However, when the factory was completed in 1855, it succeeded in producing only dark molasses. After two seasons of operation, the enterprise was abandoned as a failure and the building and equipment put to other uses.[54]

During these same busy years, Angell also designed an arsenal, a number of new homes, a schoolhouse for the Twelfth Ward, a store for merchants Livingston and Kincade, several forts for new settlements, a penitentiary, and many minor projects. To serve the needs of the Church during the construction of the temple, the Presidency had Angell supervise the erection of a simple adobe Endowment House in the northwest corner of Temple Square. William Ward assisted Angell in making the drawings for a "Big House" for President Young's family, later known as the Lion House. The castellated stone entrance vestibule drawn by William Ward illustrates the young man's ability to design in a more proper Gothic Revival style than his supervisor. The Salt Lake County Courthouse built during 1855 gives particularly clear evidence of Angell's progress as an architect. Similar to the Council House in its general form, it exhibits much greater refinement in the arrangement of doors and windows and the details of its decoration.

There were also developments in Angell's personal life. His heavy responsibilities had begun to affect his health. In 1854 he wrote that he felt as much fatigued from drawing "as I ever did a hewing timber or mowing grass, the two kinds of business that used to weary me the most in my early life."[55] Throughout that year and the next, his bad health became an increasingly frequent subject of journal entries. Another change in his life began during a trip to some of the southern settlements with Brigham Young in the spring of 1855, when the President advised him to take a second plural wife. In June he dutifully married Mary Ann Johnson, a young woman who bore him eight children over the next thirty years. This additional wife and the probability of more children may have been a factor in a letter he wrote that fall to Brigham Young asking permission to supplement his income by taking jobs on the side.[56]

Angell continued to work on the temple plans through January 1856, but the long hours of concentration finally proved too much for him. He stayed away from the office part of February and most of March to rest. Apparently President Young became concerned. While Angell was dining with him and his family around the first of April, the President suggested a working vacation—a mission to Europe. Angell's reply, recorded on the first page of his missionary journal, implies that he was more interested in a change than excited about Europe: "I told him that the labors of my office were very fatiguing and crowded upon me farther than I could attend to them, and that I did desire temporary relief."[57]

Brother Brigham may have had a motive beyond concern for Truman's health for sending Truman on a mission. In the eight years since William Weeks had left the Church, no trained architects had appeared in Utah, and President Young may have decided to train one. Setting Angell apart as a missionary, President Young promised him money and an opportunity to "view the various specimens of architecture that you may desire to see." Perhaps reflecting his own enthusiasm for England's cathedrals and other buildings, he added, "You will wonder at the works of the ancients and marvel to see what they have done; and you will be quick to comprehend the architectural designs of men in various ages . . . and you will rejoice all the time." The President also reminded Angell to "take drafts of valuable works of architecture and be better qualified to continue . . . work . . . upon the temple and other buildings."[58]

Truman Angell spent the next three weeks in preparation and departed on 22 April with an eastbound wagon company of forty-five people that included such notables as A. O. Smoot, E. T. Benson, Orrin Porter Rockwell, and the non-Mormon Judge John F. Kinney. The journey was hardly relaxing. Because of limited wagon space, Angell had to walk most of the way. By the second day, he was exhausted. Less than two weeks out, the group ran into a late blizzard that trapped them in several feet of snow for six days. Angell records: "I have been robbed of a home, I have been afflicted in body; but never did I feel in a tighter place than this journey has placed me in."[59] The remainder of the trip, however, was relatively uneventful, and Truman arrived in Liverpool on 13 July after nearly three months of travel.

From the time of his arrival in England, Angell received special treatment. Franklin D. Richards, the retiring president of the European Mission, had received word from Brigham Young that Angell was to visit many countries and places, that the mission should furnish the means for his travel, and that a companion should be chosen to accompany him.[60] The companion was James Kay, presiding elder in the Liverpool Conference.[61] Local branches provided traveling funds. Angell set his own schedule and was accorded minor celebrity status in many of the branches he visited, preaching at length in most places.

Truman's missionary journal contains many evidences of his deep feelings of devotion to the Church. He preached the "necessity of living their religion" and records with much satisfaction after a particularly strong sermon that he had "let them have the heaviest licks that I could streak."[62] When news of the Reformation of 1857 reached Britain, Angell fasted and prayed with the other missionaries before rebaptism and reconfirmation. On his return home, he wrote, "I am endeavoring to reform Truman before the Lord of Hosts."[63]

Liverpool, the European Mission headquarters, became Angell's base. He spent fifteen out of his thirty weeks in Europe in and around the city, much of the time resting, writing letters and his journal, and making preparations for travel elsewhere. He visited London three times; made a two-week trip to France and the Channel Islands, and a three-week visit to Ireland; spent nine days in Wales, two weeks in and around Manchester, and one week each around Birmingham and on the Isle of Man.

A careful reading of Angell's detailed journal yields some unexpected observations of both mission and missionary. In spite of his special calling to study architecture, Angell spent considerably more time doing traditional missionary work— visiting branches and members, attending conferences, and speaking in church meetings—than looking at architecture. And he spent nearly as much time resting and nursing his health as he did in Church work. His journal records visits to buildings or other sightseeing on only about forty days, roughly one day in five of his mission.

A second unexpected observation is that Angell was generally neither very impressed by nor very interested in the great buildings of Britain and France. He described in detail and took notes on only one structure—a theater that he thought might serve as a model for one back home. Of the new Houses of Parliament, he writes, "It was burdened with ornaments till it became sickening. I had to think the object of decorating so much was to excell rather than to display anything like a reasonable taste."[64] Westminster Abbey, he thought, "exhibited the genius of men but there was something about it very inanimate."[65] He saw the neoclassical National Gallery of Art "with which I was not impressed" and the Tower of London of which he records, "I shall not mention more of than to say that I bought a pamphlet that gives a full description of it."[66] Angell was already tired of sightseeing when he visited Sir Christopher Wren's masterpiece, St. Paul's Cathedral. "The most that I could say of it was that it was a National Show, and when the people want to make a show with their money, such buildings may be built, that can be easily matched."[67] Later in his journal, after listing a few of the buildings he saw in Paris, Angell writes, "We visited several other buildings of principle note. To mention them here would use up my patience."[68] Wren's chapel at Greenwich college, he says, "was burdened, and in fact this is one of the faults of the English Architecture."[69]

Clearly, Angell's taste in architecture seems to have been firmly set in favor of American simplicity. One of the few English buildings he praised was Hereford Cathedral, which he described as "built in a masterly style of architecture."[70] It may be significant in light of the style of the Salt Lake Temple that parts of this cathedral are outstanding examples of the Norman style, with round arches and massive, relatively simple stonework. Angell also had a few good words for a free library in Manchester, praising it for its orderly arrangement and similarity to his own design for "one of our chambers in the Plan of the State House, Utah Territory."[71]

Although neither interested nor impressed by most of the architecture he saw in Britain and France, Angell was fascinated by technological and scientific achievements. He was much taken with the Great Iron Ship under construction near London and marveled at a machine that could punch holes in a sheet of iron one inch thick as easily as a person could "put a needle through a sheet of thin strained paper."[72] He spent most of two days at the exhibit of manufactured goods at the Crystal Palace and wished he could have spent another two weeks. Museums in Dublin, Paris, and Manchester drew his special attention to their industrial displays. He also recorded details about a stone quarry, an iron works, a hat factory, a sewing shop, and a copper and lead factory. Though Greenwich's chapel left him unimpressed, he was fascinated by the observatory and described its moveable dome and some of the scientific equipment in some detail. Because of his own frustrating experiences in trying to build the sugar factory in Utah, he spent nearly two weeks arranging to visit a sugar refinery near Liverpool and wrote an extensive and technical description of it afterwards. The prospect of seeing another refinery was his main reason for going to Ireland. He spent a whole week writing his report on the two factories in a detailed letter to Brigham Young[73] and had it copied by a Church member "expert with his pen" before sending it off.

He spent a good deal of time having an engraving made of his design of the Salt Lake Temple based on a daguerrotype of the rendering made by William Ward. The work was done by Frederick Piercy, a Mormon convert in London who later became known for his illustrated guidebook to the Mormon Trail.[74] Piercy also made an engraving of Brigham Young's house from Angell's drawing.

Angell received instructions to return home in late January 1857.[75] Tired and sick from his travels, he had already spent most of January resting and rewriting his journal. His exhaustion was accompanied by sleeplessness, head and chest aches, loss of memory, and depression. "I feel as though I had not a friend on the earth," he writes, and dispiritedly records a few days before boarding the ship being as much "out of health" as "before I left the Valley."[76] On an uncomfortable night in France he had summarized his negative view of Europe: "The Saints in Zion should be thankful to the Lord, for the poor in Salt Lake are a thousand times more comfortable than they are in this town. My heart sickens at the horrors seen in this hemisphere."[77]

Arriving in Boston on 2 March after a stormy winter crossing, Angell visited his old home in upstate New York before proceeding to St. Louis. Among the Saints there he found William Ward, his former assistant in the architect's office, still relatively friendly despite his having left the Church and Utah during Angell's mission.

Angell traveled from Independence, Missouri, to the Salt Lake Valley in a wagon train which included only six teamsters and six passengers, one of them the Apostle George A. Smith; and Angell found there was room for him to ride. They passed the first train of handcart pioneers en route, and Angell left his rifle with them when he saw that they had only one gun in the camp. The wagon train traveled from dawn to midnight covering fifty miles a day. The continued rapid pace exhausted Angell. By the last day of the journey he could not eat and had wild dreams when he tried to rest. He arrived in Salt Lake City on 29 May to find his family happy and well, including a six-month-old son born in his absence.

Truman Angell's mission had taken him 16,569½ miles, by his own reckoning, and had lasted a little more than thirteen months.[78] It had been intended to enlarge his view of architecture, expand his imagination, and increase his ability to design buildings for the Mormon kingdom. It was ironic, therefore, that compared with the productive years before his mission, Angell would have few opportunities in the years that followed to use his new knowledge. Other architects would design most of Salt Lake City's new public buildings and homes. Angell's exterior designs for the temple, completed before his mission, would remain substantially unchanged, and most of the interior details he would develop for the building would ultimately be set aside. Excepting his design for the St. George Temple, most of his contributions would be made as a construction supervisor.

His new role began immediately. He had been called back to make detailed drawings so that stone could be quarried for the temple walls. He prepared master drawings and then began making full-size quarrying patterns using the spacious second floor of the Church store. He had completed part of this work by 24 July 1857, two months after his return, when word of Johnston's Army reached the Valley. Angell helped pack up the temple drawings, some to be moved south and others to be cached locally while the temple foundations were buried. Angell used the winter respite to continue planning the temple stonework and, in a letter dated 22 March 1858, assured Brigham Young that the drawings were clear enough to be understood after the passage of time "if there was a prospect of the building yet being erected."[79] Angell and his three families joined in the exodus southward, returning after the peaceful settlement of the difficulties that summer. The temple foundations remained buried, however, and other projects took priority in the ensuing months. Through the fall and winter Angell supervised the remodeling of the Old Tabernacle, moving the organ and choir seats from the north end to the center of the east side opposite the pulpit. A new "fence" between the stand and organ divided the room in half with women on the north and men on the south.[80]

Angell continued his architectural work with reluctance. In September 1858, just a few months after returning from the move south, he wrote to President Young alluding to his own poor health and expressing the hope that a change of work to farming would revive him.[81] He did change occupations for 1859, but he worked at his old trade, carpentry, rather than at farming, and he complained, "There was too much hard labour in getting wood that seemed to use me up, and all this winter I have felt a set back."[82]

In January 1860 he asked President Young in a letter if there were more projects to plan for the new year, for "if not, I want to make such other arrangements for spring as may open for me."[83] However, new projects developed. He worked on plans for a new home for John M. Bernhisel and for a handsome Gothic Revival bay window to be added to Hyrum B. Clawson's house. Probably his biggest project was developing plans for the New Social Hall, a large building for drama and dance. Although Angell prepared fairly detailed drawings, Church leaders decided to build the Salt Lake Theater instead. That same year, at the request of Brigham Young, Angell also made a study of the newly popularized system of balloon-frame construction, which used many relatively small pieces of milled lumber rather than the heavy timbers of older wood buildings. Angell's assurance that the new system was cheaper and that its thinner walls wasted less space than adobe may have influenced the President to use it for his new house at Forest Farm southeast of the city.[84]

In late 1860 William H. Folsom arrived in Salt Lake City. This old acquaintance and colleague was, like Truman Angell, a New England–born carpenter who had grown up along the Erie Canal. The two men had worked together on the Nauvoo

Temple. After the exodus, however, William Folsom had remained in the Midwest, eventually becoming a successful building contractor in Omaha. With his experience and abilities, Folsom may have been the only other man in the territory qualified for Angell's job. While Angell retained the title of Church Architect throughout the summer of 1861, Folsom made drawings for a new Seventies Hall and also began work on the Salt Lake Theater. Angell spent the year planning additions to the rear of Brigham Young's office between the Beehive and Lion House and supervising more changes to the Old Tabernacle. Angell harvested a crop of sugarcane from his farm late that season and resigned as Church Architect to devote his full energies to farming. William Folsom was sustained as his successor in October conference of 1861.

Not much information remains about Angell's years as a sugarcane farmer and sugar mill operator in Salt Lake City's Sugar House area. He summarizes the experience in a sentence: "I resigned . . . and went out on my farm and here the parts of my boddy that was not called into uce in the designing room was put into uce on the farm and for one or 2 years it seamed to do me good but alas I found I must stop."[85] In 1865 Angell took up carpentry again and worked part of the following year on the new Tabernacle under the direction of William Folsom and Henry Grow. But his old trade was hard on him, and he returned to his farm for the winter so weak that he could not do a day's work for five months.

Meanwhile, William Folsom, encountering some of the difficulties and frustrations that Angell had experienced before him, asked to be released as Church Architect. Brigham Young asked Truman Angell if he would be willing to take up the burden again. After reflecting, Angell answered on 31 March 1867: "If you do wish me to apply miself again to the Architects calling, I will do so with all my mite."[86] On 8 April he attended general conference where he was sustained once more as Church Architect. His son, Truman Angell, Jr., and William Folsom were sustained as Assistant Church Architects.

Truman lost little time getting back to work. Two days later, he moved at least part of his family back into the city and prepared a small office between two of the unfinished tabernacle's piers. Within a week he was working on drawings of the tabernacle cornice he had helped build the previous year. Angell also began keeping an office journal. Again, characteristically, at the end of his first week back on the job, he wrote that he frequently had to get out of the office for fresh air and a change of scene to avoid dizziness. Also characteristically, the second week he committed to paper an expression of his genuine humility and determination:

> I must say I feel a good deal worn out but if the Preserdent and my brethering feal to sustain a poor worm of the dust like me to be Architect of the Church let me strive to serve them and not disgrace my self. . . . May the Lord help me so to do."[87]

Angell found both the temple and the tabernacle projects in partial disarray. The construction of the Tabernacle had advanced beyond the detailed drawings, and the temple drawings were confused. The frustration of bringing order to the two projects was increased by Angell's realization that his work would probably not be appreciated: "All this is a labour of the mind and hence is a labour that no one perhaps will see."[88]

Both Angell and Folsom had examined the temple foundations when they were uncovered in 1862 following the departure of Johnston's army. Both had agreed that much of the masonry work was badly done and needed to be replaced. In the succeeding five years, the foundations had been rebuilt and work had begun on the walls without detailed plans. During the spring of 1867, Angell refined the system that he had devised ten years earlier. He prepared a master drawing of the temple, showing every stone with a number. He then made a detailed pattern of every stone so that each one could be cut to size at the quarry in Little Cottonwood Canyon, numbered, and shipped to the temple block. In this way, no waste stone would be shipped, and the number on each stone would tell the masons exactly where it should go. Angell believed that his system would be so simple that it would eliminate most of the need for trained supervision. He took great pride in the originality and beauty of his system, but had no illusions: "I beleave when this house is up my labers will then be appreciated and not before."[89]

For much of the summer, however, the Tabernacle was his first priority. Its west end, including its half-dome roof, had been constructed the previous year. The huge arched trusses that spanned the central section of the building like a row of bridges had presented fewer problems than the half arches at the ends which came together at one point in the center of the roof. This complicated connection was evidently not planned in detail before the pieces were put into place, and the result was a rather inelegant, although sturdy, patchwork. Perhaps referring to this situation as well as the interior finish work, Angell writes, "If I had charge of this building from the start it would bin my way to of found all the main troubles in a plan a head of the work but now it is otherways and I will do the best I can."[90] The east end, erected in the summer of 1867, was much neater and more workmanlike, perhaps due to Angell's supervision as well as the experience gained by the workmen the previous year.

Most of Angell's work on the Tabernacle focused on interior carpentry. He acted as foreman, summarizing his role succinctly: "I do the thinking and they have nought but to push the work."[91] The stand, based on instructions from Brigham Young, had pulpits on three levels, reminiscent of the Kirtland and Nauvoo temples. Angell also made careful arrangements for the organ and chorister. He described the stand as "quite different from the stiles of the day," resembling a "masked battery" fortification with the guns concealed behind protective walls. "You see not a gun," he notes, with a flash of wit, "but the heavest [heaviest] shots known on this earth will be there."[92] Brigham Young followed the Tabernacle's progress closely, personally revising the seating arrangement, deciding the locations for the stairs to the future galleries, and even selecting the grade of iron to be used for attaching the seats to the floor.

Although Angell made steady progress on the temple and completed the Tabernacle in time for October conference, the summer was frustrating. He had clashes with William Folsom and was understandably annoyed that Folsom's successful private business was drawing some of the best workmen away from Church jobs. Truman also felt that Henry Grow, the Tabernacle general foreman, did not supervise the work carefully enough. When Grow was given credit in an October 1867 newspaper article for most of the work on the building, Angell was so angry that he demanded and got a printed correction.[93]

Personal frustrations and sorrow added to his professional problems. Despite his years of hard work trying to support three families, he was still poor. On 4 July 1867 he records deciding not to use a five-dollar ticket to a ball at the theater because "the planness of my rig will be so much behind the company that will be there I think it best for me to stay away."[94] He worked long hours and often spent the night in town rather than walk the three miles to his house. On a weekend home he wrote that some of his younger children were afraid of him because they had seen him so seldom. In August and September, grasshoppers ravished his farm, eating even the leaves from the trees; and his two-year-old son became seriously ill and died before the end of September. In September and again in October, he was so discouraged that he asked to be released, but President Young persuaded him to stay on. By the end of the winter he was reconciled.

Angell's journal ends in the spring of 1868 with an entry stating that for the previous six months he had supervised the stonework on the temple, making diagrams of every course and every stone. In his first explanation of his system to President Young ten years earlier, he had predicted that this part of the work would require "scores of times" more labor than it took to design the building—and his predictions came true. Sheaves of drawings preserved in the LDS Church Archives and much of Angell's correspondence attest to his perseverance in this tedious task.

Another aspect of the work on the temple allowed more room for creativity—designing the interior details of the building. In the summer after his mission, Truman had made drawings of window details, columns, and cornices ornamented with carved faces. He continued this work in November and December of 1869, after a lapse of twelve years. The keystones of the arches included carved portraits of Brigham Young and Joseph Smith. In a similar undated drawing of a column capital, Angell indulged himself in the manner of some ancient cathedral architects by including a carved likeness of himself as an assurance that his contribution would not be forgotten.

President Young's announcement in 1871 that another temple would be built in St. George, Utah, presented Truman Angell with his last opportunity to design a major building. Although busy with other projects, he worked on the plans in bits of spare time. Since much of his work was done while the President and other leaders were in St. George, Angell was unsure if his design would be accepted and therefore put off completing details and specifications. His plans were accepted, however, and the building was started before he could finish his work. Because of the confusion caused by the inadequate plans, Angell found it necessary to go to the site personally several times over the next few years. These arduous journeys, some of them in bad weather, wore on his health and energy.

Angell was apparently instructed to follow the pattern of the Nauvoo Temple rather closely in his design for the St. George building. The two buildings were roughly the same size, and his drawings show that the room arrangements were also similar. The exterior style, however, followed the Salt Lake Temple in its castellated details. The walls had crenellations at the top and buttresses between the windows that were even more medieval and functional-looking than those in Salt Lake. One description classified the new temple's architecture as "English Norman."[95] In an original touch to the plans, Angell allowed the stairs on both sides of the main facade to project beyond the sides of the building in a way that recalls the fortified towers of romantic villas in contemporary pattern books. A drawing of the interior structure shows the floors supported by lattice trusses much like those used in the roof of the New Tabernacle. Angell seems to have had difficulty with the wooden tower. An early drawing shows a rather awkward octagonal spire, but the completed building had a squat-domed cupola. Brigham Young thought the tower too low and demanded a change but died before anything was done. The following year, the unchanged tower was split in half by lightning and was replaced with a higher domed structure designed by William Folsom under Angell's direction. The completed stone building was plastered and painted gleaming white, simultaneously giving it the appearance of castle and church. While evoking memories of the Nauvoo Temple, the interior at St. George also displayed many of Angell's ideas for the Salt Lake Temple that would never be realized. The meeting rooms included arched plaster ceilings, clustered Gothic Revival columns, and cornices decorated with stars and quatrafoils.

In July 1876 Angell was completely worn out once again. "Not one hour of the day am I clear of important duties and I have now allowed the work to go neglected, this has been the pride of my hart but age creeps on me and I see I fail," he writes in a letter of resignation to Brigham Young.[96] Angell proposed to homestead some public land to leave an inheritance for his family. The President accepted Angell's resignation in the hope "that the desired quiet" of a farmer's life "may restore you to your wonted health."[97] The resignation, however, produced anything but quiet. On 4 August Brigham appointed T. O. Angell, Jr., to serve in his father's place. A month later, after receiving a letter demanding a salary increase, Brigham released him with the statement: "Men that dictate the affairs of this great work in which we are engaged do not place price upon their labor."[98] William Folsom was asked to serve instead, but by the first of the year Truman, Sr., was back in his old job, reconciled to seeing it through to the end. "My health is not first rate and I do not know as it ever will be but I had rather ware out in my duty then rust out."[99]

Brigham Young's death late in August of 1877 must have been a particularly heavy blow to Angell, who had regarded him with the affection of a son and the admiration of a disciple. "The Lord . . . seames to dictate all he does," Angell had written earlier in his journal. "All I ask is to know the mind of

President Young to me and my way is clear."[100] Three weeks after the funeral, Angell wrote to President John Taylor and the other Apostles, "Brethren, you can continue me in the architect's office or not as you see fit, I am at your service."[101] They asked him to stay.

Angell's orderly system continued to guide the slow, steady process of construction of the Salt Lake Temple. In 1880, Angell reported that in ten years the walls had risen nearly seventy feet. He claimed to have saved the Church over twenty thousand dollars through his careful planning of the stonework, his personal hiring and management of the masons, his system of producing excellent mortar in a mill on Temple Square, and his use of improved boom cranes which were partly his own design. He also reported that in spite of years of faithful service, he remained desperately poor. In answer to his appeal for financial assistance, the Church granted him one thousand dollars to repair his home.

In his later years, Angell came to rely increasingly on the help of several of his sons. Truman O. Angell, Jr., made most of the later masonry drawings and diagrams for the temple and also served as scribe for much of his father's correspondence. Theodore began working as a stonemason in the late 1870s and became his father's clerk while his older brother was supervising the temple in Logan. When the foreman of stonecutters on the Salt Lake Temple was sent to prison for polygamy in 1886, Angell tried unsuccessfully to have Theodore appointed foreman and proposed another son, Leonard, to serve as clerk.

Following President Young's death, Angell was involved in several significant changes to the temple plans. A steam-heating system with boilers located outside the building replaced the less efficient and more dangerous original system of fireplaces in the stone walls. In 1885 and 1886, the interior layout of the building was changed to provide larger rooms for temple ordinances, a floor of offices, and one large meeting room with a gallery. This new plan was based on a scheme developed by Truman, Jr., for the Logan Temple. Angell, Sr., seems to have conceded these changes reluctantly.

President Taylor noted with concern in 1886 that Angell's signature did not appear on the revised interior plans and assured him, "We look upon you and sustain you as the architect of the temple . . . and wish whatever plans are submitted to be drawn out under your supervision and with your approval."[102] Church records are unclear about how Angell really felt in this case, but another incident suggests that his feelings may have been negative. Shortly after President Taylor's death in 1887, Truman, Jr., suggested to President Woodruff that the temple spires be finished in stone rather than wood covered with tin as planned. Although President Taylor had rejected the same suggestion a few years before, President Woodruff favored the idea and asked Truman, Sr., for his view. On 11 October the sickly architect asked his son to record his opposition to the change: it would alter Brigham's design, add a year to the construction time, and triple the cost. The son, however, added to the same letter his own views, disagreeing with his father and undercutting his arguments.[103] Five days later, before a decision was made on the matter, Truman O. Angell, Sr., passed quietly away.

On 17 October 1887 the *Deseret Evening News* announced his death and eulogized him as "a modest, unassuming man, of genial disposition, and a staunch and true Latter-day Saint."[104] His funeral was restrained, in keeping with his wishes. Speaking in the Third Ward Chapel, President Daniel H. Wells, for many years Angell's supervisor on the public works and a former member of the First Presidency, paid tribute to him in a paraphrase of Sir Christopher Wren's epitaph in St. Paul's Cathedral—"As long as the Salt Lake Temple stands, that is monument enough for him."[105] Truman Angell was buried in the Salt Lake City Cemetery next to his beloved Polly, who had passed away ten years before. He left behind two wives, thirteen children, and fifty-five grandchildren and great-grandchildren. Joseph Don Carlos Young, a son of Brigham Young trained in the East as an engineer, succeeded Truman Angell as Church Architect and supervised the last six years of the temple's construction, including stone spires and redesigned interiors.

Perhaps the most fitting characterization of Angell's place in Mormon history was one made by himself in a letter to President Taylor. After reviewing many events of his life, Angell modestly wrote that he had been called as architect "perhaps for want of a better man."[106] He knew that there had been stronger, healthier, better-trained, and more talented men than himself in the Church from time to time. But William Weeks and William Ward left the Saints to go elsewhere, William Folsom arrived in the Valley late and found the job too frustrating and limiting, and Truman, Jr., had neither the requisite humility nor devotion to the Church to replace his father. Only Truman O. Angell, Sr., had been willing to endure years of frustration and friction with his associates, striving to "suit the authorities of the Church" while receiving little recognition and inadequate compensation, and persisting for decades in supervising even the smallest construction details of a single building. His contribution in providing order and continuity to this important project was not the work of an architectural genius but rather the humble offering of an uncommonly loyal and devoted servant of the Church. As an architect he had achieved more than he aspired to do simply by doing what he regarded as his duty. For this monumental job, the Church had never found a "better man." In many ways, Truman O. Angell's life had been a testimony to the sincerity of his exclamation in another letter to President Taylor, "Oh that I could go to my Father in Heaven and have Him say, 'Well and faithful have you been over a few things. Enter my rest.' "[107]

Notes

1. Truman O. Angell, Journal 1857, 8 April 1867–1868, MSS, Library-Archives, Historical Department, The Church of Jesus Christ of Latter-day Saints, Salt Lake City, Utah; hereafter cited as LDS Church Archives, 24 September 1867.

2. Much of the preliminary research for this chapter was made possible by a 1973 Summer Research Fellowship from the History Division

Paul L. Anderson

of the Church Historical Department. The help and encouragement of Church Historian Leonard J. Arrington is gratefully acknowledged.

3. Most of what is known of the first half of Truman Angell's life, the thirty-seven years from his birth to his arrival in the Salt Lake Valley, is contained in a short autobiographical sketch prepared in 1845 and revised and expanded in 1875 and 1884. The longest version fills only eleven pages of typescript, telling a story with many elements common to the faithful rank-and-file who participated in the early scenes of the Mormon saga. The longest version is titled "Journal of Truman O. Angell"; hereafter cited as Angell, Journal. A shorter version is "Biography of Truman Osborn Angell, Sr."; hereafter cited as Angell, Biography. Typescripts are preserved in the LDS Church Archives.

4. Angell, Journal, p. 1.

5. Ibid., p. 2.

6. Ibid.

7. Joseph Holbrook, "The Life of Joseph Holbrook Written by His Own Hand," typescript, LDS Church Archives, p. 8.

8. Ibid., pp. 13–14.

9. Ibid., p. 14.

10. Angell, Biography, p. 2.

11. Angell, Journal, p. 2.

12. Ibid., p. 4.

13. Ibid., p. 3.

14. Ibid.

15. Ibid., p. 5.

16. Ibid., p. 4.

17. Ibid., p. 5.

18. Ibid., p. 11.

19. Ibid.

20. Ibid., p. 3.

21. Susa Young Gates, in collaboration with Leah D. Widtsoe, *The Life Story of Brigham Young* (New York: Macmillan Company, 1930), p. 24.

22. Angell, Biography, p. 3.

23. Angell, Journal, p. 5.

24. Ibid.

25. Angell, Biography, p. 5.

26. Angell, Journal, p. 6.

27. Angell, Biography, p. 5.

28. Card Index, Nauvoo Restoration; *Nauvoo Neighbor,* 23 April 1844.

29. For information on William Weeks, see J. Earl Arrington, "William Weeks, Architect of the Nauvoo Temple," *Brigham Young University Studies* 19 (Spring 1979): 337–59.

30. Joseph Smith, Jr., *History of The Church of Jesus Christ of Latter-day Saints,* ed. B. H. Roberts, 2d rev., 7 vols. (Salt Lake City: Deseret News, 1932–1951), 6:196–97.

31. Angell, Journal, p. 7.

32. Angell, Biography, p. 6.

33. Truman O. Angell to Brigham Young, 27 December 1845, LDS Church Archives.

34. Angell, Journal, p. 6.

35. Ibid., p. 7.

36. Truman O. Angell to Brigham Young, 27 December 1845.

37. Angell, Journal, p. 8.

38. Truman O. Angell, "A Journal of my Time kept by my own hand," commencing 15 December 1851, typescript, LDS Church Archives, p. 1 (hereafter cited as Angell, Journal 1851–56).

39. Ibid.

40. Ibid.

41. *Catalogue of the Utah Territorial Library* (Great Salt Lake City: Brigham H. Young, Printer, 1852), typescript, LDS Church Archives, p. 27.

42. Angell, Journal 1854–56, p. 24, refers to a work by Peter Nicholson, probably *Principles of Architecture* (London, 1848). Other influences seem to come from books by A. J. Downing, William H. Ranlett, and Edward Shaw.

43. Compare Angell's design with William H. Ranlett, *The Architect* (New York: William H. Graham, 1847), plate 6.

44. Angell, Journal 1851–56, pp. 2–3.

45. Ibid., p. 2.

46. Ibid., p. 7.

47. Ibid., p. 10.

48. Ibid., p. 13.

49. William Ward, "Who Designed the Temple?" *Deseret Evening News,* 16 April 1892, p. 4.

50. Ibid., p. 4.

51. Peter Nicholson, *The New Practical Builder and Workman's Companion* (London: Thos. Kelly, 1822). Charles Mark Hamilton has also mentioned this similarity in his dissertation, "The Salt Lake Temple: An Architectural Monograph" (Ph.D. diss., Ohio State University, 1978), p. 56.

52. Edward Shaw, *Rural Architecture* (Boston: James B. Dow, 1843), p. 51.

53. Angell, Journal 1851–56, p. 18.

54. See Leonard J. Arrington, *Great Basin Kingdom* (Lincoln: University of Nebraska Press, 1958) for details about the early attempts at building a sugar industry.

55. Angell, Journal 1851–56, p. 20.

56. Truman O. Angell to Brigham Young, 2 October 1855, LDS Church Archives.

57. Truman O. Angell, "Journal by Truman Osborn Angell 1856," typescript, LDS Church Archives (original in Daughters of Utah Pioneers Archives), p. 1; hereafter cited as Angell, Missionary Journal.

58. Ibid.

59. Ibid., p. 7.

60. Ibid., p. 20.

61. Ibid.

62. Angell, Missionary Journal, p. 51.

63. Ibid., p. 76.

64. Ibid., p. 28.

65. Ibid., p. 29.

66. Ibid., pp. 30–31.

67. Ibid., p. 32.

68. Ibid., p. 57.

69. Ibid., p. 62.

70. Ibid., p. 69.

71. Ibid., pp. 50–51.

72. Ibid., p. 24.

73. Ibid., pp. 44–48.

74. Frederick Piercy, *Route from Liverpool to Great Salt Lake Valley* (Liverpool: Franklin D. Richards, 1855).

75. Angell, Missionary Journal, p. 68.

76. Ibid., pp. 65, 70.

77. Ibid., p. 68.

78. Ibid.

79. Truman O. Angell to Brigham Young, 22 March 1858, LDS Church Archives.

80. Journal History, 2 January 1859, p. 1, LDS Church Archives.

81. Truman O. Angell to Brigham Young, 20 September 1858, LDS Church Archives.

82. Truman O. Angell to Brigham Young, 2 January 1860, LDS Church Archives.

83. Ibid.

84. Truman O. Angell to Brigham Young, 18 July 1860, LDS Church Archives. Although there has been some speculation that Angell designed the Forest Farm house, I have been unable to find any evidence for his participation in that project.

85. Truman O. Angell, Journal 1857 to 8 April 1868, MSS, LDS Church Archives, 18 April 1867; hereafter cited as Angell, Journal 1857–68. In the absence of page numbers, citations are made by date of entry.

86. Truman O. Angell to Brigham Young, 31 March 1867, LDS Church Archives.

87. Angell, Journal 1857–68, 21 April 1867.

88. Ibid., 28 April 1867.

89. Ibid., 28 May 1867.

90. Ibid., 19 June 1867.

91. Ibid., 26 September 1867.

92. Ibid., 30 August 1867.

93. Ibid., 6, 12, and 18 October 1867.

94. Ibid., Journal 1857–68, 4 July 1867.

95. Hazel Bradshaw, ed. *Under Dixie Sun* (St. George, Utah: Washington County Chapter Daughters of Utah Pioneers, 1950), p. 340.

96. Truman O. Angell to Brigham Young, 29 July 1876, LDS Church Archives.

97. Brigham Young to Truman O. Angell, 4 August 1876, LDS Church Archives.

98. Brigham Young to Truman O. Angell, Jr., 4 September 1876, LDS Church Archives.

99. Truman O. Angell to Brigham Young, 23 February 1877, LDS Church Archives.

100. Angell, Journal 1857–68, 16 March 1868.

101. Truman O. Angell to John Taylor, 25 September 1877, LDS Church Archives.

102. John Taylor to Truman O. Angell, 13 May 1886, LDS Church Archives.

103. Truman O. Angell and Truman O. Angell, Jr., to Wilford Woodruff, 11 October 1887, LDS Church Archives.

104. "Death of Truman O. Angell, Sr.," *Deseret Evening News,* 17 October 1887, p. 3.

105. Laura P. Angell King, "Truman O. Angell, Sr.," in Kate B. Carter, *Heart Throbs of the West,* 12 vols. (Salt Lake City: Daughters of Utah Pioneers, 1941), 3:71.

106. Truman O. Angell to John Taylor, December 1881, LDS Church Archives.

107. Truman O. Angell to John Taylor, 18 October 1881, LDS Church Archives.

David J. Whittaker

7

Richard Ballantyne and the Defense of Mormonism in India in the 1850s

A native of California, David J. Whittaker now resides with his wife and four children in Provo, Utah. His current position is University Archivist and Archivist of the Mormon Experience at Brigham Young University. He received his B.A. from Brigham Young University and his M.A. from California State University at Northridge. He received his Ph.D. from Brigham Young University. He has published widely in Church periodicals and professional journals. His interest in Richard Ballantyne originated in his work on early Mormon pamphleteering, which was his dissertation subject.

Richard Ballantyne's name is usually associated with the founding of the Sunday School program in the early latter-day Church. Indeed, emphasis on this important contribution has often overshadowed his other contributions and achievements.[1]

Richard Ballantyne was born in Whitridgebog, Roxburgshire, Scotland, on 26 August 1817.[2] His parents were of Scottish descent and his father died before his family heard of the restored gospel, brought to the British Isles by the followers of Joseph Smith, Jr. Young Richard was in his twenty-sixth year when his family moved to Nauvoo, Illinois, in 1843. He had finally accepted the message of Mormonism in December 1842, allowing Henry McCune to baptize him into The Church of Jesus Christ of Latter-day Saints.[3]

Prior to his conversion he had worked as a farmer and also as a baker. Both employments left little time for school, and what education he had received was during the winter months. After arriving in Nauvoo, he became the manager and bookkeeper of the Coach and Carriage Association, and in 1846 he was involved in the closing of John Taylor's printing establishment in Nauvoo.[4] He participated in the Mormon Exodus in 1846, staying in Winter Quarters until May 1848, when he migrated to the Salt Lake Valley, arriving in September. Before leaving Nauvoo he had advanced in the priesthood, first to a seventy and then to a high priest. He married Huldah Meriah Clark in 1847 and thus became a "family man" (their first son was born while they were crossing the plains) when he entered the Salt Lake Valley.

During his first year in the Great Basin he engaged in farming. In December 1849 he held the first Sunday School class in the Church. He thus engaged himself until the fall of 1852 when he was called on a mission to Hindostan, India.[5] His mission to East India lasted until September 1855, after which he returned to the Salt Lake Valley.

He arrived home during the "Reformation" and was immediately called on a "home mission."[6] These experiences undoubtedly led to his plural marriages: to Mary Pearce in 1855 and to Caroline Sanderson in 1857. He spent the remainder of his life in farming and business, and for a short time (May 1877 to November 1878) he owned and operated the *Ogden Junction*. After this, he engaged first in railroading and then in the lumber business. Some successes in these enterprises led him into real estate, but the Panic of 1893 left him a poor man. He died in Ogden on 8 November 1898.

He is best remembered for his work in the Sunday Schools of the Church, a work he continued throughout his life. But it is the purpose of this essay to examine in detail his mission to India and more specifically his writings and publications there.

The East India Mission, 1849–1856

Although Richard Ballantyne's mission call to India came in August 1852, very early in the Church's history, Mormon missionaries were already there. According to Lanier Britsch's study, the need for an LDS mission arose from the requests of two men in India (Thomas Metcalfe and William A. Sheppard), who wrote requesting tracts and other literature about the Church.[7] This request and the petitions of two sailors, George Barber and Benjamin Richey, in 1849 began the official LDS missionary work in India. Between 1849 and 1856 seventeen Mormon missionaries labored in this mission.[8]

From its founding, the Church was missionary oriented. Extending its efforts into Canada in 1832 and England in 1837, its great success in the British Isles thereafter has overshadowed many of the other missions.[9] In 1849, after the initial assault on the Great Basin, Brigham Young began a renewed program of foreign missionary work. In addition to the British Mission, elders were sent to Italy, France, and Scandinavia in 1849. In 1850 missionaries were sent to Hawaii. But the greatest effort to warn "the world" came in 1852 when, at a special conference held in Salt Lake City on 28 and 29 August, missionaries were called to Gibraltar, Siam, China, Hindostan, South Africa, the West Indies, British Guiana, and Australia.[10]

Ballantyne, like many of his coworkers, brought great zeal and testimony to his calling. Convinced for himself that God had again spoken to man after centuries of Apostolic darkness, he acted out of both conscience and scriptural injunction to warn the world of Christ's message and imminent return. To accomplish this task, early Mormons willingly responded to their leader's request to act out their part in this, the final act of this world's play.

These missionaries were attracted to Mormonism for a

variety of reasons, but they generally joined the Church because its message struck a responsive chord in breasts that had already been tuned during an age of spiritual ferment.[11] Undoubtedly, their own conversion experiences affected the way they approached others. The literature they read and the stories they heard often became the models of the material they offered to others.[12] Another important ingredient of their teaching was the influence of their mission leaders and specifically the publications of those leaders. The East India Mission is a case in point.

Setting the Stage:
Lorenzo Snow and the East India Mission

Lorenzo Snow, who became the fifth President of The Church of Jesus Christ of Latter-day Saints, was baptized into the Church in June 1836. He went on his first mission the next year and spent the rest of his long life fulfilling various mission-type calls for the Church.[13] His first mission outside the United States was to England in 1840. While there he assisted Parley P. Pratt in printing an English edition of the Book of Mormon and also managed to publish his first pamphlet, *The Only Way to Be Saved.* After three years in England, he returned to Nauvoo. He completed several short missions and was in Ohio when he heard of the deaths of Joseph and Hyrum Smith. He returned to Nauvoo, supported Brigham Young as Joseph Smith's successor, and traveled overland to the Salt Lake Valley in the fall of 1848. Early in 1849, he was called to the Apostleship by Brigham Young, and in October of the same year he was called to the Italian Mission and "to other nations and countries wherever the opportunity should present itself."[14]

Elder Snow traveled to Italy through London and Paris, and although his major accomplishments on this trip do not concern us here, his interests, assignments, and publishing activities in relationship to India must be noted.[15] From the start he seems always to have considered his call as embracing more than just Italy. For example, before he left London he called William Willes, Joseph Richards, and Hugh Findlay to India on missions.[16]

By the time he reached Italy, Elder Snow was even more concerned with the missionary efforts in India.[17] By March 1852 he was in Malta and was anxiously awaiting news from Bombay and Calcutta.[18] It was during this time that he undertook to publish several tracts and to establish at Malta a "Central Book Depot" for those countries he considered under his presidency. These publishing activities and his leadership had great influence in the Swiss, Italian, Spanish, Bombay, and Calcutta missions. In May 1852 he wrote to Franklin D. Richards of his plans:

> In view of carrying forward with efficiency those several missions that have come under my direction, and to open the road to the introduction of the Gospel into those Catholic countries bordering upon the Mediterranean, we are arranging all our publications in respect to kind, matter, quantity, and language. Our printer, who expresses much interest in the prosperity of our cause, has just made arrangements to order from England an apparatus for stereotyping, and we hope, by this means and other opportunities to be able ere long to supply economically from this point, as a Central Book Depot, Italy, Switzerland, Spain, Bombay, and Calcutta.[19]

He also told of two works he had just published: *Voice of Joseph* and the *Ancient Gospel Restored,* which was a retitled printing of his earlier *The Only Way to Be Saved.*[20] Both, he said, were to be sent to Calcutta and Bombay as soon as he had an address to send them to.

Taking his presidency seriously, he had planned to visit India himself as early as July 1851, when he was contemplating sending missionaries there. He had also planned to see his tracts printed there.[21] As he left England he told members there that he would visit Switzerland, Italy, and India.[22] His plans to visit India, Bombay, and Calcutta were changed, however, when he was unable to get passage from Malta because of an accident which damaged the East India steamer he had planned to take. By the time the ship would have been repaired it would have been too late in the year to travel east, so he headed west to England and thence to the United States.[23]

Lorenzo Snow, then, actively anticipating the establishment of a firmer missionary effort in India, sent several men to this country and attempted to set up a book supply station for Church literature in southern Europe and India. When he withdrew from Europe, he left in the hands of others the various missions he had begun, specifically instructing that "these brethren will keep up a correspondence with the Presidency at Liverpool, from whom they will receive from time to time that instruction and counsel as shall tend to promote our Master's cause under their directions."[24]

Organized Beginning in India

Despite his inability to visit India personally, Lorenzo Snow provided a catalyst to early missionary work there. Returning home to Salt Lake City, he arrived one day after the special conference had ended that called nine elders to labor in Calcutta and Hindostan.[25] The addition of these missionaries came at a critical time in the history of the mission. Although their united assault on India would prove unsuccessful, it has been said that "there is nothing more heroic in our Church annals than the labors and sufferings of these brethren of the mission to India."[26]

Richard Ballantyne arrived with the other missionaries in Calcutta on 26 April 1852.[27] As indicated previously, they were not the first Mormons there, nor were the Mormons the first Christian group to visit India. Christian visits to India allegedly date back to the Apostle Thomas, who is said to have established Christianity in India in A.D. 52. Other groups came in the succeeding centuries, but not until the sixteenth century when St. Francis Xavier was very successful in planting Catholicism there was real progress made. In the years following, Spain and Portugal, who had really come to India for its trade, received stiff competition from the English and Dutch. The Protestants failed at first to do missionary work; in fact, the few missionaries there constantly complained of the corruptness and bad example of the East India Company on the natives. But eventually the first Protestant chapel was built after 1710, and Baptists were in Calcutta by 1793. By the time Mormons first made contact with India in 1849, European Christianity did have a foothold, although it was somewhat tenuous.[28]

The LDS missionary thrust was determined by several factors, most of which resulted from the non-Western environment of their field of labor. India's population was placed at 206 million in 1872, the year of its first census. The vast majority lived in rural settings with those speaking English residing in or near the larger seaport cities where European trade flowed in and out and where British military posts were established. The difficulty of the languages meant that the Mormon missionaries would (at first anyway) have to concentrate their efforts in those areas where an English-speaking population existed and where a practical missionary effort could be sustained. In addition to the language barrier, the early missionaries recorded their frustrations about the native religions (most of which they found revolting), the caste system (which always seemed to place *them* in the middle between the numerous poor and a handful of rich), and the climate (which ultimately weakened the health of the missionaries).[29]

The initial days in Calcutta were critical for these new arrivals. Since the beginning of the eighteenth century, Calcutta had been the center of British commerce and trade in India. Its population in 1850 was a little over one million, of which some four thousand were Europeans.[30] With its government officials and substantial English-speaking population, Calcutta was and remained through the 1850s the quasi-headquarters of the East India Mission. When the missionaries arrived, an official presidency was set apart and the elders were assigned to various parts of India. These assignments were made at a special conference three days after the American elders arrived in Calcutta.[31]

Richard Ballantyne and Robert Skelton, assigned to Madras, were unable to get passage until 20 June. While awaiting passage, Ballantyne got his first taste of missionary work in India. At the same time he got his first exposure in India to anti-Mormon literature, an exposure which undoubtedly set the stage for much of the orientation of his mission at Madras.

Nathaniel V. Jones, president of the East India Mission, wrote in June 1853 of a pamphlet that was having an adverse effect on the elders' activities in and around Calcutta. One Charles Saunder and a friend had produced a work entitled *Mormonism Unveiled* which, like its 1834 counterpart, was a collection of miscellaneous items attacking Mormonism.[32] As early as 10 May the missionaries were studying it and by 16 May were writing a reply. When the 120-page reply was published on 4 August, it appeared under the authorship of N. V. Jones. But evidence now available makes it clear that it was a group effort of Jones, Amos Musser, James Meik, and Ballantyne.[33] Although Ballantyne contributed but little to the work, it was his first publishing effort to appear in India. His own journal tells of N. V. Jones's asking for his help on 18 May and of his spending the next two weeks studying the tract and in writing his assigned portion.[34] This first exposure to the anti-Mormon press in India served to set the tone for his own publishing activities during the year that followed.

Publishing in Madras

Ballantyne and Skelton were able to secure passage to Madras on 20 June,[35] arriving on the evening of 24 July 1853. The faith-promoting voyage and their quickly developed friendship with the ship's captain, Thomas Scott, foreshadowed their missionary activities in Madras. The passage to Madras was during the monsoon season, a rather perilous time to be traveling the Bay of Bengal. But with a visionary "call" to Ballantyne, telling him the time was right to travel to Madras, the two men sought passage. After five refusals, Captain Scott finally agreed to take them, and then only after they promised him safe passage. There was a near miss and a storm did threaten the ship, but they made it safely to their destination.[36]

The captain proved to be an important asset in their assault on Madras. Before the voyage he had heard of the Mormons and had refused at first to transport them because he had considered them of "bad reputation" and, therefore, not fit company for the ladies he had as passengers. Only their perseverance, a chance conversation with a merchant on Scott's ship, and their promise of safe passage finally got them on board.[37]

The passage gave them additional opportunities to get closer to the captain, and in time they were fast friends. During the voyage they lost no opportunity for teaching and were able to preach and distribute such tracts as Parley P. Pratt's *Voice of Warning,*[38] the Pearl of Great Price,[39] Lorenzo Snow's *The Only Way to Be Saved,*[40] and the Book of Mormon. Captain Scott's interest grew in proportion to their time at sea. He was particularly interested in Lorenzo Snow's tract, so much so that the day before they reached Madras he offered to pay for reprinting it.[41] Captain Scott also arranged for a room for them at a fine hotel after their arrival and gave Ballantyne a pair of shoes and some extra money above what the cost of printing would run. Further evidence of the captain's friendship was manifested the day after the missionaries' arrival when they received a note from him saying he had contacted and arranged with a printer to have Snow's pamphlet printed. These missionaries were surprised to learn that the work would be done in two days.[42] The initial agreement called for three hundred copies, but as Ballantyne worked with the printer (reading galleys, etc.) during the next few days, the price break caused him to increase the order first to six hundred and then to a thousand. He also insisted to the foreman of the Oriental Press that good quality paper be used. This was assured when the thousand copies were ordered.[43] This pamphlet of eight pages was ready on 30 July. The day before they received it, Captain Scott offered to pay for the printing of another tract; so when the Snow tract was picked up, Ballantyne was ready to give another order to the printer.

Their second publishing project in Madras was the reprinting of Parley P. Pratt's *Proclamation of the Gospel* with some extra material about the history of the Church.[44] This publishing of Pratt's work at the same time they were printing Snow's work illustrates that India in the 1850s was a kind of melting pot for Mormon literature and leadership. Elder Snow, as we have seen, was active from the European side of India and the presence of Parley Pratt's work suggests the influence from the Pacific side.

Elder Pratt had taken California and the Pacific area as part of his missionary responsibility and had, during the early 1850s, specifically written the *Proclamation* for his area of jurisdiction. Going to Chile, he had taken charge of the Australian missionary work of John Murdock and Charles W. Wandell, giving them a copy of his work in San Francisco and telling them to print it when they got to Australia. This they did as soon as they arrived in Sydney.[45] It was probably this printing that Ballantyne used for his edition.[46] Ballantyne, however, added his own personal touches, and when it appeared on 5 August 1853, it contained both a "proclamation" and a brief account of Joseph Smith's early religious experiences.[47]

The local press announced the missionaries' arrival as they busied themselves with the publishing and distributing of these tracts. These public announcements soon led to attacks on them which in turn forced them out of their hotel, the Madras House. A member from England, who was then residing at St. Thomas Mount, offered them a room to stay in. This was their first taste of opposition in Madras, which was just the beginning.

On 1 August Captain Scott told Ballantyne that a "very long article" had just appeared in a Roman Catholic paper in Madras. By 5 August Ballantyne had obtained a copy of it and had responded to these "scurrilous reports" which were affecting Captain Scott.[48] On 5 August, the day he received the *Proclamation,* he called at the Oriental Printing Office and requested Mr. Bowie, the printer, to publish his reply in the *United Service Gazette.* Mr. Bowie consented, and the issue containing his letter was out by 12 August.

As these attacks increased, the missionaries were forced more and more to defend themselves and their doctrines. On 17 August the *Madras Christian Herald* fired another volley against them, and again Ballantyne was forced to write a response.[49]

Polygamy in the Early Mormon Press

Even though their responses did not stop the attacks, these missionaries were quite aware of the publicity they were getting and sought to make the most of it. Knowing their own supply of tracts would neither last nor be sufficient to answer all questions posed to them, they ordered more from Calcutta and Liverpool.[50] At the same time, realizing that "circulating tracts alone will not do,"[51] they decided to schedule a series of lectures on various religious topics. To announce these, they had Mr. Bowie print one hundred handbills which they began to post around the area.[52] But their public meetings were small because by the time they gave their first public lecture on 2 September the charge of polygamy was being leveled against them. Ballantyne's letter to his wife on 9 September realistically describes their situation at St. Thomas Mount: "The large bone that is now being picked is Polygamy. This is a large pill for many to swallow, and in fact the very first sight of it so nauseates their stomachs, that at present they can scarcely receive anything else."[53] He had learned this from experience. Robert Skelton had been ordered out of the canonment at St. Thomas Mount because of this and other doctrines. A mob had even gathered to forcibly remove him. Ballantyne himself had just about converted a Mr. Alex Wilson, who refused to hear any more about the gospel after he heard of the polygamy doctrine.[54]

Again Ballantyne took up the pen to explain his religion to the public. He concluded on 29 August to write a piece for the newspaper. He finished it on 31 August, but the section dealing with polygamy was not published.[55]

Polygamy remained a major stumbling block to the LDS missionary work in India. Although Ballantyne was monogamous until after his mission, he began defending the doctrine soon after his arrival in Calcutta. Twelve days after his arrival, he recorded in his journal that he had commenced writing "an article on Polygamy tracing its history from the Old Testament."[56] These early days in Calcutta taught him how very little he and his coworkers knew about the doctrine and practice of plural marriage; and as the attacks on the Church tended more and more to center on this doctrine, every attempt was made to obtain information on it. Hugh Findlay reflected the concerns and needs of these early missionaries when he wrote from Bombay to N. V. Jones that celestial marriage

> is, and has been from the first a point of continual discussion here —the corrupt hearts spicing forth their own abominable ideas concerning it.
>
> I sincerely desire to know the points of said law, as to be known among the Gentiles, and any Tracts in your possession on the subject will be more acceptable indeed.[57]

Even before the public announcement of plural marriage (in August 1852), which permitted the missionaries to publicly defend and discuss the doctrine, the press in India raised the issue of its practice. The request of Hugh Findlay was based on his attempts to deal with such attacks.[58]

Rumors of plural marriage were a part of anti-Mormon literature as early as the 1830s, even though polygamy's precise beginnings are not known. There is little doubt that Joseph Smith began the practice, so much a part of LDS history after his death, but exact information is hard to come by.[59] Because of this, with two major exceptions,[60] no public statements were available until the end of 1852. At the beginning of 1853, the Mormon press began producing the defenses that continued through the 1880s.[61]

Mormon leaders, in the wake of this public announcement, sought to head off criticism by establishing new Mormon periodicals in strategic locations throughout the country. Orson Pratt was sent by Brigham Young to Washington, D.C., where

The Seer was established. John Taylor went to New York City and in 1855 began *The Mormon.* Erastus Snow published the *St. Louis Luminary* at St. Louis from 1854 to the end of 1855. On the West Coast, George Q. Cannon published at San Francisco the *Western Standard* in 1856–1857.[62] All contained defenses of polygamy, but Pratt's publication was by far the most systematic and influential in the early Church.[63]

In addition to those previously mentioned, other essays and pamphlets were potentially available as sources to early missionaries needing ammunition to defend themselves. In February and March of 1853, the *LDS Millennial Star* ran a series of letters on polygamy by John Jaques, stressing the virtue of the Mormons and defending their leaders against attacks then being made.[64] In the following months other items appeared,[65] including the first defense of the doctrine by a woman.[66] The missionaries in India in the 1850s drew on these sources for information on polygamy. Richard Ballantyne's experience illustrates this.

In addition to the public challenges, his journal and correspondence suggest his personal concerns. In May 1853 his wife wrote him a letter, which he received in September while he was dealing with the public attacks. In addition to her expressions of loneliness she expressed her personal concern with polygamy.[67] His response on this occasion was the same five months later when he wrote to her again:

> In regard to domestic relationships, and duties I would here *earnestly* recommend Brother O. Pratt's works as your constant guide. He has laid down 27 admirable, and comprehensive *rules,* in the November and December Nos. of the Seer. You wrote to me that you intended taking that work, but if you have not, I would advise you to get it, and preserve it in the family.[68]

Throughout this time he was preparing to write what became the only pamphlet published in India devoted entirely to the subject of polygamy—*Dialogue Between A and B on Polygamy*—which appeared in March 1854. The pamphlet's dialogue format came from his reading of an unpublished anti-Mormon work.[69] The contents, however, clearly reflected

Orson Pratt's influence. Ballantyne had heard Pratt's 29 August official pronouncement of the doctrine, and his journal reflects his regular habit of reading Pratt's work; the pamphlet itself shows even more clearly this debt. But in addition to Pratt's influence, traces of the influence of the early Mormon press are also evident.[70]

Although Ballantyne was the only missionary in India to devote an entire tract to the subject of plural marriage, others, just as troubled by attacks on the practice, directed their writing to the newspapers. One of the best-documented replies was that of Hugh Findlay. Arriving in Bombay in April 1852, he was immediately pelted by the local presses. These assaults continued through the coming months, with each article increasing in vulgarity as they increasingly centered their volleys on polygamy. In the midst of these Findlay called for help, as we have noted previously.[71] A complete analysis of these replies is beyond the immediate scope of this essay, but even a cursory examination of them will reveal the influence again of Orson Pratt and the *LDS Millennial Star.*[72]

In addition to polygamy, there were two other major problems confronting the missionaries in India: the governmental and religious systems of "paying" employees and converts, and the climate.[73]

The first is talked about in almost every record we have of the India Mission. Ballantyne throughout his mission records his anger and frustration at the constant threats Europeans faced from their employer (the government) when the employer learned they were investigating the Church. At the same time (because they worked primarily with natives who worked for Protestant and Catholic churches), when they tried to teach English-speaking natives, the natives too (because they were dependent upon the priest who paid them) were threatened with losing their livelihood.[74]

The second problem, that of climate, affected both the health of the missionaries and the "health" of their missionary efforts. The monsoon season, extending from June to September, assured a wetness that brought spring to India's soil and constant dampness to its people. Mormon missionaries noted their inability to keep their clothes dry. They also noted poor attendance at their meetings during these months when most people preferred to remain at home. This excessive heat and dampness played havoc with the missionaries' health.[75]

Replies to Attacks

In the midst of writing answers to newspaper attacks, Richard Ballantyne learned of a new pamphlet that was being circulated against the Church. His investigation of its contents and author led him to write a first reply, and when another tract followed the first attack, he responded with his second reply.

A pamphlet by Reverend J. Richards made its appearance in Madras about 1 September 1853. By 7 September, Ballantyne had located a copy and was studying and preparing a reply to it. He continued writing through 18 September, took the manuscript to the printer the next day, and by 27 September his *Reply* was ready for distribution.[76] The work itself was defensive and clearly reflected his earlier involvement in writing a part of N. V. Jones's work referred to above. It was primarily a collection of documents countering Richards's attacks. He therefore drew on earlier works printed both in India and America.[77] His borrowing was even more evident in his *Second Reply,* which appeared just over a month after the first.[78]

The writing of pamphlets directed at a special attack or individual usually meant that the missionaries were well enough established to have immediate interest in the attack and that the attack itself was threatening enough to warrant a more lengthy and systematic rebuttal. This was certainly the situation in Madras; a close reading of Ballantyne's journal confirms this.[79]

Hugh Findlay, while laboring in Bombay, had pursued the same course just a year before, suggesting that Ballantyne's experience was not unique. From April to June 1852 Findlay tried systematically to answer the attacks in the local newspaper, but in time found his essays getting longer and less acceptable to the editors. By August 1852 the opposition clergy were busy circulating a tract by J. G. Deck, a tract which threatened Findlay's work in Bombay. From 30 August 1852, when he commenced writing a reply, to February or March 1853, Findlay records his progress in writing and his concerns over the effect Deck's tract was having.[80]

By the 1850s the Mormons had engaged in several pamphlet "wars." Almost all important Church leaders had been involved, and examination of the pamphlets helps not only to reveal the core of the Mormon defensive position, but to put these replies in historical context.[81]

Throughout this period, Richard Ballantyne (like his co-workers), journalizes his feelings about the news from home. His wife sent him regularly the *Deseret News,* and he also received the *LDS Millennial Star* and *The Seer.* In November 1853, he records: "To look into one of these valuable papers is truly like using a telescope to magnify objects at a distance and even causing us to see much which we could not without such aid perceive. . . . The editorials are truly precious." In a letter to his wife the same month, he writes: "You cannot tell how highly we appreciate the *Deseret News.* They are as it were life to our souls. When we read them it is like placing us in your midst for a short season, and being refreshed with the Spirit and teachings of Zion." His sentiment had not changed three months later.[82]

In spite of his well-meaning publishing ventures and the fact that several individuals never really could afford to carry this part of the missionary effort on, Ballantyne became caught in a vicious circle that many others like him could not avoid. Publishing was a quick way to spread his message and advertise his presence in a given city. But once his message was received and his presence noted, he was immediately attacked. This led him first to newspaper replies and finally to separately published tracts. His letters to newspapers seldom cost him anything,[83] but when he was forced to print his own replies he found his financial status severely taxed. It was here that he found his traveling "without purse or scrip" a disadvantage. It was at this point that he screamed the loudest about those "clergy who work for hire," those "priests" who, for money, lead the people to hell.[84]

Financially he was always on the poverty level while in India. Forced to depend on the goodwill and charity of others because of his insistence on not preaching for hire, he became caught in another trap, almost beyond his control. His eagerness to preach and defend the gospel at almost all costs forced him to rely very heavily on the gifts of others, usually the very people he was anxious to convert. In several cases his insistent badgering and begging seems to have driven potential converts away. Captain Thomas Scott, as noted before, was most gracious in giving them passage to Madras, taking an interest in their cause, and then in offering to pay for the printing of several of their tracts. Although the evidence is not entirely clear, it seems probable that Captain Scott's growing coolness to the cause grew almost in proportion to Ballantyne's pleas for more financial support.[85]

Ballantyne wanted to start a newspaper as early as September, and in October 1853 tried to get Captain Scott to help pay for that venture. It was not until March 1854 that the project was planned well enough that it could be carried out. It was to be a monthly paper, but it too was on very shaky financial grounds. Ballantyne named it the *LDS Millennial Star and Monthly Visitor,* and even though he was in the middle of getting his tract on polygamy printed, he began preparing material for the first issue on 7 March. In spite of various setbacks his almost indefatigable drive pushed him to have a manuscript to the Oriental Press by 30 March. By 6 April he was distributing the three hundred copies of the first issue at a conference. He optimistically told his conference (composed of seven members) the first issue was "an omen of good to the cause" and encouraged them to support "our monthly press." The involvement of a conference in matters of publishing was not unusual in the early Church, but by this time and with only seven members Ballantyne should have sensed the futility of this effort.

He continued to publicly express optimism even though privately his pessimism grew. On 21 April, he received permission from N. V. Jones in Calcutta to take leave of India "to another country" if he so desired, but he decided to stay until 15 July and managed to publish three more issues of this newspaper. The *LDS Millennial Star and Monthly Visitor* was a scissors-and-paste job, consisting mainly of articles and revelations from other Mormon publications.[86]

Last Months in India

Ballantyne's last months in Madras were spent, in addition to working on the previously mentioned periodical, in preparing a "proclamation to the people of India,"[87] dealing with a troublesome missionary companion Robert Owens,[88] dealing with a form of "spiritualism" among potential converts,[89] and advertising and delivering a series of lectures on the Church.[90] Throughout this time Ballantyne was also very ill.[91]

On 26 June 1854, Ballantyne and Skelton received another letter from N. V. Jones "in which he gave us both permission to go home."[92] For the next month, Ballantyne prepared to leave.

Even as he made preparations to depart, he undertook two other projects related to his publishing activities. The first was to prepare for President Jones an "account of the books he sent me for sale."[93] In addition to this he was now faced with the need to obtain enough money for the passage home. On 10 July he recorded his intention of getting all the tracts he had previously published bound into one volume.[94]

He apparently was not able to sell enough copies of this bound work to obtain passage, for he finally obtained passage on the brigg *Royal Thistle* for London by convincing the captain that he was traveling without "purse or scrip." The captain took a little convincing but finally consented to take him if he would carry his own provisions and because he was sick and "a stranger in a foreign land."[95]

Even though the bound volume did not sell, Ballantyne's decision to assemble such a work was probably based on his own experiences as well as those of others. N. V. Jones had written from Calcutta to Liverpool that "bound books sell very well, but tracts we cannot get anything for."[96] Again, the already established religious groups, with ample financial backing, had gratuitously distributed thousands of tracts to anyone who wished to have a copy. This made it difficult, if not impossible, for Mormon missionaries to sell their pamphlets, especially in a country where the majority of the population existed only on a poverty level.

When Ballantyne reached London in December 1854, he wrote President Richards this summary of his mission to India:[97]

> When I left Madras we had baptized 12 persons; ordained one Elder; preached the Gospel in almost every nook and corner of that large city and several of the adjacent villages and cantonments; established a monthly paper of 8 pages; printed 1000 numbers of "Only Way to be Saved;" 1000 of the "Proclamation of the Gospel," 400 of a "First," and the same number of a "Second Reply" to the Rev. T. [*sic*] Richards, of the English Church; 400 numbers of a "Dialogue on Polygamy;" several letters in the newspapers; and a regular issue, monthly, of 300 copies of the little periodical already alluded to.

This was surely a worthy effort for his twelve months in Madras, but, wrote Ballantyne, "we saw little fruit as the result of our toils."[98]

In conclusion, Ballantyne's concern with publishing was at least threefold. In the first place, he was motivated to provide an antidote for what he considered was the poison of anti-Mormon literature being spread about the Church wherever he went. Secondly, he was concerned about "nourish[ing] the people with the written word."[99] Finally, he was (in part) financially tied to these ventures both because of the debts incurred and because of the possible profit which could help sustain the missionary cause in Madras by providing some money to the missionaries themselves. All of this is not to say that he considered publishing the only way to do missionary work. In fact, he specifically noted very early in his mission that nothing could replace door-to-door, person-to-person visits.[100] But it should now be obvious that Ballantyne and his companions in India considered the pen as important in their work as any other tool or aid they had available.

Richard Ballantyne was one of about eighty individuals who published defenses of Mormonism between 1836 and 1857. Our examination of his work as a missionary, particularly as a publishing missionary, has opened up an aspect of the early Church that has yet to be studied in great detail. As an index to its doctrinal position, its value structure, and the stresses and strains of its growth, such an analysis of these writings allows us to glimpse, from a new angle, the Church and kingdom that Ballantyne loyally defended.

Notes

1. The major sources used in the preparation of this paper are found in the Library-Archives, Historical Department, The Church of Jesus Christ of Latter-day Saints, Salt Lake City, Utah. All references herein cited by collection or source with "LDS Church Archives" following are found in this archival repository. The fuller story of the International Missions of the Church in the 1850s is told in David J. Whittaker, "Early Mormon Pamphleteering" (Ph.D. diss., Brigham Young University, 1982), pp. 236–320.

2. The primary sources on Ballantyne are the eight volumes of journals he kept from 1852 to 1858 (volumes 1–7) and 1893–1894 (volume 8), all of which are in LDS Church Archives. In addition to these, the LDS Church Archives has several folders of letters and personal papers, which contain such items as his notes of the various things he read, outlines of sermons, patriarchal blessings, and various study notes. A good many of his letters (many of which no longer exist in manuscript form) are to be found in early Latter-day Saint periodicals. His missionary companions in India also left many written items of worth, relating to both Ballantyne and the India Mission. Copies of Ballantyne's publishing ventures in India are also in LDS Church Archives and will be noted in specific footnote citations.

Secondary sources relating to Richard Ballantyne are Conway B. Sonne, *Knight of the Kingdom, the Story of Richard Ballantyne* (Salt Lake City: Stevens and Wallace, 1949); Vadis B. (Sue) Ballantyne, " 'I, Richard,' a

Biography of Richard Ballantyne" (unpublished Closure Project, Bachelor of Independent Studies, Brigham Young University, 111 pages, 1 July 1974); Edward H. Anderson, "Richard Ballantyne," *Utah Genealogical and Historical Magazine* 2 (1911): 170–77 (a good photo of him appears opposite page 170); and "Richard Ballantyne," in Andrew Jenson, *Latter-day Saint Biographical Encyclopedia,* 4 vols. (Salt Lake City: Jenson History Company, 1901–1936): 1:703–6.

3. This is the full name of the Church restored on 6 April 1830 by Joseph Smith, Jr., and several associates. In the process the Book of Mormon was produced with divine help; it is from this book that the name Mormon(s) comes. Throughout this paper the terms *Church* and *Mormon* will refer to this organization and its members.

4. For a concise summary of his Nauvoo days, see Richard Ballantyne, "With the Remnants at Nauvoo," in the *Improvement Era* 4 (Feb. 1901): 273–79. See also Journal History, LDS Church Archives under dates of 5, 12, 26 July and 17 August 1846.

5. For specific details of his life during this time, see Journal History, 20 January, 22 May, 1 June, 24 September, 31 December 1848; 24 July 1849; 23 September 1851; and 18 May, 28 August, 13 October 1852.

6. For a discussion of the "Reformation," see Gustive L. Larson, "The Mormon Reformation," *Utah Historical Quarterly* 26 (Jan. 1958): 45–63, and more recently Paul H. Peterson, "The Mormon Reformation" (Ph.D. diss., Brigham Young University, 1981). As Peterson shows, the number of plural marriages increased notably during the Reformation. Ballantyne likely became involved in the teaching of this doctrine, and his practice soon followed suit. Ballantyne's journal during this period is an excellent contemporary source of this episode in Mormon history.

7. Sources on the India missions are the "Manuscript History of the East Indian Mission," manuscript in LDS Church Archives; Letter of Benjamin Richey to George A. Smith, dated Nephi, Utah, 2 December 1865, in "Correspondence," George A. Smith Collection, LDS Church Archives; Ralph Lanier Britsch, "A History of the Missionary Activities of The Church of Jesus Christ of Latter-day Saints in India, 1849–1856" (Master's thesis, Brigham Young University, 1964), hereafter cited as "Missionary Activities in India"; R. L. Britsch, "Early Latter-day Saints Missions to South and East Asia" (Ph.D. diss., Claremont Graduate School, 1976).

8. These seventeen missionaries were William F. Carter, Richard Ballantyne, Benjamin Franklin Dewey, Allan Findlay, Hugh Findlay, William Fotheringham, Nathaniel Vary Jones, Truman Leonard, Elam Luddington, Amos Milton Musser, Robert Owens, Joseph Richards, Levi Savage, Robert Skelton, Chauncey Walker West, William Willes, and Samuel Amos Woolley. Brief biographical sketches of each appear in Britsch, "Missionary Activities in India," pp. 163–66. George Q. Cannon does suggest that as early as 1838–1839 George A. Smith set apart William Donaldson as a missionary to India, and in August 1840 a Church newspaper notes Donaldson as a "member of the army [British] bound for the East Indies." It

is at present unknown just what became of this mission. (See George Q. Cannon, *The Life of Joseph Smith* [Salt Lake City: G. Q. Cannon & Sons, 1888], p. 308; and excerpts of Donaldson's letters dated 3 July and 24 July (1840) in *Times and Seasons* 2 [15 Nov. 1840]: 229; *Millennial Star* 46 [18 Aug. 1904]: 514. See also, George A. Smith, *Rise, Progress and Travels . . .* [1869], pp. 34–35.)

The immediate impetus for the India Mission in the 1850s were letters from two people in India to Church authorities in England requesting more information on the Church. (See Benjamin Richey letter cited above; letter of Thomas Metcalfe to "Dear Christian friend of the Church of Latter-day Saints" dated East Indies, Lahore, 19 April 1849, in *Millennial Star* 11 [15 Aug. 1849]: 252, and William A. Sheppard to Orson Spencer, dated Calcutta, 6 February 1850, in *Millennial Star* 12 [15 May 1850]: 155–57. See also, Britsch, "Missionary Activities in India," pp. 9–11.) Interestingly, both Metcalfe and Sheppard had been impressed with Church tracts and had requested more. This certainly shaped Lorenzo Snow's approach to India and his choice of the missionaries who went there. According to Joseph Richards, Metcalfe died of fever and ague at Peshaivr in November 1850 as "a firm believer." (See Joseph Richards to S. W. Richards, dated Calcutta, 4 August 1852, in *Millennial Star* 14 [16 Oct. 1852]: 542.)

9. Useful studies of the early missionary thrust are S. George Ellsworth, "A History of Mormon Missions in the United States and Canada, 1830–1860" (Ph.D. diss., University of California, Berkeley, 1951); Barbara Joan M. Higdon, "The Role of Preaching in the Early Latter-day Saint Church, 1830–1846" (Ph.D. diss., University of Missouri, 1961); Brad Morris, "The Internationalization of The Church of Jesus Christ of Latter-day Saints" (Manuscript, September 1972, copy in LDS Church Archives); and those sources mentioned in James B. Allen and Glen M. Leonard, *The Story of the Latter-day Saints* (Salt Lake City: Deseret Book Company, 1976), pp. 643–44. The most successful foreign missions in the nineteenth century were England and Scandinavia. The standard studies are P.A.M. Taylor, *Expectations Westward* (Ithaca: Cornell University Press, 1966); and William Mulder, *Homeward to Zion* (Minneapolis: University of Minnesota Press, 1957).

10. A summary of these missions is in Morris, "Internationalization of the Church," pp. 13–21. The "calls" of the special conference of 28–29 August 1852 are in *Millennial Star* 14 (13 Nov. 1852): 600. The actual conference minutes were published in *Millennial Star* 15 (supplement, 1853), 64 pages. See also B. H. Roberts, *A Comprehensive History of The Church of Jesus Christ of Latter-day Saints,* 6 vol. (Salt Lake City: Deseret News Press, 1930) 4:68–76.

11. Recent studies have suggested that two major themes of early Mormonism were especially attractive to converts: the strong authoritarian basis of the movement and the primitive gospel approach of its message. The first is dealt with in two published studies by Mario S. DePillis, "The Quest for Religious Authority and the Rise of Mormonism," *Dialogue: A Journal of Mormon Thought* 1 (Spring 1966): 68–88, and "The Social

Sources of Mormonism," *Church History* 37 (March 1968): 50–69. The second, although modifying the first, is defended by Marvin S. Hill, "The Role of Christian Primitivism in the Origin and Development of the Mormon Kingdom, 1830–1844" (Ph.D. diss., University of Chicago, 1968), and "The Shaping of the Mormon Mind in New England and New York," *Brigham Young University Studies* 9 (Spring 1969): 351–72. Both DePillis and Hill lacked the detailed demographic studies yet to be done before any "final" answers can be given, though both have made valuable contributions to the subject.

12. For an overview of the literature and messages of the early missionaries, see Ellsworth, "History of Mormon Missions," pp. 35–50, and Higdon, "Role of Preaching." Also useful for the early years are James B. Allen, "The Significance of Joseph Smith's First Vision in Mormon Thought," *Dialogue* 1 (Autumn 1966): 28–45 and Gordon Irving, "The Mormons and the Bible in the 1830s," *BYU Studies* 13 (Summer 1973): 473–88. The themes of their writings will become obvious as we proceed.

13. The best sources on Lorenzo Snow are in the LDS Church Archives. These include letter books, miscellaneous personal and official papers, and parts of his diary, although the location of many of his diaries is unknown. Other useful sources include Eliza Roxey Snow, *Biography and Family Record of Lorenzo Snow* (Salt Lake City: Deseret News Co., 1884); Andrew Jenson, *LDS Biographical Encyclopedia,* 4 vols. 1:26–31; Thomas Cottam Romney, *The Life of Lorenzo Snow* (Salt Lake City: Sugarhouse Press, 1955); "Lorenzo Snow," *Utah Genealogical and Historical Magazine* 2 (1911): 145–57; and Edward W. Tullidge, ed., "The Apostle, Lorenzo Snow," *Tullidge's Quarterly Magazine* 2 (Jan. 1883): 377–98.

14. His call is discussed in Eliza R. Snow, *Lorenzo Snow,* pp. 109–10.

15. Snow's Italian Mission is covered in the sources listed in note 13. Also important is Lorenzo Snow, *The Italian Mission . . .* (London: W. Aubrey, 1851). This twenty-eight-page pamphlet contains many letters relating to this mission, several of which deal with the topic at hand. Also important for dealing with his connection with the India Mission are five of his letters published in volume 14 of the *Millennial Star* (1852) as cited in notes 16–19.

16. William Willes was sent to Calcutta. His missionary certificate was signed by Lorenzo Snow and was dated London, 29 August 1851. (A copy appears in Britsch, "Missionary Activities in India," p. 13. See also letter to F. D. Richards, dated Paris, 26 January 1852, in *Millennal Star* 14 [1 Mar. 1852]: 76–78. Snow clearly states in this letter that he is concerned about establishing the gospel in "that country." He had voiced the same concern earlier. See Lorenzo Snow to F. D. Richards, n.d., in *Millennial Star* 13 [15 Aug. 1851]: 252–53.) Before leaving London, Lorenzo Snow also appointed Hugh Findlay to the Bombay Mission. The "invitation" was dated 1 September 1851, and on 10 September, Findlay responded in the affirmative. (Originals of this correspondence, together with Findlay's missionary journals, are in LDS Church Archives. They have been conveniently

published in Ross and Linnie Findlay, comp. *Missionary Journals of Hugh Findlay, India-Scotland* [Ephraim, Utah: n.p., 1973]. Ross Findlay kindly provided me with a copy.)

17. On the work in Italy, see Lorenzo Snow to F. D. Richards, dated Italy, 18 February 1852, in *Millennial Star* 14 (1 Apr. 1852): 107–8. In this essay I have not touched on his work on getting the Book of Mormon translated into Italian.

18. Lorenzo Snow to F. D. Richards, dated Malta, 10 March 1852, in *Millennial Star* 14 (24 Apr. 1952): 141–42.

19. L. Snow to S. W. Richards, dated Malta, 1 May 1852 in *Millennial Star* 14 (5 June 1852): 236–37.

20. *The Only Way to Be Saved* had first appeared in London in 1841. (It was still in use in England in the 1850s, as one Peter Drummand attempted to refute it in *The Mormon's "Only Way to be Saved not the Way to be Saved;" or the plausible logic of Mormonism refuted* . . . [n.p., 1854]. This reply was dated Stirling [Scotland] January 1854.) It was published in French and Italian by Lorenzo Snow and again in English from the Italian edition at Malta in 1852. It was probably this English printing that was used as the basis for the three printings in India: in Calcutta in September/ October 1852 (in Bengalee); in Madras in September 1853; and in Delhi in ca. October 1853. At least one other printing was planned in India in 1855–56, but there is no evidence that it was published.

  The Voice of Joseph was first printed in French in 1850. The next year it appeared in Italian, and in 1852 Lorenzo Snow published a revised edition (from the Italian) at Malta in English. The contents and use of both printings are mentioned in *The Italian Mission,* pp. 13, 25. (See also Lorenzo Snow letter to Orson Pratt, dated the Piedmont, 4 November 1850, in *Millennial Star* 12 [15 Dec. 1850]: 370.) Another English printing was in November 1852. (See the notice in *Millennial Star* 14 [27 Nov. 1852]: 635. The whole tract is quoted in Eliza R. Snow, *Lorenzo Snow,* pp. 136–68.)

21. See Lorenzo Snow, "Address to the Saints in Great Britain," in *Millennial Star* 13 (1 Dec. 1851): 362–65, esp. 365. See also Lorenzo Snow to F. D. Richards, as cited in Eliza R. Snow, *Lorenzo Snow* pp. 184–86.

22. Lorenzo Snow to F. D. Richards, n.d., in *Millennial Star* 13 (15 Aug. 1851): 252–53. Also in Eliza R. Snow, *Lorenzo Snow* pp. 191–200. The reference to India is on page 199.

23. In his letter dated 1 May 1852, at Malta, he apologized for disappointing the "brethren in India" (*Millennial Star* 14 [5 June 1852]: 236–37). Editorial comments in the *Star* later explain the exact reason for this change in plans (*Millennial Star* 14 [3 July 1852]: 296–97). This decision to return to England then to America was probably influenced by the First Presidency's request of 22 September 1851 that all members of the Quorum of the Twelve Apostles return to Salt Lake Valley for the April 1853 general conference. (See *Millennial Star* 14 [15 Jan. 1852]: 25.)

24. L. Snow to S. W. Richards, dated Malta, 1 May 1852, in *Millennial Star* 14 (5 June 1852): 236–37. Lorenzo Snow stated "the Indian Mission

[will be left] with Elders Findlay, Willis and Joseph Richards." The shift back to Liverpool assured that this city would be looked to as the depot for Church publications. I have dealt with this in "Early Mormon Pamphleteering," *Journal of Mormon History* 4 (1977): 35–49, esp. p. 45.

25. As noted previously Snow's concern for missionary work in India found expression in a variety of ways. It it quite possible that his public requests throughout 1852 for more missionaries helped result in the special conference of 28 and 29 August. (See particularly his letter of 1 May 1852, in *Millennial Star* 14 [5 June 1852]: 236–37, and the editorial comments by S. W. Richards in the next issue, ibid. 14 [12 June 1852]: 250.)

26. B. H. Roberts, *Comprehensive History*, 4:72–73.

27. A condensed treatment of their preparation and travel to India is in Britsch, "Missionary Activities in India," pp. 28–40. Since the major focus of this paper is on Richard Ballantyne, specific reference should be made of his accounts of this phase of his mission: Volumes one and two of his journals contain the day-to-day record, MSS in LDS Church Archives. There are also five letters to his wife written at various points along the way: (1) undated letter, Provo City; (2) 3 November 1852, Parowan, Iron County; (3) 13 December 1852, Hugo Ranch, near San Bernardino; (4) 20 January 1852, San Francisco; (5) 8 February 1852, San Francisco. MSS of all these letters in LDS Church Archives.

28. Much of this is summarized from Britsch, "Missionary Activities in India," p. 108. He does not have much material on Christianity in India after 1800, which is, of course, critical to understanding the setting of Mormonism's assault on this country, especially as the Mormon elders would spend most of their time in replying to attacks made by these groups. Useful studies filling this void are contained in Ramsay Muir, ed., *The Making of British India, 1756–1858* (Manchester: University Press, 1915), which reproduces many documents, including British Military dispatches relating to religious matters in the cantonments. These are particularly important because Latter-day Saints made many attempts to get access to the military posts to preach but such access was generally not allowed. Also useful in this regard is Sir Alfred Lyall, *The Rise and Expansion of the British Dominion in India* [to 1858] 3d ed. (London: John Murray, 1960). See also Kenneth Scott Latourett, *A History of Christianity* (New York: Harper and Bros., 1953), pp. 694, 930–32, 1033–35, 1314–18; Fred D. Schneider, "Parliament, the East India Company, and the Calcutta Bishopric," *Journal of Church and State* 16 (Winter 1974): 51–71; G. A. Oddie, "India and Missionary Motives, c. 1850–1900," *Journal of Ecclesiastical History* 25 (Jan. 1974): 61–74; and Stuart Piggin, "Sectarianism versus Ecumenism: The Impact on British Churches of the Missionary Movement to India, c. 1800–1860," *Journal of Ecclesiastical History* 27 (Oct. 1976): 387–402.

29. All of these barriers and their relationship to the India Mission will be noted as we proceed. Two useful works which give insight to India in the mid-1800s are Ferdinand DeWilton Ward, *India and the Hindoos: Being a Popular View of the Geography, History, Government, Manners,*

Customs, Literature, and Religion of that Ancient People; With an Account of Christian Missions among Them (London: William Collins, 1853); and Caleb Wright, *India and Its Inhabitants* (Cincinnati: J. A. Brainerd, 1854). This last work has many engravings of all aspects of Indian culture. An early convert who lived in India, Matthew McCune, wrote a series, "Chapters on Asia," *Millennial Star* 25 (24 Jan. to 6 June 1863).

30. Britsch, "Missionary Activities in India," p. 41.

31. The conference was held on 29 April 1853. Amos M. Musser's account is quoted in Britsch, "Missionary Activities in India," p. 40. See also "Manuscript History of the East Indian Mission," under same date, MS in LDS Church Archives; and Ballantyne's Journal, vol. 2, under date of 29 April 1853. The assignments at this conference were N. V. Jones and Amos M. Musser to Calcutta; Richard Ballantyne, Robert Skelton, and Robert Owens to Madras; Wm. F. Carter and William Fotheringham to Dinapore; and T. Leonard and S. A. Woolley to Chinsurah. N. V. Jones was appointed president of the Calcutta Branch and this position eventually came to mean president of the mission. He was set apart by Richard Ballantyne, who had acted as president of the group as they crossed the Pacific. Because the focus of this essay will be on Ballantyne and the Madras area, little will be said hereafter about the other missionaries. I will, however, refer to them as related to their publishing activities. The published letter sources on them, listed by individuals, will be found in Whittaker, "Early Mormon Pamphleteering," pp. 435–45. The missionaries assigned to Burma and Ceylon (which was considered part of the India Mission) were C. West, B. F. Dewey, Edam Luddington, and Levi Savage. A map of the areas of assignments is found in Britsch, "Missionary Activities in India," p. i. N. V. Jones's account of the conference is in *Deseret News,* 26 December 1855, p. 334.

32. According to N. V. Jones it was published without the author indicated, but upon investigation the authors (or rather compilers) were found to be Charles Saunder and an unnamed associate. It was printed in Calcutta and according to Jones was a "vile production" consisting of "a mere collection of newspaper trash, Bennett's lies, etc.," (N. V. Jones to S. W. Richards, dated Calcutta, 14 June 1853, in *Millennial Star* 15 [20 Aug. 1853]: 558–59; also in *Deseret News* [12 November 1853], p. 2.) No copy of this work could be located, but Jones, et al. *A Reply to "Mormonism Unveiled"* (Calcutta: Sanders, Cones and Co., 1853) is available and it offers many clues as to the content of Saunder's work. Its title was after the 1834 work of E. D. Howe, *Mormonism Unvailed* [sic]. Howe's work was also a potpourri of documents attacking Mormonism and Joseph Smith from various angles. The Bennett referred to is John C. Bennett, author of another attack entitled *History of the Saints* (1842). Bennett's book was especially used in anti-Mormon literature to expose polygamy and what he considered the secularism of Joseph Smith in Nauvoo. The Howe book is dealt with in Richard L. Anderson, "Joseph Smith's New York Reputation Reappraised," *BYU Studies* 10 (Spring 1970): 283–314. The Bennett book is discussed in Kenneth W. Godfrey, "Causes of Mormon, Non-Mormon

Conflict in Hancock County, Illinois, 1839–1846'' (Ph.D. diss., Brigham Young University, 1967), pp. 113–23. That the pamphlet was compiled by several people is made clear in another letter of N. V. Jones, dated 5 August 1853 in *Deseret News,* 9 January 1856, p. 350. According to this letter the tract had been in circulation for about a year, and after he had finished a *Reply* he remarked: "The entire production was a tirade of abuse, a scurrilious [sic] tissue of misrepresentation and falsehood as was ever compiled in one precious bundle.'' Saunder is spelled "Sunder" in the *Reply* and both spellings occur in the sources.

33. The chronology of the production of Jones, *A Reply to "Mormonism Unveiled"* can be constructed by examining the "Manuscript History of the East India Mission," MS in LDS Church Archives and several other sources. The "Manuscript History" suggests the following schedule: From 10 to 14 May, Jones and Musser were at Elder Meiks (a convert living in Acra) "investigating" the attack. They returned again to continue writing the *Reply*. By 9 July, they sent one hundred pages of the *Reply* to the printer and on 4 August, they received 250 copies at a cost of 192 1/2 rupees for printing and binding. The cost was borne in large part by their new convert, Arthur McMahon. 192 1/2 rupees was about $96.00. A copy of this rare item is in LDS Church Archives. Musser's role is described in Karl Brooks, "Amos Milton Musser" (master's thesis, Brigham Young University, 1968), p. 39.

34. Ballantyne's Journal, vol. 2, entries from 18 to 31 May detail his involvement in this project. He never mentions just which pages he wrote, but under the date of 20 May 1853, he wrote that he was assisting Brother Jones in answering "Mormonism Unveiled" and that "the part I have been answering related to the Gold Plates and the testimony of the witnesses." This would suggest that he was responsible for pp. 33 to 44 in the *Reply*. His work was finished by 28 May. He received a copy of it in Madras on 31 August. See also his letters to Dr. Samuel Sprague, dated Calcutta, 13 May 1853, in *Deseret News,* 5 January 1854, p. 2; and to his wife, dated Calcutta, 31 May 1853, MS in LDS Church Archives. See also William Fotheringham, "Travels in India," *Juvenile Instructor* 12 (15 June 1877): 136 and ibid. 13 (15 Sept. 1878): 206. The *Reply* is referred to once again in Ballantyne's Journal when he was attempting to convert Thomas Scott, the captain of the ship that transported him and Skelton to Madras. It seems Captain Scott had some reservations about some of the arguments presented in the *Reply* and Ballantyne expressed his opinion that only sound doctrine need be accepted and not everything in this work was necessarily in that category. See his Journal under date of 22 October 1853.

35. Robert Owens, who had been assigned to Madras with them, stayed in and around the Calcutta area until he finally arrived in Madras on 3 January 1854. He was in constant trouble with his fellow workers in India. He was "tried" and his missionary license taken from him on 29 May 1853 for his "abuse to the Council, false teachings, revengeful spirit, etc" (letter of Richard Ballantyne to his wife, dated Calcutta, 31 May 1853, MS in LDS Church Archives). Owens was restored to fellowship on 13 June but was

again in trouble by 26 June 1853. See "Manuscript History of East India Mission." Owens remained in Calcutta area until late December 1853, when he was again assigned to Madras. He remained in this general area until he left to eventually return to the United States via Australia. He was a constant problem to Ballantyne, a situation which grew worse as time passed. It eventually separated the two men and was quite disruptive to the unity of the missionaries in Madras. Owens's behavior reached very serious proportions by April 1854, when his rather lewd conduct seriously undermined Ballantyne's work with several potential converts. Owens's life during this period can be traced in records kept by Ballantyne: see his letter to his wife dated Madras, 8 October 1853, p. 6, MS in LDS Church Archives; and his Journals under these dates: 29, 30 May 1853; 3, 27 January; 14, 23 February; 23, 26 March; 6, 14, 29 April; and 9 July 1854. On 14 April 1854 Ballantyne wrote to N. V. Jones in Calcutta of Owens's activities in Madras. This letter was copied into the first pages of vol. 4 of Ballantyne's Journal, under date of 3 May 1854. For the serious moral charges against him see Ballantyne's Journal, 29 April 1854. Owens arrived in Sydney, Australia, in the fall of 1854 per the letter of William Cook dated 13 October in *Millennial Star* 17 (17 Feb. 1855): 105. He left Australia on brig *Tarquenia* for San Pedro, California, on 27 April 1855 per a letter of Augustus Farnliam, dated Sydney, 31 May 1855 in *Millennial Star* 17 (15 Sept. 1855): 591. He labored in Australia for over five months. He was the first Mormon elder to go to Tasmania. See John Douglas Hawkes, "A History of the Church . . . in Australia to 1900," (Master's thesis, Brigham Young University, 1965), pp. 44ff. Owens appears to have been a loner, and I have not been able to locate his letters or diaries. See also Britsch, "Missionary Activities in India," p. 96, n. 3.

36. The faith-promoting side of this voyage is told in Richard Ballantyne, "A Promise Fulfilled," *Improvement Era* 6 (June 1903): 590–93. The fuller account is in his Journal between dates 20 June and 24 July 1853. Much of the ship's log is quoted in Ballantyne's Journal. Also, Britsch, "Missionary Activities in India," pp. 81–86.

37. Ballantyne, "A Promise Fulfilled," pp. 590–93; and Britsch, "Missionary Activities in India," pp. 81–86.

38. Originally printed in New York in 1837, this book (216+ pages) was probably one of the most influential works outside Mormon scripture in the nineteenth century. A brief bibliographical description is in Peter Crawley, "A Bibliography of The Church of Jesus Christ of Latter-day Saints in New York, Ohio, and Missouri," *BYU Studies* 12 (Summer 1972): 516–18, Item no. 36.

39. The Pearl of Great Price was first published in Liverpool, England in 1851. Compiled by Franklin D. Richards, the British mission president at the time, it was essentially a compilation of extracts of the writings and revelations of Joseph Smith. It was a very popular tract and was canonized as the fourth standard work of the Church in October 1880. A convenient study of its history and contents is James R. Clark, *The Story of the Pearl of Great Price* (Salt Lake City: Bookcraft, Inc., 1955).

40. See note 20.

41. Robert Patch's comment that "Brother Ballantyne's expedition into publications was taken as a result of unsuccessful missionary work in the vicinity [of Madras]" is not correct. Ballantyne's Journal makes it quite plain that publishing was a major part of his conception of proper missionary work, *not* a substitute when it failed. Patch's work contains many inaccuracies, especially when dealing with LDS publications in India. See his "An Historical Overview of the Missionary Activities of The Church of Jesus Christ of Latter-day Saints in Continental Asia," (Master's thesis, Brigham Young University, 1949). His comments on Ballantyne are on p. 55.

42. This information is summarized from Ballantyne's Journal, dates of 23–25 July 1853.

43. Ballantyne's Journal, dates of 24 July to 30 July 1853 when the thousand copies were ready, contains the details of his work with the printer. He noted on 27 July, the day he examined the proof-sheets: "In case it might appear before the Public as a sort of anonymous publication having no one to sustain the doctrines contained in it, in this place, I have added to the title page the following words, 'Republished by R. Ballantyne, presiding Elder of the Mission to Madras.' This is all I have added to Bro. L. Snows production." Ballantyne's missionary companion also tells of this printing: letter of Robert Skelton to Thomas Bullock, dated 5 September 1853 in *Deseret News,* 2 February 1854, p. 2.

44. Actually Ballantyne had contemplated publishing a part of the Proclamation the day before Captain Scott had offered to pay for its printing. He had, according to his journal of 29 July 1853, already begun selecting material to be included in it. Ballantyne felt that Captain Scott's offer was literally an answer to prayer.

45. As at Madras, the Australian mission began with publishing activities. More will be said of this, but the best overview of the early printing in Australia is Peter Crawley, "The First Australian Mormon Imprints," *Graduates Review* 2 (Fall 1973): 38–51. (The *Graduates Review* is a publication of the BYU Graduate Student Association of Library and Information Sciences.)

46. Ballantyne brought at least one other Australian work with him from Calcutta to Madras. He records reading Wandell's, *Reply to "Shall We Believe in Mormon?"* on 27 July 1853, just two days before he mentions the Proclamation. The influence of other Australian publications will be noted later.

47. The contents of it were described in Ballantyne's letter to S. W. Richards, dated 3–16 August 1853, in *Millennial Star* 15 (22 Oct. 1853): 700–702. The manuscript was given to the printer on 30 July; the proofs were examined on 2 August; and one thousand copies were received on 5 August. The original *Proclamation* had six sections (or "chapters") and these were faithfully reprinted by Wandell, probably in November 1851. Ballantyne extracted sections 1, 2, 3, 6 (which he published as 1, 2, 3, 4) and

then added a three-page section entitled "Rise and Progress of the Church," which consisted of extracts from the *Times and Seasons* 3 (1 Mar. 1842): 706–8. See also Ballantyne's Journal 30 July 1853. According to his journal, Captain Scott paid twenty rupees for the printing. According to William Fotheringham, a rupee was the value of two English shillings or forty-eight cents. See *Juvenile Instructor* 17 (15 May 1882): 157.

48. With the possibility of losing their best supporter, Ballantyne wrote both to the newspapers and to Captain Scott. His letter to Scott appears in his Journal, under date of 2 August 1853. See also his letter to his wife, dated 9 August 1853 (MS in LDS Church Archives) where he says his publishing was trying to correct the poor treatment they were receiving at the hands of "priests and editors."

49. Extracts of the attack were copied into Ballantyne's Journal of 22 August 1853, and appear in slightly modified form in Britsch, "Missionary Activities in India," pp. 89–90. His response was published in the "Madras Circulation" on 7 September 1853. It was copied into his Journal of 22 August and recopied for the publishers on 24 August.

50. This whole "pipeline" of Church literature needs further study, but it should be noted that these India missionaries ordered "outside" Church literature for a variety of reasons, but primarily to maintain contact with the outside world and to continue to receive instruction themselves. This is especially so in regards to polygamy, a doctrine officially announced at the same conference from which they received their mission calls. Ballantyne's thinking and writing on this subject was influenced by the literature he continued to receive while on his mission.

51. Ballantyne Journal, 9 August 1853. He specifically notes on 12 August that they had distributed over three hundred tracts, but had collected money for only eleven of them and really did not know if those that had been distributed were having the desired effect. He probably felt that the use of tracts left an impersonal void they would try to make up through personal contact.

52. The wording of the handbills, for which they obtained free printing, is in Ballantyne's Journal, 22 August 1853. The lectures were scheduled for Friday nights, and the first was held on 2 September 1853. Fifteen people came.

53. Letter of R. Ballantyne to his wife, dated Madras, 6 September 1853. MS in LDS Church Archives.

54. These experiences are detailed in Ballantyne's Journal, 28 and 29 August 1853.

55. The entire piece, begun on 30 August, was really a long editorial or "an article for the Public, to remove if possible some reproach from this cause. . . ." The whole essay was copied into his Journal under date of 30 August 1853 and occupies pp. 39–67 of Vol. 3. From the date at the end of the essay it seems he finished it on 31 August. Pages 40 and 41 are blank, Ballantyne having skipped over them. At the top of page 60 is a penned

note: "This far the foregoing was published in the Madras 'Circulation' on Monday the 12 September 1853 without comment—May the Lord bless the Editor." This meant that about three-fifths of the article was published, but interestingly enough it was the *un*published part that dealt with polygamy. Six months later he would print a tract on the subject but his arguments would change but little. What he did publish took almost two weeks to get printed. This episode can be followed in his Journal, 31 August to 12 September 1853. Robert Skelton was listed as the coauthor when it was published although it was clearly the work of Ballantyne. For Skelton's positive judgment of the essay, see his letter to Thomas Bullock dated 5 September 1853, in *Deseret News,* 2 February 1854, p. 2.

56. R. Ballantyne's Journal, 7 May 1853. In his first two letters to his wife from India he told her of the problems the missionaries were encountering over this doctrine. On 2 May he told her of his giving a talk on the subject, and on 4 May he mentioned that attacks were being made against him. This no doubt convinced him that a published defense would be necessary.

57. Letter of Hugh Findlay to N. V. Jones dated Bombay, 24 June 1853. Original is copied into Findlay's Journal, LDS Church Archives. A convenient printing of this is Ross Findlay, pp. 150–51.

58. H. Findlay copied into his Journal several of these attacks: *Bombay Guardian* 16 April 1852; *Bombay Gazette* 21 April 1852; and the *Bombay Telegraph and Courier* 26 April and 6 May 1852. All of these are in Ross Findlay, pp. 7–19. Findlay's reply to the *Bombay Guardian* piece, denying as he did the doctrine and practice, surely placed him in a precarious position after the public announcement in August. His request of 25 June no doubt reveals the growing uncertainty of his public position.

59. The complex problem of the origin of plural marriage, also called "celestial marriage" by Latter-day Saints, is beyond the scope of this essay. Useful places to begin are Andrew Jenson, "Plural Marriage," *The Historical Record* 6 (May 1887): 219–40; Stanley R. Ivins, "Notes on Mormon Polygamy," *Western Humanities Review* 10 (Summer 1956): 220–39; Kimball Young, *Isn't One Wife Enough?* (New York: H. Holt & Co., Inc., 1954); more recently, Daniel W. Backman, "A Study of the Mormon Practice of Plural Marriage Before the Death of Joseph Smith" (Master's thesis, Purdue University, 1975). A useful evaluation of studies on polygamy is Davis Bitton, "Mormon Polygamy: A Review Article," *Journal of Mormon History* 4 (1977): 101–18.

60. The two exceptions were the revelation on the subject given 12 July 1843 to Joseph Smith and first printed in the *Deseret News* Extra, 14 September 1852; and the little-known pamphlet *The Peace Maker,* published in Nauvoo in 1842.

61. The first public statement from Church leaders came on 29 August 1852 when Orson Pratt, at a special missionary conference, delivered a sermon on the doctrine. The text was printed in the *Deseret News* Extra, 14 September 1852 and after in *Millennial Star* 15 (Supplement, 1953): 32–36;

and in *Journal of Discourses,* 26 vols. (Liverpool: F. D. and S. W. Richards, 1854) 1:53–66. Pratt quickly became the major public spokesman for the Church on this doctrine. The arguments he gave in August 1852, although expanded in his monthly periodical *The Seer* (Washington, D.C., 1853–1854), were fivefold: (1) God commanded it; (2) raising up "seed" unto Christ; (3) fulfilling God's promises to Abraham; (4) providing tabernacles (i.e., bodies) for "noble spirits"; and (5) reforming society both morally and spiritually. His expanded series on "Celestial Marriage" still provide the most detailed examination of this doctrine: see *The Seer* 1 (Jan. 1853–Dec. 1853): 7–16, 25–32, 41–48, 58–64, 73–80, 89–96, 105–12, 122–28, 135–44, 152–60, 169–76, 183–92. For a fuller treatment see Whittaker, "Early Mormon Pamphleteering," pp. 321–94.

62. A convenient summary of these periodicals and their publishers is in B. H. Roberts, *Comprehensive History* 4:55–68.

63. Also available was Orson Spencer's, *Patriarchal Order or Plurality of Wives,* . . . (Liverpool, 1853). His death in October 1855 probably lessened the influence of this work.

64. See "Polygamy" series, letters of John Jaques to J.— G.— in *Millennial Star* 15 (12 & 26 Feb. 1853): 97–102, 133–36 and ibid., 15 (5 and 12 Mar. 1853): 145–49, 161–66. In the midst of this series Jaques was assigned to the editorial office of the *Star* and in that capacity authored numerous items in the following issues. These letters were the source of his sixteen-page pamphlet *Polygamy,* probably printed in 1869. See also his poem "Celestial Marriage," *Millennial Star* 18 (12 Apr. 1856): 240.

65. See for example "Nelly and Abby—A familiar conversation between two cousins on Marriage," by "L." in *Millennial Star* 15 (9 and 16 Apr. 1853): 225–29; 241–44; and "Monogamy, Polygamy, and Christianity," ibid. 15 (6 Aug. 1853): 513–17. The first is representative of the dialogue-type propaganda which became very popular in the Church in the 1850s; the second is an example of the proof-texting the defenders of polygamy soon adopted, using as they did non-Mormon sources to prove their position.

66. See Belinda Marden Pratt, *Defence of Polygamy, By a Lady of Utah in a Letter to Her Sister in New Hampshire,* (Salt Lake City: 1854). This nine-page letter is dated 12 January 1854. It was reprinted in the *Millennial Star* 16 (29 July 1854): 475–80 and in *Zion's Watchman* (Australia) 1 (15 Nov. 1854): 171–80. It also appeared in Richard Burton, *The City of The Saints* (London: 1861), pp. 484–93.

67. Although her letter is not extant, Richard Ballantyne's journal entry for 26 September 1853 (the day he received her letter) makes it plain what her concerns were.

68. Letter of Richard Ballantyne to his wife dated Madras, 2–6 February 1854. MS in LDS Church Archives. The "rules" referred to are in *The Seer* 1 (Nov., Dec. 1853): 174–76; 183–87.

69. On 3 December 1853 he recorded: "In the evening, I examined a manuscript, which Mr. Mills gave me, written by a Baptist, being a dialogue between the Minister and Member concerning the impropriety of admitting an unbaptised person or a Polygamist to what they call the Lord's Table."

70. The actual writing of the eight-page tract was done on 8 March 1854. On 13 March a printer's copy was prepared, and although an exact date is not known, it seems obvious it was out by the end of March. Its cost was borne by a Mr. Brown, the man from whom they were then renting an apartment. In addition to the argument from the Old Testament, two lengthy quotes are given in the tract, one in the text of the pamphlet and the other as an "Appendix" to it. The first quote appears on pp. 4–5 and was undoubtedly obtained from either Pratt or the *Millennial Star* or both. This material first appeared under the title "Luther on Polygamy" in *Millennial Star* 15 (6 Aug. 1853): 526–27 and in expanded form as "Christian Polygamy in the Sixteenth Century," in *The Seer* 1 (Dec. 1853): 177–83. The Appendix, "Milton on Polygamy," appeared in longer form under the same title in *Millennial Star* 16 (27 May 1854): 321–24, and ibid. 16 (3 June 1854): 342–45; in the *Deseret News* 4 (10 Aug. 1854): 1–2; in the *St. Louis Luminary* 1 (3 Feb. 1855): 41; and in *Zion's Watchman* 2 (15 Jan. 1855): 209–10, in exactly the same form as printed by Ballantyne. I have not been able to trace just where Ballantyne got this, but after his work appeared it was reprinted in several Church works. Milton's arguments are treated in Leo Miller, *John Milton Among the Polygamaphiles* (New York: Loewenthal Press, 1974). Milton was trying to get out of a bad marriage.

Orson Pratt's influence again shows up in another early defense of plural marriage: see Jesse Haven, *Celestical Marriage, and the Plurality of Wives* . . . (Capetown: W. Foelscher, 1853). Written between May and June 1853, this eight-page tract clearly shows Pratt's influence (see pp. 5–8). Haven was President of the South African Mission and in that capacity wrote this and several other works. An examination of his Journal suggests that it appeared about 17 June 1853. See Haven, "Journal A," MS in LDS Church Archives under dates of 20 and 26 May and 13–15, 18 and 20 June 1853. A copy of Haven's pamphlet on plural marriage was in India by October 1853. N. V. Jones called it "a sound work" in his letter to Hugh Findlay dated Calcutta, 7 October 1853, in Ross Findlay, pp. 164–65. I have found no evidence that Haven's work circulated beyond Calcutta. Although some of the same arguments show up on pp. 88–105 of N. V. Jones, *A Reply to "Mormonism Unveiled"* (Aug. 1853), it is not likely Haven's tract was available in India until September or October 1853.

71. See note 57.

72. Fortunately Findlay copied into his Journal both the attacks and his replies to them. The first attack he recorded came from *Bombay Guardian,* 16 April 1852. Findlay's reply appeared on 27 April. Both are in Ross Findlay, pp. 7–11. On 21 April 1852, *The Bombay Gazette* spoke of the "debaucheries" of Mormonism. Findlay replied on 23 April 1852. See Ross Findlay, pp. 12–14. On 26 April and again on 6 May 1852, the *Bombay*

Telegraph and Courier attacked the doctrine, and Findlay replied to both (no date given in his journal for the first reply; the second was dated 10 May 1852); see Ross Findlay, pp. 14–30. These newspapers continued their attacks and finally refused to print any more of Hugh Findlay's replies. This explains, in part, why he was forced to print separate pamphlets. A quick examination of the anti-Mormon material reveals two things: the influence of John C. Bennett's book (*History of the Saints,* 1842) and the tendency of non-Mormon Christian groups to rely on anti-Mormon material imported from England.

73. Both are touched on by Britsch, "The Latter-day Saint Mission to India, 1851–1856," *BYU Studies* 12 (Spring 1972): 272–78. Britsch adds to the list the social consciousness of Europeans and the caste system.

74. This aspect can be traced in Ballantyne's Journal under the following dates: 28 May 1853; 30 September 1853; 2, 8, 9, 17, and 26 October 1853; 9 December 1853; 28 April 1854 (a conversation with a native on this); 1 May 1854 (three members: Mills, McCarthy and Barnett lost their Tract Society jobs over their conversion to the Church). See also Ballantyne's letters to his wife: 8 October 1853, and 9 December 1853. Ballantyne made his "gripes" about the protestant clergy using this kind of force in his pamphlet *Dialogue Between A and B on Polygamy,* pp. 1–2. For other comments on the same problems see: Letter of Hugh Findlay to William Gibson, dated Bombay, 13 November 1853, in *Deseret News,* 27 April 1852, pp, 2–3; Letter of Samuel A. Woolley, dated 14 November 1853, Delhi, in "Manuscript History of the East Indian Mission," MS in LDS Church Archives under date of 14 November 1853. Robert Skelton, the last Mormon missionary to leave India, left several comments about these problems. See letters of Skelton to F. D. Richards, dated Calcutta, 8 March 1856, in *Millennial Star* 18 (31 May 1856): 348–49, and to George Q. Cannon, dated 16 August 1845 in *The Western Standard* 1 (30 Aug. and 6 Sept. 1856): 3; and letter of N. V. Jones to S. W. Richards, dated Calcutta, 4 October 1853, in *Millennial Star* 15 (10 Dec. 1853): 812–14. Even after returning to the United States, Samuel A. Woolley, in an interview with the *Boston Times,* sarcastically commented that in India "the missionaries who have the most cash always [are] the most successful in making converts." As quoted in *St. Louis Luminary* 1 (3 Mar. 1855): 57; see also letter of N. V. Jones, n.d., *Deseret News* 23 April 1856, p. 56: "The universal means adopted by the missionaries [non-Mormon] to obtain converts has been to hire them." When their missions were over, most would have agreed with Amos Musser: "The greatest work we accomplished was in saving ourselves." Letter of A. M. Musser to Orson Pratt, dated Birmingham, 10 March 1857, in *Millennial Star* 19 (4 Apr. 1857): 220.

75. From November to February the season is cool and dry, and these were the months of the successful missionary work. The health problem of the missionaries is discussed in Britsch, "Missionary Activities in India," pp. 2–3, 49, 96–97, 112, 113, 138, 159. "From the time the Elders arrived in Calcutta until the end of 1853 [and after] there are only a few entries in the Journal [of Amos Musser] which do not record someone as being ill. Often

the sickness of the brethren were so severe that they were completely bedridden for several days. None of the Elders escaped being sick at least part of the time. The common diagnosis was that they were suffering from fever and chills. However, it was not unusual for them to have boils, blotches, and other maladies" (p. 49).

76. The production of the first reply, *A Reply to a Tract Written by the Rev. J. Richards, M.A., Giving a More Correct Answer to the Question "What is Mormonism?"*—*purporting to be answered by him* . . . (Madras: S. Bowie, Printer, 1853), can be followed through several contemporary sources: Ballantyne's Journal dates of 7, 14–16, 17–18, 19, 23, and 27 September; Ballantyne's letters to his wife: 6 September 1853; 8 October 1853; 4 November 1853. Four hundred copies of this eight-page work were printed, and they were bound with an equal number of his first two publishing ventures *The Only Way to Be Saved* and *The Proclamation*. . . . The printer was to be paid via the sale of the pamphlet; see Ballantyne Journal, 18 September 1853.

77. The largest quote in the *Reply* occurs on pp. 2–3 and it comes from the *Times and Seasons* 1 (Jan. 1840): 47. It is the testimony of the widow of Solomon Spaulding (Mrs. Matilda Davidson) regarding the relationship of the writings of her husband to the Book of Mormon. The testimony had been taken by Jesse Haven. Ballantyne's immediate source was an earlier India publication, *What is Mormonism* published by Wm. Willes in Calcutta in October or November 1852. A recent treatment of the Spalding theory is Lester E. Bush, Jr., "The Spalding Theory, Then and Now," *Dialogue* 10 (Autumn 1977): 40–69.

78. The production of the *Second Reply* can be followed in Ballantyne's Journal: 5 October 1853 (he learned of Rev. Richards's second tract); 9, 17 October (one Samuel Pascal told him that John Mills had offered to pay for the printing of the second reply); 13, 14 October (spent compiling it); 17 October (examined and corrected the proof sheets); 28, 29 October (he received 397 copies of the *Second Reply*). In a letter to Mr. Mills (copied into his Journal on 14 October,) Ballantyne described the contents: "The tract will not only be a reply to Mr. Richards, but is designed, especially on the subject just named [the trinity], to be a standard work." The estimated cost, on 15 October, to print it was 17 rupees. Its final cost was just over 26 rupees. All but 11 rupees had been paid by 10 December 1852. Eleven of the eighteen pages of the *Second Reply* (pp. 6–17) contain Lectures three through five of the "Lectures on Faith" from the Doctrine and Covenants.

79. See especially Ballantyne's Journal under dates 7, 13, 14, 27 September; 5, 9, 11, 14, 24, 30 October 1853.

80. See Findlay's Journal, as printed in Ross Findlay, under dates of 30 August; 6, 28 September; 26 October; 1, 4 November 1852 and 5, 6, 7, 9 January; 3, 4, and 13 February 1853. The twenty-page work was finished by end September 1852, but problems with finances and the printer delayed its publication until February or March 1853. Note Findlay's letter of 13

September 1852, in *Millennial Star* 14 (27 Nov. 1852): 635–36. A copy of this rather rare pamphlet is in LDS Church Archives under the title of *"The Mormons or Latter-day Saints." A Reply by Hugh Findlay To a Tract Bearing The Above Title by J. G. Deck and Reprinted at the Bombay "Time Press"* (Bombay: Duftur Ashkana Press, 1853).

81. A complete listing of early Latter-day Saint authors who wrote pamphlet-length replies to specific attacks is beyond the scope of this essay. A partial listing would include the following writers: George J. Adams, William Appleby, Richard Ballantyne, James F. Bell, S. Bennett, James Flanigan, Hugh Findlay, Dan Jones, N. V. Jones, David W. Kilbourne, Reuben Miller, Julian Moses, Orson Pratt, Parley P. Pratt, Erastus Snow, John Taylor, and Benjamin Winchester.

82. His comments on the LDS press appear throughout his journals and letters and could be the subject of a separate essay. The quotes cited above are found, in order of their appearance, in the following: Journal, 3 November 1853; letter to his wife, dated Madras, 4 November 1853, MS in LDS Church Archives; and Journal, 11 February 1854.

83. A possible exception would be the reference contained in his journal under the date of 8 September 1853: "Today Subscribed for the 'circulator' a paper published three times a week. I wish to encourage it as the Editor is friendly and publishes my letters, to which I have attached great importance." See also his comments in his letter to S. W. Richards, dated Madras, 4 October 1853, in *Millennial Star* 15 (9 Dec. 1853): 796.

84. Undoubtedly these kinds of judgments were unfair generalizations, but their existence in Ballantyne's (and others') journals does suggest a kind of scapegoat or escape mechanism that enabled these missionaries to rationally deal with situations that were often beyond their ability to control or understand. By the end of Ballantyne's Madras mission there is an almost paranoia about his failure there. For Ballantyne's comments on the failure of the India mission see his Journal under dates of 23 November 1853; 22 February; 16 March; 12, 24 April; 28 May, and 26 June 1854; see also his letters to his wife, dated Madras 9 and 18 December 1853, MS in LDS Church Archives; to S. W. Richards, dated Madras, 6 February 1854, in *Deseret News,* 19 October 1854, pp. 2–3.

85. This can be traced through Ballantyne's Journal beginning in June 1853. The fact that his first two publishing efforts totaled one thousand copies each, but the next three were only four hundred copies each may suggest this lack of financial support. His concerns over money to publish reached his dreams on 25 September 1853.

86. Ballantyne's Journal gives most of the information on the dates this periodical appeared. The first issue appeared by 6 April 1854; the second issue was out by 28 April 1854; the third and fourth issues seem to have appeared around the first of June and July 1854, respectively. Ballantyne left Madras in July, and his companion, Richard Skelton, continued the publication for at least three more issues: August, October, and November 1854. Copies of the first six are in LDS Church Archives; a copy of the seventh is in the Bancroft Library, University of California, Berkeley.

87. Ballantyne's Journal, 12 May 1854. I have been unable to find any proof that it was ever printed.

88. See note 35.

89. On 12 December 1853, Ballantyne noted in his journal that a Mr. McCarthy had been dabbling with "evil spirits and hat moving." On 16 December he took notes on "Moving, Rapping, and Kindred Phenomena." Ballantyne had earlier encountered this when his missionary group had arrived in San Bernardino in December 1852. See his Journal for 23 December 1852. This was an interesting part of early Mormon social history which eventually caused great concern to Church leaders. Orson Pratt's concern was reflected in his "Second Epistle to the Saints," *The Seer* 1 (Nov. 1853): 167. See also Davis Bitton, "Mormonism's Encounter with Spiritualism," *Journal of Mormon History* 1 (1975): 39–50. Ballantyne, like Pratt, simply relegated these experiences to the devil.

90. He announced to the public a series of twelve lectures through three hundred printed handbills he distributed on 14 May 1854. Twelve lectures were to be given in Madras and also in neighboring Vepery. He describes these lectures in a letter to John Taylor, dated Madras, 29 May 1854, in *Deseret News,* 19 October 1854, pp. 2–3. He had tried a similar approach in August 1853 (see note 52), and N. V. Jones had tried this also in Calcutta in November–December 1853. Ballantyne records that few attended the lectures in Madras. The use of handbills was quite common in the early missionary effort. A non-Mormon mention of these early handbills is by Daniel Kidder: "It is not an uncommon thing to see handbills posted up in our streets, setting forth various items about the fulness of the gospel, and promising to gratify the curiosity felt to know what the Latter-day Saints do believe" (*Mormonism and the Mormons* . . . [New York: Lane and Scott, 1852], p. 311).

91. Beginning on 15 May 1854 his Journal almost daily records his illness. From 4 June to 25 June he was so ill he could not keep up his journal. He recounted the critical period of this illness in a letter to his wife, dated 4 July 1854. MS in LDS Church Archives.

92. They had written Jones on 28 May requesting his counsel in regard "to the propriety of leaving Madras. We stated that our labors here seem to be at an end . . ." (Ballantyne's Journal, 28 May 1854). By 26 June he noted that every door in Madras had been closed against them. Ballantyne's certificate of release was dated 4 August 1854 and was copied into his Journal, Vol. 5, 9 January 1855. He requested this from N. V. Jones on 9 July after he had been "released." The First Presidency had prepared the way for their release in "To the Missionaries From Utah," *Deseret News,* 31 August 1854; and *Millennial Star* 16 (18 Nov. 1854): 721–22.

93. Ballantyne's Journal, 9 July 1854. As I have suggested elsewhere, this was a necessary part of the distribution system of Church literature. See my comments in *Journal of Mormon History* 4 (1977): 46–47.

94. "I am now getting 106 Volumes of the Series of Tracts which I have published here bound, with the intent to sell them to help me home. The volume contains:

1st A Proclamation of the Gospel, by P. P. Pratt
2nd The Only Way to be Saved, by Lorenzo Snow
3rd A Reply to the Rev. J. Richards
4th A Second Reply to Rev. J. Richards
5th 1st No. of the Millennial Star and Monthly Visitor
6th 2nd No. of the Millennial Star and Monthly Visitor
7th 3rd No. of the Millennial Star and Monthly Visitor
8th 4th No. of the Millennial Star and Monthly Visitor
9th The Dialogue on Polygamy
    These comprise all that I have published in Madras during the last 11 months with the exception of four letters which were published in the 'Gazzette,' and 'Circulator:' Making in all 4,300 pamphlets'' (Ballantyne's Journal, 10 July 1854). A title page was prepared for this edition: *Tracts &c. Published by Richard Ballantyne, Elder in the Church of Jesus Christ of Latter-day Saints; Consisting of* . . . The price for the collection was one rupee. LDS Church Archives has a copy of this edition.

    95. See his Journal, dates of 15 and 17 July and 16 August 1854.

    96. Letter of N. V. Jones to S. W. Richards, dated Calcutta, 17 March 1854, in *Millennial Star* 16 (13 May 1854): 303. As early as 9 September 1853, Ballantyne complained of a lack of books to sell, especially copies of the Book of Mormon. See his Journal for that date. See also his letter to his wife, dated 9 December 1853, p. 7. MS in LDS Church Archives.

    97. Letter of R. Ballantyne to [F. D.] Richards, dated London, 13 December 1854 in *Millennial Star* 17 (13 Jan. 1855): 28.

    98. Ibid.

    99. Ballantyne's Journal, 5 October 1853. His comment on the "poison" is in his letter to his wife dated Madras, 2–6 February 1854, pp. 2–3. MS in LDS Church Archives. For a list of Mormon imprints published in India see Whittaker, "Early Mormon Pamphleteering," pp. 446–49.

    100. There are several such references in his Journal, and since my emphasis in this essay has been on his publishing activities, there is the possibility the reader will think he did nothing else. Although his writing did play a major role in his missionary work it must not obscure his day-to-day preaching, visiting, and other such activities which he recorded in his journal. His specific concerns about the *limits* of publishing were voiced in a letter to S. W. Richards early in his mission: "The most effective way to remove the prejudices of the honest, we find to be to visit from house to house. In this way they discern the spirit we are of." See the letter dated Madras, 3 August 1853 in *Millennial Star* 15 (22 Oct. 1853): 700–702. By 12 August 1853, they had distributed three hundred of their tracts (only received pay for eleven). He recorded on that date: "I feel that circulating Tracts alone will not do. The people must be awakened." Also important, and I have not developed it here, is the story of the attempts to get material published, which material never appeared in printed form. See Whittaker, "Early Mormon Pamphleteering," pp. 450–53, for a listing of the items that were either not completed or never published.

Thomas E. Lyon

8

John Lyon:
Poet for the Lord

Thomas E. Lyon was born in Salt Lake City, Utah, the fifth
son of T. Edgar and Hermana Forsberg Lyon. He graduated
magna cum laude from the University of Utah in 1963 and
completed Ph.D. studies at U.C.L.A. in 1967, with a
specialty in Latin American Literature. He has taught at
U.C.L.A., the University of Oklahoma, the University of
Wisconsin, Madison, and the University of Glasgow in
Scotland. He came to Brigham Young University in 1972
and directs service programs in Mexico and Guatemala. He
is currently chairman of the Department of Spanish and
Portuguese. He and his wife, Cheryl Larsen Lyon, are
parents to five children.

It is rare that Death lays his hand upon one who, without
special official position in the Church, was so widely known
personally or by reputation as Father John Lyon."[1] At Lyon's
death in 1889 his name *was* widely known by most Latter-day
Saints: his sixteen-year tenure as territorial librarian, superintendent (secretary, recorder) of the Endowment House for
thirty years, theater and poetry critic for the *Deseret News,*
composer of many early LDS hymns, author of the first book

of poetry published by the Church, all made him well known in the nineteenth-century Church. The twentieth century has forgotten most of his writing and has allowed his name to slip into dusty catalogs and files, if not into dark anonymity.

John Lyon was born in the gray slums of old Glasgow, Scotland, on 4 March 1803, to Janet McArthur and Thomas Lyon.[2] Years earlier Thomas had ceremoniously forsaken the family farm in nearby East Kilbride, gone "a 'soldiering" to the romantic West Indies and returned ailing, to eke out a poverty existence in urban Glasgow. Janet carried on a small hand-weaving enterprise but was never able to save more than enough to buy cotton or wool yarn for the next project. Young John, the only surviving child of four children, was needed to help with the heddles, shuttle, and loom, attended only one and a half years of formal schooling as a youth, and was barely able to read a few simple words. When John was eight, his father died of asthma; a few years later his mother began seeing another man. John, at age seventeen, in disaccord with his future stepfather left the dingy, two-room tenement forever. He took employment as an apprentice weaver but also delighted in bare-knuckled boxing in the shabby bars of decaying Glasgow.

In 1824, John suffered from frequent dizzy spells. The doctors of the Royal Infirmary proceeded to bleed a pint of blood from him every other day. Getting no better from this "cure," he visited another doctor who advised him to leave Glasgow and take up residence in any town "six miles from the sea; drink plentifully of sweet milk, and take all the fresh air morning, noon and night."[3] John left his hometown and almost by chance took up residence in Kilmarnock, twenty-one miles southwest of Glasgow. He had never been so far from home but confidently rented a loom, began weaving, and never again complained of dizziness or prolonged ill health. In the 1820s Kilmarnock bustled with industry, and Lyon prospered at the loom. The town also bustled with young lasses, and in 1826 John married sixteen-year-old Janet Thomson, daughter of one of the "established" families in the community.

In Kilmarnock John joined in verbal debate with some college students and soon realized that he would have to learn to read and write. He enrolled in night classes and after three years pronounced himself literate. Like many weavers he debated and argued politics while at the loom, and in the evening he read poetry, particularly the sentimental works of Robert Burns. Although he was from nearby Ayr, Burns had published his first poems in Kilmarnock in 1786, and the local intelligentsia considered him a kindred spirit, if not a native son. Lyon read and pondered Shakespeare and Cervantes; he also kept abreast of current happenings, now joyously reading of them firsthand in the county newspapers.

From 1826 until 1849, Janet bore twelve children. She and the older children learned the weaving business and were able to assist in keeping the family loom working as many as sixteen hours a day. Prices for woven blankets, paisley and worsted shawls, bonnets and outerwear, all of which John and Janet wove, had fallen sharply in the 1830s so the entire family had to cooperate to earn sufficient for food. In economic straits, John decided to try his inexperienced hand at writing for the county newspapers. He visited historical sites in the region, chatted with local eccentrics and covered current news stories. Paganini played in Kilmarnock in 1831, and John reported his concert. In 1832 Lyon championed the cause of the poor in the passage of Britain's first major reform bill; his report on poverty in Ayrshire was read in Parliament and published in the London *Times*. He worked for at least eight different short-lived newspapers, contributing articles, canvassing for new subscriptions, penning an occasional original poem, collecting bills, securing advertising, adding a few meagre pence to the family income from each endeavor.

Three major themes emerge from his early years: (1) a vital concern for the poor (likely learned and felt from his own young years); (2) a fetish-like admiration for the "self-made man" who had risen above what birth or circumstance might dictate; and (3) a fascination with those who maintained deep religious conviction, particularly the "Covenanters," the "Cameronians," the "original Seceders," and especially Thomas Chalmers and the 480 ministers who in 1843 finally dissented and formed the Free Church of Scotland. These three concerns united in 1843 when William Gibson, a Mormon from nearby Paisely, came to Kilmarnock to preach a new "restored" religion. The LDS faith had only been expounded for four years in Scotland and counted few members; the general religious fervor of the 1840s had broken traditional barriers and allowed many incipient groups to win new members from established Presbyterianism. John Lyon attended Gibson's first preaching meeting in Kilmarnock and quite naturally engaged in debate; after six months of study he became the first "convert" in Kilmarnock, on 30 March 1844. William Gibson tersely recorded, "This evening I baptized the first two [people] John Lyon, [Sen.], and Ivy Thomson."[4] Years later, John recalled the moving moment when he truly felt the newfound truth:

> How sweet the Gospel message came,
> When first I learn'd its light and pow'r;
> 'Twas all the anxious heart could claim,
> It and the Scriptures were the same:
> I was a "Mormon" from that hour![5]

Janet had just given birth to her ninth child on 27 March 1844 and could not be baptized into the Church until 4 May, with her oldest son, Thomas. As the other children developed a testimony of the Church, those thirteen years and older also received baptism at the hands of one of John's newfound friends.

John now became a lion for the Lord, dedicating as much time to preaching as to newspapering and weaving. He and Elder Gibson held scores of public debates throughout Ayrshire, challenging the Presbyterian church and "all other takers."[6] Local ministers hired the services of Alexander Robertson, an early Mormon convert from Paisely, Scotland, who had been to Nauvoo, left the Church, and returned to his native lands, to try to thwart missionary work. No victor was declared in the debates but the rapid growth of the Church in Kilmarnock indicates Lyon's success. The Church headquarters in Liverpool named John the presiding elder in Kilmarnock (and indeed all of county Ayrshire) in February 1845, just ten months after he had joined the Church. He preached and baptized wherever he could. One longtime resident of Kilmarnock recalled of Lyon:

> I often met with him at Paxton's Brewery at the Waterside, and had disputes with him on all subjects—Stewart's Philosophy, Locke's. For some years I had not seen much of Lyon, and when we did meet he was with some Mormons in a neighbouring village trying to make converts to the new faith. Of course I did laugh heartily to find him, of all men, a Saul among the prophets, and ridiculed in no measured terms the new imposture.[7]

The LDS *Millennial Star* records a similar incident from quite a different point of view. Lyon "opened" neighboring Stewarton to Mormonism in 1847. He first obtained a meeting-house free of charge, but after some success in attracting new members the church building was denied him. A local gentleman bought a copy of the Doctrine and Covenants for the purpose of convincing the town of its absurdities. Lyon met him in public debate where "the truth bore him down to an acknowledgement that such were the laws in ancient times, and the man of loud words became a perfect infant in the Lyon's paw."[8] The pun is obviously intended; Lyon felt a nobility in his name and often "roared" his beliefs aloud. A pre-Mormon friend in Kilmarnock observed that "John Lyon was a poet worthy of his name" but also that he was "very disputatious as well as pugnacious."[9] John enjoyed the public contests and the exposure they gave the Church. And they obviously bore fruits; the branch in Kilmarnock grew to 107 members in four years under Lyon's missionary efforts, and approximately 190 converts were baptized in nearby villages from 1844 to 1848, John being responsible for most of these eager new members.

The Lyon house in Kilmarnock was a well-known stopping place for visiting Church authorities in Scotland. Diaries and letters of brothers Samuel W. and Franklin D. Richards, as well as their uncle Dr. Levi Richards, indicate that they visited with John and Janet and always participated in a delightful evening of entertainment in the home, a change from most other houses in which they lodged. Lyon was usually encouraged to read his poems; songs, both religious and otherwise, were performed by invited Church members; especially popular were the lilting melodies and words of Robert Burns. Invariably each diarist recorded his delight in the Kilmarnock home. A single example from young Franklin D. Richards in 1846 points up the varied nature of the evenings: "Spent the evening there [home of John Lyon] and saw experiments on mesmerism."[10]

Yet popularity and prosperity in the Church did not guarantee joy and blessings at home. Different from most couples of the time, Janet and John enjoyed the first twenty-two years of their married life without the death of a child. During the winter of 1848, however, one-year-old Margaret died and two months later her infant sister, Agnes, also passed away. The death of these girls, the tenth and eleventh children in the family, were evidence of Janet's tired, overworked body. One more child would be born, but he too would not live to maturity.

John's poetry written before his joining the Church was much in the vein of the Romantic movement—exultation in nature, eulogy of local people and places, sentimental, personal, and often written in the Scottish dialect. "The Auld Man's Lament," "The Laboring Man's Song," and "Reflections on a Bank Note" are but a few published examples.[11] After joining the Church, he continued the search for rhyme and easy metaphor but directed his lyric efforts to the thrilling doctrines, the exciting people, and the inspired activities of the new gospel. The few poems of his pre-Mormon years gave way to an effusion of pent-up poetry in praise of God and man. The *Millennial Star* now became Lyon's main vehicle of publication; its pages trace his lyric outburst, thirty-two poems between 1845 and 1852. Many are occasional poems, written for a specific person,[12] for a unique occasion (the death of Orson and Sarah Pratt's infant son, for example), or a particular place. Most of the poems reflect an optimistic view of life and many point to a future millennial reign on earth. Lyon sensed the Mormon mood of the day, feeling that he was part of a new order which would very soon usher in the second coming of Christ. His poems reflect the themes that he was preaching to his non-Mormon neighbors—gathering to Zion, fleeing "Babylon," repenting, and so forth.

In 1850 Orson Pratt, then president of the British Mission, urged John to collect his scattered poetry and publish a single volume of LDS poems. With continued encouragement from Franklin D. Richards, John collected thirty poems that had previously appeared in the *Millennial Star,* added seventy-four more and delivered the package to the new British Mission president, Samuel W. Richards. Lyon dedicated the book to his dynamic young Apostle friend Franklin D. Richards and agreed to donate any proceeds to the Perpetual Emigration Fund (P.E.F.). The office in Liverpool paid the printing costs for 3,400 copies, and in January 1853 *The Harp of Zion* was delivered for sale throughout Great Britain. "It is got up in superior manner, printed in new type, on beautiful thick paper, and splendidly bound. No Saint will be satisfied to be destitute of a copy."[13] Lyon and indeed the entire Church in Great Britain were proud of this, the first complete edition of poetry published by the Church.[14] For the first time the Church entered the realm of publishing creative literature. Nearly every issue of the *Millennial Star* had featured a poem or two by an LDS writer, but now an entire book was published with Church money and approval. Mormon authorities had previously printed newspapers, tracts, general epistles, an emigrants' guide, and standard scriptures, but not a book of poetry. *The Harp of Zion* indicated that many authorities felt that the Restoration must be captured in aesthetic form, as well as rhetorical and scriptural discourse.

The Harp of Zion, despite its claim to fame as a "first," did not sell well in Great Britain. George Q. Cannon, reviewing the enormous inventory of publications in the Liverpool office in

1861 noted that "of books: there is the *Harp of Zion,* out of 3404 copies 21 have been sold in three years."[15] It may have sold better in the first years of its publication but at two shillings and six pence the book was likely too expensive for most of the Saints, strapped by poverty and already expected to contribute to the Perpetual Emigration Fund, to the fund to build the Salt Lake Temple, to the traveling elders, and to pay tithing and buy the *Millennial Star* and scores of doctrinal tracts. George Q. Cannon packed up most of the copies of the *Harp* and, with Eliza R. Snow's 1856 *Poems: Religious, Political, Historical,* which had sold even fewer copies, sent them to Utah. Many copies of Lyon's book were sold throughout the territory; a few were given to friends. The book achieved a fame in Utah that it had not experienced in Great Britain, likely due to the author's visibility in high Church circles, as well as an improving economy that permitted the luxury of purchasing a book of poetry.

It was likely Lyon's visibility as a poet in the *Millennial Star,* as well as his success as a "baptizer" in Ayrshire and his friendship with Franklin D. Richards, that had brought his name to Orson Pratt. In 1849 President Pratt called Lyon to full-time missionary service to preside over and preach to the Worcester (England) Conference. John had ample reason not to accept the assignment: his wife was pregnant with child number twelve; his two youngest daughters had died just a few months earlier; his two oldest children had just married and were expecting; weaving was not producing profits and Janet would have a near-impossible time supporting the family by herself; and two sons were seriously sick with cholera. Nevertheless, he put his affairs in order, sadly left Kilmarnock, visited Orson Pratt in Liverpool for instructions (where President Pratt told him to push the tract project of getting one LDS pamphlet in every home in Great Britain), and on 11 February 1849 John Lyon reported for three years of purseless, scripless missionary work. He kept a detailed diary during the first four months of his mission, recording branches visited, baptisms performed, sermons preached, letters written, and people contacted. During his mission, Lyon wrote some 1,000 letters, walked approximately 5,445 miles, delivered 420 formal sermons, and baptized approximately 360 people—all in thirty-five months![16]

Once again, however, Church successes were clouded by family tragedy. On 27 March, just two months after leaving home, John received a letter which

> gave me intelligence of the death of my son David who died on the 23 at half past 11 a.m. This news gave me exceeding pain; I wept aloud and slept very little during the night thinking of my family and their mother. I prayed for them and felt to ask the Lord to strengthen her in this bereavement.
>
> March 28 Wednesday
>
> This day I wrote a consolatory letter to my family condolling them on the Death of my son over which I shed many bitter tears of regret in not having it in my power to carry his remains to the silent grave.[17]

Two months later another letter from home informed

> of my son Roberts, departure, which took place on Saturday evening the 26th [of May 1849] at 1/2 past 6 evening for which I felt to be thankful to my heavenly father for removing him from his long and severe affliction.[18]

Robert, age sixteen, and David, age ten, both died of the lingering illness of cholera. The diary entries are brief but the pain that John and Janet suffered is incalculable. John surely asked why. When he was doing the Lord's work, why should he be so plagued? No answer came immediately; he continued working. In June of the same year Janet delivered a son; she and John selected the name of Franklin D. Richards Lyon in honor of their Apostle friend, a further affirmation of their trust in the Church.

In December 1851, President Franklin D. Richards reassigned John to preside over the large Glasgow Conference. Lyon joyously packed his bags, returned to Kilmarnock, and soon took up residence in Glasgow for the next thirteen months. As conference president, he collected and recorded donated monies, blessed scores of babies, organized quarterly conference meetings, and continued preaching to his long-forgotten friends. He was now a "somebody" in Glasgow and felt that his "self-made rise from poverty" was chiefly a result of his religious convictions. During his short tenure in Glasgow, he baptized approximately 35 people, making a total of 715 he converted and baptized in Great Britain.

Finally, after preaching the doctrine of the gathering, writing poems about fleeing Babylon to congregate in Zion, and baptizing many who had already left for America, John received official permission to gather with the Saints in Salt Lake. He, Janet, and their five surviving single children sailed on 28 February 1853, in the ship *International* with 417 other excited LDS emigrants. Samuel W. Richards recognized John's leadership talent and named him first counselor to the ship's LDS president, Christopher Arthur. Lyon kept an accurate log of the fifty-four-day crossing, with its too-frequent calms and occasional serious storms; he recorded the fifty-three-day sea-sickness of Richard Waddington, the second counselor to President Arthur, and noted the scarcity of water and provisions as a result of unfavorable winds, as well as understandable quarrels between tightly berthed passengers.[19]

Upon arriving in New Orleans, the company boarded a steamer journeying upriver to St. Louis, then to Keokuk, Iowa, where Isaac Haight, the Church's agent, organized them into various companies for overland travel. Lyon's leadership and speaking abilities again caused that he be named captain of one hundred in a ten-pound P.E.F. company, as well as chaplain for the entire Jacob Gates company. They purchased oxen, wagons, and provisions, and set out on a four-month, fourteen-hundred-mile journey across Iowa, Nebraska, and the wilderness of Wyoming and Utah. Various diaries indicate slow but constant progress, and plagues of grasshoppers, mosquitoes, and flies. Lyon's family reached "the Valley" on 28 September 1853, the completion of a more than ten-thousand-mile journey from Scotland; they had been "on the road" for more than eight months but joyously entered an autumn valley with high and happy hopes for a reunion with the Saints of God.

The John Lyon family barely scraped through the first hard winter in the Valley, existing on potatoes and on roots grubbed from the nearby hills. In 1854 Lyon built a log home in what was soon to be the Twentieth Ward and settled into making an adequate living. Brigham Young gave him part-time work as his family weaver and also requested that Lyon teach all Brigham's daughters to weave.[20]

John's literary fame had preceded him, and he began volunteer work with the newly created Territorial Library. The librarian, William C. Staines, married John's daughter, Lillias, in 1854, the same year in which John was named assistant librarian. When Staines was called on an extended mission, Lyon took over as head librarian, receiving an annual salary of $400 for the relatively short hours he put in. As librarian, he met Sir Richard Burton, Mark Twain, and Artemus Ward—a few among the many dignitaries and literatti who passed through Utah. The Church authorities showed off Lyon as a literate Scottish convert whose erudition did not keep him from exercising the new faith. Lyon also earned a meager salary as superintendent of the Endowment House from its dedication in 1855 to 1884. He continued his newspapering work, writing as a critic for the *Deseret News.* He gave elocution and "Dramatic Art" lessons to Maude Adams and many other actors on the stage of the Salt Lake Theater. In short, he dominated much of the literary realm in early Salt Lake City.

While steamboating up the Mississippi en route to the West in 1853 John had heard of a new Church doctrine, referred to cryptically as the D.O.P.O.W. (doctrine of the plurality of wives), or celestial plural marriage. He resisted for three years but was frequently aware of its preached importance from the highest levels of Church leadership. His close friendship with Brigham Young and other authorities and his organizing work at the Endowment House brought plural marriage to mind daily. In 1856 John had a dramatic dream:

I thought [dreamed] . . . that I was in company with the First Presidency, as a guest at dinner, when Brigham Young asked me why I did not take another wife, as I was losing time. I replied that I did not know where I could find one willing to have me. Said he, "Will you take one, if I find one?" I said "yes" so I dreamed he took me out to the street and told me to go as far as I saw the rise of the road, and there enquire for a lady of the name _____. In my dream I arrived at the house in quick time but it seemed to be evening and rather dark. So I rapped at the door but got no answer. . . . I rapped again and a voice said, "Come in." I was in the middle of a small room having one bed in the corner, where a woman was sitting in her nightgown. I enquired "if there was a lady of the name of _____ [who] lived here?" when all in chorus, rang out a loud laugh, from the lady in bed, and what I supposed other three, who were hidden in the room. This merry introduction wakened me out of my pleasant anticipations.[21]

The dream reveals John's desire to comply with Brigham's wish, but he must have worried about the reaction of others, particularly his acceptance by women, as indicated by their derisive laughter as he approached the lady in bed.

Near the small Lyon family cabin lived another Scotsman, Robert Crookston; John frequently visited with his fellow countryman and observed a sixteen-year-old English girl who served as a maid. Her father had died in Nauvoo and her mother in Winter Quarters, and the kindly Crookstons brought her to Salt Lake City in 1852. "Often visiting this family, my mind was drawn to this girl, and *plural marriage* being a subject on my mind as *sacred as baptism for the remission of sin,*"[22] John timidly thought of marriage with the sixteen-year-old orphan.

Although I never put much faith in my dreams as revelation still I looked upon it as strange that this [house of the dream] was in the vicinity of my Scotch acquaintance's dwelling, where I had seen this girl. Some months later I was indeed invited to dinner [by the First Presidency]. After dinner Brigham Young addressed me in the exact words, "Why did I not take another wife as I was getting old?" To this question I answered by a laugh, when he sternly asked me what I meant. I told the three gentlemen my dream.

Brigham told John that the dream was from the Lord and that he ought not be concerned about ridicule. That very night, John went to the Crookston home, talked with the young girl and "proposed to her . . . if she would be my wife for time and all eternity, to which she answered in the affirmative. This was all the courtship we had."[23] On 28 March 1856 Brigham Young sealed fifty-three-year-old John Lyon to sixteen-year-old Caroline Holland in the Endowment House. Janet had also been sixteen when she married John thirty years earlier. She was not present at the sealing ceremony.

Little if any specific consultation took place between Janet and John prior to this plural marriage; considerable occurred after! Young "Carrie" (Caroline) continued living with the Crookston family until John was able to build another tiny cabin on the corner of Oak and Bluff streets (3rd Ave. and F St.), adjacent to his "first home." Janet must have resented her husband's frequent evening absences; when Caroline finally did move in as neighbor and husband-sharer, forty-eight-year-old Janet moved out to Tooele with her recently arrived married daughter, Janet Lyon Spiers. After a year, however, Janet returned to help teenage Caroline care for her children. During the next fifteen years Caroline bore seven children, the last one born in 1872, when her husband was in his seventieth year and she in her thirty-third. Natural jealousies often overcame the need to cooperate, to express love, and to sacrifice for the expanding family.

John felt some of the tensions that existed among two women living under nearly the same roof and captured these in poetic form. He does not attack the rather sacred doctrine of plural marriage but through literary displacement exposes the not unexpected human strife and struggles. Most non-Mormons viewed polygamy as a crude throwback to a less-civilized era, one of the relics of barbarism. Others, among them Mark Twain and Artemus Ward, whom Lyon had met personally, turned polygamy into fun and frolic.[24] Lyon was directly aware of its serious human conflicts, its joys and doctrinal importance, but chose to emphasize the humorous.

Most of Lyon's poetry is a very serious examination of the "Mormon experience." In Scotland he had observed and later challenged a former Saint who had gone to Nauvoo, become disillusioned, and returned to Glasgow. This individual was likely the previously mentioned Mr. Robertson. John wrote a poem, a poignant examination of what happens to an individual who has "walked in the light" and later "fallen on into darkness":

The Apostate

I knew him, ere the roots of bitterness
Had grown to putrid cancer in his soul.
Then Revelation's light gleamed o'er his mind
In strange fantastic dreams of future bliss;
. . . .
Precocious, in a day from childhood to
A man, he grew a giant of his kind;
. . . .
All knowledge, ere it was revealed, he knew.
The knotty points in Scripture he could solve,
By presto touch of talismanic wand,
And, Patriarch like, had the discerning gift
To know the ancient seeds of Israel's race.
. . . .
The gathering was his constant theme; for he
Had dreamed at golden gates, and pearly walls,
. . . .
And so he left, to seek this fairy land
Uncounselled, in his *own* imaginings.
But ah! he thought not of the fiery path
Where persecution, poverty, and death,
Await the just, ere they can sing the song
Of ransom'd ones, by suffering perfect made.

Thus, full of novelty's romance, he found
The city of the Saints, and with it all

The stern realities of life. His hope,
Like morning mist, evaporated quite,
And with it, all his dreams of phantom bliss
. . . .
Still disaffection's deadly 'venomed sting
Withered his schemes, till every sense became
Corrupt, and dead. He neither saw, nor felt,
Nor heard, nor savour'd of the things of God.
Then falsehood came, and with it came distrust;
Truth error seemed, and lies appeared as truth!
And holy men mere swindling vagabonds!

Like smould'ring embers still the hatred burned
In his foul mind, till every passion burst
Their prison'd fire, and blazed one sulph'rous flame
Of malice, hotter than the Stygian lake!
And so he fell from his gigantic height,

As we have seen a falling meteor fall
From out the starry vault, which never had,
'Mong constellations, a fixed residence,
Save the combustive fluid of scattered gas,
That, kindled by the windy current, flashed,
And falling, seemed a blazing orb of heaven!
. . . .
Forgotten, nearly twenty moons he'd left
Nauvoo! when lo! in Scotland I beheld
This strange, outlandish looking man at church
Among the Saints. I wondered much, I watched
Him when the congregation sang in praise
The songs of Zion! but his lips moved not,
And when they knelt, he stood a statue mute
Amidst the prostrate throng of worshippers.
His bas'lisk eye in rolling anguish told
The gnawings of the bitter worm within.
I met him after service, and he strove
To imitate the Saints' fond welcome greet,
But when his hand touched mine,—Lord save me, how
I shook! Touched with his influence of despair;
It ran like lightning o'er my mortal frame,
Benumbing all the energies of life.

The Prophet, Saints, and all their labours, were
His theme of execration and contempt.
. . . .
He raved, and counted o'er his money lost;—
The turning period of his selfish soul—
And like old Shylock, grinned in bitter spite
To have his "pound of flesh." We parted thus.
'Twas past all patience, longer to endure.

(Harp of Zion, pp. 53–56)

The vibrant images—a cancered soul, dead corrupted senses, smouldering embers of hatred, a muted statue, lifeless lips—re-create an agonizing human tragedy. John felt the loss for and to the individual and vividly created an anguished being who had lost so much of his former self.

Lyon also wrote scores of shorter lyric poems praising God and nature, man and mountains, and individual friends and fellow believers. Most of his poetry is hope-filled—a positive response to the glorious doctrines he found in The Church of Jesus Christ of Latter-day Saints. Much of the poetry is hastily written for a specific occasion; most poems are based on a strong need to rhyme, at times ignoring other necessary components of good poetry. When he is at his best, he is a very good poet; the sonnet "Lust" represents an excellent combination of lyric expression and meaningful thought:

Lust

Lust is the offspring of a thousand sighs,
Intrigue, deception, and as many lies;
A strange compound of hidden, plotting ill,
To fire with rage, to torture, or to kill;
Fraught with distrust, anxiety, and care,
Jealousy, revenge, and unconsoled despair:
The softest passion of a menial's heart,
That ebbs and flows, as impulse plays its part;
At times o'ercome with feelings proud and mean,
That lurk in secret, yet are ever seen
In looks, and gestures, thoughts, and strong desire,
That live, and burn unquenched; undying fire,

> That e'en in death, with all life's powers destroyed,
> Still longs, and lusts, yet never is enjoyed.
>
> <div align="right">(<i>Harp of Zion,</i> pp. 155–56)</div>

John Lyon's extant poetic production numbers more than 350 poems. He wrote at least twenty-five short stories and prose sketches which were published in the *Mountaineer, Tullidge's Quarterly Magazine, The Contributor,* and the *Deseret News.* Some of his poetry was put to music and appeared in the *Juvenile Instructor.* The LDS hymnbook of 1851, more like a book of poetry because it was published without musical notation, carried eight of his hymn-poems. Subsequent editions continued most of these hymns, originally selected by Franklin D. Richards; however, the 1948 revision of the hymnbook eliminated all of Lyon's songs. John maintained an intimate poetic friendship with Eliza R. Snow, exchanging poems and puns with her for thirty years, and both Eliza and John regularly acted live roles in the temple endowment ceremony. Lyon met with all the aspiring writers and poets of the territory, encouraging them to produce and publish. In the intellectually oriented Twentieth Ward he batted ideas and doctrine with William C. Staines, Karl G. Maeser, Phineas H. Young, William S. Godbe, Eli B. Kelsey, and Edward Tullidge. Lyon discussed and wrote with these men but never went to the extremes that caused Godbe and others to leave the Church. He became known to all as Father Lyon, an endearing term of respect for his age, his office of patriarch, and his continuing poetic and personal contributions to the Church.

John Lyon received many official Church callings in Utah. In January 1854, he became a seventy and was sustained as one of the presidents of the Thirty-seventh Quorum, meeting every Friday evening in the Fourteenth Ward schoolhouse.[25] On 12 February 1867 he received the fulness of the priesthood in the Endowment House.[26] Brigham Young, John Taylor, George Q. Cannon, and other Apostles, with Wilford Woodruff as "mouth" ordained him a patriarch on 7 May 1873.[27] He served in this capacity until his death. As were other early Church members, John Lyon was baptized more than once. Of one baptism John simply recorded on a scrap of paper, "Baptised in the ED house for the N order 1876."[28] This was his third baptism, performed to signify a new life in the United Order. (The first baptism occurred in 1844 in Scotland; the second, upon his arrival in Salt Lake City in 1853). In his waning years, Brigham Young pushed very hard to establish the cooperative orders that he felt should characterize true Saints. As a friend of the great organizer, Lyon entered into a covenant to live more closely the laws of mutual production and sharing.

John "retired" from his supervisory work at the Endowment House in 1884 at age eighty-one, having served for thirty years. During that span, he had examined recommends, organized sessions, and accurately recorded the comings and goings of thousands of Saints who came to be sealed. He was intimately associated with Presidents Brigham Young, John Taylor, and Wilford Woodruff. "Brother Brigham" included John Lyon in a now-famous portrait "Brigham Young and his Friends," hanging in the Church Museum in Salt Lake City.[29] Wilford Woodruff paid him the honor of setting Lyon apart as patriarch. John Taylor, a fellow British Islander, loved Lyon's poetry and responded by writing a fine poetic response to John:

> Thou Lyon of the East! I've heard thy roar;
> Thy voice hath sounded Britain's Isles all o'er;
> And in Columbia's land a Lyon's known,
> Not by another's works, but by his own.
> . . . .
> Let those less noble rack their creaking lyre,
> And try in vain to light the Poet's fire
> 'Tis thine to take a more exalted stand,
> And touch the living chords with master hand.
> With Pope, or Milton, Shakespeare, Mills or Snow
> . . . .
> A thousand tongues shall reverb'rate thy praise.[30]

While the sentiment and comparison with other great English writers is overblown, John Taylor honestly viewed the contribution Lyon made to the interpreting and understanding of LDS doctrine to be of incalculable, even eternal, worth.

As a man who did not have early educational opportunity and who did not learn to read and write until his mid-twenties, Lyon achieved the goal he had early admired, that of being at least partially "self-made." For forty-five years he lent his entire spiritual, personal, and literary energies to The Church of Jesus Christ of Latter-day Saints, giving much to it and receiving more from it. He was a poet for the Lord. "Father" John Lyon was known and admired by most of the members of the Church in the nineteenth century. He died in Salt Lake City on Thanksgiving day, 28 November 1889.

Notes

1. Announcement of Lyon's death, *Millennial Star* 51 (23 Dec. 1889): 813.

2. Information concerning John Lyon's early life comes from forty-two pages of fragmented reflections on his early life, written in Utah in the 1880s, in my possession.

3. Ibid.

4. Information taken from the journal of William Gibson, Library-Archives, Historical Department, The Church of Jesus Christ of Latter-day Saints (hereafter cited as LDS Church Archives) and records of the Kilmarnock Branch.

5. This poem, written in 1875 and awkwardly titled "Reminiscence of My Early Ignorance of 'Mormonism,' " was published in a posthumous collection of Lyon's writing entitled *Songs of a Pioneer* (Salt Lake City: Magazine Printing Co., 1923), p. 81.

6. Lyon manuscript in my possession.

7. "Senex" (pen name for Matthew Wilson), "Mormonism—A Kilmarnock Bishop in Utah," 9 April 1881 Supplement to *The Kilmarnock Standard.* Wilson visited Utah in the 1870s and wrote a very scathing article on Lyon and Mormonism.

8. John Lyon to Thomas D. Brown, *Millennial Star* 10 (15 July 1848): 221.

9. John Kelso Hunter, "Retrospects," *The Kilmarnock Standard,* 20 April 1895, p. 6.

10. Diary of Franklin D. Richards, 5 December 1846, in LDS Church Archives.

11. The poems were published in the Kilmarnock *Journal,* the *Western Watchman* and the Edinburgh *Witness,* the latter two papers published for the purpose of religious reform.

12. Among the many poems of this nature are three written to Franklin D. Richards, one to Eliza R. Snow, one to Eli B. Kelsey, another to Samuel W. Richards, and a poem of encouragement to two lonely sisters in a remote corner of Scotland.

13. *Millennial Star* 15 (29 Jan. 1853): 73.

14. In 1840 Parley P. Pratt published a 140-page collection of his poems and miscellaneous writings, which may be considered *the* first book of poetry published by a nineteenth-century Mormon. It did not, however, have the certification of the Church, which is tacitly implied in Lyon's 1853 work, published by and for Church members. In later years, newspapers in Utah hailed Lyon as the first Mormon to publish a complete book of poetry, likely because he was so well known, Parley P. Pratt was dead, and Lyon's *Harp of Zion* "was in many homes in the territory" (*Millennial Star,* December 1889, p. 183).

15. George Q. Cannon to Brigham Young, 31 March 1861, original in LDS Church Archives, cited by David J. Whittaker, "Early Mormon Pamphleteering," *Journal of Mormon History* 4 (1977): 48, n. 39.

16. Diary in Archives of Harold B. Lee Library, Brigham Young University, Provo, Utah. Figures are extrapolated from the diary and branch and conference records.

17. Ibid.

18. Ibid.

19. Log book in Archives of Lee Library.

20. Recollection of Maria Young Dougall, "True Pioneer Stories," *Juvenile Instructor* 62 (Nov. 1927): 611.

21. This quote comes from one of the many incomplete fragments John Lyon wrote about his life. These fragments are in my possession.

22. Ibid., italics added.

23. Ibid.

24. See Richard H. Cracroft, "Distorting Polygamy for Fun and Profit: Artemus Ward and Mark Twain among the Mormons," *Brigham Young University Studies* 14 (Winter 1974): 272–88, for other writers who saw humor in plural marriage.

25. Journal History of The Church of Jesus Christ of Latter-day Saints, 12 January 1854, LDS Church Archives.

26. Lyon manuscript in my possession.

27. Ibid.

28. Ibid.

29. Lyon family tradition holds that John and one other were painted in some years after the original was completed.

30. Reproduced in Lyon, *Harp of Zion,* pp. 3–4.

Chad J. Flake

9

From the Diary of
Lucy Hannah White Flake

Born in Snowflake, Arizona, Chad J. Flake is the grandson of
Lucy Hannah White Flake. He attended Northern Arizona
University and received a B.A. degree from Brigham Young
University in 1953. Chad received an M.A. degree from
Denver University. He is the author of *A Mormon
Bibliography, 1830–1930,* and editor of *Mormon
Americana 1960–1980.* He is also the author of articles and
book reviews in various journals.

When Andrew Jenson toured the various stakes in 1893,
advising members to keep diaries, he drew a responsive commitment from Lucy Hannah White Flake. She began a day-by-
day diary, while at the same time recording a summary of her
life up until that time. The story of her life in Utah, her move to
Arizona, and the summary of her life to January 1894 are contained in the first volume of her writings. Two subsequent
volumes record her day-to-day activities from January 1894
until shortly before her death in January 1900.[1] The quotations
used herein are taken from her three-volume journal, using the
punctuation and spelling as found in the diaries in order to
maintain the flavor of the original.

Lucy Hannah White was born 23 August 1842 in Knox County, Illinois, the oldest daughter of Samuel Dennis and Mary Hannah White. Her parents joined The Church of Jesus Christ of Latter-day Saints before Lucy was born. Her earliest recollection was of being shown the city of Nauvoo from the top of the Nauvoo Temple. Her father was chosen as one of the men who remained in Nauvoo to aid the poorer Saints in preparing to leave for the West. The family crossed the plains in 1850 and settled thirty-five miles south of Salt Lake City in an area which was later to be called Lehi. Here they were reunited with their relatives, only to be separated again in 1853 when they were called as part of the Iron County Mission. Her mother's sorrow at having to leave her family after being reunited in Utah previews Lucy's own sorrow at leaving Beaver some twenty-four years later.

In February 1858 Lucy met William Jordan Flake; they were married 30 December 1858. William Flake was the oldest son of James Madison and Agnes Love Flake, who had converted to Mormonism in Mississippi. Freeing their slaves,[2] they came to Nauvoo in 1844. In 1848 they moved to Utah. James Madison was killed while on the gold mission to California, and Agnes died of consumption while living in San Bernardino. After her death, the three children lived with Amasa Lyman and returned with him to Utah when the Saints were recalled from the San Bernardino Mission.

Lucy and William started marriage with very few possessions. For the first three months they lived with the Lymans in Cedar City before accompanying them in their move to Beaver. According to Osmer Flake's biography, the couple had "a bed-stead made with an axe as the only tool, two log benches he made, a frying pan, a case knife he found and for which he whittled a handle, two tin plates, and a spoon that he cut out of wood with his pocketknife."[3] Though colorful, this seems highly apocryphal inasmuch as both her family and the Lymans were living in close proximity. Lucy merely records "we had verry little to keep house with but we were just as happy as could be. . . . my parents lived close by and greatley asisted us" (p. 9).

Lucy's first sorrow was the death of her second son. William Melvin was born 20 January 1861 and seemed to be a fine, healthy child, but he died 20 March of the same year. Lucy writes, "It seemed my prairs had alway been answered before but in his sickness it seemed like my prairs did no good but still I kept trying to get my Hevenly Father to here me kept praying but it seemed he could not here me" (p. 10). This was the first of five children to die before their third birthday. Lucy found this very difficult, particularly since none of her mother's children had died in infancy.

In the fall of 1867 Lucy's husband concluded to take a second wife. Asked by Eliza R. Snow if she were willing to accept "the principle," Lucy replied, "I said am quite willing to try. . . . My Mother and sister live in it and I think [I] can do as much as them and besides I wanted my Husband to go into that principal before I was old because I think it right" (p. 16). Of the marriage of William and Prudence Kartchner, O. D. Flake records, "The two women lived in the same house, or in close proximity and often helped each other when their work permitted."[4] However, this seemingly tranquil and whole-hearted acceptance of the second marriage does not accurately portray Lucy's feelings. She mentions Prudence in her journal in the fall of 1874, but Prudence is seldom mentioned again until the day before Prudence's death on 7 February 1896, when Lucy writes, "in the evening went in to see sister Prudence she is very low and week I fear she will not recover." On 8 February Lucy records, "Prudence was very low all night," and then, "Pa dedicated her and she Passed away like an babe going to sleep" (p. 159). Then follows a description of Prudence's funeral.

Lucy's not mentioning Prudence at family gatherings, church meetings, parties, and other such functions, leads one to feel that she largely ignored Prudence. This estrangement can also be detected in subtle passages of the diary. In discussing a trip back to Utah in 1878, Lucy records, "we were just our own familey" (p. 26). Concerning a visit of Edward Stevenson to Snowflake, Arizona, she records, "Brother Stevenson preached in Beaver in pourfull sermon on polygamy and retrenchment in the Sisters Hall 26 years ago. That surmound gave me great comfort. It was healing balm to my soal. He said poligamy is the greatest trial our Hevenly Father has in store for his daughters'' (p. 141). After the death of their mother, Prudence's four daughters refused to move to the ranch if Lucy were going to live there also. So Lucy remained in town for the first month of the summer. A reconciliation seems to have been accomplished since she did move to the farm later in the year, but both families continued to have separate homes in town, and it is doubtful that the girls spent another summer on the ranch as long as Lucy lived. They were, however, finally included in family gatherings such as that of the Christmas of 1897.

As a result of accepting polygamy, William was eventually arrested and was sentenced to six months in the Yuma prison. Polygamy, therefore, was an ambivalence in Lucy's life. On one hand it was a visible acceptance of the will of God; on the other hand it was a practical hardship to be dealt with every day.

In 1877 William was called to help settle northern Arizona. This was a severe blow to the family for several reasons. First, they had worked hard to provide themselves with comfortable surroundings both in town and at the ranch. Second, there was the sorrow of leaving her family, particularly her mother, with no idea of how long they would be away. Finally, it was difficult because in 1873 William had been called to explore northern Arizona and had concluded that it was not very fit for colonization. He then had been promised by Brigham Young that he would not be expected to settle in Arizona. As Lucy summarizes it, "Oh the thought of leaveing my poor Widowed Mother who had stood over me night and day in my dreadfull sickness and never gave me up when all others did it was cruel it seemed to me and William said he had rather go to England" (p. 21). But, like others before them, they accepted the call and began selling their property and disposing of their cattle and sheep.

The trip to Arizona was a difficult journey. Leaving Beaver in November, they traveled over the Buckskin Mountains of northern Arizona in deep snow. Early in the trip their two oldest girls contracted diphtheria, and Prudence herself had three very bad spells of sickness. At the death of a child in the group, Lucy was called upon to wash the body. "They called on me to wash it the watter would freeze as quick as it touched the child it was the first time I ever washed the dead" (p. 23). The drive was very difficult for the livestock, so they were forced to abandon them, leaving their son Charles and a hired hand to take care of them until the spring. Lucy relates, "After this was all over and so much anxiety and care and leveing Charles hard work and constant strain on my nerves and strength I took down sick and was several days could not get out of bed" (p. 24).

Arriving at the Little Colorado settlements of Brigham City and Sunset, the group rested for a few days and then continued up the river twenty miles to start a new settlement, which they named Taylor. After the fifth dam was washed away, William concluded that it was not a good place for a settlement and made a trip to the Silver Creek Ranch, which he had seen in 1873, to see if it were available. The ranch, owned by James Stinson, was located in a valley to the south. During William's three-week absence, their son, George, became ill. Lucy's narration of this event is one of the most sensitive passages in her diary:

> I did all I could with medicen and also with faith my prairs did not seem to be herd but several times each day I went a way from my wagon in secret and prayed our wagons was our home often had the Elders administer but it seemed they had no faith I was sad indeed away from home and kindred and my Husband a way my Dear sons James and Charles was willing to do all they could and for a long time I did not blow out the candle at night and the boys would tell me when I wanted them they would stay with me I was so tired out they did stay with me one at a time through the night on the morning of July 6th 78 I was so deep in sorrow it seemed I could not bare it any longer I went out in some brush

out of site and asked my Father in Heven to take him home for I could not bare it any longer my burden was hevier than I could bare that prair was simple but from my hart I wint to him he breathed afew times and passed a way so sweetly my own hands made his clothes dressed him fixed some paint and painted his coffin in one hour after he passed away his Father came (p. 26).

William Flake purchased the Silver Creek Ranch from James Stinson for $12,000 (Lucy has 1,200 in her diary), and three families moved from the Taylor settlement. A humorous anecdote is noted in O. D. Flake's biography:

"Now Mr. Flake, [Mr. Stinson talking] there is just enough water here for this small farm. If you will keep the place for your family alone, you will have a fine place, but if you let anyone else in, you will all starve." Flake said, "You could not give me the place, if I had to live here that way. I am going to have a town and farm all of the land." Stinson then answered, "You won't have enough water. I use it all, and then don't have enough in the dry season." To this Flake replied, "When the Mormons come, the water will increase." Shortly after that the rains came, and it kept coming. They had a hard time gathering the barley and beans, and lost some on account of rain. Stinson said, "I wish the hell the Mormons had stayed away until I had my crop gathered."[5]

The purchase of Silver Creek Ranch necessitated William's return to Utah for more stock. Knowing of Lucy's homesickness, he allowed her and all the children except James to return to Utah.

When William had pulled his stock out of the United Order at Taylor, he was accused of being an apostate, a designation which troubled him greatly. On this return trip to Beaver, the company met Erastus Snow a few miles below Brigham City. William counseled with Apostle Snow concerning moving to a new location, relating a dream he had had, in which Brigham Young appeared to him. In his dream he told Brigham about purchasing the ranch after which "President Young ran his hand in his pocket as if to pull out money he said Bro Young I don't want money I want to know if I done right" (p. 27). After relating this dream to Erastus Snow, the Apostle replied that

that was all the counsel he needed. William continued to Utah to secure stock while Apostle Snow continued to the new settlement to organize a ward and stake. It was Erastus Snow who gave the settlement its name: "Snow" in honor of his being the Apostle in charge of the Southern Utah-Northern Arizona colonization, and "Flake" to honor its founder.

In 1880 the stake and ward Relief Societies were organized in the Snowflake Ward and Stake.[6] During the organization of the Society, Lucy was made first counselor to Mary J. West, a union which sustained her during many of her dark periods. When Mary J. West was put into the stake Relief Society twenty-six years later, Lucy was made stake Primary president. In these capacities, the sisters would travel great distances, sometimes with a male driver, but most often on their own. Some of these visits are recorded in Lucy's diary as follows:

11 January 1896: "Myself and first counceler Sister Willis Went to Shumway and met with the Primary" (p. 156).

24 January: "We went to Pine-dale and met with the Primary at four o clock that evening after meeting we Sister Willis she went with me called on some of the sisters then after dark we went to the dance" (p. 158).

5 June: "Myself Sisters Willis Belle Flake and Basheba Smith we started for Woodruff nine o clock in the Morning" (p. 180).

6 June: "Erley in the morning we started for St Joseph arived in Hole brook a little after eleven. . . . We ate a lunch then started for St Joseph where we arived half past three at four went to Primary" (p. 180).

They returned on Monday, 8 June. In one of their subsequent trips to Joseph City, in which they had to cross the Little Colorado River, the river was so high that they had to wait until someone came along who could drive them across the river. On 27 June "half past eight Sisters Willis Belle Bashey Smith and myself Satarted for pinetop went to Showlow stoped two hours . . . arived at pinetop just after sundown" (p. 183). They continued to organize the Primary there before continuing to the Ellsworth settlement, two miles south. They returned home on Tuesday.

Lucy was always critical of her own performance, particularly during stake meetings. On 29 May 1897 she records, "I with my councilors had to preside [at the Primary Conference] I made such a poor out of it broke down and almost cried and felt so shamed to think I made such a poor out but I am wery Week I tried to put my trust in our Hevenly Father but perhaps I was lacking on my part" (p. 240).

In October 1897 she, along with William, Albert Minerly, and William Willis traveled to Tuba City about 150 miles to the north. William performed his duties as home missionary while Lucy organized the Primary at their conference. On this occasion she felt better about her performance: "I presided the Lord helped me and things went off nice" (p. 263). On 11 September 1898 she and Fanny Willis went on an extended trip, stopping at Pinetop, then on to Adair (a settlement which was north of Showlow but which no longer exists), Ellsworth (also no longer in existence), and Woodland (a dependent branch south of Showlow, later incorporated as part of Lakeside), then back to Ellsworth and Adair, returning home on 15 September. In a later trip to Pinetop, 12 September 1899, she records, "The bishop said the people was so dissatisfied he did not think it would do any good to try and have any primary" (p. 378).

In addition to her work with the ward Relief Society, Lucy worked as a Sunday School teacher both in Beaver and Snowflake. She received a great deal of satisfaction in her church work and on the whole seems to have had a good opinion of her performance, always, of course, giving the credit to her Heavenly Father.

Her most memorable religious experience was a trip to the dedication of the Salt Lake Temple in April 1893. The family went by wagon to Beaver, where they stopped for a few days in order to wash, iron, and mend their clothes. In company with many of Lucy's relatives from Beaver, they continued to Milford by wagon and then "took the cares [train]" (p. 52) to Salt Lake City where they stayed with other relatives. There they attended conference and on 6 April Lucy and William attended the "Great council meeting," the first of thirty-one dedicatory services for the Salt Lake Temple (p. 53). On 8 April they attended another session in the temple with the Beaver and outlying wards. Of these experiences she records, "After being absent from Salt Lake so many years to go to that Grand Tabernicle and here that great Organ it brings tears of joy to my eyes. . . . The Temple was grand and butifull its descriptio[n] has been given to meny time for me to discribe it or even try but it is beond discription butifull in every part" (pp. 53–54).

On that same day they did some temple work. Concerning this, Joseph F. Smith said to them, "Isent that nice Brother Flake yor names Will go on the record as the first work done in this Temple that is a great credit to you" (p. 55). He then led them on a tour of several different rooms and gave them temple cards so that they could attend a session the next morning. After spending several days in Salt Lake City participating in the various meetings during the dedication and in visiting relatives, they returned to Beaver on the train. On 18 April they started back to Arizona. "We dared not stay any longer," Lucy records, "for fear the Big Colorado would be so high we could not cross it" (pp. 56–57).

Throughout her life it was Lucy's religious work that sustained her, but it was the day-by-day drudgery which gradually took its toll on her health. Because they had the only house of any size in Snowflake, there was always a multitude of guests. Army officers from Fort Apache and travelers from "every station in life partook of their hospitality," recalls O. D. Flake. "Although the greater majority were strangers they had never met before, they often supplied whole families for long periods of time. Don't ask me how they did it. I was there (part of the time) but I do not know. A quilt on the floor was our lot; in a year or two, when we had more room, and I could sleep on a bed stead (home made), they often brought in a stranger to share my bed. Sometimes, when there were many of them, I was told to put on my clothes and go up, and crawl in bed with the Hunt boys."[7] Their son John tells that he never knew who would be in his bed when he returned late. On one such night, going to bed without any light to see, he inadvertently got into bed with two women but was happily able to slip out in the morning before they awakened.[8]

Besides the labor of having many guests, the quantity and variety of the everyday work, often with only primitive tools available, made life hard. In addition to the usual housekeeping, including the almost daily churning of butter using milk from as many as nine cows, which she often had to milk alone, Lucy made all the family clothes as well as the blankets and mattresses, using both feathers and corn husks. She also made the usual household furnishings such as rugs, curtains, cushions, and endless "Tidys" (coverings for just about everything). The woolen clothes usually began with raw wool which she picked, carded, spun, and dyed. Much of the sewing was for other members of the family. In addition to working in the house, she incubated chickens and eventually sold their eggs; raised ducks, pigs, and the family garden; husked and shelled the corn; made candles and cheese; and did other chores too numerous to mention.

Lucy's diary reflects the effect that this work had on her.

11 October 1895: "John and me milked as usual then got breakfast then went and picked sixteen Ducks then came in and done up my work" (p. 134).

18 April 1897: "I work to hard am tired all the time but if I dont work I would study till I would go crazy so it seemes I have to work in order to keep from doing worse" (p. 234).

25 May 1898: "I have worked so hard all day til 6 o clock cleening then cleaned the cupbord the doors and meny other cleaned my bed stead and floor I'm very tired" (p. 308).

23 December 1898: "I made 17 pies done up all my work nice . . . came home and fixed a cushion for rocking chair and now 11 o clock I must go to bed" (pp. 340–41).

13 April 1899: "Done up work cleaned kitchen floor made pie and after went to sisters meeting. . . . I bought screen to make me some screen doors as I never had any. . . . it seems

we have worked hard and we ought to have some comforts in our declining years" (p. 357).

14 April: "Done my ironing and other work and was dredful tired" (p. 357).

On 22 December 1899, during the month before her death, she records: "Swept both floors and chored a round the house most all day. . . . We have concluded to have a Christmas Dinner here at our Home for the Familey" (p. 390).

23 December: "I made some pies ironed a little cooked beets done up my work and finished Joel mittens knit them this week and Reginold a pair of Stockings I think that is good for a person that is called sick" (p. 390). She carried this heavy workload almost to the end of her life.

Besides the hard work, the weather made living on the frontier hard. Inadequate heating and poor insulation made the house uncomfortable during much of the year. Lucy talks of the heat in summer but is more affected by the cold. On 25 January 1898 she writes, "Last night was the coldest night we have had I sewed today it seems like we cannot leave the fire it is so cold" (p. 286).

26 October 1899: "It is very cold last night was the coldest this fall . . . this house is very cold" (p. 384). But it was the spring season that was the real problem. In the spring, in the vicinity of Snowflake, the wind blows for about three months. It begins in March and blows almost continually (at least during the day) until well into June. This often makes it necessary for farmers to haul the first hay crop during the night to try to keep it from blowing away. Local residents feel that by June all the dirt from Snowflake has been blown to Holbrook, only to be replaced by that from Taylor and Shumway.

Lucy was bothered greatly by the wind. Following are a few of her many (almost daily) references to the constant wind.

15 June 1895: "It seems dreary when the wind blows and everything is makeing a rackit" (p. 113).

5 May 1896: "I washed and it is a dredfull day I could not hang out one peace" (p. 175).

6 May: "Wind very bad could not hang out my clothes yet" (p. 175).

7 May: "The wind is dredfull" (p. 176).

9 May: "The wind blows very hard in the evening it was very cold we suffered with the cold coming home" (p. 176).

10 May: "Brother Flake and John Started for Apache this morning with freight and the wind blows very hard I am on the place all a lone it seems like this country was going to blow a way" (pp. 175–76).

2 June 1898: "The wind blows very hard to day I feel quite miserable" (p. 309).

The wind particularly bothered her when it was combined with her loneliness and her poor health.

13 March 1898: "The wind blows all to day—I did not go to meeting it blows so hard" (p. 295).

16 May: "The wind blew all night and today it is just fearful we have not had such a day this spring the men folks can t work it look like it would tare the trees all to peaces" (p. 307).

12 October 1899: "It is lonely when it is such stormy wether" (p. 382).

Offsetting the loneliness and the ill health brought on by overwork and the weather was her association with family and friends. January 1896 (pp. 152–59) provides a sufficient sample to see that these associations were apparently important to her peace of mind:

1st: "We all our familey took our food and went over to Marys and had a familey Dinner there Was fifty two of us . . . eleven that did not belong to our familey."

2d: "I fasted and went to fast meeting and Sisters meeting."

3rd: "I was invited to spend the day at Sister Frisbys to day also Mary."

5th: "Sister Whipple has been spending a few days with me . . . after meeting went to help wash and change Sister Oakley."

6th: "In the evening went to conjoint meeting."

7th: "Mary came and spent the day with me in the evening

helped to make up a diagram for our department in Sunday School for three month."

8th: "All well but John . . . we expect William home to day this is seven days he has been gon In loking over some of my papers or letters I find Charles Confermation also a letter he wrote me."

9th: "I invited Belle and her children to come and spend the day and they came."

10th: "William took me up to Brother Whipples I spent the day."

11th: "Myself and first councler Sister Willis Went to Shumway."

12th: "We are prepareing for a review in Sunday School."

14th: "Aunt Mary came and slept with me last night today I went and helped Elsie to quilt."

15th: "This afternoon I went and set with Mary her baby is quite poorly."

16th: "This is Sister Gemima Smiths birthday . . . after the meeting was out we had a pass around."

17th: "Brother Flake came home this evening feeling first class. I was called to go to a prair meeting for Sarah Freeman."[9]

18th: "William is going to Woodruff as home mishonary I with my counclers went to Taylor to meet with the Primary."

19th: "This is Ward Conferance I was caled to represent the Releier Society of this ward."

20th: "William came home this afternoon."

22d: "William and myself are invited to Brother Ramseys birthday supper."

24th: "We went to Pine-dale and met with the Primary."

25th: "Came home this afternoon at three o clock stratened up the front room then met with the Primary in this place after supper got a note from Maria Bushman Smith that her mother was here and it was her birthday they wished me to come and spend the evening."

26th: "We went to Sunday School . . . in the evening the Sisters had officers meeting. . . . Sister West came home with me from afternoon meeting and took supper."

28th: "Elsie and her girls spent the day with me." It is on the days that she did not have visitors or did not go visiting that she talks of loneliness and ill health. Such a picture reveals the common lot of many pioneers.

A fellowship similar to her immediate family and friends was the unity of the sisters of the ward. Although this unity was important to Lucy, it was her association with Mary J. West which provided her with endless pleasure and spiritual aid. She had served as Mary's first counselor in the ward Relief Society from its organization until November 1895. On 17 November she records that Sister West had been chosen second counselor in the stake organization (p. 140). Commenting on this on 1 December, Lucy states, "Sister West is a dear good women she is the Warmest friend I have and it was a seavear trial to us both when she was chosen to fill her new place as second councler in this stake" (p. 146).

Again, on 23 February 1896, Lucy records, "I went to my dear Sister Wests We went up stares and prayed togather I was feeling very much tired in my feelings after we had prair Sister West said she felt impressed to bless me which she did and she gave me one of the greatest blessing I ever got" (p. 163).

13 September: "Went to Sunday School after it was out went up and saw Sister West we went up stares and had secret prair togather" (p. 197).

7 January 1898: "Went up to My Dear Sister Wests and we talked and then went up stares and poured out our soles in prair. . . . I put my hands on her head and blessed her and she blest me" (p. 282).

On 5 May 1899 she records, "My Dear Friend Sister West came and stayed till six o clock we had such a good visit talking over our past life and labors to gather We have been one for 20 years" (p. 359).

On 28 September she spent the day with Sister West before her departure for Salt Lake City: "It seemed hard to say good by" (p. 380).

1 October: "When it [teachers meeting] was out went to

Sister Wests House. She had gon it seemed so sad to have her go" (p. 381).

On 29 October she records, "I wrote a letter to my Dear Friend Sister West it seems lonely without her" (p. 384).

It is not mere coincidence that Lucy died soon after Sister West departed for Salt Lake City. In a letter from Mary J. West to May H. Larson, Mary states, "We have heard several times that sister Flake was not well but when Annie said in her letter that their play was put off on account of her serious illness and told us how bad she was I felt like a bolt of electricity had struck me, and I can hardly think of any thing else. Oh! we have been together so much I can almost feel her by my side, encouraging me on to good works. She always called *me* the comforter, but *not* so—she never knew how much comfort and support she was to me. . . . I felt like I was encircled by a bond of gold when she was near me" (p. 396).[10] The loss of the spiritual union between these two women undoubtedly had an effect on Lucy's illness as she did not have someone to raise her spirits and bolster her with the fortitude to continue.

Harder to bear than the daily hardships of the frontier and even the loss of Mary West was the death of Lucy's son Charles Love Flake. Charles received a telegram concerning an outlaw wanted for killings in New Mexico. He and James, his brother, attempted to arrest the man, and in the struggle James was shot in the ear and Charles in the neck. Charles lived for an hour and a half. "No other person would not be missed more or caused more sorrow than did his death," Lucy records (p. 49). His untimely death was a terrible blow to Lucy, one she could not forget. In the autobiography, even the sorrow at leaving Charles on the Colorado River as they were moving to Arizona was colored by her feelings concerning his death. In the letter from Mary J. West to May Larson, she continues, "But if her work is unfinished she will yet live. Yet I thought for several months before I left that she was not so ambitious for the future as she used to be and she told me once that sometimes she wanted to see Charley so bad she could hardly endure it"

(p. 396).[11] Each year on Charley's birthday, Lucy would mention Charley's name, something she did not do for her other dead children.

Poor health was always a problem for Lucy. In 1874 she had an illness that kept her in bed for weeks. At one point her children had to be kept from her for three weeks, and her husband was recalled from a mission working on the St. George Temple. She did no housework for four months. The nature of the illness is not clear. Some of her statements in her daily diary concerning her illness include the following.

29 March 1895: "I was sick all night was very sick all day Friday Did not eat one bit nor drink and was sick all night" (p. 100).

12 July 1895: "I did not feel very well and at night was very sick with sick head ache" (p. 118). The headache she often had is similar to a migraine and seemed to get progressively worse as she aged.

1 February 1896: "I am feeling quite poorley with pain in my sholders and back I beleave my liver is affected also my kidneys have sent for some Medicen to salt lake" (p. 159).

5 February: "Yesterday worked very hard and went to bed with the sick-head ache and was dredfull sick threw up" (p. 160).

2 June: "I fell very tired and my back aches very much to day but I have my work to do" (p. 179).

25 November: "I tryed three times to get up but was so very sick could not set up sick to my stumick and dizzy could hardley open my eyes and such a head ache" (p. 208).

11 January 1897: "I was sick in bed all day with a bilious spell and sick head ache" (p. 218).

2 May: "The Bell rang for afternoon meeting my head ached so bad I did not go" (p. 235).

9 June: "I was very Sick all night Pukeing and purgin and very sick all day" (p. 242).

2 June: "The wind blows very hard to day I feel quite miserable I have so much pains and aches since conference" (p. 308).

13 June: "I had a very sick head ache last night" (p. 310).

5 December 1898: "Have been lame in my back and hips for a month" (p. 338). In the spring of 1899 she went to St. Johns to see a dentist and had all her teeth pulled—a result of the deterioration of her health.

Finally, there is the drudgery of living on the frontier. She relates traveling during the winter, having gone between Snowflake and Beaver nine times—four hundred miles and a difficult road to travel. Traditionally these trips were made during the winter since all were needed on the farm during the summer.

11 September 1896: "It seemes so lonely I can hardley endure it sometimes it seems like I cant stand it . . . if it was not for the consolation we get in prair we could not stand our trials but our Hevenly Father is so mercifull we dont have to call on him in vain" (p. 196).

6 January 1897: "It has froze in the kitchen nights all this week" (p. 217).

30 December: "It takes so much time chooring no one to bring in a stick of wood or any choores at all" (p. 276).

21 January 1898: "Jeff Adams and his companion came here last night and this afternoon they comenced to repair our Well it caved in two years agoae and We had no use of it since" (p. 285).

18 August: "The wether is very warm and flies are very bad one can hardley write" (p. 322).

30 January 1899: "I boilt over pork brian and melted snow to wash with" (p. 346).

A fine example of her coping with such situations seems to be summed up in an entry for 17 April 1899: "I dont feel well had a very bad head ache all night did not sleep till after 12 o clock cleaned a chicken churned done up my work and got dinner it dont do any good for me to feel bad I have to work" (p. 357). Again on 29 September: "I was in much pain all night but had to church and Wash when I got done could hardley hold up and layed on the bed most all the afternoon and had a hot feavor and it lasted most all night I have to much hard work to do and work to hard" (p. 380).

As the year wore on, her diary entries became more and more of a combination of her hard work and her loneliness.

9 October: "The wind blows it seems lonesome up hear now" (p. 382).

10 November: "I dont feel well done up my work and was sick the rest of the day" (p. 386).

13 November: "Was on my feet all day putting things in order it takes so long" (p. 386).

7 December: "Worked so hard yesterday am sick today" (p. 389).

The diary breaks after the eighth, and she does not attempt to catch it up except for this entry: "Dear Journel since I wrote last I have been very sick took sick on the ninth of this month had been feeling very bad for a week was very sick. . . . I got worse and worse till the Twelfth that morning I changed for the better but was very week but have been improving slowly" (p. 390).

But this improvement was not to continue. Lucy Hannah White Flake became ill again after the first of the year and died Saturday, 27 January 1900. The exact nature of the illness is not known, but it has been suggested by many who have read the diary that it was a combination of hard work, loneliness, the death of her son Charles, the loss of the ministration of Mary J. West, rigors of frontier, and her chronic headaches and other health problems. The final entry in her diary is 31 December 1899: "I went to Sunday School this is the first time since Conferance I invited Samuel Smith and John Rodgers home with me they came and we had good visit and went to meeting this closes the year with all its cares and sorrows and its Joys we will say good bye" (p. 391).

Notes

1. The original holograph volumes of the Lucy Hannah White Flake Diary are located in Special Collections, Harold B. Lee Library, Brigham Young University, Provo, Utah. I have used the pagination from the typed manuscript hereafter cited parenthetically in the text.

2. They freed all of their slaves but two: Green, who entered the valley with the Vanguard Wagon Train of 1847 in order to build a home for the family, and Liz, who stayed with the family until the death of Agnes Love Flake in San Bernardino.

3. Osmer D. Flake, *William J. Flake, Pioneer–Colonizer*. (Phoenix: Published by the author, [1948?], pp. 30–31.

4. Ibid., p. 49.

5. Ibid., pp. 74–75.

6. Although the Relief Society of The Church of Jesus Christ of Latter-day Saints had been organized in Nauvoo in 1842, its implementation in the West was very slow. The first Societies were formed as early as 1853 but continued sporadically through 1857, when the Utah Expedition interrupted again. In 1866 Brigham Young recommended that Societies be organized in every ward and branch, and in 1877 stake organizations were beginning to be formed. Although the range of the Relief Society work was broad, from silk culture, cooperative stores and granaries, disaster relief, cultural halls, suffrage, donations to hospitals, and later on, war work, the Society on the Arizona frontier seemed more modest, with spiritual comfort being the most important facet. Snowflake Stake would later, however, purchase a woolen mill as part of its activities.

7. Flake, *William J. Flake,* p. 75–76.

8. Interview with John T. Flake.

9. The use of Brother Flake instead of William predominates the last part of her diary. One can only speculate on its reason. Was it due to age and a less intimate relationship? or was it that the Church terminology had begun to dominate her writing? or was she just following the convention common to the nineteenth century?

10. Extracts of Mary J. West's letter to May H. Larson dated 30 January 1900 were copied into the third journal by Roberta Flake Clayton.

11. Ibid.

D. Gene Pace

10

Elijah F. Sheets:
The Half-century Bishop

D. Gene Pace was born in Salt Lake City. He now lives in
Kentucky with his wife and four children, where he teaches
history at Alice Lloyd College. He has taught at the high
school, community college, and college level. He received
his B.S. and M.A. from Brigham Young University and a
Ph.D. from Ohio State University. Gene has published
articles related to Mormon history in the *Journal of the
West* and *Brigham Young University Studies.* This article on
Bishop Elijah Sheets grew out of his doctoral dissertation on
the roles of nineteenth-century Mormon bishops in selected
communities.

Elijah F. Sheet's forty-eight-year tenure as bishop exceeded
that of any other bishop ever to serve in The Church of Jesus
Christ of Latter-day Saints. He served as bishop of the Salt Lake
City Eighth Ward from 1856 to 1904. He also served at the
central Church level as a traveling bishop, as the Church's head
livestock agent, and as an assistant trustee-in-trust.[1] Elijah
Sheets became one of the most influential bishops in Mormon
history.

Born on 22 March 1821, in Charlestown, Pennsylvania, Elijah was the son of Frederick Sheets and Hannah Page. Orphaned when only six years old, he resided with his grandparents; after approximately two years he moved in with the Edward Hunter family.[2] The Hunter-Sheets "father-son" relationship paralleled their subsequent interaction in Church administration. Edward Hunter rose to the position of Presiding Bishop and Elijah Sheets emerged as one of Hunter's most prominent subordinates. Appropriately, Presiding Bishop Hunter assisted in ordaining Sheets as a ward bishop in 1856.[3]

In 1840 nineteen-year-old Elijah entered the Church through baptism. He demonstrated his loyalty to the Church by moving to Nauvoo, Illinois, in 1841 and becoming an elder in 1842. The Nauvoo years brought maturity to the Church in general and to Sheets personally. While in Nauvoo, Sheets performed a half-year of voluntary labor on the Nauvoo Temple without compensation. Prior to moving with the Saints to Utah in 1847, he served proselyting missions to Pennsylvania and Great Britain.[4] In 1850 Sheets took part in the settlement of Iron County, Utah.

After returning to Salt Lake City to live, Elijah F. Sheets became bishop of the Eighth Ward in 1856. During his tenure as bishop, however, Sheets did not reside continuously within the Eighth Ward boundaries or even in Salt Lake City. While still bishop, he moved to Provo where he became a counselor in the stake presidency, serving under Abraham O. Smoot.[5] Sheets later left the Provo area, but his stay there illustrates that in the nineteenth century a bishop was not necessarily released when residing in another city. Even when Sheets served a proselyting and genealogical mission to Pennsylvania in 1869 and 1870, he was not released as bishop. Perhaps it is appropriate that when he finally was released in 1904, Bishop Sheets did not reside in the ward he presided over.[6]

Elijah F. Sheets, like many other nineteenth-century bishops, practiced plural marriage. Although he married four wives, at no time was Sheets married to more than two living wives. His practice of plural marriage led to his imprisonment during the federal government's anti-polygamy "raid" in the 1880s.[7] Imprisoned Mormons chose obedience to religious law over adherence to what they considered an unconstitutional violation of their religious freedom. As did other imprisoned Mormons, Bishop Sheets seemed to consider his incarceration as more of an honor than a condemnation. While in the penitentiary he posed for a photograph with other inmates in his prison apparel, and following his release from the "pen" his ward gave him a hero's welcome at a social gathering they held in his honor.[8] Abraham A. Kimball, an imprisoned bishop who was in poor health, mentioned Bishop Sheets in his journal. In one entry reflecting Sheet's concern for the ailing bishop, Bishop Kimball noted that "Bp E. F. Sheets gave me a Peice of homade cake." In the same entry Bishop Kimball wrote:

> I also received a nice peice of cheess which I was wishing for while at Supper. Bp E. F. Sheets called with Some grapes and asked me if I would like a peice of Cheess I Said yes he said his partner cell mate had Some he Came in a few minutes. he was the man hansen who runs the Cache Valley Cheese factory.[9]

Sheets was not simply an ordinary ward bishop. He became the senior ward bishop in the Church, in addition to playing prominent roles in central Church leadership. This chapter focuses on the administrative activities of Bishop Sheets in order to provide insights into his leadership abilities, his personality, and his character. It also seeks to broaden our understanding of LDS administrative practices in the nineteenth century. In dealing with his activities as a ward bishop, this chapter explores several themes: Sheet's attempt to promote spiritual and temporal unity within his ward, his use of teachers to extend his influence, and his attitudes and practices regarding social welfare.

Spiritual and Temporal Unity

As bishop of the Eighth Ward, Elijah Sheets sought to promote both spiritual and temporal unity within his congregation. His desire for social homogeneity reflected his strong support for the central Church leadership. During the 1850s when Jedediah M. Grant and other General Authorities made a concerted effort to purify the Church spiritually, Bishop Sheets carried out this "reformation" on the ward level. Taking his cue from the upper-echelon Church leadership, Sheets stressed the reformation. At an 1856 Sunday evening service, Bishop Sheets told his ward "that President Grant . . . gave the bishops instructions to get up a reformation in their wards that they might reform and be honest, pay their debts and tithing, and live as Saints of the most high, . . . to be more faithful and keep all of the commandments."[10] He continued to stress the reformation in subsequent church meetings.[11] In 1857 many of the members of his ward demonstrated their desire for personal reform by being rebaptized.[12]

Bishop Sheets also demonstrated his support for his ecclesiastical superiors by supporting their position regarding temporal self-sufficiency. In 1867 he stated that "he wished the teachers to encourage home manufactures."[13]

Besides encouraging the Saints to produce their own goods, Sheets also gave strong backing to the Church's policy of boycotting gentile merchants. Anticipating the completion of the transcontinental railroad, which reached Utah in 1869, Brigham Young advocated preserving Mormon independence from outside financial control by supporting Mormon businesses and avoiding those owned by Gentiles. As a part of this effort, Zion's Cooperative Mercantile Institution (Z.C.M.I.) was established in Salt Lake City. Branches of this parent store sprang up in many other Mormon settlements.[14]

Advocating President Young's stance on economic self-sufficiency, Bishop Sheets, at a Utah Stake bishops' meeting on 23 March 1869, expressed support for the idea of limiting consumer patronage to a single store in order to "dry up all the retail trade."[15] The following day at a meeting of bishops, their counselors, and the presiding Relief Society officers of Provo's four wards, Bishop Sheets spoke concerning the blessings he felt would accompany adherence to the Church's position. He felt that the Church's plan would "unite the faithful" and expose those who refused to submit "to the control of the holy priesthood."[16] And Bishop Sheets wanted to begin immediately. "We ought to go into business within one week from this. Such a society cannot fail, for we ought all to understand that it becomes our duty to invariably trade at our own store and in this manner build it up." He suggested that the bishops and their counselors serve on the board of directors of the proposed retail store.[17]

At a Utah Stake bishops' meeting held 31 August 1869, Bishop Sheets stated that he did not consider a certain merchant to be a friend of the Church. He recommended "that the teachers visit every man and warn them that their fellowship is in danger if they continue trading with [the merchant under consideration]"[18] Later, at a teachers' meeting held in the Salt Lake Eighth Ward on 26 October 1869, Sheets stated that "cooperation to some seemed to be a bug bear, but he was satisfied that it was only a stepping stone to greater things that will come."[19]

Sheets's Use of Teachers

Bishop Sheets used his teachers, the nineteenth-century parallel of modern-day home teachers, to enable him to maintain contact with ward members. Sheets met with his teachers personally to hear their reports, to make recommendations to them, and to provide personal direction for solving the problems of the ward. He was convinced that the service which the teachers provided was fundamental to the well-being of the ward. "There was no more important position in the Church than that of a good faithful teacher," he once remarked.[20] At a teachers' meeting held in 1880, Bishop Sheets instructed his teachers to visit every member of the ward "at least once a month and as much oftener as possible." To emphasize the importance of their service, he told the Eighth Ward teachers that they were "as much on a mission as if they were sent to the nations of the earth and God required as much diligence from them."[21] And Bishop Sheets did not exempt himself from needing visits from the teachers. At an 1875 teachers' meeting, Sheets notified the teachers that probably a year had elapsed since the last time teachers had visited his house. Because he felt that "the teachers had an influence that was good among the people both old and young,"[22] Sheets missed their visits and did not want the teachers to overlook visiting his house.

Sheets believed that the teachers must live sufficiently righteous lives to merit the responsibilities of their office. At a teachers' meeting held in 1879, Sheets dealt with a teacher who previously had been "suspended as acting as a teacher because he was fighting." Because of these actions Sheets and his counselors had called the teacher before the bishop's court. The teacher had become offended at the proceedings of the court. Sheets maintained that the teacher's behavior left the bishopric no other choice than to act as they had. Their action is not specified in the minutes of the teachers' meeting. Sheets argued, "We would not be justified in receiving [the teacher] into our bosoms without some restitution." The bishop stated that he was "willing to take [the teacher] in full fellowship if he will manifest a penitent Spirit and make suitable reparation." The wayward teacher responded by apologizing for hurting the bishopric's feelings, requesting they forgive him, and assuring them he would try to do better. Following his statement he "was restored to full fellowship."[23]

Besides using his teachers to assist him in his general overseeing of the ward, Bishop Sheets called on them to fulfill specific assignments, such as enlisting their aid in carrying out his responsibilities regarding tithing. At an 1873 teachers' meeting, Bishop Sheets's counselor, Isaac Brockbank, explained that the meeting's primary objective was to ask the teachers to visit the members of the Eighth Ward in order to learn what occupations they had, how much remuneration they had received for their work, and the amount and kind of tithing they had paid thus far in 1873. Following Brockbank's introduction of the subject, Bishop Sheets and his other counselor, John McAllister, followed by addressing the same theme. The inquiry began in the meeting itself with Sheets and others reporting their income and tithing paid during the year. The following week the teachers returned to report their findings. Although not all of the desired information had been acquired, the status of twenty-five ward members was disclosed.[24]

Bishop Sheets also called upon his teachers to encourage political participation. At an 1874 teachers' meeting, he "referred to election matters and wished the brethren to see that the folks were urged to go to the polls and vote."[25] In 1885 the bishop told the teachers he appreciated the vigilance of the people at the previous school trustee election, and now that another election was at hand he "urged the teachers to be as vigilant as before in getting the people to vote."[26] In 1889, prior to another school trustee election, he "urged the Brethren to see that all the voters turn out."[27]

In addition, Bishop Sheets relied on his teachers to settle problems within the ward. The teachers were to be tolerant but not to the point of improperly condoning unrighteousness. However, Sheets displayed a sensitivity to different circumstances of persons within his ward. In 1883 he referred to an unspecified difficulty between two parties and stated that he wanted the teachers to attempt to settle the matter without resorting to a bishop's court. Although willing to hold courts when he deemed it necessary, Sheets in this case advised the teachers "to be lenient toward them as they were very ignorant in the principles of the Gospel and like little children and needed more teaching than others of more experience."[28]

But Sheets did not believe that the teachers could simply overlook serious transgression without becoming personally responsible before God for such neglect of duty. At an 1875 teachers' meeting, Sheets remarked that "he thought that *mercy* ought not to rob *justice.*" In the case being considered, Sheets stated that "he wished the teachers to find out if the parties that had been reported wished to belong to the Church." He then warned that "the responsibility was upon the teachers until they were brought before the bishop and council."[29] In 1882 two teachers wrote Bishop Sheets a letter stating that they had been unable to resolve a difficulty with a brother in the ward and consequently desired to turn the matter over to the bishop "that sin may not be attached to [them] as teachers in longer tolerating such unchristianlike conduct."[30] Elijah Sheets taught his teachers to balance tolerance with inquiry into unacceptable conduct and with the application of necessary religious sanctions.

Social Welfare

Caring for the poor constituted one of the most important responsibilities Sheets assumed as bishop of the Eighth Ward. Consequently, understanding his attitudes toward social welfare is not only important in understanding Bishop Sheets but also in understanding nineteenth-century bishops in general, assuming that his thinking was representative. Because bishops held, to a significant extent, the purse strings in their wards, the social attitudes they espoused were of particular importance.

Elijah Sheets was personally charitable. He believed that "all that we have is the Lord's and when He wishes it, to gather the poor from the nations or perform any work to build up the kingdom of God, it should be on hand."[31] At an 1859 teachers' meeting, Bishop Sheets and twelve others each donated one-half cord of wood for the benefit of the poor. At an 1864 meeting, Bishop Sheets and others spoke regarding fulfilling the needs of the poor, and Sheets again donated one-half cord of wood for their benefit.[32] In 1863, Sheets spoke concerning "raising means to send to the Frontiers for the Poor" and then pledged a yoke of oxen, a wagon, and three hundred pounds of flour to that end.[33] In responding to the need for similar assistance in 1864, Sheets spoke on the subject at the teachers' meeting and then followed by promising to furnish one yoke of cattle, one hundred pounds of flour, and a dried beef.[34] Following the arrival of a train of immigrants in 1865, the *Deseret News* reported that "Bishop Sheets, Elder Goddard and others of our citizens were busy with the new comers, finding them homes, looking to their welfare and otherwise having them properly cared for."[35]

Besides being willing to part with his own means when he felt the occasion warranted, Sheets was also convinced that the Church should help provide for the legitimate needs of the poor. As a bishop he contributed Church funds to their welfare. In January 1882, the bishop spoke concerning "the many poor" which the Eighth Ward supported totally or partially and told the teachers "the poor must not be neglected."[36] Also in April of that year, a report made at the teachers' meeting indicated that the funds used to support the ward's poor were low. The minutes stated, "At present we were in debt but still the poor never have suffered in this Ward."[37] Sheets felt that the Latter-day Saints should be willing to produce not only for themselves but also for others. "The man who raises a bushel of wheat more than he needs for his own consumption has done so much for the general good," he explained. "He must be a slothful servant who produces nothing more than he consumes."[38]

Sheets's brand of charity, however, did not include over-generous giving. At a July 1882 teachers' meeting, Sheets listened to a statement regarding a man whose wife had argued that her husband needed hospitalization, apparently to be funded by the ward. After several of those present disagreed with the woman's request, Bishop Sheets remarked that this case was "peculiar" and had "two sides." "In the first place," he explained, "the man's family had ought to care for him in his affliction." Besides, he continued, "This Ward is out of funds and are now owing for the care of the poor already."[39] In 1889, Bishop Sheets explained that he favored assisting "all worthy poor." He did not favor helping persons who could work but were simply lazy.[40] Sheets advocated providing assistance for those who would otherwise suffer, but he opposed aiding those who could take care of their own needs. "The more we help some people," he once said, "the more they need help."[41] The bishop also believed that poverty involved not only actual conditions but also depended to some extent on one's attitude concerning his circumstances. According to Sheets, "Those who feel poor always will be poor."[42]

In spite of his philosophical sympathies toward the poor, the reality of providing for their assistance seemed to temper Sheets's idealism. The bishop's statements at an 1884 teachers' meeting illustrate this dualism in his attitudes toward the poor. The immediate matter at hand was a bill Bishop Sheets had received from the teacher of the "Day School" requesting payment for the schooling of poor children. Sheets counseled those present "that if they fetch people into the ward that are too poor to provide for themselves they should see that they are maintained and not burden the ward with them." Sheets's counselor, Joseph McMurrin, remarked that no ward should be burdened disproportionately for the care of the poor, although he realized that poor people had as much right to choose in which ward to reside as rich people did. He personally favored assisting any poor that he might bring into the Eighth Ward. Bishop Sheets then explained "the difficulties that arise by allowing too many poor people to crowd into any ward without a bishop's knowledge or consent." He thought that as bishop he had the right to make sure "that the ward was not imposed upon." Sheets attempted to clarify his position concerning the poor by arguing that he was not unfair to them. He noted that he had instructed two brethren in the ward "never to deny anyone whenever they applied [for assistance] or it was known in any way that they needed help."[43]

In 1889 Sheets told the teachers, perhaps with some sarcasm, "We must be doing better to the poor than others; hence the reason why they flock in."[44] Sheets's thinking reflected support of a safety-valve philosophy: overcrowded wards and the poor could benefit from relocating the poor into less settled areas, commonly referred to as "the country." Several months after his ordination as bishop in 1856, Sheets recommended that the poor be counseled "to go into the country." He did not want poor persons brought into the Eighth Ward by anyone who was unable to provide for their support, and he hoped to prevent the ward's becoming over-burdened with "more than [its] share of the poor."[45] Sheets still seemed to be trying to implement this safety-valve philosophy in 1880 when he stated that provision for housing in the country had been made for a brother but that the man was unwilling to accept the arrangement.[46]

In the life of Bishop Sheets we see the paradox that he faced as an administrator of voluntary donations made to the Church. He walked a philosophical tightrope. On the one hand, because of personal charitable feelings and adherence to Mormon doctrine, which advocated proper care of the poor, he dared not neglect the poor. On the other hand, he was philosophically opposed to doing too much for the poor. The paradox he faced and the balance he attempted to maintain were reflected in his statements and actions while bishop. The charitable Sheets donated for the relief of the poor, yet wished he were not "blessed" with more than his due share of the needy in his ward. He continually stressed the need not to overlook the needs of the poor, but also wished more of them would move out into the country. Sheets apparently saw no inconsistency in his social welfare attitudes and practices. To him the overriding philosophy of doing what was best for the poor encompassed both the need for charitable donations and the obligation to act in the best interests of the poor by not providing too much, to their detriment.

Expanded Leadership Duties

Sheets was more than an ordinary bishop. He stood somewhere between the local ward bishops and the General Authorities over the entire Church. In 1871 Sheets became a traveling bishop, the last one to be called in the Church. With his appointment to this position, Sheets became one of a small group of men who served as traveling bishops in nineteenth-century Utah, including John Banks, Alfred Cordon, Nathaniel H. Felt, David Fullmer, Abraham Hoaglend, A. Milton Musser, David Pettigrew, Daniel Spencer, and Seth Taft.[47] Sheets's letter of appointment, written by the First Presidency, detailed the duties which presiding officers expected him to assume.

> Salt Lake City U[tah] T[erritory]
> 28 April 1871

Elder Elijah F. Sheets
   Dear Brother.

You are hereby authorized and appointed to act as a Traveling Bishop throughout the settlements in Utah, Juab, San Pete and Millard Counties, and such other places as the First Presidency shall direct to take a general supervision of all Tithing donated in the district to which you are or may be assigned, and to see that all tithing butter, eggs, cheese, cash &c, be forwarded to the General Tithing Store in kind as received as well as all grain, vegetables, stock, &c, unless otherwise directed by the First Presidency, you will also counsel and advise with the Elders and Saints where you are, or may be appointed to travel, in such manner as the Holy Spirit may inspire, and advice from us from time to time may direct in temporal matters pertaining to the well-being of the Saints and the upbuilding of the Kingdom of God upon the earth.

That you may be constantly guided by the Spirit of the Lord to be as a father to the people, that your labors may prove a blessing to them, and to yourself, and that you may be an instrument in the hands of the Lord in doing a good work in the mission to which you are assigned

   Is the Prayer of your Brethren

> Brigham Young
> Geo. A. Smith
> Daniel H. Wells[48]

As noted in his letter of appointment, Sheets became an agent designated to service under the direction of the First Presidency. Traveling Bishop Sheets, like local ward bishops, received an assignment regarding tithing administration. Unlike ward bishops, however, Sheets served as a traveling representative to the General Tithing Storehouse in Salt Lake City. As such, he was not subject to the geographical limitations on his authority which he faced as bishop of the Eighth Ward. An example of his service as a traveling bishop comes from Sheets's brief account of his life. In 1871 he wrote, "Prest B. Young Invited me to take a trip with him and his company to Cache Valley & Bare Lake & Soda Springs, Which I did & seen to the Tithing &c."[49] Following his service as traveling bishop, Sheets maintained the conviction that the First Presidency and others under whom he had served were pleased with his performance.[50]

Present information concerning Sheets's activities as a traveling bishop is scanty. Presumably, he carried out the duties assigned him in his letter of appointment. Sheets does not state clearly when he ceased to be a traveling bishop, or even if he were ever released, although his service as a traveling bishop did not continue past 1880. In that year, Orson Pratt stated that there were no traveling bishops currently serving in the Church.[51] The difficulty of discovering what Sheets did as a traveling bishop is increased because of two additional calls he received during the same period. Several months after his call to be a traveling bishop, Sheets replaced Briant Stringham as the Church's livestock agent. He continued in this second position until 1887.[52] Sheets also assumed the prestigious position of assistant trustee-in-trust in April 1873 and continued to act in this central-leadership capacity until September 1875.[53] Because all three callings related to the temporal affairs of the Church, his activities may well have merged and overlapped. Conceivably, Sheets could have dealt with the livestock of the Church, for example, because of his authority as a traveling bishop, livestock agent, or assistant trustee-in-trust.

During the presidencies of Brigham Young and John Taylor, a relatively small number of men served as assistant trustees-in-trust. Elijah Sheets was one of an even smaller number of non-General Authorities to hold that position.[54]

In reflecting on his service to the Church during the administration of President Young, Sheets seemed most proud of his accomplishments with the Church livestock. He recalled, "Our cattle and sheep increased to the thousands during this time

[1871–1877] and the blessing of the Lord was upon them."[55] Following President Young's death, John Taylor retained Sheets as Church livestock agent. From 1878 onward, Sheets was responsible for all the Church's livestock in Utah, Idaho, and Arizona, as well as on all Church farms.[56]

In 1877 an administrative system involving a network of regional bishops, called bishop's agents, was introduced in the Church. This may have alleviated the need for traveling bishops.[57] Nevertheless, on at least one occasion, Sheets received an assignment which resembled his previous calling as a traveling bishop. In a letter written 1 March 1881, President Taylor and Presiding Bishop Hunter wrote to Sheets: "You are hereby requested to proceed to Utah and other Stakes, and in connexion with the Bishops Agents and Bishops to Ascertain the condition of the Tithing hay, Potatoes and other vegetables, and so far as possible make such disposition of the same as will be the most beneficial in the interest of the church."[58] While the reassignment did not call him as a traveling bishop on a permanent basis, it seems to have demonstrated the confidence which the General Authorities placed in this experienced bishop and their desire to utilize his talents and experience.

The Quorum of the Twelve Apostles, the Church's governing body during the interim period between the death of President Young and the ordination of John Taylor as Church President, also continued to take advantage of Sheets's abilities. In 1878 they appointed him to serve on a special committee to study the wages being paid to employees of the trustee-in-trust, including "all Clerks, Laborers, Carpenters, Blacksmiths, Teamsters, and other employees of the Trustee in Trust of the Church . . . in Salt Lake City and vicinity." Following their investigation, the committee was to report to the Quorum of the Twelve.[59] Within a week of the first instructions written to the committee, Sheets and his fellow committee members received expanded responsibilities. The Apostles "unanimously decided to extend the scope of the labors of the Committee on wages." The committee was now also to consider needed changes in the number of employees and in the "mode of doing Church business."[60] The members of the committee, "Bishops L. W. Hardy, Robert T. Burton, E. F. Sheets and John Sharp and Elder A. M. Musser,"[61] ranked among the most prominent men in the Church. The appointment of Sheets to this committee, as well as his continued work as Church live-stock agent, demonstrates the confidence which Elder Taylor and the other Apostles placed in him.

Conclusion

Elijah F. Sheets is unique in the history of the Church because of his forty-eight-year tenure as bishop of the Eighth Ward. Sheets may also be seen as a symbol of an age in which bishops differed from present-day bishops in several notable respects. Sheets typified an era in which a ward bishop could play an important role in Church administration outside his immediate ward. At a time when a number of ward bishops doubled as regional presiding bishops, Sheets rendered signif-icant administrative service on the central Church level with-out being released as head of his ward.[62]

Elijah Sheets differed from modern bishops in his personal contact with the President of the Church and other General Authorities. Sheets valued the praise of his leaders and prided himself on his close association with them.[63] In 1897 he spoke to the members of the Eighth Ward "of his intimate acquain-tance with the prophets from Joseph Smith to Wilford Wood-ruff."[64] Sheets's proximity to Church headquarters, his high-level responsibilities, and the relatively small size of the Church in his day gave him opportunities for personal association with the General Authorities that modern-day bishops do not com-monly enjoy.

Remaining in office for an indefinite, extended period of time, Bishop Sheets could bring more personal influence to his position than if he had been called to serve for a definite, short term as are modern bishops. Sheets's long tenure provided more opportunity for ward members to develop loyalty and emotional attachment to him as a man, and not simply as a bishop, than if he had served for a predetermined short tenure. Under present practices a ward would see about ten bishops called and released with clocklike regularity during the same period of time in which the Eighth Ward came under the leadership of a single personality. Bishop Sheets retained his position for an era, not a brief interval; for a half-century, not a half-decade.

Bishop Sheets expanded his influence in his ward by meeting personally with his representatives, the teachers. He heard their reports and gave suggestions directly rather than communicating through intermediary administrative officers. The less bureaucratic nineteenth-century Mormon ward allowed the bishop an opportunity to personally train his teachers. Elijah F. Sheets could thus impose his personal mode of thinking—his desires for spiritual and temporal unity, his view of the place of teachers in the Church, his social welfare attitudes—on his personal representatives. Elijah Sheets's release as bishop in 1904 resulted not merely in a routine leadership change; it symbolized the end of an era in which a single bishop had personally influenced the nature of the Eighth Ward for decades and had filled key roles in Church administration outside his ward as well.

Notes

1. Elijah F. Sheets, Journal, Elijah F. Sheets Collection, Library-Archives, Historical Department, The Church of Jesus Christ of Latter-day Saints, Salt Lake City, Utah (hereafter cited as LDS Church Archives); Andrew Jenson, *Latter-day Saint Biographical Encyclopedia: A Compilation of Biographical Sketches of Prominent Men and Women in The Church of Jesus Christ of Latter-day Saints,* 4 vols. (Salt Lake City: Andrew Jenson History Co., 1901–36) 1:614–16. For additional information concerning Bishop Sheets and the Eighth Ward, see D. Gene Pace, "Community Leadership on the Mormon Frontier: Mormon Bishops and the Political, Economic, and Social Development of Utah before Statehood" (Ph.D. diss., Ohio State University, 1983).

2. Sheets, Journal; Jenson, *LDS Biographical Encyclopedia,* 1:614.

3. Sheets, Journal.

4. Sheets, Journal; Jenson, *LDS Biographical Encyclopedia,* 1:614.

5. Sheets, Journal; ibid. 1:615.

6. Eighth Ward Historical Record, 12 June 1904, LDS Church Archives.

7. Jenson, *LDS Biographical Encyclopedia,* 1:615; Elijah F. Sheets, Family Group Records Collection, Genealogical Library of The Church of Jesus Christ of Latter-day Saints, Salt Lake City: Sheets, Journal.

8. Sheets, Journal; photograph, Utah State Historical Society. For general background on the government's anti-polygamy efforts, see Leonard J. Arrington, *Great Basin Kingdom: An Economic History of the Latter-day Saints, 1830–1900* (Cambridge: Harvard University Press, 1958), chap. 12, "The Raid," pp. 353–79.

9. Abraham A. Kimball, Journal, 3 December 1888, Harold B. Lee Library, Brigham Young University, Provo, Utah.

10. Eighth Ward Historical Record, 27 September 1856. Punctuation and capitalization edited.

11. For example, see ibid., 1 October 1856, 4 October 1856.

12. Ibid., 7 March 1857.

13. Ibid., 28 February 1867. Capitalization edited.

14. For general background on the Mormon response to the coming of the transcontinental railroad, see Arrington, *Great Basin Kingdom,* "Part Three: The Kingdom Threatened (1869–1884)," pp. 233–349.

15. Meetings of Bishops and Lesser Priesthood, Utah Stake, 23 March 1869, LDS Church Archives.

16. Ibid., 24 March 1869. Spelling edited.

17. Ibid. Punctuation edited.

18. Ibid., 31 August 1869.

19. Eighth Ward Historical Record, 26 October 1869. Spelling and punctuation edited. For excellent background on the priesthood office of teacher, see William G. Hartley, "Ordained and Acting Teachers in the Lesser Priesthood, 1851–1883," *Brigham Young University Studies* 16 (Spring 1976): 375–98.

20. Eighth Ward Historical Record, 14 November 1872. Punctuation and capitalization edited.

21. Ibid., 20 May 1880. Spelling edited.

22. Ibid., 24 June 1875. Capitalization edited.

23. Ibid., 24 April 1879.

24. Ibid., 7 July 1873.

25. Ibid., 31 July 1874. Punctuation and capitalization edited.

26. Ibid., 25 June 1885.

27. Ibid., 5 July 1889.

28. Ibid., 8 March 1883. Capitalization edited.

29. Ibid., 29 April 1875. Punctuation and capitalization edited. Italics in original.

30. Ibid., 9 August 1882. Capitalization edited.

31. Journal History, 9 February 1868, p. 2.

32. Eighth Ward Historical Record, September 1859, 27 October 1864.

33. Ibid., 8 March 1863.

34. Ibid., 3 March 1864.

35. Journal History, 15 November 1865.

36. Eighth Ward Historical Record, 12 January 1882.

37. Ibid., 5 April 1882.

38. Journal History, 9 February 1868, p. 2.

39. Eighth Ward Historical Record, 27 July 1882.

40. Ibid., 3 January 1889.

41. Ibid., 10 December 1885.

42. Ibid., 5 July 1866.

43. Ibid., 26 June 1884. Spelling and capitalization edited.

44. Ibid., 3 January 1889. Punctuation and spelling edited.

45. Ibid., 29 September 1856. Capitalization edited.

46. Ibid., 20 May 1880.

47. For a discussion of traveling bishops, see D. Gene Pace, "Changing Patterns of Mormon Financial Administration: Traveling Bishops, Regional Bishops and Bishop's Agents, 1851–88," *BYU Studies* 23 (Spring 1983): 184–86.

48. Brigham Young, George A. Smith, Daniel H. Wells to Elijah F. Sheets, 28 April 1871, Brigham Young Letterbooks, Brigham Young Papers, LDS Church Archives.

49. Sheets, Journal.

50. Ibid.

51. Orson Pratt, *Journal of Discourses,* 26 vols. (Liverpool, England, 1854–86) 22:34–35. Pratt made his statement on 10 October 1880.

52. Sheets, Journal; Jenson, *LDS Biographical Encyclopedia,* 1:614–16.

53. Sheets, Journal; ibid., 1:42, 614–16.

54. See D. Gene Pace, "The LDS Presiding Bishopric, 1851–1888: An Administrative Study" (Master's thesis, Brigham Young University, 1978),

appendix E, p. 189, for a list of trustees-in-trust sustained at general conferences from April 1851 to October 1891. This list was derived from reports of the conferences found in the *Deseret Weekly News,* the *Deseret Evening News,* and the Journal History, all available at the LDS Church Archives.

55. Sheets, Journal.

56. Ibid.

57. For a discussion of bishop's agents, see Pace, "Changing Patterns of Mormon Financial Administration," pp. 187–90.

58. John Taylor and Edward Hunter to Elijah F. Sheets, 1 March 1881, Edward Hunter Letterbooks, Presiding Bishopric Collection, LDS Church Archives.

59. John Taylor to Bishop L. W. Hardy and Associates, 28 January 1878, Council of the Twelve Apostles, LDS Church Archives.

60. Ibid., 2 February 1878.

61. Ibid., 28 January 1878.

62. The use of regional presiding bishops is discussed in Pace, "Changing Patterns of Mormon Financial Administration," pp. 186–87.

63. Sheets, Journal.

64. Eighth Ward Historical Record, 19 September 1897. Spelling and capitalization edited.

William G. Hartley

11

Edward Hunter: Pioneer Presiding Bishop

A native of California, William G. Hartley now resides with his wife and six children in Sandy, Utah. Hartley is a research historian for BYU's Joseph Fielding Smith Institute for Church History. For eight years he was a historian on the staff of Church Historian, Leonard J. Arrington. William Hartley is a frequent contributor to the *Ensign* and *BYU Studies,* and is a specialist in the history of LDS priesthood and Church government. With Dr. Arrington he is editing a forthcoming collection of essays about LDS administrative history. He received bachelor's and master's degrees from Brigham Young University and completed doctoral course work at Washington State University. This essay on Bishop Edward Hunter stems from Hartley's research into the historical development of the office of Presiding Bishop.

When Heber J. Grant was young, his mother once crossed the street diagonally. Presiding Bishop Edward Hunter met her and said with the usual twinkle in his eye and double phrase on his lips: "Rachel, Rachel, go straight, go straight. Be careful. Cut a corner and miss heaven, cut a corner and miss heaven. Keep in the straight path."[1] Young Heber and other youths of his day grew up mimicking the double phrases of the bewhiskered Pennsylvanian, and they repeated many proverbs and aphorisms they knew were his. Although forgotten today, Edward Hunter was a well-known and well-liked General Authority in his day because he was colorful and a bit eccentric, and because his fair but kindly ways of performing as Presiding Bishop pleased so many Saints.

He was a pioneer Presiding Bishop in two ways. First, he presided during most of the Mormon pioneering years and longer, from 1851 to 1883. His firm hand on the Church's temporal reins helped steer it through dramatic transformations in size and procedures. During his thirty-three-year term, the Rocky Mountain Saints' population grew from 11,000 to over 120,000, and the number of wards increased from forty to about three hundred.[2] Because he had direct responsibility for people and resources, such explosive growth in the basically cashless desert oasis taxed his executive talents.

He also pioneered in terms of the office and calling of Presiding Bishop. The office had barely developed beyond an embryonic stage when Hunter's predecessor, Bishop Newel K. Whitney, died in 1850. During the next decades, Bishop Hunter firmly carved the Presiding Bishopric's niche into the Church's General Authority hierarchy. Of concern here are Bishop Hunter's two most demanding responsibilities: tithing supervisor, with the corollary task of caring for the worthy poor, and president of the Aaronic Priesthood.

The Call

When Elder Heber C. Kimball announced to the April 1851 general conference that Bishop Edward Hunter would succeed Bishop Whitney, he warned: "I wish Bro. Hunter to understand that he has now got into a place, where he will be thumped and pulled about. Can you go it?" The large fifty-eight-year-old bishop—he weighed over 250 pounds—replied, "I will do the best I can." Elder Kimball continued: "I can recommend him to fill that office, as a man of God, and a man of business."³

After Edward's conversion to Mormonism in 1839–1840, his commitment to the gospel never wavered. Once socially and financially prominent in Pennsylvania, he surrendered the good life of country squire to emigrate to Nauvoo and there consecrated great wealth to the Lord. His loyalty and generosity to Joseph Smith were unbounded, causing Joseph to tell him in the name of the Lord to cease donating. "In all of early Church history," writes a Hunter biographer, "we find no other convert past middle age who had comparable wealth that consecrated his material wealth and mortal life to a similar extent."⁴ On another occasion Joseph Smith told Edward: "I have enquired of the Lord concerning you, and you are favourable in His sight."⁵ When Joseph was martyred, Edward passed his loyalty from Joseph to Brigham Young, in part because he witnessed the mystical moment when the mantle of Joseph descended upon Brigham and transformed his appearance. During the trek west Edward Hunter, who had been Nauvoo Fifth Ward bishop, served as a Winter Quarters bishop and then in 1848 captained a company of a hundred into the Valley.⁶

In 1849 when Salt Lake City was divided into wards, he became the Thirteenth Ward's bishop. When called as Presiding Bishop in 1851, he was judged to be a careful and thorough businessman, a person with "great knowledge in temporal things." By background he was a farmer, leather curer, a cattle expert in terms of breeding, handling, judging, and a businessman.⁷

In 1851, the time of Edward Hunter's call, the office of Presiding Bishop was not well defined. The Bishop's role when the law of consecration was being practiced in Missouri was fairly clear, but its role in Nauvoo's temporal affairs was less so. When Newel Whitney, "a most upright and thorough business man," became Presiding Bishop in 1848, President Young directed him to manage tithing, establish home industry, and care for the poor; but the confusion caused by the Utah migration seems to have precluded firm procedures by the time Bishop Whitney died.[8] President Young said that bishops in Nauvoo "never seemed to understand the duty and office of a bishop." Regarding Bishop Whitney, he confessed: "I did often chastise him severely, to try to get him to understand his office." He added that Bishop Whitney, near the end of his life, seemed "to have waked up out of a deep sleep, and began to understand something of his office and duty." By contrast, Brigham once said, Brother Hunter never was chastised like Bishop Whitney. Why?

> Because I knew . . . he came into this Church, and had transacted business on a large scale, was a good and competent judge of Horses, Cattle, Cows, Grain Etc; and therefore did not need those severe chastisements that some of you bishops are obliged to take from time to time.[9]

Edward served as Presiding Bishop for one year on a trial basis and then was ordained. Brigham Young and Heber C. Kimball were his counselors. In 1854 Edward was released as Thirteenth Ward bishop. In 1856 Leonard W. Hardy and Jesse C. Little became his counselors, and at that point the three-man Presiding Bishopric as we know it today emerged. Hardy also continued as Twelfth Ward bishop until 1877. Little was replaced in the Presiding Bishopric in 1874 by Robert T. Burton, bishop of the Fifteenth Ward.[10]

We look in vain for indications of formal meetings between the Presiding Bishopric and the First Presidency. Available daybooks for the Historian's Office and the Presidency's Office keep good track of Brigham Young's activities, but mentions of Brigham's meeting formally with Bishop Hunter are rare. Informal consultations seem to have been the rule. During Edward's first years as Presiding Bishop he met regularly on Sunday afternoons with the First Presidency and members of the Twelve in a prayer circle, where leaders discussed Church problems and where Edward evidently obtained occasional instructions. After receiving formal counselors in 1856, Edward was told by the First Presidency "to come into the councils of the first presidency, and feel that there was his place and pre-rogative and not for one moment to think he was intruding."[11]

Bishop Hunter continued a tradition, started by Bishop Whitney, of meeting regularly with the Salt Lake Valley bishops and others from more distant wards who could attend. These "town meetings" of bishops, or bishops' quorum meetings, provided Bishop Hunter and the First Presidency a regular forum for instructing and for receiving feedback. The First Presidency attended, but not regularly. At times they gave Hunter instructions before the meetings, as in 1857 when he "informed the meeting that he had an interview with the first presidency a short time prior to the meeting and they expressed themselves satisfied with the labors of the Bishops." Bishop Hunter frequently took policy-type questions, raised at the meetings, to the First Presidency for clarification.[12]

During most of this period, the First Presidency's headquarters were in Brigham Young's office on Brigham's block. Bishop Hunter had an office a block west in the General Tithing Office. Both offices had their own clerks and record books. As near as the system can be pieced together now, the main finance books for the Church were the trustee-in-trust ledger books in the President's office. These master records included records received from daybooks and account books kept by the Church public works clerks and the General Tithing Office clerks. But Hunter's office daybooks, which recorded tithes on hand at the General Tithing Office, evidently were turned in periodically and made permanent records in the trustee-in-trust master books.[13]

Bishop Hunter knew his role was subordinate, second level, a carry-it-out type job rather than a policy-making job. While some members and bishops believed that temporal matters should shift from the First Presidency to the Presiding Bishopric, and that temporal matters ought not to be the concern of the Melchizedek Priesthood, the First Presidency thought otherwise.[14] Said Heber C. Kimball in 1854:

> Many wish for the time when President Brigham Young and his brethren would be relieved from attending to temporal matters

and to attend to spiritual matters altogether. You will have to wait for this until we get into the spiritual world. . . . All things pertaining to this world, both spiritual and temporal, will be dictated by the Prophet.[15]

Brigham Young made his position clear, too. He told a Parowan group in 1855 that Bishop Hunter was called "to help the 1st Presidency in temporal matters." But if the First Presidency could be in two places at once, he added, "they would attend to the Bishop's business." But even God could not be in two places at once, he said, "hence the necessity of helps and governments in the priesthood to aid the presiding authorities."[16] In 1860 Brigham Young said the Presiding Bishopric had charge of temporal matters "and were under the immediate dictation of the 1st Presidency."[17] Willard Richards said that if Bishop Hunter should counsel wrong "it is the business of the First Presidency . . . to correct him, from whom he receives his instruction."[18]

One temporal activity the First Presidency did not turn over to the Presiding Bishop was the public works projects. Through the trustee-in-trust office, the Presidency supervised the temple, tabernacle, and other construction projects and workers, paying the workers in tithing goods and scrip issued from Hunter's office.[19]

Tithing Manager

Tithing was the portly Bishop's number one responsibility —encouraging, receiving, storing, allocating, and accounting for animal and produce tithes, properties, labor tithes, and some cash.

From Bishop Whitney he inherited no smoothly working tithing operation. So, with the First Presidency, he had to develop, refine, and manage a complicated non-cash tithing system that pumped economic life into the basically poor Church. His first summer in the saddle, 1851, he saw tithes barely trickle into the new tithing storehouse's cellars and apartments. Skimpy donations meant Church projects suffered for want of lumber, materials, and laborers. Even a tithe of the tithing due, said the First Presidency's epistle that fall, "would have enabled us to enclose the Temple Block as we had anticipated."[20]

A new tithing push soon came. That September Bishop Hunter and the First Presidency announced a new program that required not just tithing on increase and labor but once again, as in pre-exodus days, on *all* that a Saint possessed, even if he had tithed on all upon conversion—as was then expected. Fall 1851 general conference attenders voted to comply. To launch the stepped-up tithing program three special traveling presiding bishops were sent to help gather in and forward tithes to the general office.[21] A November circular said that Bishop Hunter "has charge of all receipts and expenditures relating to tithing," and the appraising of properties and recording of donations.[22]

So Hunter's first year proved to be a busy one that left him overwhelmed. "Many times I am so crowded with business," he lamented in October 1851, "that I have not time to treat my brethren with that civility and kindness that they are entitled to and which would be congenial to my feelings."[23] Besides receiving goods and recording them, he had to handle a wave of questions from bishops. How much were cows worth this year? Oxen per yoke? Could wheat be taken in place of property tithing? How should perishables like butter and eggs be stored? Could there be regional storehouses built? The results of the push, announced in April 1852 conference, earned Brigham Young's praise: "There has been more done by the Bishops in the last 7 months than in the previous 7 years, and I feel to bless you." "Never before," the First Presidency broadcast, "has the Lord's storehouse been so well supplied."[24]

The Seventh Epistle by the First Presidency in April 1852 provides one rare disclosure of Church tithes. From 1847 to 1851, the letter noted, $390,261 had come in as tithes. Expenditures, amounting to $354,000, went for public-works shops (blacksmith, carpenter, paint), for a barn and storehouse for tithes, for a bowery and a tabernacle, for factories and lands, for clerks and superintendents, and for provisions for emigration. "Little had been received in cash," the report concluded.[25]

The tithing success earned Bishop Hunter a permanent job. "I am going to present the case of Bishop Hunter," President Heber C. Kimball, First Counselor in the First Presidency, told the April 1852 conference. "He has never been ordained to that calling. We thought we would prove him before we ordain him." They then ordained him on 11 April "to preside over the temporal affairs of our God on the earth," and blessed him with powers to discern, to judge righteously, and "to lift the hearts of the Saints." More traveling bishops were called that conference to assist the Bishop.[26]

Not wanting another year-end inundation at the General Tithing Office, Bishop Hunter changed tithing procedures so that henceforth local bishops settled with tithepayers and made up annual ward tithing ledgers. Tithe-paying thus was localized. But local record keeping posed a serious problem. "There never has been a bishop yet who has made a report that would give me any knowledge of the condition of his ward," Brigham Young complained in 1855.[27] He wanted records good enough "that Bishop Hunter can read it right; and know how [much] Oxen, Horses, Cows, Sheep, Lambs, Pigs, Fowls . . . Eggs, Butter, and Cheese, Produce of every kind, and money" was given. Bishop Hunter therefore issued a circular letter that explained record keeping, the disbursements of tithing, and answered typical tithepayer questions. From 1852 to 1854 wards received record books and built local tithing storehouses. By 1854 storehouses stood or were being built in Provo, Lehi, Springville, Palmyra, American Fork, and elsewhere.[28]

In 1854 the tithing requirement was turned up another notch when President Young announced in April conference that Saints could move beyond tithing to voluntarily consecrate all their property to the Church. The Saints voted to comply with this law "first given to Brother Joseph." But much interest and sermonizing produced little consecrating, mainly because of legal snags in the deed form. Scripture and tradition place the Presiding Bishop in the role of manager of consecrated properties, as Bishop Edward Partridge was in Missouri. Many Utahns wondered if Edward Hunter would assume the role Bishop Partridge had held. But the deeds were conveyed to Brigham Young as trustee-in-trust and not to the Presiding Bishop. What Bishop Hunter's reactions were to his backseat role in the renewed consecration effort is not known.[29]

However, that Bishop Hunter thought he should play a bigger role in Church temporal management is shown by his proposal in the late 1850s that the Twelve cease earning their own livelihoods and be sustained from general Church funds. Two liked the idea, others were neutral, but some adamantly insisted on earning their own livings. One warned that "if we could do as Bishop Hunter spoke of, we might become dry and dull" and unable to advise Saints on temporal matters. The proposal died.[30]

Today's cash tithing operation seems rather simple when compared to Bishop Hunter's system. Table 1 shows the basics of the complex system.

Labor tithing, which originated in Nauvoo, meant laboring one day in ten for the Church. "When [a man] has worked nine days for himself," said one explanation, "then let him take his team and work a day for public works. . . . If he idles 150 days of his time in riding and pleasure, he owes 15 days work for the Lord." Labor tithing could be used to pay off tithes in kind. It could be commuted and paid by goods or cash. A tithepayer might even hire someone to perform the labor tithing for him. The labor tithe required not just a man with his work clothes and bare hands but also the labor of his work animals and equipment—wagons, teams, shovels, hammers, and drills. The most frequently mentioned type of labor tithing was hauling, either hauling tithing produce from ward storehouses to the General Tithing Office or hauling building materials to or from public work sites.[31]

Underdeveloped regions needed labor, and labor tithing let able-bodied men make projects happen even when there was no cash. Frequently Bishop Hunter issued urgent calls for labor

LOCAL

Refunds for
Overpayments in ◄─────────────
Labor Tithing

Spoilage ◄─────────────

COMMODITIES & CASH	
Grain	Salt
Fruit	Chickens
Eggs	Lumber
Butter	Coal
Milk	Land
Wool	Tools
Meat	Cattle
Vegetables	
Minerals	CASH

WARD

TITHING

LABOR	(Every 10th Work Day)

Teamsters
Laborers
Craftsmen
Mechanics
Patrols
Herdsmen

► Aid the Poor

► Local LDS Expenses

► Local Work Projects

► Families of Public Works
  Laborers, of Missionaries

► Compensate Bishop

► Sell for Cash

► Trade Locally for Needed
  Items

► Loans

► Storage

Shipped to Regional or
SLC Storehouse; Tithing
Labor to Haul It

Sent to Help on Public
Works

Sent to Aid Immigrants

► Local Improvements

► Maintain Local Tithing
  Office

► Assist the Poor

► Earn Credits or Tithing
  Scrip

► Cut Community Firewood

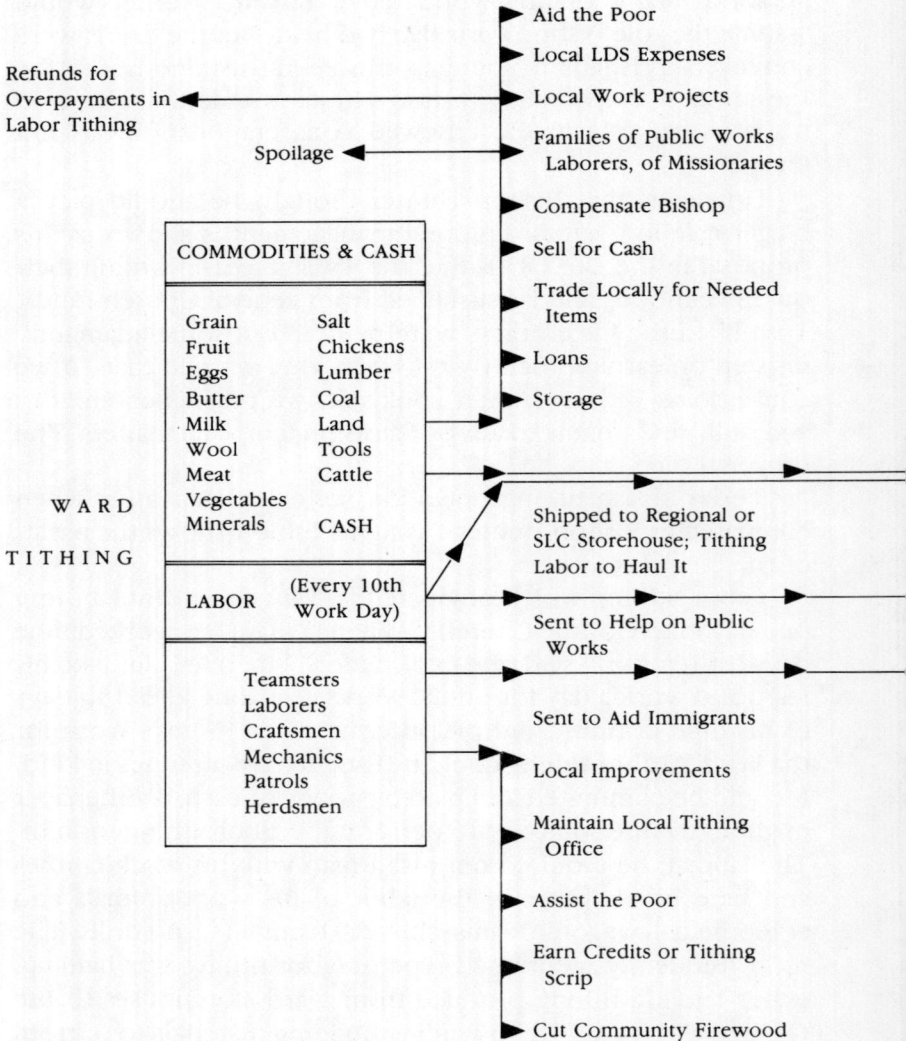

TABLE 1. Tithing System During the Era of
Presiding Bishop Edward Hunter, 1851–1883

REGIONAL OR GENERAL

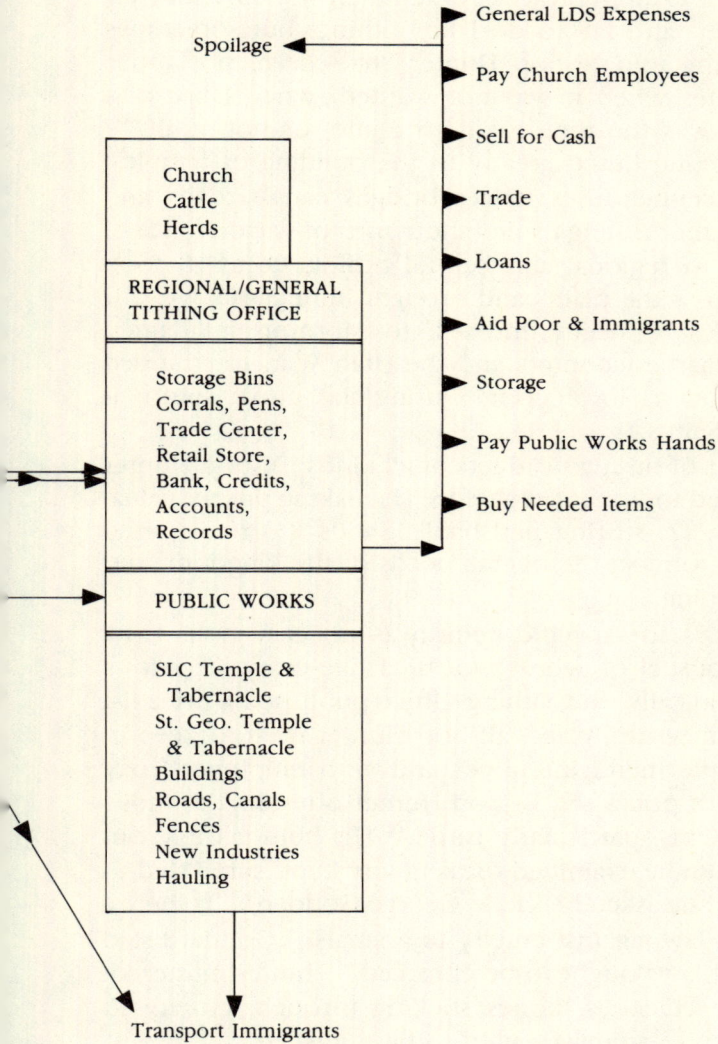

Spoilage ←

General LDS Expenses

Pay Church Employees

Sell for Cash

Trade

Loans

Aid Poor & Immigrants

Storage

Pay Public Works Hands

Buy Needed Items

Church
Cattle
Herds

REGIONAL/GENERAL
TITHING OFFICE

Storage Bins
Corrals, Pens,
Trade Center,
Retail Store,
Bank, Credits,
Accounts,
Records

PUBLIC WORKS

SLC Temple &
  Tabernacle
St. Geo. Temple
  & Tabernacle
Buildings
Roads, Canals
Fences
New Industries
Hauling

Transport Immigrants

tithing, and notices were read from the stand each Sunday telling what days Salt Lake wards were assigned to provide labor tithing for Church projects. Often men waited until after spring, summer, and fall to do labor tithing, but sometimes President Young told Bishop Hunter "to receive no labour tithing in winter when it was not wanted, when labor was needed, then was the time for it to come, or not at all."[32] Labor tithing contributed greatly to the building of temples, tabernacles, meetinghouses, fences, bridges, canals, roads, and storehouses. Labor tithing hauled thousands of wagon loads of tithing goods to regional and central tithing stores. It took goods east across the plains and brought immigrants west. It carried supplies to needy Indians, to Mormon militiamen during the Indian encounters and the Utah War, to stranded immigrants, and to local poor. During the move south, it helped many Saints.[33]

As manager of tithing products of all kinds, Bishop Hunter constantly faced four main problems: (1) making proper valuation of goods, (2) storing perishable goods, (3) transferring goods around to meet the overall needs of the kingdom, and (4) record keeping.

Fixing prices for specific items was no easy task. How much was a bushel of wheat worth? a five-year-old cow? a chicken? Periodically, the Tithing Office published a price list by weight or measure, prices Bishop Hunter tried to keep in line with gentile merchant prices and with employers' pay rates. Even with prices set, Bishop Hunter often had to judge the value of items, particularly cattle.[34] His humor came out sometimes when he examined the scrawny items submitted to the Lord. Once he asked his clerk, George Goddard: "Is there a law, is there a law, against cruelty to animals?" Goddard said yes. "All good laws ought to be enforced," Hunter muttered; "tithing office chickens, bones sticking through, cruelty to animals, cruelty to animals, ought to be punished."[35]

Tithing's main purpose was to provide for the Church's financial needs. As the First Presidency explained in 1855:

The tithing furnishes our resources for all of our public improvements, and this is generally paid in grain, vegetables, stock, wagons, labour, and other property, and but very little in money, and with the exception of what is needed for the use of the men employed, has to be turned into cash to procure such other articles as are necessary for properly prosecuting business. The constant investment of the funds of the Church in permanent improvements, trouble of changing, and delay in converting into cash, sometimes unavoidably involve us in debt; but if the brethren will be faithful and punctual in paying their tithing in kind, it will relieve us of all embarrassment, and furnish sufficient for the needful purposes.[36]

"While it required much wisdom and labor to collect [tithing]," one bishop said in 1875, "it required much more wisdom to righteously disburse it, so as to bring about the greatest possible good to the greatest number."[37] Bishop Hunter monitored needs and surpluses, weather and insect reports, immigration and crop projections. Balancing supply and demand throughout hundreds of Mormon settlements was tricky. His first priority was supplying the needs of Church headquarters, and the General Tithing Office had standing orders for tithes to come in if not specifically approved by Bishop Hunter for local use and if no more than one hundred miles distant. Conferences provided ideal opportunities for wheeling the goods into the General Tithing Office.[38] Beyond reminders for regular tithes, Bishop Hunter issued emergency appeals whenever the General Tithing Office ran short. Particular bishops often were picked on to provide products he knew their people produced. In 1874, for example, facing a fuel shortage in public buildings and among the poor, he urged the Coalville bishop to send several train carloads of coal.[39]

The quantity of tithing goods flowing into the General Tithing Office cannot be tallied (tithing account books are not available to the public). But an 1852 report of a fifteen-week period of tithes totalled them this way: 5000 pounds of butter, 2200 pounds of cheese, 1150 dozen eggs. At one time Pleasant Grove shipped fifteen wagon loads of hay and Springville six hundred bushels of wheat. A wagon train from Fort Ephraim brought six wagon loads of wheat, pork, and eggs.⁴⁰

Public works projects proved to be an expensive drain on the treasury. Although historian Leonard Arrington says that public works employees provided bread for themselves, records make clear that many of them depended in whole or large part upon tithing foodstuffs. In 1853, for example, President Young called for tithes because a public works push meant the need for more "provisions to feed the laborers." An appeal in 1854 asked Saints to "allow the men upon the public works the blessing of comfortable meals." In 1857 the Tithing Office was dealing out seven tons of flour weekly to workers. In 1874 Bishop Hunter asked Bountiful leaders to send vegetables quickly, "having many families to supply who labor on the temple."⁴¹

For most of his term as Presiding Bishop, Hunter employed agents to help funnel the tithes, including traveling bishops, regional presiding bishops who managed regional tithing stores, and various traveling agents. Bishop Hunter and his counselors traveled too. Bishop Hunter had direct contact with regional bishops in Utah and Cache counties, and his traveling bishops and agents supervised outlying counties. Historian Gene Pace has identified twenty-seven regional presiding bishops who served before 1877.⁴²

From the early days of temple ordinances, members needed to tithe in order to receive recommends. "Not another soul (will) get an endowment until he has paid his tithing to the utermost and has got his receipt to put in the records," President Heber C. Kimball warned in 1851. Similar statements punctuate the records during the Brigham Young era.⁴³

Beyond his duty to receive, store, transfer, and record tithes, Bishop Hunter served as the leading "drummer" for tithing, particularly during lean agricultural years. For example, when the surplus of 1857 was depleted by late 1859, and the General Tithing Office had no bread, he put a get-tough policy into effect. Also, during the United Order push in the 1870s the tithing program continued, and Bishop Hunter still functioned as chief tithing officer.[44]

Bishop Hunter devoutly believed in tithing. No hypocrisy tinged his appeals for people to pay. People churchwide knew and repeated his slogan, spoken over and over again: "Pay your tithing and be blessed, pay your tithing and be blessed." Teach the people that the payment of their tithing is doing themselves good, he told the bishops.[45]

As chief caretaker of Church tithes, Bishop Hunter had scriptural duty to aid the Lord's poor. He spent much time helping two types of needy: needy immigrants coming to Zion and the needy already there.

Starting in 1850, when Bishop Hunter brought the very first Perpetual Emigrating Fund train of emigrants to Utah, he actively worked to aid the annual immigration effort. He supervised the welcoming of immigrant trains to the Valley, sometimes escorting them in. With the help of local bishops and Saints, he tried to offer places to lodge the first night or two and to provide vegetables and other edibles to gladden the weary travelers.[46] An 1866 account depicts Hunter's role when a wagon train arrived:

> Most of the passengers went with the wagons, having friends northward. Some remained with friends in this city and a few were cared for by Bishop Hunter and his counselors, who attended to their wants in a fatherly manner. The bishop and his council were indefatigable in their exertions for the welfare of the passengers.[47]

When word came that wagon companies were having difficulty in Wyoming, Bishop Hunter called on his bishops to send out relief wagons and cattle. Taking orders from the First Presidency, Bishop Hunter, during the 1860s, orchestrated a vast operation of "down and back" Church team trains, calling on wards to provide wagons and teams to go east to pick up immigrants and bring them to Utah. In 1861 he sent out two hundred wagons, a total that grew to five hundred wagons and teams by 1866.[48]

The First Presidency expected Bishop Hunter, with other bishops' help, to be a population traffic manager, steering new immigrants away from Salt Lake and into valleys where they were needed or where they could find decent livings. In 1852, for example, Bishop Hunter told bishops that some immigrant mechanics could stay in Salt Lake City but that other new-comers had a duty "to move out of the city to those localities where strength is needed, and their labors can be useful."[49] In 1854 Brigham Young requested bishops to inform Bishop Hunter how many new settlers their wards could take. Some of the reports were Pleasant Grove, 40 to 50 Saints; Provo Third, 22; Nephi, 20; Palmyra, 25 or 30 families; Mill Creek Ward, 13 families; Payson, 75 to 80 persons; an Ogden ward, 4 to 5 families.[50] In late 1855 Bishop Hunter told the bishops' meeting that "we are distributing the migration companies very well" and added: "Some are very destitute and ignorant as to the methods of getting a living; they should go into the country. They must be taught, for they are full of faith, but not many works."[51] In September 1861 he reported that he "had been busy for two weeks past in making a distribution of the Emigration through the Territory." Bishop Hunter had to solve problems like that created in the Salt Lake Second Ward when more poor Danes settled there than Bishop Hill could handle; Bishop Hunter arranged for several to move to Sanpete County. In 1869, when the railroad first brought in immigrants all the way to Zion, Bishop Hunter arranged for local Ogden leaders to host and distribute the newcomers. In 1870 he sent twenty Swiss Germans to Cache Valley to start cheese production there.[52]

The poor already in Utah were also a big concern for the big Bishop. Pioneer poverty is an underrated factor in pioneer history. Life stories of pioneers, if read by the bushel, give the feeling of precariousness for common folk. Accidents ruined workers, including fathers; crickets in 1848, 1849, 1850, and grasshoppers in 1855 and later; famine in 1856; regional short-ages; crop diseases; too-hot summers and too-long winters knocked pioneers on their backs financially. Even Provo, an area as developed as any outside of Salt Lake Valley by 1870, had difficulty at that late date raising funds needed by its bishop—the people honestly pleaded poverty.[53] A case might be made that most pioneers lived at or below a poverty level. Most of them suffered silently, aided at times by local bishops, Relief Society sisters, or relatives and friends.

Bishop Hunter's approach to the general poor was constantly to encourage bishops to be sensitive. "Do not make beggars of the poor," he warned. "It has always been my chief object to find employment for the poor," he said by way of advice. He urged bishops to seek out the "modest unassuming people" who silently suffer hunger. "We must watch over the poor." Devise employment or place them in families who have employment for them, he counseled. Every summer he reminded bishops to stockpile wood for winter fuel for the poor.[54]

Only the desperate cases reached the Presiding Bishop's attention, including the handicapped, retarded, and orphaned. Still, the cries of the poor reached the General Tithing Store constantly, some in letter, others in person. One sampling of Hunter's letterbooks from 1872 to 1875 shows him giving attention to hardship cases involving a woman with children needing a home, two boys ages four and six needing a home, a blind sister wanting to reach St. George, a blind and poor man needing clothing, an "idiot or foolish boy," a blind seventy-year-old immigrant, a poor widow who was not paid back a loan, a feeble woman without family, a begging woman with three children, and a blind man from Denmark.[55] In 1873 Bishop Hunter chided a bishop for stinginess in caring for an addled lady and then editorialized: "She like some other unfortunates who need a little aid have no more claim on one ward than another, but wherever they happen to be, there we expect the Bishop to look after them and not allow them to suffer."[56] Referring to a wife who was mistreated and poor, he said, "such cases absorb nearly half of our time."[57] Incoming letters told of more situations of abuse, neglect, handicaps, misfortune, and even a drug addict who pleaded with Bishop

Hunter, "Don't let me die for a few ounces of opium" and then requested that the Bishop or "some other good brother will supply me."[58]

Until asylums and hospitals were built in Utah, the basic method for caring for the handicapped, the retarded and insane, the feeble elderly, and the long-term ill was the cottage system—finding households that would take these cases in return for tithing credits, Church payments, or blessings in heaven.[59]

By the 1860s the problem of housing and feeding the desperately poor had become too burdensome for some bishops. In 1867 President Daniel H. Wells read seventy names of those receiving weekly allowances at the Tithing Office at a total cost of $200 per week—these were in addition to hundreds aided by local bishops. Traveling Bishop Milton Musser surveyed the Church in 1869 and found 1,054 of 109,000 were acutely poor and two-thirds of those, or about 700, were entirely dependent. An idea was discussed that a central poorhouse be set up in wards or in the Valley or that a poor farm be built. The cost of keeping the increasing number of gentile and LDS needy in single rooms was too great. Why not put them in one house? Brigham Young opposed the poor farm idea, but bishops did not drop the matter. At one point the bishops tried to turn a ten-acre city lot into a poor farm and home where the able could work, but the plan fizzled.[60]

Bishop Hunter's constant commitment was that none should suffer, and whenever bishops ran out of fast offerings to aid the poor, he approved the use of tithing for that purpose. Although basically kindhearted, he had little patience for lazy and shiftless Saints who loafed around. One time he wearied of seeing women hanging around the tithing storehouse steps "showing their dirty legs" and asked bishops either to pick up the food and deliver it to the women or else have men pick it up "and let the women stay at home."[61] Another time he complained of "chronic beggars, chronic beggars. No good. No good. We have the Lord's poor, the devil's poor, and the poor devils."[62] Of vagrants hanging around the Tithing Office, he remarked humorously: "Hunting work, hunting work; yes, yes, but they don't want to find it very bad." But then he instructed his staff. "Feed them, brethren, feed them—mustn't let them starve."[63]

President of the Aaronic Priesthood

Priesthood theory, in Hunter's day, held that the Presiding Bishop was "President of the Aaronic Priesthood in all the World" and therefore presided over all bishops, priests, teachers, and deacons. But in practice how did that presiding occur? In Bishop Hunter's case, he and the First Presidency agreed on some Aaronic Priesthood matter, and the Presidency then directed him to see that the work was carried out in the stakes. Bishop Hunter, assuming the cooperation of stake officers, in turn instructed bishops and sometimes stake leaders to implement the Aaronic Priesthood work. Bishop Hunter's task as president divides into three activities: (1) presiding over bishops, (2) presiding over Aaronic Priesthood quorums, and (3) participating in ceremonial activities.[64]

"It is the duty of the Presiding Bishop to preside over all Bishops" the First Presidency instructed as early as 1851. However, as president of the bishops, Hunter had no regular voice in selecting them. "There are several Wards without Bishops," he said in 1856 but admitted that he did not know when they would have them. The First Presidency chose the new bishops and then let Bishop Hunter know who they were, sometimes instructing him to ordain the newly chosen men, often instructing him to teach them their duties. Hunter's office kept an up-to-date list of Mormon settlements with their presiding officers, for reference and for correspondence purposes.[65] Newly appointed bishops received instructions from Bishop Hunter and his counselors. An 1877 instruction letter, for example, advises about tithing, meetings ("let them be short and spiritual"), fast offerings and testimony meetings ("have no preaching sermons"), calling block teachers ("select the best and wisest men"), solving disputes ("have all their grievances and disputes settled by the lesser priesthood"), and organizing the lesser priesthood properly ("in your stake . . . a full quorum of 48 priests, 24 teachers and 12 deacons").[66]

If one thing made Bishop Hunter feel like a president, it was when he presided at the twice monthly bishops' meetings in the city. Because a large percentage of the Church's bishops lived in the Salt Lake Valley and came to these meetings, he had an effective forum. Normally twenty to thirty wards were represented, but during general conference or when the territorial legislature sat, the bishops' meetings' ranks swelled with many "outside" bishops. Although the majority of Church bishops could not attend these meetings, those attending served as a representative body. Their decisions became policy churchwide. Proceedings and decisions were published in the *Deseret News* or capsuled in circular letters for all bishops to read. The main topics treated in these meetings were tithing, emigration fund donations, public works assignments, specific cases of poor and needy persons, Aaronic Priesthood labors (specifically ward teaching), and domestic manufactures. Also, a wide range of other matters received attention less often: sacrament, baptizing, wheat storage, innoculations, marital and family advice, stealing, voting, land-owning, naturalization, and water problems. These "town meetings" of bishops produced vigorous questioning, challenging, criticizing, disagreeing, and open expressing of opinions.[67]

In addition to the bishops' meetings, Bishop Hunter communicated with bishops by mail. He received and answered many personal letters. He issued circular letters over his signature, which sometimes were cosigned by the First Presidency. After 1861, the Deseret Telegraph sped up communication and reduced the senior bishop's mail pile. Bishop Hunter and his counselors also paid personal visits to stakes and wards. In addition, he had a good, personal, one-to-one contact with bishops who visited his General Tithing Office. Now and then he requested written reports from all bishops, reports containing tithing totals, census figures, or immigration assignment lists. In the bishops' meetings he sometimes called for oral reports from bishops about the numbers in the ward who sustained the Word of Wisdom, numbers rebaptized, numbers of poor, block teaching patterns, and the spirit in ward meetings.[68]

Bishop Hunter often became the man in the uncomfortable middle. That is, he would try to defend bishops against First Presidency criticisms, and then he would have to criticize the bishops. Empathetic and appreciative of bishops generally, and aware of their heavy burdens, he remembered that his ordination called him to lift the drooping spirits. Nevertheless, he disliked foot-dragging by bishops. Home manufacturing, for example, was not a popular topic in the bishops' meetings, causing Counselor Little to admonish that "he did not want to hear any cold water remarks thrown upon it" and that whenever a call came from Brigham Young through the Presiding Bishopric he wanted "a hearty and immediate" support from the bishops. Hunter blamed some of the 1856 Reformation's chastisements on "the heedlessness of the Bishops." In 1862 he issued them "a sharp but sensible reproof" for neglecting Aaronic Priesthood matters.[69] Knowing bishops sometimes ignored Bishop Hunter, John Taylor once reminded them: "You bishops are subject to your head, Bishop Hunter, and you cannot shake off the responsibilities that he lays upon you."[70]

Regarding Hunter's role as president of the Aaronic Priesthood quorums, Brigham Young reminded him that "it was the duty of the Presiding Bishop to have a full quorum of Priests, Teachers and Deacons, properly organized in every stake of Zion, and hold there regular meetings."[71] (Notice he said *stake,* not ward.) In Salt Lake Stake, where Hunter served somewhat like a stake bishop, he influenced the calling of its Aaronic Priesthood presidencies. During his term, Salt Lake Stake held stake Aaronic Priesthood meetings, stake deacons quorum meetings, stake teachers quorum meetings, and stake priests quorum meetings. At general conference, when Salt Lake Stake officers were sustained, voters sustained presidencies for a deacons, a teachers, and a priests quorum—one quorum of each in a stake of about twenty thousand Saints.[72]

In some stakes quorums existed; in others they did not. Bishop Hunter said he labored many years to make the lesser priesthood function, to make it "honorable," and in 1873 he won Brigham Young's backing for a pointed epistle instructing him as Presiding Bishop to order stakes to organize quorums.[73] One person Bishop Hunter *gently* ordered was Apostle Orson Hyde in Sanpete Stake, the acting stake president. "This is not done to gratify a personal ambition to dictate [to] President Hyde who is above me," his letter respectfully began, "but simply to discharge a duty imposed upon me. . . . You will therefore please to have 3 quorums filled."[74] President-Apostle Hyde responded, and soon his stake had one priests quorum— twenty-four priests from Manti and twenty-four from Ephraim (the stake's two leading towns); one teachers quorum—twelve teachers from Manti and twelve from Ephraim; and one deacons quorum—six from each town.[75]

Aaronic Priesthood work was considered adult work. Frequently, high priests, seventies, and elders served as acting deacons, acting teachers, acting priests, much as high priests served as bishops; and a common phrase heard among acting Aaronic Priesthood men was "We are called to act in both priesthoods."[76]

After the Priesthood Reorganizing of 1877, stakes became better organized and expanded the number of quorums, especially deacons units, so that practically every ward had a quorum.[77]

Bishop Hunter propounded a lofty concept of lesser priesthood work. In Zion, Melchizedek Priesthood bearers had little to do in wards unless they performed "acting" lesser priesthood work, such as block teaching. Hunter's generation believed that only ordained teachers had priesthood power to reconcile differences between two parties; bishop's courts could make decisions, but decisions often did not produce reconciliations. The Aaronic Priesthood had power to discern iniquity and help people repent. It had the obligation to watch over the members. It could have the ministerings of angels. While many Saints considered the lesser priesthood to be lesser and lower, Bishop Hunter considered it vital to the Church, and particularly helpful to overloaded bishops.[78]

Bishop Hunter supervised bishops and encouraged Aaronic Priesthood work, and he also performed ceremonial functions as Aaronic Priesthood President. He made official appearances on public occasions. He accepted speaking invitations. He helped dedicate chapels and buildings. He participated in funeral programs. At general conference and at the Sunday Tabernacle sacrament meetings he and his counselors sometimes took charge of the sacrament. Occasionally he spoke at general conferences and priesthood gatherings. When the Salt Lake Temple cornerstones were laid, he orated and then dedicated a stone on behalf of the Aaronic Priesthood. At the St. George Temple dedication he represented the Aaronic Priesthood.[79]

Somehow a hosting role developed for him, too, perhaps because his management of the General Tithing Storehouse made him a food czar. Starting in 1864 he hosted a series of annual reunions for the Zion's Camp survivors. He also hosted reunions for the Mormon Battalion survivors. Sometimes he was chairman of the Twenty-fourth of July program for the Salt Lake Valley. During the 1870s he helped launch an annual Old Folks' Day that became a fine Utah tradition. In 1876, to cite one outing, Bishop Hunter and his committee arranged for about six hundred excursionists, half over sixty-five years old, to go by train to Provo. Half the company went free; the others paid $1. At Provo spring-seated wagons and a band met them and off they went to a big picnic. The program included a speech by Bishop Hunter, band numbers, and songs. Dancing, swings, and reminiscing under shady trees occupied the afternoon, and then the group returned to Salt Lake, enjoying cake and lemonade, and singing on the way back. Bishop Hunter became well known as the annual producer of the Old Folks' Days.[80]

Because of his position and his wisdom, Bishop Hunter received requests to arbitrate, not in the formal court setting, but by way of opinion. Such requests usually involved money or property disputes beyond the jurisdiction of local bishops, such as problems between the bishops, or those involving General Authorities or people outside of Utah.[81]

Leader and Follower

President Brigham Young and Presiding Bishop Hunter worked basically smoothly together as a temporal team, but not without some differences. On occasion Brigham asked for more than the Bishop was doing. In 1855 the President severely chastised the bishops, including Bishop Hunter, giving them a "few reproofs." In 1857 Brigham became impatient for 1856 tithing to be settled, and Bishop Hunter responded that he would "take measures to ascertain [it] as soon as possible." Bishop Hunter evidently told bishops to put cellars in the tithing houses, something Brigham Young contradicted. In 1863 Hunter admitted that "he himself had been severely reproved 'by his superiors' and could only account for it on the principle, that Whom the Lord loveth, he chasteneth." In 1872 President Young ordered Bishop Hunter to send a circular to country bishops because the President disliked the waste and spoilage of tithing hay and fodder he saw during a recent trip.[82] When he was chastised for neglect of duty, the Bishop was heard to say: "Thank the Lord, thank the Lord, true son, true son, no bastard, no bastard, whom the Lord loveth he chasteneth."[83]

The yoking of the younger ex-Vermont glazier with the older Pennsylvania squire seemed both compatible and successful. Both men seemed to understand the subordinate position of the Presiding Bishopric relative to the First Presidency. If Bishop Hunter ever disagreed strongly with the President, he and Brigham must have worked it out, or else Bishop Hunter suffered in silence. Possibly on occasion Hunter failed to enforce or emphasize some policies that the President favored, a form of passive resistance. But there is no evidence that Bishop Hunter ever took a strong opposition stance or that he recruited bishops to go against President Young's policies. He played his team part well. He was an able man, who conscientiously sought to perform well and "delighted to labor in the Kingdom," although many times he felt "weary" from it all.[84]

When Brigham Young once praised him while scoring others, Bishop Hunter while walking away was heard to say: "Bishop Hunter, Bishop Hunter, look out, devil's after you, don't get the big head, been praised, been praised, flattery, flattery, stubby toe, fall down, break your neck, look out praise, be humble, Bishop Hunter, be humble, devil catch you sure." Another time he said, "Don't get the big head, Kill you sure, Kill you sure, Killed more men than anything else in the Church."[85] The universally high opinion held of him at his death in 1883 indicates that Edward Hunter's selection as Presiding Bishop thirty-two years earlier was an excellent decision by President Young. Edward Hunter was a well-liked leader who by 1875 was regarded as "fatherly" and "kindhearted." Liberal responses by bishops to his calls, he said, "melt my feelings." During his bishopric career, he had tried to do what his setting-apart blessing instructed: "There is nothing so pleasing to me," he said, "as to cheer up the drooping spirit— it was in my blessing by Prest. Young, and I felt it at the time in a remarkable degree."[86]

Edward's personal life, his industries, farms, cattle raising, his plural marriage and family life, his involvement with city government and territorial affairs, and his personal involvement in the Deseret Agricultural and Manufacturing Association are explored well in a published biography,[87] so are not part of this assessment.

One day Clio, the Greek goddess of history, interviewed many second-level leaders in world history. She tabulated her findings and concluded that one of the world's toughest jobs is being a number two leader—vice-president, executive-secretary, counselor, junior partner—anyone who must administer and execute while lacking independence to frame policy.

Many number two men have failed. Clio filed her survey and then whispered to historians to be sure to give credit to number two men who do good jobs. Clio or no Clio, Edward Hunter earned a reputation during his lifetime for being a great man because he learned how to be a good number two man to the strong-willed Brigham Young. In the process, his time, energy, and ideas contributed greatly to moving Utah through the pioneering stage, and he pioneered in the office of Presiding Bishop, shaping that position into one of the vital executive offices in the restored Church.

Notes

1. Heber J. Grant to Edward H. Anderson, 9 July 1901, notes in author's possession.

2. William G. Hartley, "The Priesthood Reorganization of 1877: Brigham Young's Last Achievement," *Brigham Young University Studies* 20 (Fall 1979): 3, 6, 27.

3. LDS General Conference Minutes Collection, 7 April 1851, Library-Archives, Historical Department, The Church of Jesus Christ of Latter-day Saints, Salt Lake City, Utah; hereafter cited as LDS Church Archives.

4. William E. Hunter, *Edward Hunter, Faithful Steward* (Salt Lake City: Publishers Press by the Hunter Family, 1970), pp. 70, 268.

5. Ibid., p. 73.

6. Ibid., pp. 78, 80, 89, 91.

7. Ibid., p. 133, and Presiding Bishopric's Meetings with Bishops, Minutes, LDS Church Archives, 24 April and 13 July 1851; 11 April 1852; and 7 April 1855. Hereafter cited as Bishops' Minutes.

8. D. Michael Quinn, "The Evolution of the Presiding Quorums of the LDS Church," *Journal of Mormon History* 1 (1974); 31–38; First Presidency, Fourth General Epistle, 27 September 1850, in James R. Clark, ed., *Messages of the First Presidency,* 6 vols. (Salt Lake City: Bookcraft, 1965), 2:60; Bishops' Minutes, 7 April 1855.

9. Bishops' Minutes, 7 April 1855.

10. Andrew Jenson, *Latter-day Saint Biographical Encyclopedia,* 4 vols. (Salt Lake City: Jenson History Co., 1901–1936), 1:236–43.

11. Journal History of The Church of Jesus Christ of Latter-day Saints, LDS Church Archives, Sunday entries during 1852; Bishops' Minutes, 7 October 1856.

12. The Bishops' Minutes covering the period 1849–1884; ibid., 27 October 1856.

13. Willard Richards, "Circular on Tithing," 5 November 1851, in Journal History of that date; Ronald G. Watt, "The Presiding Bishopric," typescript, in author's possession.

14. Bishops' Minutes, 11 February and 15 March 1875.

15. Bishops' Minutes, 16 July 1854.

16. LDS General Minutes, taken during conference held in Parowan, 21 May 1855.

17. Bishops' Minutes, 6 October 1860.

18. Richards, "Circular on Tithing," 15 November 1851.

19. Watt, "The Presiding Bishopric."

20. First Presidency, Sixth General Epistle, 22 September 1851, in Clark, *Messages,* 2:78.

21. Ibid., 2:90.

22. Richards, "Circular on Tithing," 15 November 1851.

23. Bishops' Minutes, 12 October 1851.

24. LDS General Minutes, 9 April 1852; First Presidency, Seventh General Epistle, 18 April 1852, in Clark, *Messages,* 2:92.

25. Clark, *Messages,* 2:96.

26. Bishops' Minutes, 11 April 1852 and 6 July 1857; First Presidency, Seventh General Epistle, 18 April 1852, in Clark, *Messages,* 2:97; a full discussion of traveling and regional bishops is in Donald Gene Pace, "The LDS Presiding Bishopric, 1851–1888: An Administrative Study" (Master's thesis, Brigham Young University, 1978), pp. 62–63.

27. Bishops' Minutes, 7 April 1855.

28. Philip K. Smith to Edward Hunter, 12 January 1853, Hunter Incoming Correspondence, LDS Church Archives; First Presidency, Ninth General Epistle, 13 April 1853, in Clark, *Messages,* 2:113; various Journal History entries during 1854.

29. First Presidency, Eleventh General Epistle, 10 April 1854, in Clark, *Messages,* 2:139–40; First Presidency, Twelfth General Epistle, 25 April 1855, in Clark, *Messages,* 2:169–70; Leonard J. Arrington, Feramorz Y. Fox, and Dean L. May, *Building the City of God: Community and Cooperation among the Mormons* (Salt Lake City: Deseret Book, 1976), pp. 69–76.

30. Journal History, 22 February 1859.

31. Ibid., 8 September 1850; Thomas Bullock Minutes Collection, 5 November 1854, LDS Church Archives; General Tithing Store Letterbook, 1872–1875; Bishops' Minutes, 18 June 1873.

32. Bishops' Minutes, 25 October 1853 and 8 October 1863.

33. Ibid., 8 and 22 December 1857.

34. Ibid., 6 January 1870 and 6 November 1873; A. M. Musser, "Tithing Data in 1880," holograph; "List of Tithing Offices Prices, Weights, and Measures, 1863," printed announcement, all in LDS Church Archives.

35. H. J. Grant to E. H. Anderson, 9 July 1901.

36. First Presidency, Twelfth General Epistle, 25 April 1855, in Clark, *Messages,* 2:168.

37. Bishops' Minutes, 11 February 1875.

38. Circular to Bishops, 20 July 1854, in Journal History for that date; Journal History, 19 March 1853.

39. Edward Hunter to Bishop William W. Cluff, 19 September 1874, General Tithing Store Letterbook.

40. Leonard J. Arrington, "Paying the Tenth in Pioneer Days," *Instructor,* Nov. 1963, p. 387; Journal History, 16 December 1854 and 26 November 1860.

41. Ibid., p. 386; Clark, *Messages,* 2:153; Journal History, 7 June 1857; Edward Hunter to Bishop Anson Call, 10 September 1874, General Tithing Store Letterbook.

42. Bishops' Minutes; Pace, "The LDS Presiding Bishopric"; Provo Bishops' Meetings, 1868–1872, LDS Church Archives; Cache Stake, Bishopric Meetings Minutes, 1872–1876, LDS Church Archives.

43. LDS General Minutes, 7 September 1851; Bishops' Minutes, 24 June 1851.

44. Bishops' Minutes, 8 October 1859; General Tithing Store Letterbook, 1872–1875.

45. Thomas C. Romney, *The Gospel in Action* (Salt Lake City: Deseret Sunday School Union Board, 1949), p. 75; Bishops' Minutes, 7 April 1855.

46. Hunter, *Edward Hunter, Faithful Steward,* pp. 119–25.

47. Journal History, 13 October 1850 and 18 March 1868; Bishops' Minutes, 27 August 1860 and 6 November 1855; Manuscript History of Brigham Young, 29 August 1866, p. 710, LDS Church Archives.

48. Bishops' Minutes, 25 April 1860, 13 August 1863, and 25 January 1866; Journal History, 31 December 1861, Supplement.

49. Bishops' Minutes, 12 September 1852.

50. Hunter Incoming Correspondence for 1854; Bishops' Minutes for 1854.

51. Bishops' Minutes, 6 November 1855.

52. Ibid., 26 September 1861, 6 November 1861, and 24 June 1869; Hunter, *Edward Hunter, Faithful Steward,* p. 301.

53. Provo Bishops' Minutes for 1870.

54. Bishops' Minutes, 12 February 1856, 1 September 1870, 29 January 1856, 3 June 1856, 7 June 1853, and 27 July 1865.

55. General Tithing Store Letterbooks, 1872–1875.

56. Ibid., 27 October 1873.

57. Ibid., 16 September 1874.

58. Hunter Incoming Correspondence, 19 February 1856.

59. General Tithing Store Letterbook, 1872–1875.

60. Ibid.; Bishops' Minutes, 5 December 1867, 15 April 1869, 25 January and 8 February 1866, 5 December 1867, 24 September and 5 November and 3 December 1874.

61. H. J. Grant to E. H. Anderson, 9 July 1901.

62. Bishops' Minutes, 27 October 1857.

63. Romney, *Gospel in Action,* p. 75.

64. Bishops' Minutes, 6 October 1860 and 11 January 1877.

65. Willard Richards, Circular on Tithing, 15 November 1851, in Journal History of that date; Bishops' Minutes, 22 April 1856. When Jordan Ward needed a bishop, Hunter said he would "inquire of the President" about "appointing a bishop there" (Bishops' Minutes, 7 January 1852). On 14 March 1857, Brigham Young wrote to Hunter that "we have nominated and appointed Richard Cook a Bishop to succeed Bp. Thomas Kington of W. Weber, and wish you to give such instruction and counsel as you may deem necessary and attend to his ordination" (Hunter Incoming Correspondence). In 1877 Brigham Young stated that Bishop Hunter presided over all bishops, not just those attending the bishops' meetings. (See Bishops' Minutes, 23 August 1877); Bishops' Minutes, 22 April 1856.

66. Bishops' Minutes, 10 July 1877.

67. Ibid., 1849–1884.

68. General Tithing Store Letterbook, 1872–1875; Hunter Incoming Correspondence; Presiding Bishopric, Circular Letter File, 1851–1883, LDS Church Archives; and Bishops' Minutes, 1851–1883. Hunter left Salt Lake City to visit outlying wards in 1851, 1853, 1854, 1856, 1861, 1864, 1867, and probably many other times.

69. Bishops' Minutes, 30 July 1863, 13 February 1862, and 30 September 1856.

70. Bishops' Minutes, 11 January 1877.

71. Bishops' Minutes, 11 September 1873 and 10 July 1877.

72. Bishops' Minutes, 25 November 1852; see also Presiding Bishop's Office, Aaronic Priesthood Minutes, 1857–1877 (which are Salt Lake Stake Minutes) and Salt Lake Stake Deacons Quorum Meeting Minutes, both in LDS Church Archives.

73. Bishops' Minutes, 13 August 1874.

74. Edward Hunter to Apostle Orson Hyde, 17 October 1873, General Tithing Store Letterbook.

75. Sanpete Stake Aaronic Priesthood Minutes, 1873–1877, LDS Church Archives.

76. Hartley, "Ordained and Acting Teachers in the Lesser Priesthood, 1851–1883," *BYU Studies* 16 (Spring 1976): 375–98.

77. Hartley, "The Priesthood Reorganization of 1877: Brigham Young's Last Achievement," *BYU Studies* 20 (Fall 1979): 3–36.

78. Hartley, "Ordained and Acting Teachers," pp. 381–86.

79. Journal History, 15 July and 19 August 1860, and 4 April 1877; *Deseret News,* 16 April 1853.

80. Journal History, 19 October 1864 and 10 October 1870; Hunter, *Edward Hunter, Faithful Steward,* p. 137; George Goddard Journal, 8 June 1876, LDS Church Archives.

81. Hunter Incoming Correspondence.

82. Bishops' Minutes, 15 May 1855, 7 April 1857, 17 December 1862, 18 June 1863, and 10 October 1872; Jane Rollins to Edward Hunter, 17 December 1862, Hunter Incoming Correspondence.

83. H. J. Grant to E. H. Anderson, 9 July 1901.

84. Bishops' Minutes, 23 September 1856 and 12 May 1857.

85. Heber J. Grant remarks at funeral of Oscar F. Hunter, 28 August 1931, notes in author's possession.

86. *Millennial Star* 45 (19 Nov. 1883): 737–46; Journal History, 3 June 1875; Bishops' Minutes, 26 October 1851 and 31 July 1855.

87. Hunter, *Edward Hunter, Faithful Steward.*

Carol Cornwall Madsen

12

Emmeline B. Wells:
Romantic Rebel

Carol Cornwall Madsen is currently a research historian with
the Joseph Fielding Smith Institute for Church History at
Brigham Young University. She is a native of Utah and lives
in Salt Lake City with her husband, Gordon A. Madsen, a
Salt Lake City attorney. They have six children. She was
educated at the University of Utah, receiving a B.A. in
English Literature and an M.A. and a Ph.D. in American
History; her doctoral dissertation "A Mormon Woman in
Victorian America," is a study of the life of Emmeline B.
Wells. She has published widely in LDS periodicals and is
coauthor of *Sisters and Little Saints.* Carol Madsen became
interested in Emmeline B. Wells while she was writing her
master's thesis, entitled "A Study of the Editorial Content of
the *Woman's Exponent,* a Mormon Woman's Journal,
1872–1914." Emmeline B. Wells edited this periodical for
thirty-seven years.

As the steamship neared the bend of the Mississippi River,
which bordered the city of Nauvoo, the young Mormon convert eagerly watched the crowd of people gathering on its
banks. From her home in Massachusetts to her journey's end in
Nauvoo, Emmeline Woodward Harris, newly married to James

Harris, had listened to the missionaries and other Latter-day Saints talk about the Prophet Joseph Smith. Many had known him personally and had described his charismatic power. "As we stepped ashore," Emmeline recalled years later, "the crowd advanced, and I could see one person who towered away and above all the others around him; in fact I did not see distinctly any others." She remembered that

> his majestic bearing, so entirely different from any one I had ever seen . . . was more than a surprise. It was as if I beheld a vision. . . . Before I was aware of it he came to me, and when he took my hand, I was simply electrified—thrilled through and through to the tips of my fingers, and every part of my body, as if some magic elixir had given me new life and vitality. . . . The one thought that filled my soul was, I have seen the prophet of God, he has taken me by the hand.[1]

The memory of that gripping moment had years to season before she wrote of it. But the experience of meeting Joseph Smith validated Emmeline's decision made two years earlier to become a Latter-day Saint. It became the cornerstone of her faith. In the years to come she would repeatedly encounter disappointment, disillusionment, and even despair because of that decision; but she would rise to become one of Utah's and the Church's strongest defenders and would devote her life to the cause of women, also because of that decision.

Emmeline was born in Petersham, a small village situated in the hill country in central Massachusetts. Her birthdate was auspicious, 29 February 1828, a rare date auguring an exceptional life for the seventh child and fifth daughter of David and Diadama Woodward. At her father's death six years later, Emmeline's family moved to New Salem, a few miles north of Petersham. In later years she claimed that she had been born a woman's rights advocate because her mother had long believed in "the emancipation of women" and when left a widow fully realized the disabilities of a woman's rearing a family alone.

Her literary precocity was noted early, as she preferred to roam the fields and hillsides of Petersham or sit under the hemlock boughs that swept the banks of the small stream that flowed near her home in New Salem. In these outdoor settings she wrote childish verses and recited stories to her nature friends. Her enduring ambition to write poetry was kindled by the natural beauties that surrounded her in the wooded hills of her New England home.

Her talent was rewarded by an education not offered her brothers and sisters. Studying first at the common schools in the towns where she lived, she was eventually enrolled at the New Salem Academy, a private institution, from which she graduated at age fourteen with a teaching certificate.[2]

In 1841, while Emmeline was away at the Academy where she boarded during the school session, Diadama and the three younger children of the family were baptized into The Church of Jesus Christ of Latter-day Saints with several other New Salem families. None of Emmeline's older brothers and sisters, by then all married, ever joined the Church. Joining the Church was a difficult decision for Emmeline, who looked forward to a teaching and literary career in her beloved New England. Her mother's entreaties and the persuasive preaching of Elder Eli P. Maginn altered Emmeline's plans, and she was baptized on 1 March 1842, the day of her birthday celebration.

When she returned to school, she suffered intense ridicule and criticism along with many appeals to abandon her new faith for the promising future that awaited her. In Nauvoo she looked back on the difficulty of those days:

> As soon as Mormonism began to flourish were they not harassing me on every side did they not tear me from my beloved home and the arms of a tender parent to keep me from Mormonism and then the Good Spirit interposed and provided a way for me to be released from the hands of a cruel guardian who pretended so much respect for me that he did not wish me to associate with my own mother and sister because they were Saints of the Most High God.[3]

Emmeline resisted the importunings of her well-meaning friends. After receiving her teaching certificate, she taught school until she married James Harvey Harris, son of the presiding elder of the branch in New Salem, where Emmeline's mother lived. The marriage, which had been arranged by their parents, took place on 29 July 1843, when Emmeline and James were both only fifteen.

In late spring the following year, the young couple, along with James's parents, left Massachusetts to join the Saints in Nauvoo, Illinois. There Emmeline's testimony was born and then tested in a dramatic way. Her contact with the Prophet, whose welcome had so affected her, was brief. Only a few weeks after her first meeting with him on the banks of the Mississippi, he and his brother Hyrum were killed by assassins' bullets. In the following months Emmeline's parents-in-law apostatized; her newborn son, Eugene Henri, died, and her husband James, hoping to find work, took a steamer up the Mississippi, never to return, as he died a short time later. By November 1844 Emmeline found herself alone in Nauvoo, with only a few former neighbors to rely on.

Her response to these tragic events reflects the dramatic aura she imposed on most of the experiences of her life:

> When will sorrow leave my bosom? All my days have I experienced it. Oppression has been my lot. When O when shall I escape the bondage Is not my life a romance? Indeed it is a novel strange and marvellous. Here was I brought to this great city by one to whom I ever expected to look for protection and left dependent on the mercy and friendship of strangers. Merciful Providence, wilt thou long suffer this? Will I forever be unhappy? Will the time never come when happiness and enjoyment will be the lot of this lump of clay, when thralldom and oppression will be cast off?[24]

Her education rescued her from dependency. She resumed teaching school. Among her students were the children of Elizabeth Ann and Newel K. Whitney, whom she had met through Elizabeth's cousin who had traveled to Nauvoo on the steamer with Emmeline. Elizabeth Ann, many years her senior, became not only a lifelong friend and surrogate mother at the death of Emmeline's own mother in 1845, but also her sister-wife in the bonds of polygamy. Marrying Newel K. Whitney on 24

February 1845, Emmeline traveled with the Whitneys to Utah in 1848 and there gave birth to two daughters, Isabel and Melvina, before Whitney's death in 1850.

Emmeline revered the man she had married, thirty-three years her senior. He was "as good a man as ever lived, a father to all within his reach and more than father to me," she recounted on the twenty-fourth anniversary of his death. "I looked to him almost as if he had been a God; my youth, my inexperience of life and its realities caused me to trust most implicitly in one who had power and integrity always at his command."[5] An anchor of calm and security following her personal anguish in Nauvoo,

> He took her in his arms, as her own father might,
>   This stranger patriarch, and comforted and blest
> Her aching heart, and showed her greater truth and light,
>   Even where to seek a haven of sweet rest.[6]

Thus in poetic form Emmeline characterized the man to whom she was sealed in marriage in the Nauvoo Temple and who would remain a fixed point of spiritual and emotional reference throughout the turbulent events that patterned her life.

Left once again to her own resources at her husband's untimely death in 1850, Emmeline began teaching once more to support herself and her daughters. But two years later a brighter prospect suggested itself to her. Remembering her late husband's close friendship with Daniel H. Wells in Nauvoo, she decided to utilize the advantages of plural marriage, publicly acknowledged that year, and appeal to Wells's sense of obligation and friendship. In a note, "A Letter from a True Friend," Emmeline wrote to the prominent Wells, reminding him of his friendship with Newel K. Whitney and asking him to "consider the lonely state" of his friend's widow. She wrote that she had often hoped to be "united with a being noble as thyself" and requested him to "return to her a description of his feelings for her."[7] His feelings must have been favorable, or at least his loyalty to Whitney enduring, for within six months of this correspondence, Emmeline became the seventh wife of Daniel H. Wells,[8] he performing a duty that many Church leaders and others exercised in providing a home, support, and family for faithful widowed Saints. Three daughters were born to this union over a nine-year period—Emma, Elizabeth Ann, and Louisa.

The prosperous Wells was at various times a counselor to Brigham Young, mayor of Salt Lake City, superintendent of Public Works, chancellor of the University of Deseret, and lieutenant general of the Nauvoo Legion. His other wives shared a large home on South Temple Street known as the "big house," while Emmeline and her five daughters lived in a smaller home a few blocks away. Enjoying financial security and stability for the first time in her life, Emmeline was distressed when her husband's investments began to fail. In 1878 Emmeline made several entries in her diary suggesting the need "to practice the most rigid economy" and the possibility of being "thrown upon my own resources."[9] A few years later, financial worries were still gnawing at her. "I feel if I had my home and means independent," she wrote, "I would be much more comfortable and it would be better in every way."[10] When finally in 1888 she was obliged to sell her home, she found the loss overwhelming.[11]

Though family tradition suggests that Emmeline lived apart from the family by choice, visits from her husband seemed to be less frequent than she had expected.

> This evening I fully expected my husband here but was again disappointed. . . . He is not in want of me for a companion or in any sense, he does not need me at all, there are plenty ready and willing to administer to every wish caprice or whim of his, indeed they anticipate them, they are near him always, while I am shut out of his life. . . . It is impossible for me to make myself useful to him in any way while I am held at such a distance.[12]

The joy when he came was almost indescribable:

> My husband came, my heart gave one great bound towards him; O how enthusiastically I love him; truly and devotedly if he could only feel towards me in any degree as I do towards him how happy it would make me.[13]

Often she lamented the loss of her only son, who could have been the "shelter and protection" needed by his "nervous and delicate Mother."[14] Time did not ease the loneliness. For more than a decade during the 1870s Emmeline struggled with longings for more companionship. "I felt dreadful," she wrote at one time; "it seemed as if I wanted some kindness shown to me—I am shut out from all that others enjoy. No wonder I'm forced to be strong-minded."[15] That last phrase is a key to Emmeline's ultimate response to a situation she clearly could not change. Her loneliness and forced independence had begun to generate within her a new sense of self-reliance and determination. A resolution confided to her diary regarding her daughters became her own course of action: "I am determined to train my girls to habits of independence so that they never need to trust blindly but understand for themselves and have sufficient energy of purpose to carry out plans for their own welfare and happiness."[16] The opportunity for Emmeline to develop some of this independence and "energy of purpose" was already beginning to unfold.

In 1872 the *Woman's Exponent,* a biweekly periodical edited and written by Mormon women, was established. At almost the same time entries in Emmeline's diary read, "I sent a manuscript to the office today," or "I submitted a piece to the *Exponent,*" or "prepared my piece for the paper." While the entries were sporadic, they intimated the change that was stirring in Emmeline's life and would ultimately catapult her from an inexperienced, private "scribbler of verse" to a leader of women in political and religious affairs. Early in her life she had acknowledged a desire to achieve something significant:

> Was it under the hemlock boughs . . . that I sat on a summer's day with proud ambition burning in my soul, ambition to be great and known to fame, when a gentle whisper came, . . . "There is no excellence without labor."[17]

Emmeline was forty-four when the *Exponent* was founded. Although she had contributed a few poems to various Church publications and given many to friends and family prior to that time, the avenues she would soon follow were not clear to her then. If the childhood ambition to do something significant remained, it was not evident during the early years of her marriage to Daniel Wells. But by 1878 she seemed to see the direction she was to follow. Her distress at the growing disparagement of Mormon women by eastern papers, along with her sensitivity to the social and legal disabilities of all women and a growing empathy for the woman's movement, set her course for her. "I desire to do all in my power to help elevate the condition of my people, especially women,"[18] she wrote in January of that year. Woman's cause became her cause, one to which she would devote all her energies through her long life. In the *Exponent,* Emmeline had found the vehicle which would help her accomplish this goal. She was a writer, and she would use her pen like a sickle to cut away the thickets of prejudice, custom, and ignorance that defamed Mormon women and undermined the position of all women.

She was well equipped for the labor that would bring "excellence to her ambition." Her dominant characteristic, one contemporary wrote of her, was "her supreme will. . . . She might differ in methods or be widely separated from her associates in matters of procedure, for her ambitions were high, her purposes lofty."[19] Barely five feet tall, with dangling earrings at her ears, rings on her fingers, and pastel scarves and furbelows adorning her neck, she was "exquisitely delicate and dainty, in her writing, her living, and in her life."[20] The fragile exterior, however, camouflaged an "exceedingly frank" nature.[21] She could be "sarcastic at times, not to say caustic," but this quality was softened by a show of repentance afterwards.[22] She was credited with a faultless memory and was frequently sought after for forgotten pieces of information about events in the early history of the Church. Her home became a meeting place for young and old who enjoyed the company, conversation, and congeniality of Emmeline and her daughters. A typical Sunday was spent amidst family and friends:

> Stormy and dark Louie went down to show Millie's servant how to arrange breakfast, Annie took Daisie and Onie to Sunday

School, it was prize day Lou. came home and went—Ort, Budd Hebe & Heber Grant called, Ort. staid and spent the day, Adeline & Inez were here to dinner, Will. & Mill called on their way up to Lib's to dinner; Ort. has been playing and singing nearly all day; this evening Charlie Adelie & May called as they were going to church. Mr. Hendrie arrived today at eleven; it seemed lonely without Will & Millie.[23]

As more and more references to her writing for the *Exponent* appear in her diaries, there are fewer notations about her marital disappointments and loneliness. The *Exponent* became a natural outlet for her creative and intellectual capacities. Chided by her daughters for working so long at the *Exponent* office one day, "as if I had to earn my living," Emmeline explained that she was eager to acquire a "thorough knowledge of an Editor's duties."[24] It would be useful information, for two years later, in 1877, she was appointed editor of the *Woman's Exponent,* holding that position for thirty-seven years. She was evidently pleased with the new opportunity. When Eliza R. Snow had invited her to join the committee of the *Exponent* in 1874 and also asked her to write an editorial in the temporary absence of the editor, Lula Greene Richards, Emmeline expressed concern in her diary that her piece might not please the committee. "For my own part," she concluded, "I would not be at all afraid, I love this kind of work."[25]

Tracing the writings of Emmeline Wells in the *Woman's Exponent* reveals an interesting dichotomy, one which not only characterized her writings but defined her personality as well. Before becoming editor of the *Exponent,* she wrote under the pseudonym of Blanche Beechwood, most of her articles advocating the advancement of women and discussing other issues of the woman question of her time. Emmeline gave up the pseudonym soon after becoming editor, but in her editorials she continued Blanche's strong advocacy for woman's rights. But about the time that Blanche Beechwood disappeared from the pages of the *Exponent,* another persona took her place—"Aunt Em." For the next thirty-six years Aunt

Em served as Emmeline's (Blanche's) alter ego. Each reflected the competing forces that struggled to define women in the nineteenth century.

Aunt Em, the traditional Victorian woman, wrote stories, poems, and articles on topics popularized by *Godey's Lady's Book,* a famous ladies' magazine of the day. Sentimental, nostalgic, and romantic, they were typical Victorian pieces extolling nature's beauties, eulogizing friends, romanticizing the past, and idealizing love. One typical essay by Aunt Em evoked memories of a happy childhood:

> O, yes, we went gipsying in our young days, or nutting and berrying, gathering autumn leaves. . . . A merry crowd we were, with full lunch baskets and light hearts, tripping gaily over the rough pastures or hillsides, climbing on our way the quaint old rail fences, bedecking ourselves with floral treasures, singing in the merriest strains snatches of songs and rhymes, and querying if gipsies themselves, of whom we had read but never seen, enjoyed with as keen a relish the open air and bright sunshine.[26]

Had the circumstances of her life been different, Emmeline Wells may have remained one of these Victorian "scribbling women." In spite of her professed ambitions for fame and recognition, and a desire to work in behalf of women, her nature initially seemed inclined toward the quieter pursuits of family rather than public life. She was subject to moods of depression and, if not quite succumbing to the fashionable "vapors," she often took to her bed with a "nervous disorder" or spells of despondency and uncontrollable crying:

> I never remember to have had so many disagreeable feelings in one evening in all my life. . . . I was alone feeling to[o] gloomy even to write crying most of the time, and my heart nearly bursting, I shall never forget it if I live to be a thousand years old; I never remember of suffering like that before, with the same feelings, O how hard it is to endure unto the end, I am not sure if it be possible for me or not sometimes I think I have to[o] much to bear.[27]

Her somber moods, more frequent than others, grew out of an enduring sorrow that began with the loss of James and Eugene and with Whitney's death a few years later and intensified with the unexpected death of Emma at age twenty-five and the long suffering and death of Louisa in childbirth.

She distinguished between chosen, reflective moments alone in her garden, which she loved, and the frequent times she was compelled to be alone, which brought only gloom. "I do not like sitting alone," she wrote, as "it makes one conjure up all sorts of weird fancies," but enjoy being "alone in the out-door air with plenty folks within call."[28] She often evoked the memory of dead loved ones—James, her youthful husband; Eugene Henri, her son; her mother; her daughters; and Newel K. Whitney, her second husband—who, she felt, had they lived, would have helped assuage her suffering from the constant trials and disappointments that confronted her.[29]

Emmeline adored her daughters and worried about what she would do without them. When Emmie was sick Emmeline was fearful:

> I felt very uneasy about her, she is so precious to me in many ways, so perfectly congenial in temperament the thought of ever being seperated from her is very painful to me, how can I ever bear it, we have been so much to each other, in our dull lonely common-place life.[30]

But she was to be separated not only from Emmie but also from Louisa, her youngest daughter, both of whom died as young women. Their deaths were devastating to her, shadowing even the bright moments of her life.

Though Emmeline undoubtedly had confidantes to share her griefs and problems with, it is unlikely that many were privy to her emotional vulnerability. "Some lives go on in tragedies" was the first line of an autobiographical poem, which continued:

> . . . each part
> To be sustained by human effort grand;
> Though 'neath the outward seeming lies the broken heart,
> That only One above can understand.[31]

Emmeline seldom blurred the boundaries of the dual role she made for herself. Her public responsibilities continued unabated almost to her death, literally sustained by an enormous force of determination that belied her fragile emotional status.

In many aspects the dainty, diminutive Emmeline was a typical Victorian woman. She was pious and pure, two dominant Victorian female qualities, and also deeply sensitive. She was not, however, domestic and was only selectively submissive, in opposition to two other expected Victorian female traits.[32] Her Victorianism partook more of the traces of an earlier romanticism, which lingered throughout the century. She gave expression to it in the romantic fantasies of her poetry and stories, in her quaint dress, in her effusive correspondence, in the self-examination of her diary entries, and in her attention to ambiance—in a room, a garden, a home, or natural setting.

Against the harmonic euphony of Aunt Em's world, Emmeline's feminism imposed a dissonant counterpoint. This dyadic nature is nowhere more startlingly exposed than in two pieces of her writing, one an *Exponent* article and the other a diary entry, written within days of each other. On 1 October 1874, the *Exponent* ran an article by Blanche Beechwood which asked,

> Is there then nothing worth living for, but to be petted, humored and caressed, by a man? That is all very well as far as it goes, but that man is the only thing in existence worth living for I fail to see. All honor and reverence to good men; but they and their attentions are not the only sources of happiness on the earth, and need not fill up every thought of woman. And when men see that women can exist without their being constantly at hand, that they can learn to be self-reliant or depend upon each other for more or less happiness, it will perhaps take a little of the conceit out of some of them.[33]

On the day this article appeared in the *Exponent,* Emmeline wrote in her diary:

> O if my husband could only love me even a little and not seem so perfectly indifferent to any sensation of that kind, he cannot know the craving of my nature, he is surrounded with love on every side, and I am cast out O My poor aching heart where shall

it rest its burden, only on the Lord, only to Him can I look every other avenue seems closed against me. . . . I have no one to go to for comfort or shelter no strong arm to lean upon no bosom bared for me, no protection or comfort in my husband.[34]

Always lying just below the bright and visible surface of Emmeline's strong self-possession were the dark depths of the brooding romantic, longing for a life and love perpetually beyond her grasp.

The roots of Emmeline's feminism lay not only in the circumstances of her personal life but also in the Relief Society, organized in Nauvoo in 1842 by Joseph Smith. Though not a member herself in Nauvoo, Emmeline shared its Nauvoo birth and demise vicariously through Elizabeth Ann Whitney, her sister-wife, who was not only a charter member but a counselor to Emma Smith, the first president. From Elizabeth, Emmeline learned of Joseph's instructions to the sisters, of the growth of the organization, and of its suspension just before his death. She learned that it was not intended to be just another of the benevolent societies that proliferated New England, but was organized "under the priesthood after the pattern of the priesthood" and "according to the law of heaven," as John Taylor, who was present at its inception, observed. When Joseph spoke the significant words, "I now turn the key to you in the name of God and this Society shall rejoice and knowledge and intelligence shall flow down from this time— this is the beginning of better days to this Society,"[35] he opened new vistas of promise and opportunity for women. To Emmeline this event heralded the dawn of a new age and literally opened the dispensation in which women would regain their lost status as man's equal. Knowledge and intelligence would be the birthright of women from that time forward. Women would be absolved from the supposed effects of Eve's transgression, long used to justify their subordinate position in the home and in society, for women now had the key to effectuate their own redemption.

Thus, Joseph Smith's turning of the key for women in 1842 and the organizing of the woman's rights movement in Seneca

Falls, New York, just six years later were no coincidence. The "Declaration of Sentiments" drawn up at Seneca Falls, enumerating woman's disabilities in society and proposing appropriate redress,[36] was construed by many Mormons as part of a grand design whose impetus was the prophetic uttering of Joseph Smith. "Men no longer [had] the same absolute sway" after that time, Emmeline observed, rejoicing that "a new era [had] been ushered in, mainly through the exertions of self-made women, acted upon by an influence many comprehend[ed] not, which [was] working for their redemption from under the curse [of Eve]."[37] Through the years Emmeline took pride in the fact that the Relief Society had opened

> one of the most important eras in the history of woman. It presented the great woman-question to the Latter-day Saints, previous to the woman's rights organizations . . . not in any aggressive form as woman opposed to man, but as a co-worker and help-meet in all that relates to the well-being and advancement of both, and mutual promoting of the best interests of the community at large.[38]

Among those who, like Emmeline, perceived a connection between the organization of Mormon women and the beginning of the woman's rights movement was Sarah M. Kimball. An active suffragist, she declared in 1870, when Utah women were enfranchised for the first time, that she had always been a "woman's rights woman" and later stated that "the sure foundations of the suffrage cause were deeply and permanently laid on the 17th of March, 1842."[39] Lula Greene Richards, first editor of the *Woman's Exponent,* wrote in 1901:

> [Joseph] declared when he organized the Sisterhood of the Church into the Relief Society, that he "turned the key in favor of woman." Since that time what a noble work has been accomplished in woman's favor by hundreds of heroic women in this and other nations, including many of the Society which the Prophet organized.[40]

Susa Young Gates, writer, editor, suffragist, and daughter of Brigham Young, remarked, "From the hour the key was given, great and restless activity has marked every phase of womanly life."[41]

Some of the Brethren concurred. Elder Orson F. Whitney declared, "The lifting of the women of Zion to that plane, was the beginning of a work for the elevation of womankind throughout the world. 'I have turned the key,' said the Prophet on that historic occasion," Elder Whitney continued,

> and from what has since taken place we are justified in believing that the words were big with fate . . . the spirit of woman's work has spread, until other nations are interested in the growing movement, . . . But who ever heard of such things until after the establishment of "Mormonism," until the turning of the key by the Prophet of God, and the setting up in this Church, of women's organizations, as one of the signs of a new era, one of those sunbursts of light that proclaim the dawning of a new dispensation?[42]

As late as 1945, George Albert Smith told the sisters in a Relief Society conference that "when the Prophet Joseph Smith turned the key for the emancipation of womankind, it was turned for all the world."[43]

Woman's cause, for Emmeline, thus encompassed a theological dimension and, though her rhetoric was often indistinguishable from that of national proponents of women's rights, her motivations derived from a different source. Woman's roles as wife, mother, homemaker, worker, citizen, and individual were inextricably bound together within an eternal framework. Progress toward perfection, an eternal quest, gave significance to the most common experience. With this enlarged view of human purpose and the promise of eternal reward, Emmeline embraced the woman's movement as a means to break the bonds of repression which had for so long kept women from reaching their highest potential. "Let [woman] have the same opportunities for an education, observation and experience in public and private for a succession of years," she challenged, "and then see if she is not equally endowed with man and prepared to bear her part on all general questions socially, politically, industrially and educationally as well as spiritually."[44]

Sensing what seemed to her to be an unprecedented opportunity in her religion for female participation, initiative, and leadership, especially through the programs Brigham Young outlined for the newly revitalized Relief Society, Emmeline found a natural coalescence of Mormon and feminist goals for women. An appraisal she made of the Relief Society in 1889, when she was serving as general secretary, indicates the impact she felt it had on the lives of Mormon women:

> It has given to woman, in its rise and progress, influence on almost all subjects that pertain to her welfare and happiness, and opportunities for expressing her own thoughts, views and opinions; all of which has had a tendency to make her intelligent in regard to matters which before were considered incompatible with "woman's sphere" and unintelligible to her "weaker" mind.[45]

Observing women all about her responding to Brigham Young's call to study skills beyond housekeeping—accounting, telegraphy, typesetting, even medicine—and to obtain an education at the highest level possible, reinforced Emmeline's assessment of the progressive attitudes of Mormonism toward women.[46] Elder Joseph F. Smith in a Relief Society conference endorsed this broad view of women's potential and usefulness. "Why," he asked,

> shall one [sex] be admitted to all the avenues of mental and physical progress and prosperity and the other be prohibited, and prescribed within certain narrow limits? . . . It is all right for them to be qualified for any and all positions, and possess the right or privelege to fill them, but that they *must* do so does not follow.

Then, chastising those who would restrain women from exercising their option to be what they had capacity to be, he concluded:

> Women may be found who seem to glory in their enthralled condition, and who caress and fondle the very chains and manacles which fetter and enslave them! Let those who love this helpless dependent condition and prefer to remain in it and enjoy it; but for conscience and for mercy's sake let them not stand in the way of those of their sisters who would be, and of right ought to be *free.*[47]

320

By interpreting from her Mormon perspective the theories enunciated by Mary Wollstonecraft, Margaret Fuller, Elizabeth Cady Stanton, and other feminists, Emmeline developed her own canon of beliefs. "Woman must be instrumental in bringing about the restoration of that equality which existed when the world was created," she wrote in a Relief Society handbook in 1902. "Perfect equality then and so it must be when all things are restored as they were in the beginning."[48] Moreover, equality began in the home. Though thrice married, Emmeline only briefly experienced the typical monogamous marriage of her time in which husband ruled and wife served, so much extolled by pulpit and press. Yet it was to this kind of relationship that she directed her criticism. A man too often saw his wife as "simply a necessity in his establishment," she observed,

> to manage his house, to cook his dinner, to attend to his wardrobe, always on hand if she is wanted and always out of sight when not needed. He doesn't mind kissing her occasionally, when it suits him; but he never thinks she has any thoughts of her own, any ideas which might be developed; she must not have even an opinion, or if she has she mustn't express it, it is entirely out of place; she is a subject, not a joint-partner in the domestic firm.[49]

Her concept of a satisfying marriage was one in which both partners supported and uplifted the other. This view digressed sharply with the formulas proposed for proper wifely behavior by the women's magazines of her day, which encouraged women to be submissive, self-sacrificing, and silent. Emmeline felt that honest love promoted a different kind of relationship. "Why," she asked, "is it not possible for man and woman to love each other truly, and dwell together in harmony, each according to the other all the freedom of thought, feeling, and expression they would grant to one who was not bound to them by indissoluble ties?"[50] She regretted the existence of those marriages in which the wife gave all, merging her life into her husband's to the "extinguishing and crushing out of all desires, ambitions, tastes, or capabilities." Her challenge to husbands was to prove themselves "noble enough to share with [their wives] such laurels as *either* may be able to win in the battle field of life, instead of arrogating to [themselves] the right to dictate . . . in all things, saying, 'thus far shalt thou go and no farther.' "[51]

Emmeline admonished women to become "enlightened on all points pertaining to life and its purposes," and she decried the influences that made women reluctant to break the "silken cord" which bound them to the "proprieties and delicacies of . . . life" beyond which they dared not step.[52] She argued that

> in the name of justice, reason, and common sense, let woman be fortified and strengthened by every possible advantage, that she may be adequately and thoroughly fitted not only to grace the drawing room, and manage every department of her household, but to perform with skill and wisdom the arduous and elaborate work of molding and fashioning the fabrics of which society is to be woven.[53]

Education was a duty as well as a privilege for women and the only means to truly develop their latent capabilities, Emmeline declared. Education was essential in order for a mother to act with intelligence within the confines of her home and for a woman to exercise her greatest influence for the betterment of society. It was through the advanced education of women, she believed, that these goals could be attained and the entire world could realize a higher civilization.[54]

Thus she extended her views of equal partnership in the home to the community. Women were not asking for their rights simply because of "place or power," she wrote,

> or to crowd men out of the ranks of the wage earners or professions but that they may be acknowledged as being an equal in the work and business of the great world in which all must live and take part. . . . This great work can never be done well by one half of the human family; it is the opinion of all who think deeply that men and women must do the work together, and unitedly.[55]

For Emmeline, as for most of her feminist contemporaries, the fight for equal rights came to center on suffrage as the

means of achieving their goals. Though she had been expressing her views on the woman question for nearly a decade in
articles for the *Woman's Exponent* and the *Boston Woman's
Journal,* a national suffrage paper, she did not take an active
role in the national suffrage movement until 1879 when John
Taylor appointed her and Zina Young Williams as delegates to
represent Mormon women at the national suffrage convention
in Washington.

Utah women had been given the vote in 1870 without peti-
tion or demonstration. For the previous three years members
of Congress had suggested granting suffrage to women in the
territories not only as an experiment in woman suffrage but
also as a ploy to enable Mormon women in Utah territory to
unshackle themselves from the bonds of polygamy. While
Congress vacillated over the proposal, the Utah territorial legislature acted upon the idea and passed the measure unanimously. It became law on 12 February 1870.

The motives for adopting such progressive legislation may
have been varied, but it was obvious that such a gesture mea-
surably countered the "enslaved" image of Mormon women.
A hidden bonus came in the form of unintended support for
the Mormon cause when suffrage became the scapegoat of
polygamy. For, unlike the prognosis of anti-polygamists, who
encouraged suffrage for polygamous Mormon women to free
themselves, Mormon women did not rise up *en masse* and
vote against plural marriage. Now the agitation in Congress was
to strengthen anti-polygamy legislation by increasing its penalties. Disfranchising Mormon women became one of these. Declaring they were ready to "render all the aid in their power to
fight this proposition,"[56] national suffragists stepped up their
lobbying efforts each time Congress considered a measure to
disfranchise Utah women.

When the United States Supreme Court decided to hear the
Reynolds case in 1878 challenging the constitutionality of the
anti-polygamy act of 1862, the time seemed propitious for
Mormons to strengthen their Washington representation. Heretofore the only Utah women involved in national suffrage

activities were Charlotte Godbe and her estranged sister-wives Annie and Mary, all married to William Godbe, founder of the liberal splinter group, the Godbeites. These women made the initial contact with national suffragists as early as 1869, when the first annual suffrage convention was held in Washington, D.C. Their independent efforts during the decade before Emmeline and Zina Williams were appointed delegates to the national convention, however, were not considered representative of the Mormon-dominated territory.

Emmeline and Zina had another mission to perform in Washington besides attending the suffrage convention, however. They were charged with an assignment to carry a memorial to Congress and the President against proposed anti-polygamy legislation that would invalidate existing marriages and illegitimatize the children of these marriages. Undoubtedly it was hoped that their efforts would influence in some way the decision of the Supreme Court on the Reynolds case. However, the Supreme Court rendered its decision while the two women were on their way to Washington. Thus, their mission became even more imperative.

It was no easy task for these two representatives of the much maligned women of Utah to brave the ridicule and derogation of Easterners. The cordiality with which they were met by Elizabeth Cady Stanton and Susan B. Anthony, however, assuaged their fears. Recognition of their capabilities even before they visited Washington perhaps helped pave the way for them. Suffragist Sarah Spencer had drawn attention to Mormon women in an article in *Woman's Words* in 1878 praising their abilities:

> At our next Convention in Washington, let us by all means have one or more of the enterprising, public-spirited women of Utah present. If we mistake not our Gentile sisters have much to learn from these heroic women. What we read of their business ability, courage and patriotism is an inspiration to us.[57]

But not everyone was pleased to have the controversial Mormons join the suffrage cause. An article in the *Boston Woman's Journal* criticized the presence of Mormon women at the convention, noticeably disturbing Elizabeth Stanton, especially since editor Lucy Stone's silence appeared to condone the criticism. Elizabeth Stanton answered, "If George Q. Cannon can sit in the Congress of the United States without compromising that body on the question of Polygamy, I should think Mormon women might sit on our platform without making us responsible for their religious faith."[58] Suffragists always made clear, however, that their sympathies were not with the Mormon cause per se, only against the move to use woman's suffrage as a weapon to strike at polygamy.[59]

Both Emmeline and Zina Williams spoke at the convention, and Emmeline was appointed one of a committee of three to call upon President Hayes to present the resolutions of the conference. "But the beauty of the interview," one non-Mormon delegate observed, "was when the two Mormon ladies laid their case before the President and he showed such kindly sympathy with them when they proved what misery would follow in Utah the enforcement of the act of 1862 against polygamy." When they finished their appeal, the President seemed "pained," the reporter observed, "reflecting how little he could do to help them since the United States Supreme Court has rendered a decision within a month against polygamy in Utah."[60] This would be the first of many interviews Emmeline B. Wells would conduct on behalf of Mormon women, appealing the case of the Mormons to Congress, to judiciary committees, and to Presidents themselves and often their wives. While she was always greeted with respect and even sympathy, neither she nor all the other delegates sent on the same mission were able to stem the tide of events that was building force against the Mormons and would culminate in the devastating Edmunds-Tucker Act of 1887, which, among other stringent penalties, abrogated women's suffrage in Utah.

From 1879 on, Emmeline was a frequent delegate to both the National and American Women's Suffrage conventions, becoming vice-president for Utah shortly after her return from her first convention and serving in various capacities during the next thirty years.

Emmeline also regularly represented the Relief Society, with other Utah delegates, at the meetings of the International Council of Women, organized in 1888, and the National Council of Women, which she joined in 1891. She also served in various offices in these organizations, and with her fellow Mormon delegates she presented papers on the Relief Society and life in Utah. During the Chicago World's Fair in 1893, a special congress of representative women was held under the direction of May Wright Sewall, president of the National Council of Women. Both the Relief Society and the Young Women's Mutual Improvement Association were represented. At one of the sessions Emmeline spoke on "Western Women in Journalism" and was given the honor of presiding at another of the sessions. She reflected on this opportunity:

> This morning I presided over the General Congress in the Hall of Columbus—an honor never before accorded to a Mormon woman—if one of our brethren had such a distinguished honor conferred upon them, it would have been heralded the country over and thought a great achievement.[61]

A highlight of her national work for women was the invitation to speak at the International Council of Women convention held in London in 1899 as one of the official delegates from the United States.

One of the most memorable of the suffrage conventions Emmeline attended was in Atlanta in January 1895. There she was to speak on the progress of Utah women in claiming their place in the new Utah State Constitution which was to be decided upon at the constitutional convention in March. With the suspension of polygamy in 1890, the way had been opened for statehood. Since Utah women had lost their franchise under the Edmunds-Tucker Law in 1887, it was imperative it be regained in the new organic law of the state. Arguing in the *Woman's Exponent* that "the women of Utah had the ballot wrested from them without adjudication, and no redress has ever been offered for that wrong," Emmeline reasoned that "it would be but a simple act of justice for that wrong done in the past, to restore the right of franchise now."[62]

Before leaving for the convention, once again with the blessings and financial support of the Church, Emmeline, as president of the Utah Woman's Suffrage Association, outlined her plans for putting woman's suffrage in the new constitution. Essentially, the strategy was to work quietly among individual delegates to the convention to gain their support. She also used the *Exponent* to warm converts to the cause. "Now that a new political era has come in the history of the Territory," she wrote in one editorial, "what is to be the outlook for the recognition of women as citizens? They pay their taxes as well as men and we have never heard that women were ignorant in regard to paying taxes; that is one of the privileges they are permitted."[63]

She urged women to qualify themselves to be useful and active on the political scene and to be ready when the rights of citizenship would be given to them. When the delegates were being chosen for the constitutional convention, using for her an uncharacteristic feminine ploy, she posed the question:

> How will [the delegates] consider the interests of the sex who have no representation save through them? Will their [women's] claims to citizenship be guaranteed to them through these great, grand, noblehearted sons of the soil? They must be trusted with this live question, it cannot be ignored for this is the woman's age of the world, and now the imperative need of the hour, is pending.[64]

At that time, Emmeline was anticipating opposition primarily from the gentile population of Utah, who feared a swelling of the majority voice in Utah politics, but she would later be surprised to find that the most vehement opponent would be a Church leader.

In the meantime, with the situation looking favorable for woman's suffrage, Emmeline began her six-week journey to Atlanta and then to Washington for the meeting of the National Council of Women. At the conclusion of her report to the Atlanta convention, she was gratified to feel the strong support of her fellow suffrage workers. "Miss Anthony came forward, put her arms around me, and made such an eloquent appeal," she wrote in her diary, "that some of the ladies were moved to tears; it was a tribute of personal affection as well as a flattering compliment to the Territory."[65]

Upon her return to Utah she was plunged immediately into a battle over suffrage she could not possibly have foreseen. Beginning with a vocal few in the convention, the argument against the vote for women moved from one of expediency to one of principle, led by the delegate from Davis County, Brigham H. Roberts, a member of the First Council of Seventy. His eloquence threatened to sweep confirmed suffragists to his point of view, which enunciated first the danger to passage of the constitution if it contained a woman suffrage clause and second the impropriety of women at the polls or embroiled in politics. Emmeline's response was swift and pointed:

> It is pitiful to see how men opposed to woman suffrage try to make the women believe it is because they worship them so, and think them far too good, and one would really think to hear those eloquent orators talk, that laws were all framed purposely to protect women in their rights, and men stood ready to defend them with their lives. . . . We can only say they have been bold and must answer to their own consciences; . . . let us hope the practical experience that will come with the ballot may convince even them that good may follow and they and their children receive the benefit of what they could not discern in the future progress of the world.[66]

While prolonging the debate over what some had considered a rubber-stamp endorsement of woman suffrage, Roberts's oratory did not succeed in defeating the proposition. Emmeline happily reported in an editorial on 1 May 1895 that the section on equal suffrage had passed.[67] That fall, while the ratifying votes were still being counted, she proudly proclaimed Utah as "the third free state for which another star will be placed in the woman's flag, and the forty-fifth star in the flag dear to every patriot."[68] But problems still remained.

The breaking up of the unified Mormon People's Party in 1891 so that Mormons could align themselves with national parties caused strain and hard feelings. For the women of the

Church it created the first real schism in the sisterhood. Emmeline observed the problems that developed:

> The division into two political parties of the Peoples' Party is the principal subject under discussion at present and considerable feeling is manifested and some ill will, or dissension is being developed already. It seems too bad that it should be so.[69]

In 1895, while most of her associates in the Relief Society general presidency (she was the secretary) and her suffrage associates became Democrats, Emmeline chose to become a Republican. This decision, on the surface, seems strange since it set her apart from virtually all of the women with whom she had been so closely allied. But there were compelling reasons for her to become a Republican. Her motive certainly had an ideological basis. According to a Republican Party document to which her name was affixed, the party declared its support of protective tariffs, bounties, and bimetalism and invoked past Republician achievements such as the Homestead Act and the abolition of slavery, urging the women of Utah who believed in these political principles to join the Republican Party. She was consistently vocal in support of this platform.

Since the political allegiances of her family were divided, Emmeline did not fall naturally into a political identity. One son-in-law was a Democrat; another was a Republican. Orson F. Whitney, a close Whitney relative, was an active Democrat, but Emmeline's husband Daniel, who died in 1891, was considered the father of Republicanism in Utah.

The most compelling reason for the choice was, undoubtedly, to satisfy her own self-interests. She was fervently courted by prominent Republicans to declare publicly for their party. Though she had evidently aligned herself with the Democratic Party earlier,[70] there is no indication that she was recruited with such fervor by the Democrats. Moreover, without the competition of her suffrage colleagues who also had political ambitions, Emmeline may have felt herself in a better position to become a candidate herself for some political office. She had always looked forward to women holding office, and who was better qualified than herself?

Thus it was that she became instrumental in organizing the Woman's Republican League, and she worked in behalf of Republicanism throughout the soon-to-be state. She was, as she had hoped, chosen by her party to be a candidate for the legislature along with Lillie Pardee for the senate and Emma McVicker for state superintendent of education. When a court ruling prohibited women from voting in the ratifying election scheduled for November 1895, and by implication prohibited women from running for office, since the constitution permitting their candidacy had yet to be ratified, public pressure forced them to withdraw their names. It was with great reluctance that Emmeline bowed to this pressure. "I am thoroughly worried about my resignation," she wrote in her journal on 17 October 1895. "I believe it is wrong. . . . I think moreover I have a right to be elected to the Legislature—as also other women—I yield unwillingly to the pressure brought to bear against the name of women on the Ticket."[71] She had hoped to make her nomination a test case of "the principle of women's equality," but that issue would be left to another election.

An aftermath of the prolonged and heated debate over inclusion of woman's suffrage in the constitution centered on the election of B. H. Roberts to Congress in the 1898 election. Emmeline and B. H. Roberts, though not personally confronting each other in the constitutional debate, were political adversaries over the issue of woman's suffrage. Though Roberts lost the cause, his nomination and subsequent election to Congress occurred with the deep regret and embarrassment of Utah's newly enfranchised women. Emmeline looked on his nomination as an insult to the women of the state, and her office entertained an army of indignant women with similar sentiments. "It is an outrageous thing for him to expect women's votes,"[72] she told her diary shortly after his nomination. Because of the number of women seeking advice on how to proceed in the campaign, she took the problem to the First Presidency of the Church. She found them opposed to Roberts's candidacy and willing that women should work, either privately or publicly, to defeat him.[73] Despite their efforts, however, B. H. Roberts won the election. Emmeline's response reflected her disappointment. "I cannot understand," she wrote, "how the women of the State can be so unscrupulous as to vote for such a man."[74]

Ironically, nearly twelve years later, at a public celebration in honor of Emmeline's eighty-second birthday, B. H. Roberts presented her a bouquet of white roses with a brief speech of tribute. A few days later, Emmeline penned him a letter of appreciation. She thanked him for the "delicate gift of roses . . . the most beautiful [gift] by far" and then explained that "coming from one who knew me so distantly (in a way) it was such a surprise that it was really like discovering a treasure— finding a beauty disguised in one, where we had only anticipated a quantum of reserve. I feel that I know you better, if only because of the selection of flowers, that I love most of all—white roses." She expressed a desire that some day she would be able to converse with him, to exchange thoughts "with one of superior intelligence," a "luxury in this barren world of cold communication."[75] Both had evidently laid their differences to rest.

In October of that same year Emmeline Wells, nearing her eighty-third birthday, reached another milestone in her eventful life. She was appointed general president of the Relief Society. Two years earlier, during a serious illness of then president Bathsheba W. Smith, Emmeline had discussed possible successors in a letter to Romania Pratt Penrose, a Relief Society general board member who was in England. Both Emmeline's daughter, Annie Wells Cannon, and Romania herself had been mentioned as possibilities by Bathsheba Smith, along with Clarissa Williams and Julina Smith. Emmeline did not consider herself a candidate.[76] But when the time came, she was selected. Her appointment came on Sunday, 2 October 1910, at the conclusion of the monthly fast meeting in the temple, when President Lund, counselor to President Joseph F. Smith, told her she had been chosen by President Smith to preside over the Relief Society.[77] She found the moment both "embarrassing" and surprising, fully expecting a younger woman to be appointed. Yet despite her age, or maybe because of it, no one was better qualified than Emmeline Wells to lead the Relief Society, nor more deserving, since to a large extent the office was also honorific.

For nearly forty years she had been active in that organization, holding the position of general secretary for more than twenty of those years. In 1876 Brigham Young had given her charge of a grain-saving program which she implemented through the Relief Society and encouraged in articles in the *Woman's Exponent.* Speaking of this assignment some years later, she recalled that during an illness in Nauvoo, she was given a blessing, part of which said, "You will live to do a work that has never been done by any woman, since the Creation.' "[78] She believed that heading the grain-saving mission was the work envisioned for her. Her timid efforts in organizing the grain-saving mission developed into a significant program, ultimately administered by the Relief Society. The stored grain was used for the poor at home and for relief abroad and soon became associated with the Relief Society as its major relief effort. During World War I, while Emmeline presided over the Relief Society, more than 200,000 bushels of wheat were sold to the United States government. After the war, when President Woodrow Wilson and his wife visited Salt Lake City, they called on Emmeline in her apartment at the Hotel Utah, where she was recuperating from an illness. Going directly to her bedside, President Wilson shook hands with her and expressed his personal appreciation for turning over the stored grain to the nation during its hour of need.[79] Five times Emmeline Wells had visited presidents in the White House, asking for their help in behalf of Mormon women. Now a president had come to her to thank her for the help of Mormon women in behalf of the nation.

Even in this last calling in the service of women, Emmeline would not be free from the disappointments that accompanied her through life. Continuing as editor of the *Woman's Exponent* after becoming president of the Relief Society, she proposed at the April conference in 1913 transferring the *Exponent* to the Relief Society as its official organ. She would continue as editor with her daughter Annie Wells Cannon as assistant. Her proposal was not acted upon at that time, but a year later a decision was made. The minutes of the Relief Society general board meeting, 12 January 1914, convey the disappointment Emmeline felt at the decision:

> President Wells announced that it was her present intention to discontinue the *Woman's Exponent* with the February Number. She had desired the privilege of giving the good will of her paper and the name to the Society, she had also desired that her name be used as editor of the Relief Society organ. These privileges had been denied her, and she had given up the paper, the name of the paper, and the idea of having her name used as editor.[80]

Susa Young Gates, a member of the board and founder of the *Young Woman's Journal,* was chosen to edit an interim bulletin in 1915 and the newly launched *Relief Society Magazine* in 1916.

It might have seemed an overextension of responsibility for one woman to preside over a large organization and edit its official organ at the same time, especially at age eighty-six. But age did not diminish Emmeline's expectations of herself, and the *Exponent* was more than just a publication to her. It had been her voice, her companion, even her child, whose life she had struggled to preserve for thirty-seven years. From the beginning, it had reported news and business of the Relief Society, and in later years had increasingly become the unofficial publication of that organization. It had even carried on its masthead, during its final years, the words, "The Organ of the Latter-day Saints Woman's Relief Society." But the *Exponent* had completed its work. A new magazine with a new format and a new editor was to take its place.

On 12 January 1914, Emmeline wrote a single sentence in her diary: "I had to get my editorial ready for the paper." That editorial would be the last she would ever write for her beloved paper. It was her valedictory. She called it "Heartfelt Farewell":

The aim of the paper has always been to assist those who needed assistance in any or every line. . . . For women, it has been a standard bearer, proclaiming their worth and just claims throughout the long years of its existence. . . . We love the readers of this paper as a part of ourselves; we love women and would ever strive to uplift and help them to attain their ideals; . . . [The *Exponent*] has surely performed a mission in the midst of Zion for the women of Zion, holding as it does within its leaves the history of their work. To lay aside the editorial pen, even after so many long years, seems a hard task, but though the pen may be idle, the mind will ever gratefully remember all the associations which this little paper has been instrumental in creating.[81]

Emmeline Wells's life bridged two centuries. Outliving most of her contemporaries, she was revered as one who knew the Prophet Joseph by a generation one step removed from that personal knowledge. Every birthday in her later years was publicly noted, particularly during leap years, when the actual day, 29 February, occurred. Her book of poetry, *Musings and Memories,* was published in 1896; its popularity demanded a second edition in 1915. For her, the most signal honor came in 1912 when she was eighty-four. She was selected to receive an honorary doctor of literature from Brigham Young University, an event "unique in Mormon history," she noted. The Blanche Beechwood in her rose to the fore as she responded to the large crowd assembled in the auditorium of the Bishop's Building in Salt Lake City. Such an honor meant much to her, she said, "not only as a personal tribute, but as an honor to her sex." She had always regretted, she continued, that "great educational institutions had withheld this distinction from women," and she hoped that this event would show the world that "Utah withheld nothing from the women of the State."[82] Forty-four years would pass before another woman would be so honored by that institution.

One final tribute was presented posthumously. On 29 February 1928, the one hundredth anniversary of her birth, a number of religious and community organizations representing the women of Utah commissioned a marble bust of her to be sculpted and placed in the rotunda of the State Capitol. It was inscribed simply, "A Fine Soul Who Served Us."

Armed with the satisfaction that successful achievement brought to her public efforts, Emmeline met the bittersweet ending of her private life with equanimity. Separated from her husband for most of the thirty-seven years of their marriage, Emmeline was joyous, though undoubtedly confused, by his inexplicable reemergence in her later life. In 1888, a year after returning from presiding over the European Mission, Daniel H. Wells was appointed president of the newly constructed Manti Temple. On his frequent visits to Salt Lake City, he sought Emmeline's company and often stayed at her home. "Strange indeed . . . ," she wrote after one of his visits, "that after all my younger years have been past in comparative seclusion that when I am past three score even he should seem so devoted."[83] Letters followed these visits, urging her to come to Manti. In March 1890, she decided to combine a Relief Society assignment to Ephraim with a visit to Manti. Her words glow with the warmth of the rekindled attraction:

> O the joy of being once more in his dear presence—his room is so nice and we are so cosy by the large grate and such a comfortable fire in it. We are more like lovers than husband and wife for we are so far removed from each other there is always the embarrassment of lovers and yet we have been married more than 37 years—how odd it seems I do not feel old neither does he— we are young to each other and that is well.[84]

Emmeline was sixty-two; Daniel, seventy-six. More visits followed throughout the summer and fall of 1890. Then, early in March 1891, when Emmeline returned from a meeting in Washington, she was shocked to learn that Daniel Wells was in Salt Lake City, seriously ill. She spent the next few days with his other wives at his bedside and saw him die on 24 March 1891. Alone in her own house afterwards, she reflected on her life with him, now

> only memories, only the coming and going and parting at the door, the joy when he came the sorrow when he went as though

all the light died out of my life. Such intense love he has manifested towards me of late years. Such a remarkable change from the long ago, when I needed him so much more, how peculiarly these things come about.[85]

The last few years of her life were shadow without substance. Her enormous energy had finally begun to wane. When Heber J. Grant became President of the Church in 1918, Emmeline Wells had served eight years as general president of the Relief Society. She was ninety. A long-time friend, President Grant approached her about the possibility of a release. Her only response was that such a move would be fatal to her, and so he took no action. Then, three years later, when she suffered a serious illness and moved to her daughter Annie's home, President Grant decided to approach her again about a release. Their meeting at the Cannon farm was a painful experience for them both. After learning his purpose in coming, Emmeline felt compelled to recite the history of the Relief Society from its beginnings, as if to prove that the legendary keenness of her memory was still sharp. But this time President Grant was firm. He had hoped to convince her of "the wisdom" of his decision, made for "the good of the work of the Lord."[86] But the release stood in her mind only as a public humiliation. All of her predecessors, except Emma Smith, had died in office. It was customary for Church authorities to serve until death. She could not be reconciled, but the release stood. When President Grant left, she started up the staircase to her room. Before reaching the top, she suffered a stroke and fell to the stairs unconscious. She lay nearly comatose for the next three weeks and died on 25 April 1921.

Emmeline B. Wells was the second woman to be honored with a funeral in the Tabernacle, the first on a weekday, making the occasion a unique "tribute to a woman."[87] Remembered as "one of the finest products of Mormonism," a woman who "had the mental force to be a pillar of strength, perhaps more than has been given to any other woman of her day," she was honored for being as "unyielding as the granite of her native New England in her devotion to that which she considered duty."[88] A complex and dynamic force veiled in lavender and lace, Emmeline Wells accomplished the task she had set about nearly fifty years before. She once wrote that she hoped historians would "remember the women of Zion when compiling the history of this Western land."[89] Emmeline B. Wells is one who will be remembered.

Notes

1. *Young Woman's Journal* 16 (Dec. 1905): 554–56. See also 23 (Aug. 1912): 435–38.

2. Augusta Joyce Crocheron, *Representative Women of Deseret: A Book of Biographical Sketches* (Salt Lake City: J. C. Graham & Co., 1884), p. 67.

3. Emmeline B. Wells, Diary, 20 February 1845, Special Collections, Harold B. Lee Library, Brigham Young University, Provo, Utah.

4. Wells, Diary, 20 February 1845.

5. Ibid., 23 September 1874.

6. Emmeline B. Wells, "Faith and Fidelity," *Musings and Memories,* 2d ed. (Salt Lake City: Deseret News, 1915), p. 210.

7. Daniel H. Wells Papers, Library-Archives, Historical Department, The Church of Jesus Christ of Latter-day Saints, Salt Lake City (hereafter cited as LDS Church Archives), as quoted in Patricia Rasmussen Eaton-Gadsby and Judith Rasmussen Dushku, "Emmeline B. Wells," in Vicky Burgess-Olson, *Sister Saints* (Provo: BYU Press, 1978), p. 459.

8. His first wife, Eliza Rebecca Robison, chose not to become a Mormon and remained in Nauvoo with their son when Daniel joined the Church and moved west.

9. Wells, Diary, 7 January 1878 and 3 February 1878.

10. Wells, Diary, 9 December 1881.

11. Bryant S. Hinckley, *Daniel H. Wells and Events of His Time* (Salt Lake City: Deseret News Press, 1942), p. 395. See also Orson F. Whitney, *History of Utah,* 4 volumes (Salt Lake City: George Q. Cannon & Sons, Co., Publishers, 1904), 4:179. Daniel H. Wells had invested heavily in a gas works company which evidently failed, and by selling most of his valuable property holdings he was able to pay off debts amounting to several thousand dollars, leaving enough to provide modest homes for his wives.

12. Wells, Diary, 13 September 1874.

13. Ibid., 11 October 1874.

14. Ibid., 1 September 1874.

15. Ibid., 6 January 1878.

16. Ibid., 7 January 1878.

17. "Midnight Soliloquoy," *Woman's Exponent* 8 (15 Apr. 1880): 175–76.

18. Wells, Diary, 4 January 1878.

19. Susa Young Gates, "President Emmeline B. Wells," *Improvement Era* 24 (May 1921): 719.

20. Susa Young Gates, "Emmeline B. Wells," *History of the Young Ladies' Mutual Improvement Association* (Salt Lake City: Deseret News, 1911), p. 53.

21. Crocheron, *Representative Women of Deseret,* p. 67.

22. Gates, *History of the Young Ladies' Mutual Improvement Association,* p. 53.

23. Wells, Diary, 8 November 1874.

24. Ibid., 24 March 1875.

25. Ibid., 24 August 1874.

26. "When We Went Gipsying," *Woman's Exponent* 9 (1 June 1880): 7.

27. Wells, Diary, 7 January 1875.

28. Ibid., 18 September 1874.

29. Ibid., various entries scattered throughout the diaries.

30. Ibid., 6 September 1874.

31. Wells, "Faith and Fidelity," *Musings and Memories,* p. 221.

32. Barbara Welter, "The Cult of True Womanhood," *Dimity Convictions, The American Woman in the Nineteenth Century* (Athens: Ohio University Press, 1976), pp. 21–41. Welter has explored the prescriptive writings of this period and determined that piety, purity, domesticity, and submissiveness were the primary qualities of true womanhood during the Victorian period.

33. "Why, Ah! Why," *Woman's Exponent* 3 (1 Oct. 1874): 67.

34. Wells, Diary, 30 September 1874.

35. Minutes of the Nauvoo Female Relief Society, 28 April 1842, transcript copy, LDS Church Archives, p. 32.

36. The "Declaration of Sentiment," drawn up by Elizabeth Cady Stanton for the Seneca Falls convention held in Seneca Falls, New York, in July 1848, was patterned after the Declaration of Independence. It cited man as having usurped woman's autonomy by denying her "her inalienable

right to the elective franchise''; by declaring her civilly dead upon marriage, thus denying her any claim to her own or her husband's property, wages, or children; by limiting her access to education and employment; by subordinating her position and participation in the churches; and by assigning her to a sphere of action independent of her own choice, thereby "destroying her confidence in her own power, lessening her self-respect, and making her willing to lead a dependent and abject life." Susan B. Anthony, et al., *History of Woman Suffrage,* 6 vols. (Rochester, N.Y.: Susan B. Anthony, 1887), 1:70–71.

37. "A Wonderful Age," *Woman's Exponent* 27 (1 Feb. 1899): 100; and "Self Made Women," *Woman's Exponent* 9 (1 Mar. 1881): 148.

38. "Women's Organizations," *Woman's Exponent* 8 (15 Jan. 1880): 122. See also "Stray Notes," *Woman's Exponent* 8 (15 July 1879): 28, for her ideas on how the Relief Society qualified women for the responsibility of suffrage and other rights. See also John A. Widtsoe, *Evidences and Reconciliations: Aid to Faith in a Modern Day* (Salt Lake City: Bookcraft, 1943), p. 245, for a further interpretation of the broad purposes of the Relief Society.

39. Woman Suffrage Leaflet (Salt Lake City, Jan. 1892), p. 3.

40. *Woman's Exponent* 29 (1 Jan. 1901): 69.

41. Ibid., p. 71.

42. "Woman's Work and Mormonism," *Young Woman's Journal* 17 (July 1906): 295–96.

43. *Relief Society Magazine* 32 (Dec. 1945): 717.

44. "Action or Indifference," *Woman's Exponent* 5 (1 Sept. 1876): 54.

45. "Women's Organizations," *Woman's Exponent* 8 (15 Jan. 1880): 122.

46. See, for example, Brigham Young's statements in *Journal of Discourses* (Liverpool, England, 1856–1886), 12:31–32; 13:61; 16:16; *Millennial Star* 31 (24 Apr. 1869): 269; *Woman's Exponent* 2 (15 July 1873): 37.

47. "Relief Society Conference," *Woman's Exponent* 24 (15 Aug. 1895): 45; italics in original.

48. *The General Relief Society, Officers, Objects and Status* (Salt Lake City: The General Officers, 1902), pp. 74–75.

49. "Real Women," *Woman's Exponent* 2 (1 Jan. 1874): 118.

50. "Woman's Progression," *Woman's Exponent* 6 (15 Feb. 1878): 140.

51. Ibid.; emphasis added.

52. "Woman, A Subject," *Woman's Exponent* 3 (1 Nov. 1847): 82; and "Noble Work for Women," *Woman's Exponent* 7 (1 Apr. 1879): 218.

53. "Impromptu Ideas of Home," *Woman's Exponent* 4 (15 May 1876): 191.

54. "Progress of Women in the Last Seventy Years," *Woman's Exponent* 40 (Feb. 1912): 44.

55. "Responsibility of Woman Voters," *Woman's Exponent* 26 (15 Sept. and 1 Oct. 1897): 196.

56. George Q. Cannon to John Taylor, 14 January 1882, Cannon Papers, LDS Church Archives, as quoted in Beverly Beeton, "Woman Suffrage in the American West, 1869–1896" (Ph.D. diss., University of Utah, 1976), p. 101.

57. Quoted in "Our Relief Societies," *Woman's Exponent* 7 (15 Oct. 1878): 76.

58. "Mrs. Stanton and Mormon Women," *Woman's Exponent* 7 (15 May 1879): 240.

59. "Mormon Ladies Calling at the White House," *Philadelphia Times,* 19 January 1879, reprinted in the *Woman's Exponent* 7 (15 Mar. 1879): 212.

60. Ibid.

61. Wells, Diary, 20 May 1893.

62. "An Appeal to Women," *Woman's Exponent* 23 (1 and 15 Nov. 1894): 204.

63. "Which Party Will Recognize Women?" *Woman's Exponent* 19 (15 June 1891): 188.

64. "The Need of the Hour," *Woman's Exponent* 23 (1 Sept. 1894): 180.

65. Wells, Diary, 2 February 1895.

66. "Woman Suffrage," *Woman's Exponent* 23 (Mar. 1895): 244.

67. "Equal Suffrage in the Constitution," *Woman's Exponent* 23 (1 May 1895): 260.

68. "The New State," *Woman's Exponent* 24 (1 and 15 Nov. 1895): 76.

69. Wells, Diary, 2 June 1891.

70. *Salt Lake Herald,* 28 July 1895.

71. Wells, Diary, 17 October 1895.

72. Ibid., 20 September 1898.

73. Ibid.

74. Ibid., 10 November 1898.

75. Emmeline B. Wells to B. H. Roberts, 20 March 1910, Roberts Collection, Marriott Library, University of Utah, Salt Lake City, Utah.

Roberts's explanation of his position concerning woman suffrage at the time of his nomination can be found in *Young Woman's Journal* 10 (Mar. 1899): 104–5.

76. Emmeline B. Wells to Romania Pratt Penrose, 15 March 1908, Emmeline B. Wells Papers, LDS Church Archives.

77. Wells, Diary, 2 October 1910.

78. *Relief Society Magazine* 2 (Feb. 1915): 47.

79. *Deseret Evening News,* 24 September 1919.

80. Minutes of the Relief Society General Board Meeting, 12 January 1914, LDS Church Archives.

81. *Woman's Exponent* 41 (Feb. 1914): 100.

82. *Woman's Exponent* 40 (Mar. 1913): 51.

83. Wells, Diary, 9 April 1890.

84. Ibid., 13 March 1890.

85. Ibid., 26 March 1891.

86. Heber J. Grant to Annie Wells Cannon, 25 April 1921, Heber J. Grant Collection, LDS Church Archives.

87. *Deseret News,* 27 April 1921.

88. Charles W. Nibley, *Deseret News,* 30 April 1912; editorial, *Deseret News,* 25 April 1921.

89. *Woman's Exponent* 40 (July 1911): 4.

James R. Christianson

13

Jacob Spori: Nineteenth-Century Swiss Missionary, Educator, and Kingdom Builder

Born in Provo and reared in Spanish Fork, Utah, James R.
Christianson now resides with his wife and nine children in
Provo, Utah. His current position is Associate Professor of
Church History at Brigham Young University. He received
his B.A. and M.A. from Brigham Young University and his
Ph.D. from the University of Kansas. He has published in
LDS periodicals and is coauthor of *The International
Church.* His interest in Jacob Spori grew out of several years
of residence in Europe.

In November 1879 a rather substantial article dealing with
The Church of Jesus Christ of Latter-day Saints appeared in the
Volksblatt, a weekly publication of the Reformed Church of
Switzerland. The article was precipitated by the fact that one
Jacob Spori, the principal of a *Primarschule* in the state of
Bern and a former member of the *Kantonsynode,* or state
synod, had converted to the largely American church. It there-
fore seemed proper, wrote *Volksblatt* editor Reverend Gott-
lieb Joss, for the religious press to take a second, more in-depth
look at these "Saints."[1] That the attention of Reverend Joss

was drawn to the activities of a former parishioner is evidence that Mormons of nineteenth-century rural Switzerland did not go unnoticed by the ecclesiastical hierarchy. It is also an indication that Jacob Spori, both in 1879 and for many years thereafter, was acknowledged as being more than just an ordinary convert to the Mormon movement.

Born 26 March 1847, Jacob grew up in adequate but not opulent circumstances. His father, Jacob (1810–1876), was a schoolteacher, a real estate broker, and an elected city official. In 1846 the elder Jacob Spori married Susanna Katharina Böhlen (1827–1880), a member of the "Dorf aristocracy." This helped secure his election in 1851 and subsequent reelections to public office. His marriage may also have enhanced his credibility as a buyer and seller of houses and lands.[2] Father Spori first saw his future wife when she was an elementary-age student in the school where he taught. He determined then that he would one day marry her and later did so though she was seventeen years his junior.

Grandfather Jacob Spori (1777–1845), like his father, Johannes (1740–1789), was employed as sexton at the local church and cemetery. At age seventy-eight, in a state of depression, he hanged himself in the family barn. His daughter, who was the first to find him, took her own life that same day in a nearby river.[3] Family tradition indicates that great-grandfather Johannes, though himself uneducated, also had been a teacher in the local school. Jacob's maternal grandfather, Daniel Böhlen, was a prominent figure in both the community and the church, as was Jacob's great-grandfather, Samuel Böhlen.[4]

Jacob himself was born in Oberwyl at the family home, called the *Stuckli im Dorfli,* across the lane from the church where his grandfather and great-grandfather Spori had been employed sextons.[5] He was reared in the *Standen,* a beautifully located home somewhat isolated from the community.

Following the completion of his schooling in the Oberwyl *Secondarschule,* Jacob applied in 1863 for admittance to a state teachers' college in Munchenbuchsee, a village near the city of Bern. But the young applicant, who had just turned sixteen, was rejected because of his age. He reapplied the following year and was admitted, passing his entrance exams with a score that was just two points less than the highest recorded over a three-year period.[6]

School records indicate that during the three years of his advanced study, the value of his father's property was more than that of any other student except one. The amount, 15,563 franks, was not, however, an indication of wealth as much as it was a testimony that the school was not popular among the financially well-off. A full 40 percent of those attending listed the value of their parents' property at zero. In light of this, it is of interest to note that Jacob received 120 franks a year for spending money, an amount equal to that given the average student.[7]

When he graduated with honors in April 1867, Jacob had received a well-rounded education, his report cards indicating he was thoroughly schooled in German, French, mathematics, history, music, penmanship, drafting, geography, religion, psychology, and the natural sciences.[8] On 2 May he was employed to teach elementary education in the village of Hausern, near St. Stephan. He moved the following year to Erlenbach and in 1869 to the village of Lenk. In both Erlenbach and Lenk he taught on the secondary level. His first three teaching positions, as well as his next one in his hometown school in Oberwyl where he started teaching in 1871, were all in Niedersemmental and were part of the same school district.[9]

Besides being an able teacher, Jacob was an avid student of history and languages. In addition, the writings of the eighteenth-century Pietists, with their emphasis on a future kingdom of righteousness and on the second coming of Christ, were a special fascination to him. He himself wrote of an ideal world where the priests, teachers, and intellectuals of every level of society would work and walk together in an effort to benefit all mankind. In recognition of his excellence as a thinker and teacher, Jacob Spori was honored in 1873 by an article in the Reformed Church of Switzerland's official publication, the *Volksblatt,* and the following year he became principal of the school where he taught. Shortly thereafter, he was chosen for a seat on the prestigious *Synodalrath* for the State of Bern.[10]

In October 1874 at the very crest of his popularity, Jacob, seemingly everyone's young man of promise, took a further step in the enhancement of his career by marrying Magdalena Roschi. She was the attractive daughter of a well-to-do land-holder who, like his father before him, was a prominent political figure in the area.[11] The following year, Jacob was selected to serve as a member of the town council, and when father Spori, who was city clerk, died in early 1876, the towns-people elected Jacob to that office.[12]

By 1876, one would suppose that his spirits, like his reputa-tion, would be soaring among the clouds. He and Magdalena were the parents of two children; they were living in the "Zelg," a lovely home purchased by his father at a bankruptcy sale; and they enjoyed an excellent standing in the community.

For Jacob, however, a storm was brewing that would greatly alter the course of his life. For a number of years he had viewed with despair the bitterness with which the several divi-sions that existed within the Reformed Church referred to each other. Greatly troubled by what he read and observed, he began searching elsewhere for what he perceived was the ideal society. Writing retrospectively in 1888, Jacob, in a letter to his former students in Oberwyl, reminded them of how "we examined together the various religious movements of the day and found good in all of them; but when we compared the teachings of these competing churches with the biblical teach-ings and promises, we discovered that some day additional light would be shed on a happier and more righteous man-kind."[13] Convinced that the men representing the multiple factions were honorable and good and worthy of his admira-tion, he was, nevertheless, forced to conclude that truth was to be found in neither their words nor their writings and that, because of the current state of affairs, the sacred character of the church was greatly diminished in the eyes of the people.[14]

In a manner fascinatingly reminiscent of the questions and conflicts which Karl G. Maeser grappled with twenty years earlier, Jacob Spori struggled to the conclusion that he could no longer represent in the eyes of his students and those who had entrusted him with his seat on the Synod Council that which he himself did not believe.[15] Pursuant to this, as an act of conscience, he resigned his position with the church and stepped down as principal of the Oberschule in Oberwyl. He did continue to teach at the elementary level for a greatly reduced salary.[16] In consequence of all this, Spori's world in December 1876 was a far cry from what it had been in January, and the new year brought even greater change.

As Jacob related it, early in 1877 he heard

> . . . that God had sent an angel and the great kingdom of the future was being established and a people was gathering in Americas' Far West. This people was again enjoying all of those blessings which were upon the earth at the time of the apostles, the absence of which had been the cause of so much misfortune throughout Christianity for hundreds of years. Many terrible things were being said about this people, the Mormons. I fully expected this, knowing that all the powers and lies of darkness would be rushed to the battle once God initiated the restoration of all things which Peter prophesied by the spirit of truth as recorded in Acts 3:21. As a teacher and servant of the people I was responsible to you and all my fellowmen to thoroughly examine this new message. After many weeks of study, biblical comparisons, prayer and exhausting, lonely, thought filled nights, God led me to the truth, exactly as promised in James 1:5 and John 14:21–23.[17]

Convinced beyond doubt, Jacob was baptised into The Church of Jesus Christ of Latter-day Saints. He then joined with the few Saints and other interested persons who met at the home of Peter Hoffman in the nearby village of Ringoldingen. Neither his wife nor any of his family shared his interest in Mormonism, but this does not appear to have alienated them from him. He and his wife continued to live at the Zelg, where a third child was born to them. One year later they moved to the Bruggmatte, the home of his wife's parents. It was there that their fourth child was born.[18]

The relatively peaceful circumstances experienced at home were not mirrored in the community or at the school where Jacob taught. Although technically independent of the church, the schools were, in fact, viewed as being rightfully subject to ecclesiastical influence. The same was true for all elected offices. Both Spori's competence and his right to continue as a teacher were immediately questioned, and school officials ordered an investigation that continued into the summer of 1877. Apparently, in the end Jacob offered his resignation and his contract was canceled. School officials were convinced that he could not do justice to his profession and represent the Mormon faith at the same time.[19]

Jacob continued in his position as city clerk until the November 1877 election, in which he was soundly defeated. His becoming a Mormon seems to have been the primary reason for his defeat: Jacob had received the support of an overwhelming majority in his first election; in 1877 he obtained less than one-tenth of the vote.[20]

Swiss Mormons in 1877 were few in number and were generally ignored or, when attention was drawn to them, viewed with considerable contempt. However, the truly difficult days of the 1850s and 1860s, when members were regularly abused and the elders were driven from the country were past. In 1864, the Swiss government had decreed that Mormons were Christian and, therefore, protected in their right to worship by the 1848 constitutional provision which guaranteed freedom of religion for all Christian nationals. This, plus a similar finding in a court case in 1876 involving John U. Stucki, president of the Swiss-German Mission, had established that the rights of the Swiss Saints were no longer to be ignored. By 1880 considerable tolerance was in evidence and, though a climate of mistrust and disdain continued, the well-being of members and missionaries was rarely in jeopardy.[21]

Jacob was jobless for just a few months during 1878 before he was employed by the president of the Swiss-German Mission to act as an emigration agent for the Church. Despite the considerable attention he received from government officials who brought charges against him for supposedly disadvantaging the gullible and for acting without a license, he was successful in helping organize an emigrant company made up of proselytes to the Mormon faith.[22]

By 1 July 1879 Spori himself was prepared to leave Switzerland and seek out the Zion he had envisioned as a young man and later identified through the teachings of the Mormon missionaries. As was true of many who had preceded him, this decision meant leaving his wife and children behind. While many took this action because they could not afford ship's passage for the entire family, in Jacob's case the problem was more than a matter of finances. In addition to the fact that Magdalena did not share his acceptance of Mormonism, she was a potential heir to her father's lands and home and was, so it appears, far too practical to disinherit herself by emigrating. According to descendants and relatives of the Spori family in Switzerland, it was primarily for this last reason, and not the oft-reported claim that his wife and children were taken from him by his father-in-law, that Jacob journeyed alone to Utah.[23]

The venture Jacob was about to undertake was by no means novel, having been experienced by thousands of his fellow Europeans. As "seekers," they discovered that the message of this strange sect was both exciting and original because its American representatives testified not of dead but of living prophets and not of a future restoration but of a kingdom then building. They spoke of a gathering already in motion which each need only step forward to join and be brought to holy places, where the God of Heaven would protect, direct, and prepare them for the trying times ahead and for the coming of his Son.[24] Though the elders' reports were at times exaggerated and tended to color the arid wastelands of the Great Basin a verdant green, the convert's commitment or determination to act on the question toward which early preaching was directed—that of emigration—was usually fortified by the words, "I have been there."[25] For the true "seeker," there was magic in the message of the missionary who could declare, "I have been there! It exists! Zion flourishes!" At every stage their witness of a real and working gathering encouraged strength and decisiveness in place of indecision and even apostasy, these being the fruits of the poverty, tradition, or persecution that often accompanied the proselyte as he stepped from the waters of baptism.

With this message ringing in his ears, Jacob willingly exchanged the lush valleys and snowcapped mountains of the "Oberland" for the water-starved expanses of a land that humbled its most ardent masters. Almost as though he were immune to contrasts, immigrant Spori, finding no market for his teaching or linguistic talents, labored with his hands at a variety of unskilled jobs, accumulating neither land nor home in the process. Most of his early years in Utah were spent in or near Logan. Although these years were hard, they were not barren. In addition to learning English and making numerous acquaintances, Jacob gained many experiences on the farms, railroads, and in the mills and mines of the area, experiences that were a decided asset years later when he made the American West his permanent home.[26]

During his five years' absence from Switzerland, Jacob was often lonely and depressed. Magdalena, or "Mädeli" as he affectionately called her, and the children were ever on his mind. Distances, however, were shortened and time weighed less heavily because of letters from home and the regular arrival of the *Volksblatt,* which contained considerable local news.

In fact, his response to the article appearing in the 15 November 1879 edition led to Jacob's being characterized as a stalwart defender of the faith, an assessment that was justified on repeated occasions during the remainder of his life.[27] In his letter to Reverend Joss, editor of the *Volksblatt,* Jacob revealed a sharpness of tongue and intellect that was combative, but sincere. Swiss relatives whose natural curiosity causes them, even after more than a hundred years, to have a lively interest in this "Spori Jacob who went to America with the Mormons," think of him as one who was fearless in his convictions and one who, once his mind was made up, could never be made to change it. Clearly evident in the letter was Jacob's total commitment to his new faith and his willingness to engage any foe in its defense.[28] Because of this, he welcomed the call that came in September 1884 to serve in the Swiss-German mission.[29]

Elder Spori left Logan on 11 October 1884 and arrived in Liverpool on 27 October. After a brief stay in England, he journeyed to Switzerland where he was allowed several weeks to become reacquainted with his wife and children before commencing his missionary labors. He and his family had been separated for five years; Jacob was now thirty-seven years old.

On 18 November 1884, Edward Schoenfeld, president of the mission, received a message from European Mission head, John H. Smith, inquiring concerning the cost of travel to Constantinople and asking if Jacob Spori spoke quality German and French. Learning from Jacob that his linguistic abilities were more than sufficient and that he had some financial reserves (most likely from his father's estate), President Schoenfeld sent an affirmative reply to President Smith. On 27 November, having received instructions to do so, President Schoenfeld informed Elder Spori and Elder George Conrad Naegle that their mission call was being extended to Turkey.[30]

On 29 November, President Schoenfeld recorded, "Brother Spori with wife and child appeared, and we had a comfortable time together. His child is sick since 17 months caused by a fall from a swing, and it will be a matter of great faith to have it healed by the prayer of faith and administering." On the thirtieth he noted, "baptism of Br. Spori's wife, I have confirmed her."[31]

Jacob and his companion set out for Constantinople on 6 December, just a few days after Magdalena's baptism. Several days later, Elder Naegle returned to Bern with the report that upon their arrival in Genoa, Italy, they had learned that Constantinople was under quarantine. Following hours of painful deliberation, they decided that since they did not have sufficient funds for both of them to wait out the travel ban, Jacob would continue the journey alone.[32]

The nearly month-long journey to Constantinople, which included an eleven-day delay necessitated by the quarantine, was almost more than Jacob could endure. Toward the end of December his enthusiasm had waned to the point that efforts to occupy himself with the study of history, geography, and languages could not spare him days filled with thoughts of home, troubled memories of his experiences in America, and periods of self-doubt and self-incrimination. It appears that his brief visit with his wife and children awakened in him, now that he was again separated from them, feelings of guilt for having remained in America so long. With much time on his hands, he tormented himself with the thought that had the Lord not blessed him he might have forsaken his family and in turn proved himself unworthy of missionary service. Such thoughts of America reminded him of those long years when the only work he could find was as a laborer on the railroad in Idaho and Montana, or when he was reduced to shoveling snow or doing other forms of manual labor in order to live and not be dependent upon others. His early lack of facility with the language and his inability to find employment befitting his training as a teacher or as one skilled in writing and keeping records was a real blow to his pride. He also remembered with feeling the times of sickness when he was "half dead and frozen and sick and no one but a few of the brothers seemed to care."[33] His mission to Turkey and a total sense of dependence on the Lord brought all this into focus, causing him many sleepless nights and troubled dreams.[34]

The one positive note revealed in his diary during the final week of the voyage concerned the forty-six bottles of wine served with his meals during the twenty-three-day sea voyage. On 31 December, the day he disembarked, he wrote, "While on the ship I did not touch any wine. 23 days = 46 bottles.

Now that is something. It was paid for, included as part of the ticket, made available daily. One sees that God does help."[35]

Immediately upon arrival, Jacob went to the home of Hagop T. Vartooquian, a resident of Constantinople of Armenian descent who, representing himself as the minister of a sizable congregation, had written President John Henry Smith in England and requested missionaries. Jacob's initial impression of and experiences with his host were mostly positive. After a brief stay in previously arranged housing, he moved in with the Armenian family.

Vartooquian, who spoke English, his wife, Phipsmac, and their two older children Sisak and Ormais, were baptized on 4 January, and what appeared to be a friendly relationship developed between the two men.[36]

Sensitive to the need for a command of the languages he would be required to use in declaring the gospel, Jacob turned to Hagop Vartooquian for help. Initially, the Armenian was eager to oblige, but he soon began to resent having to take time to teach his guest. Jacob, who shared the family's two-room apartment and ate his meals with them, became increasingly ill at ease. On 23 January, Spori recorded in his journal:

> I have already spelled out a fair amount of Armenian and, if one had time, it warranted much cause for laughter. He [Vartooquian] was kind enough to listen to me and was satisfied. He did suggest that I go through it two or three more times, as if I had not already done so thirty or forty times. Mr. V. comes home late at night. I do not know what he is doing during the night time, but his look is false and shallow.
>
> It's a miracle! He gave me another lesson in Turkish. Wait just a few more weeks, then I will hardly need your charity. If I only had time and it were not half a sin, I would turn the things I have to observe here into a comedy.[37]

The following day he correctly analyzed his problem when he wrote: "My miserable situation is, by the way, my own fault. If I had just followed the advice of President Smith, rented a small room and lived on bread and water, I could have held out for a long time."[38]

Jacob's concerns were not simply due to his deteriorating relationship with his convert host. His diary reveals a lonely, cold, depressed missionary. Letters from "Mädeli" were "miserable," telling of her own doubts and of her worry for their injured child. The weather was cold and damp, as was the small crowded Vartooquian apartment. Jacob's days were crowded with worries about home and finances and with the study of the Turkish, Armenian, French, Italian, English, Greek, and Danish languages. His nights were crowded with violent, unsettling dreams, or were often sleepless. The only thing that kept him going was an occasional ray of light that shone through, such as on the morning when he wrote: "I slept warm . . . dreamed of John Taylor. He was friendly and encouraged me. This made me very happy and gave me new courage."[39]

Just one month after the date of their baptism, Vartooquian and his wife declared that they wished to have nothing more to do with the Church. Even though he had paid considerable sums in advance, Jacob was presented with a statement covering twenty-five days' lodging and meals and he was invited to leave. During several drunken flare-ups, the Armenian—who, Jacob learned, was not a minister and had not been one for the past eight years—made it clear he had expected the Church to aid him financially. His disenchantment with the Church stemmed from the disappointment of that expectation. For this he blamed his guest. Spori's response to leaving was to the point: "This evening will be the last night here. Thank God!"[40]

Jacob moved to the home of a German family, and his mission really began. His dreams and sleeplessness subsided. He made contact with a number of individuals with whom he exchanged language instruction. He was introduced at the German Working Men's Union, where he had an occasional opportunity to teach the gospel. On 15 April he summarized his new outlook when he wrote, "I studied Turkish and desire to continue. I feel only peace and clearness of thought. Happy is the man who is in the service of God."[41]

About this same time, Jacob learned that his injured daughter, "Katheli," had died. Since the death of the child was not unexpected and he knew that his family was being cared for by his in-laws, he was able to accept her death. The additional news, however, that he might be asked to return from his mission was greeted with protest. He expressed the wish to continue his efforts to teach the gospel and to master the languages.

As the weeks passed, opportunities to share the gospel began to multiply. Jacob was even called on to give blessings, and with positive results. Of one such occasion he wrote:

> On the 12th of April I was called on to visit two other sick persons. I promised to fast for them, and call again and see what to do. In the evening I had a good opportunity of explaining the Gospel. I was treated like a pasha which was quite different from my simple way of living. But people think it foolish for me to refuse such good coffee, such fine tobacco, such wonderful wine, and such good, sweet 'Racky' [Liquor] and fine beer. On the 13th the old sick lady mentioned before was out of her bed, and said she was perfectly well. This result caused a veritable Turkish astonishment. A doctor called upon her to convince himself, and she told him a few words for which the Lord will bless her.[42]

In time, Jacob became rather well known. His forthright style, the incomprehensible doctrine of the Word of Wisdom, and the more familiar teaching of plural marriage gained him considerable attention if not converts. He was also successful in having articles about the Church and even portions of the *Voice of Warning* by Parley P. Pratt published in local newspapers. Toward the end of the year, he was extremely busy with teaching, writing pamphlets, and studying the necessary languages. There was no concrete payoff for these months of work, however, as his only baptisms in Constantinople came just four days after his arrival in Turkey when the four members of the Vartooquian family joined the Church.

On 6 December 1885, Joseph M. Tanner, an elder from the Swiss-German Mission, joined Elder Spori in Constantinople. Elder Tanner was in the city for two days before he met his new companion. When they finally did get together, Jacob's months of isolation were over.[43]

The arrival of Elder Tanner brought a new vigor and direction to the work. The elders began to make additional use of the newspapers and to hold more public meetings. A number of newspaper editors were suddenly anxious to give the message of the elders a fair hearing. It soon became necessary to rent a room where they could meet with those who came to inquire further. Even the Minister of Public Instruction, Munif Pasha, requested an interview with them in order to learn more of their religious beliefs and history. For the most part, however, their conversations were in French and German with French and German natives living in Constantinople.[44]

The two missionaries wanted to work with Turkish nationals whom they usually found were more Christlike in their habits than the Christians, but their interest level rarely went beyond a few courteous questions. Regarding this, Elder Tanner sent the following report to Elder Franklin D. Richards in Salt Lake City:

> So far as I have the spirit of discernment the Turks are the only ones, as a nation, that live so as to receive the gospel. They are far above Europeans in real Christian ethics. . . . I cannot say what the will of the Lord may be regarding the spread of the Gospel among the Turks; but I have a great desire that they should have it in their own language, for I feel that if an opening can be made among them, there will be a great work accomplished in these lands. They are very reticent, but very courteous.[45]

Upon his return from a visit to the Holy Land in the company of Elder Francis M. Lyman, Jr., Elder Tanner, after sharing his impressions with Spori, requested the permission of President Wells in Switzerland to have Elder Spori travel to Haifa and work with the German-speaking colonies located there. Elder Tanner had been greatly impressed by these devout people who, several years earlier, had gathered in Palestine to await the second coming of Christ.[46]

President Wells gave his consent, and Elder Spori took passage for Jaffa on 29 July 1886. After a pleasant, uneventful voyage, he arrived at his destination on 8 August. His initial reception by both the Germans and his fellow Swiss was neither warm nor hostile but was characterized more by a general feeling of disinterest. They saw no need for either authority or baptism, and, like many people, were conditioned because of a prior knowledge of the doctrine of plural marriage to not take Mormonism seriously. Jacob, however, was not discouraged. For him, just being in the Holy Land was reward enough for his efforts. Within a few days of his arrival he journeyed to Jerusalem and to other sacred sites. And while marveling at being in the very places he had once talked about with his students, he used the occasion to discuss the gospel with and bear testimony to numerous Jews, Arabs, and German-speaking pilgrims.[47]

By 14 August, he was back in Jaffa, concerned with how he might successfully approach members of the German-speaking community. Having just arrived in the city after a long, dry journey, and wishing to refresh himself, he approached a well, which the Europeans owned. As he paused to obtain water, he was attacked by two massive dogs. In an effort to defend himself, he began pelting the beasts with a number of large stones. As the animals retreated, he let fly with one last missile that sailed beyond the dogs and over a nearby fence. Immediately he heard a cry and the sound of angry German voices. In an instant the dogs, two Germans, three Arabs, and a black man were facing him. "I stood there rocks in hand," wrote Jacob, "with the old Berner blood rising and my instinct for self preservation awakened. I was ready to take on the whole group, including the dogs."[48] Fortunately, after a brief exchange, the group retreated behind the fence; and Jacob, no longer angry, but overwhelmed with feelings of guilt, shame, and fear of God for his unmissionary-like behavior, hurriedly left the area. Fearing that he had seriously injured someone, Jacob eventually went to the office of the American consulate and confessed his actions. It was with great relief he learned that no complaint had been registered and that he was free to continue his missionary labors.

Shortly after this troublesome incident, Jacob traveled to Haifa, where he was happy to find a more open and receptive group of German immigrants. Aided by references from the few friends he had won in Jaffa, he was busy teaching and bearing testimony from the time of his arrival. On 16 August he met George Grau, a blacksmith who, along with his wife, showed an immediate and mature interest in the gospel. During the next two weeks, Elder Spori met with Grau and his wife on a near-daily basis. They became close friends, and he was often invited to dine with them.[49]

At this time, Jacob was destitute of funds—he found it necessary to leave his wedding ring with the postmaster as security for a twenty-frank loan—but refused offers of aid from Grau and others. Jacob preferred to work long hours cleaning Grau's goat pens and blacksmith shop to pay for his meals and eventually for a place to sleep. The latter became necessary when he was stung by a large scorpion and became very ill.[50]

George Grau was baptized on 29 August; on 3 September he was ordained an elder. Shortly after Jacob's return to Jaffa, on 16 September, Grau baptized his wife. The Graus were a happy, positive couple, and from the very outset, they became the heart of the missionary effort in Haifa and the surrounding area. They attracted other interested persons to the Church, and, in time, with the help of Joseph Tanner, who labored in Palestine throughout most of 1887, a small branch was established. Eventually, most of those baptized emigrated to America and settled near Provo, Utah.[51]

During the next three months, Jacob traveled widely. When he left for Constantinople in early January 1887, he had delivered his message in every German community in Palestine. Although Jacob was generally well received, there is no record of any further baptisms being performed.[52]

Shortly after boarding ship at Jaffa for his return voyage, Jacob met and was eventually responsible for the baptism of Mischa Markow, a young man who became one of the most interesting and able of all early Mormon emissaries. A Hungarian with Serbian ancestry, Mischa, himself a seeker, had earlier moved to Alexandria, where he worked as a barber. About the same time that Jacob was preparing to leave Palestine, Mischa was admonished in a dream to leave for Constantinople. Acting immediately, he sold his business and belongings and, after considerable difficulty, boarded a ship sailing for Constantinople by way of Jaffa. After meeting Elder Spori (the two were able to converse in German), Markow eagerly listened to the stranger's message of the restoration. By the time they reached Constantinople, he was ready to become a member of the Church. Following his baptism, he was encouraged by the elders to emigrate. However, he refused to do so, expressing a desire to preach the gospel before going to America.[53] Mischa's colorful service as a missionary for the Church is best described in a paragraph he appended as a flyleaf of his life story.

> I, Mischa Markow Preach the Gospel in 8th Kingdoms: 1. Belgien, 2. Hungary, 3. Romanien, 4. Bulgarien, 5. Germany, 6. Turkey, 7. Russia, Serbia. I was 11th times in to City court. 4th Times in to Magistrate, 2. Times in to High Cort. I was 3 Times guardet Police stud by the Gate and if somebody wants to come to hear me police did not Let him in. And that was in Romanien, Bulgarien, & Serbien. 2 Times I was banished that is in Hungary and in Serbien. I was 2 times in the jail in Romanien and Hungary.[54]

Following his return to Constantinople, Jacob had but a short time remaining before being released from his mission. He busied himself during these weeks studying Hebrew and Russian and teaching French to Elder Tanner and Turkish to a newly arrived elder, Ferdinand Hinze. He was also responsible for the publication of several pamphlets in German, Turkish, and Armenian. As no other funds were available, Jacob used his travel money to pay for the printing. This delayed his return to Switzerland until he was able to earn the necessary amount for passage by giving language lessons.[55] On 23 March 1887, he finally left for Switzerland, where he rejoined his family and began preparations for their eventual emigration to America.

During the ensuing months, Jacob was called on to use both voice and pen in defending the reputation of the Church and the rights of its members, as he previously had done while in America and while on his mission. There are, for example, more letters on file in Swiss government archives from Jacob Spori addressing state and national officials on matters concerning the Church and its members than from almost all other nineteenth-century Mormon spokesmen combined. One reason for this may be that while numerous additional letters might have been written but were not saved, Jacob's, because of who he was during his pre-Mormon days, warranted preservation.

One such letter, written from Constantinople on 18 May 1886, was in response to an article in a Bern newspaper, *Der Freien Oberlander,* in which the writer suggested that "the Mormon apostles of plural marriage who were pursuing their business of death" should not only be warned but prosecuted and punished.[56] Referring to the article, Jacob eloquently reminded the Bern heads of state that the Swiss had fought for, won, and now exemplified the role of freedom before the world. Religious freedom, he suggested, was either to be honored or the whole of the concept was stripped of significance. Reviewing the history of the persecution of the Church members in detail and picturing the blissful, happy circumstances of the hardworking Swiss emigrants after taming, as they had, the most raw of climates and conditions, he asked why anyone would endure all that was required for his own and his religion's sake and then, as the news article charged, be base and immoral. "In the name of sound reason," he wrote, "could not a man with immoral motives achieve his purposes much more cheaply by spending a few pieces of gold in any of the civilized Christian cities?"[57] It appears that in this, as in other letters, petitions, and requests, Jacob Spori was sought out by Swiss mission leaders in the hope that in certain critical situations, where the attempts of others might go unacknowledged, both his reputation and eloquence would serve to open doors, gain a hearing, or divert an action.

Jacob also labored during the fall of 1887 and winter of 1888 to form an emigrant company that would leave for Utah in the spring. This accomplished, he sailed from England on 26

May 1888 with his family and his sister Anna, who had joined the Church and decided that she too would gather to Zion.

Upon his arrival in America, Jacob took his family to Rexburg, Idaho. The city had been established about five years earlier and had become a center for the growth and development taking place throughout the Snake River Valley. It was also the residence of Henry Flamm, a Swiss immigrant who had befriended Jacob in America during a period of severe illness in 1879. They had also worked together in Bern just prior to Jacob's departure for Utah in 1879.[58]

Some weeks after his arrival in Rexburg, Jacob Spori was called as a member of the stake board of education. As part of an ambitious program to expand Church education, LDS leaders had commissioned the organizing of schools or academies throughout several of the western states and the Mormon colonies in Mexico. The Bannock Stake, headquartered in Rexburg, was one of these; the board, under the direction of President Thomas E. Ricks, worked vigorously so as to be ready for the upcoming school year. Although somewhat late in beginning, they were successful, and history was made as the first classes of the Bannock Stake Academy were welcomed on 12 November 1888.[59]

Much to his surprise, Jacob was selected as the principal of the fledgling school. There was no question about his being qualified, but, as he had learned during his earlier years in Zion, what the European immigrant did and what he was capable of doing often bore little relationship to one another. This perception appears to have so impressed itself upon his mind that throughout his mission he always referred to himself as a simple woodchopper, never mentioning either his education or his teaching experience except as he wrote to Swiss government officials. Jacob was a good principal. He cared about and sacrificed for the Academy. After three years, however, he resigned his position, having determined he must get his own financial house in order. The salary promised him each year ranged between $300 and $700 and was usually paid out of the tithing house. Since his salary depended on the tithing house's having either funds or commodities, he was never sure of his income. But perhaps his most significant reward during his years as principal was his occasional association with Karl G. Maeser at the campus of Brigham Young Academy in Provo, Utah.[60]

After leaving the Academy, Jacob immersed himself in a number of interesting, although sometimes controversial, ventures. On 15 December 1892 a letter he had written to a Church member in Switzerland appeared in *Der Stern,* a monthly publication of the Swiss-German Mission. It was introduced to the magazine's readers with the comment that the editors wished to show what an active, dedicated person could accomplish in a short time. In the letter, Spori detailed how he and several brethren were working a mine near Logan, which, according to best reports, could become one of the most productive in Utah. He was also involved in the purchase of lands and the laying out of lots for the establishment of a community to be settled, hopefully, by his "good German brethren." Under his direction, canals and fences were being built, crops were being planted, and shares in a steam saw and coal mine had been purchased. In closing he wrote, "Zion is moving busily ahead; the Lord may soon appear and we must hurry our preparations."[61]

Following the appearance of this letter, Jacob was accused of writing it in an attempt to entice immigrants into investing in his schemes. Responding to this charge, he immediately wrote to *Der Stern,* asking that he be allowed to defend himself. Point by point, he justified each of his activities, stating that his sole purpose was to aid his brethren in the kingdom to help themselves. By becoming independent of the world, they could work together under the influence of the Spirit and prepare for the day when the Lord would once again entrust his people with the lost keys to the United Order.[62]

Events of the following years seem to indicate that Jacob's apparently well-intended efforts to strengthen the kingdom were greeted with continued criticism, in spite of the fact that a valuable canal system bearing the Spori name was completed, making possible the development of thousands of acres of rich farmland.[63]

In a December 1894 letter to his former missionary companion George Naegle, who was then serving as president of the Swiss-German Mission, Jacob wrote of those who came to Zion thinking it a place where one "sang psalms continually and rested peacefully" but who, when they found it to be otherwise—a place where the "called" worked to become chosen, and enduring to the end was the only path available to the righteous—"sprouted evil tongues and bred unrest." Referring to how Satan would sift some as wheat and to the suffering borne by Christ and Joseph Smith, he seemed to be saying that though he too had suffered and been sifted, he was still firm in his conviction that the gospel was true. At this time, he was again teaching and had been called to serve on the Bannock Stake High Council.[64]

Spori's last letter to appear in *Der Stern* was written to George Naegle 10 November 1895 and stated, "I am once again in the state of Montana and have two contracts, one for nine months and one for a year; one of the Twelve knows where I am and what I am doing here."[65] What happened to Jacob's mine, sawmill, and land development schemes, and why he went to Montana to work on the railroad are not clear. Also, why an Apostle knew where he was and what he was doing is a small mystery.

Upon returning from Montana late in 1896, Jacob again took up teaching during the winter months and pursued his mining interests throughout the summer. His wife, Magdalena, died 14 September 1900. Three years later, on 27 September 1903, at age fifty-six and suffering from diabetes, Jacob died. That his age was not advanced when he died and that death came rather suddenly led to rumors being circulated among family members and acquaintances in Switzerland that he was murdered.

Jacob Spori was in his day, and has remained, an enigma. Acquaintances dating from his pre-Mormon years were impressed by his intelligence, strength of character, teaching skills, and piety. When these very qualities led him to embrace what was perceived as the most objectionable of sects, Mormonism, those same people were distressed but not angered. He retained their guarded respect, and his voice was acknowledged as one to be listened to. In fact, Jacob's most difficult hours were not spent among Gentiles but in Zion among a people in the process of becoming Saints, a people with much room for growth. He recognized this and was, therefore, able to shrug off those who misunderstood his sincerity and genuineness regarding lots, land, mines, mills, and communities for immigrants. Thinking him greedy, they pictured him as one who preyed on the misfortunes of others. Some, among them descendants and admirers, have mistaken his fascination with languages as being a matter of pride and perhaps fuel for his ego. In reality, however, Jacob saw language as a necessary medium for teaching the gospel. It hardly seems likely that any other motivation could have driven him to labor as his diary reveals he did in an effort to master so many. In the end, his vision was greater than his grasp as time and opportunity limited his fluency to English, German, and French, and a better than average ability in Turkish and Armenian.

If Jacob had a public relations problem, it was that he was simply not believable—he was so genuine as to be suspect. This led to numerous disappointments for him and to misunderstandings with his fellow Saints. As his daughter Elizabeth noted some years after his death:

> He was generous to a fault, both in material and ethical things. Too generous, many would say for his own good, but he always believed that only when we give do we receive and only that which makes another happy can bring happiness to ourselves.
>
> His honesty and integrity cannot be questioned now in the light of these passing years and could he speak for himself, he would say,
>
> "Here is my life; whatever of fault and mistake there is in it, pass it by; whatever of worth take it for your own; it is yours!"[66]

Jacob Spori, a truly great man, believed in and was prepared to sacrifice all for that which he prized most—the gospel of Christ. He cared about others, all others, and did something about it. Because in the cosmopolitan city of Constantinople there were those who spoke Greek, Danish, Italian, Turkish, and Armenian, he studied each language in order that all might hear his message. He made himself rich, not in a material sense, but as a teacher and a builder and a man of vision. Jacob Spori was indeed a kingdom builder.

Notes

1. "Einiges über die Mormonen," *Volksblatt für die Reformirte Kirche der Schweiz,* XI Jahrgang, nr. 21 (15 Nov. 1879): 181–82. Hereafter cited as *Volksblatt.*

2. City records show the elder Spori winning elections following his marriage in 1846 and continuing to do so until shortly before his death in 1876.

3. "Protokoll über die Versamlungen der Einwohner von Oberwyl, 1845–1895," Gemeinde Oberwyl, pp. 262, 429.

4. Ibid., and Jacob Spori Pedigree Chart, in possession of the author.

5. Some homes were given names and were so known and are so identified at the present time.

6. "Lehrerbuildung, Seminarin, Lokales, Munchenbuchsee," 1862– 1870, Stadt Archives, Bern, BB III b 5208. 1863 VI/XII.

7. Ibid., 1864, 1865, 1866.

8. Ibid., 1866.

9. "Primar and Secondar Schülen, Lokales, Amtsbezirk Nieder- semmental, Gemeinde Oberwyl," 1856–1896, Stadt Archives, Bern, BB III b, 690155, 1867–1871.

10. Jacob Spori, "Offener Brief an Hrn. Pfarren G. Joss in Herzogen- buchsee, Schweiz," *Der Stern,* vols. 12–15 (4 Jan. 1880): 56–57.

11. Magdalena's father, Michael Roschi, held the positions of Ge- meinde Rath and Sittensrichter. The latter was a form of justice of the peace and was responsible to admonish, judge, and punish the youth regarding their moral behavior. Grandfather Michael Roschi had occupied these same positions as well as that of Chorrichter, a form of judge, and Kirchmeier.

12. "Protokoll der Einwohner Gemeinde Versamlung, 1832–1890," Gemeinde Oberwyl, 328–29.

13. Jacob Spori, "Einige Wörter an Meine Gewesenen Schulkinder," *Der Stern,* vols. 18–21 (May 1888): 157.

14. Spori, "Offener Brief an Hrn. Pfarren G. Joss," p. 57.

15. Douglas F. Tobler, "Karl G. Maeser's German Background, 1828–1856: The Making of Zion's Teacher," *Brigham Young University Studies* 17 (Winter 1977): 170–71.

16. "Nachrichten und Korrespondenten," *Volksblatt*, VIII. Jahrgang, nr. 34 (Samstag, 19 Aug. 1876): 136, and "Spori to Joss," *Volksblatt*, 57.

17. Spori, "Einige Wörter an Meine Gewesenen Schulkinder," *Der Stern*, vols. 18–21 (May 1888): 157–58.

18. "Protokoll der Einwohner Gemeinde Versamlung, 1832–1890," Gemeinde Oberwyl, 342.

19. "Brief von [indecipherable] an Herren Jakob Spori in Oberwyl," 9 June 1877. Primar u. Secondar Schulen, Lokales, Amtsbezirk Niedersemmental, Gemeinde Oberwyl, 1856–1896. Stadt Archives, Bern, BB III b, 690155.

20. "Protokoll der Einwohner Gemeinde Versamlung, 1832–1890," Gemeinde Oberwyl, 328–42.

21. James R. Christianson, et al., *The International Church*, (Provo, Utah: BYU Press, 1982), p. 34. See also, *Millennial Star* 38 (27 Mar. 1826): 203.

22. "Anzeige gegen Jacob Spori und Missionar Flamm," Richter Amt Thun, Kanton Bern, 19 July 1879, nr. 748–49.

23. Interviews with numerous Spori family members, Niedersemmental, Switzerland, June–July 1980.

24. Christianson, *The International Church*, p. 51.

25. Ibid., p. 52.

26. "Jacob Spori Tagebuch," October–December 1884; and Denton Brewerton, "Istanbul and Rexburg," *Ensign*, June 1980, p. 26.

27. "Einiges über die Mormonen," *Volksblatt*, XI Jahrgang, nr. 46 (Samstag, 15 Nov. 1879): 181–82.

28. "Ein Brief aus Utah," *Volksblatt*, XII Jahrgang, nr. 21 (Samstag, 22 Mai 1880): 81–82.

29. "Jacob Spori to the Utah Journal," Logan, Utah, Journal History of The Church of Jesus Christ of Latter-day Saints, April 11, 1885, p. 13, Library-Archives, Historical Department, The Church of Jesus Christ of Latter-day Saints, Salt Lake City, Utah.

30. Diary of Edward Schoenfeld, Vol. 1, 18 to 27 November 1884.

31. Ibid., 29 November and 30 November 1884.

32. Ibid., 6 December and 8 December 1884.

33. "Jacob Spori Tagebuch," 2 August 1885, p. 149.

34. Ibid., 22 December 1884 to 30 January 1885, pp. 25–122.

35. Ibid., 31 December 1884, p. 36.

36. Ibid., 4 January 1885, p. 54.

37. Ibid., 23 January 1885, p. 54.

38. Ibid., 24 January 1885, p. 86.

39. Ibid., 13 January 1885, p. 73.

40. Ibid., 3 February 1885, pp. 137–49.

41. Ibid., 15 April 1885.

42. "Abstract of Correspondence from Constantinople," *Millennial Star* 47 (18 May 1885): 317.

43. Joseph M. Tanner to Daniel H. Wells, 9 December 1885, *Millennial Star,* 48 (11 Jan. 1886): 29–30.

44. See numerous letters from Jacob Spori and Joseph M. Tanner to Daniel H. Wells in *Millennial Star,* 48 (1886): 75–76; 108–9; 443–44; 479.

45. Joseph M. Tanner to Franklin D. Richards, 31 August 1886, *Deseret News,* 6 October 1886, p. 606.

46. "Tanner to Daniel H. Wells," 22 June 1886, *Millennial Star,* 48 (12 July 1886): 443.

47. "Spori Tagebuch," 8 August to 14 August 1884.

48. Ibid., 15 August 1884.

49. Ibid., 16 August to 29 August 1884.

50. Ibid., 16 August to 21 September 1884.

51. "Turkish Mission 1884–1900," Church Historian's Office, 6 September 1887. Also "Spori to Wells," 12 October 1886, *Millennial Star,* 48 (15 Nov. 1886): 731.

52. "Spori to Wells," *Millennial Star,* XVIII (13 Dec. 1886): 14.

53. Mischa Markow, "Life and History," LDS Church Archives, (n.p., n.d.).

54. Ibid.

55. "Spori Tagebuch," 15 January 1887 to 23 March 1887.

56. "Mormonen," *Der Freien Oberlander,* Nr. 37 (8 May 1886): 2.

57. "Jacob Spori an den Titl. Regierungsrath des Kantons Bern," *Bestands Register* 11/1, 7175 (A) 1, National Archives, Bern, 18 May 1886.

58. "Spori Tagebuch," 31 August 1884, p. 72.

59. "Bannock Stake Minute Book," 12 November 1888, pp. 282–83. See also Jerry C. Roundy, "Ricks College—A Struggle for Survival" (Ph.D. diss., Brigham Young University, 1975), 25–26.

60. Roundy, "Ricks College," pp. 27, 33, 37.

61. "Aus einem Brief von Bruder Spori," *Der Stern,* vols. 23–24 (15 Dez. 1892): 377.

62. "Spori an Präsident J. J. Scharrer," *Der Stern,* vols. 25–27 (11 Jan. 1893): 58–60.

63. "Spori an den Regierungsrath des Kantons Bern," Bestands Register 11/1 in 7175 (A) 1 National Archives, Bern, 22 März, 1894.

64. "Spori an Präsident George Naegle," *Der Stern,* vols. 25–27 (21 Dez. 1894): 30–31.

65. Ibid. (10 Nov. 1895), p. 238.

66. Elizabeth S. Stowell, "A History of Jacob Spori, by His Daughter," (18 November 1926), MS, Paper for the Daughters of the Snake River Pioneers (located in Special Collections, Ricks College Library, Rexburg, Idaho), p. 18.

Donald Q. Cannon

14

Angus M. Cannon:
Pioneer, President, Patriarch

Donald Q. Cannon was born in Washington, D.C., and grew up in Salt Lake City. He now resides with his wife and six children in Orem, Utah. Currently he serves as Professor of Church History and Doctrine at Brigham Young University. He received his B.A. and M.A. from the University of Utah and his Ph.D. from Clark University. He has published several books, articles, and book reviews, including the *Far West Record*. A great-grandson of Angus M. Cannon, he has spent considerable time studying Angus's papers and journals.

Angus Cannon often came to visit his son, Jesse F. Cannon. After dinner on one visit Angus went out in his fine Prince Albert coat and hat and tried to flag down the trolley. Unknown to Angus, the trolley company had recently changed that route to an express line, so the train failed to stop. Immediately, Angus went inside and called the president of the Utah Traction Company and told him to make sure all trains stopped for him. After all, he was President Angus M. Cannon! From then on the trolley did stop for Angus, wherever and whenever he flagged it down.[1] This incident, indicative of

Angus Cannon's aggressiveness and ability to command the respect of others, was related by his grandson, T. Quentin Cannon. Quayle Cannon, Jr., another grandson, recalls his impressions of Angus. He remembers that Angus was fastidious in his dress, rather stern, and religious in manner.[2]

What was Angus M. Cannon really like? What impact did he have on nineteenth-century Utah? What does the life of this pioneer, president, and patriarch tell us about Utah and the Latter-day Saints? In order to answer these questions a brief survey of his life will be presented, followed by an in-depth analysis of Angus as churchman, specifically as a member of The Church of Jesus Christ of Latter-day Saints.[3]

Biographical Sketch

Angus M. Cannon, the second son and fourth child of George Cannon and Ann Quayle, was born in Liverpool, Lancashire, England, 17 May 1834.[4] The Apostle John Taylor, who had married Leonora, sister of Angus's father, converted and baptized the Cannons on 11 February 1840.[5]

In September 1842 the family took passage to America with a company of Saints on the ship *Sidney*. After six weeks of serious illness, Angus's mother died and was buried at sea. A voyage of eight weeks' duration brought the Cannons to New Orleans, and then they proceeded up the Mississippi to St. Louis, where they spent the winter.

In the spring of 1843 they arrived in Nauvoo. Because of the change of climate, Angus and his brothers and sisters became seriously ill with fever and chills. Fearful that he would die not having been baptized, Angus requested baptism, but his desire was not realized until the next year when he had recovered. Meanwhile his father had died, and his sister Mary Alice and her husband Charles Lambert became guardians of the orphaned children.

With the remnant of the Nauvoo Saints, Angus and his family took refuge across the Mississippi River in Iowa Territory. There, in the fall of 1846, exhausted and suffering from hunger, these pioneers experienced the "miracle of the quail," when thousands of quail came into camp, providing badly needed sustenance. While crossing Iowa, Angus worked for supplies, and at Winter Quarters he helped build a house for the winter. After what must have seemed an endless delay, they departed for the Great Basin in the spring of 1849, arriving in Salt Lake in October 1849.

Angus spent the next year farming and cutting wood, after which he went with George A. Smith's company to Iron County. After helping to establish Parowan, Angus returned to Salt Lake in the spring of 1851.

In the fall of 1854 Angus received a call to serve a mission in the eastern United States, in company with Elder John Taylor. In New York City, he assisted Elder Taylor in publishing *The Mormon.* Following his labors in New York, Elder Cannon preached in Connecticut, New Jersey, Pennsylvania, and Delaware, baptizing several people.

As a consequence of the Utah War, Angus returned to Salt Lake City, arriving on 21 June 1858. Later that summer he married two sisters whom he had met in the mission field—Ann Amanda and Sarah Maria Mousley. After establishing a home for his family, Angus started a pottery business.

His roots had scarcely begun to take hold when Church leaders interrupted his life with another call to serve. Predictably, Angus M. Cannon responded in the affirmative. Angus and his family had been called to the "cotton mission," which meant moving to southern Utah to assist in colonization. In company with Erastus Snow and Jacob Gates, Angus helped select the site for St. George. In the newly created community Angus served in several responsible positions, including mayor, city marshal, county prosecuting attorney, and major in the militia. In December 1864, he went south with a military and exploratory expedition which established Call's Landing on the Colorado River.

In consequence of Angus's feeble health, he and his family returned to Salt Lake City in 1867. Getting reestablished, Angus worked at various jobs. He managed a lumber mill, took a freight wagon team to Montana, and worked in the coal business. During the last quarter of the century, he earned a living from a variety of occupations, including business manager of the *Deseret News,* farmer, stock raiser, and miner.

Meanwhile, his church service continued unabated. He filled a second mission to the eastern states from 1869 to 1870. He was ordained a high priest and set apart as a high councilor in the Salt Lake Stake on 9 May 1873. Then in April 1876 President Brigham Young called Angus and set him apart as stake president of the Salt Lake Stake. During his twenty-eight-year term as stake president, Angus M. Cannon presided over the largest stake in the Church, and he and his counselors and high council established many important precedents in Church government.

As he served in the Church and earned a living, his family responsibilities increased substantially. He had married the Mousley sisters in 1858, and he subsequently added four additional wives to his family: on 16 June 1876 he married the widow of William Mason, Clarissa Cordelia Moses Mason, and during the 1880s he married Martha Hughes, Maria Bennion, and Johanna Cristina Danielson. His six wives bore him twenty-seven children, and with the five Clarissa brought to their marriage, he had thirty-two children to rear.

During the anti-polygamy crusade, President Cannon came under scrutiny of the law, and in January 1885 he was arrested on charges of unlawful cohabitation. His trial in April resulted in a guilty verdict, and in May Judge Charles Zane sentenced him to six months in the penitentiary and fined him three hundred dollars. He served his sentence as well as some extra time in order to allow for an appeal and was released on 14 December 1885.

In 1904 Angus began serving as stake patriarch in the Salt Lake Stake, following his release as stake president. He also spent much of his time performing temple work and doing genealogical research. In 1906 he made a lengthy visit to his ancestral home, the Isle of Man, where he gathered genealogical records and tried to convert his relatives. He died 7 June

1915, and his funeral services were held in the Assembly Hall on Temple Square, 11 June 1915. Concerning his death, a *Deseret News* editorial expresses: "The death of President Angus M. Cannon . . . removes from mortality one of the most valiant, useful and prominent men of the intermountain country."[6]

Churchman

Although he engaged in a multiplicity of activities, Angus M. Cannon was first and foremost a churchman. This Utah pioneer served as a missionary, high councilor, stake president, and stake patriarch.

At the impressionable age of six, Angus, with his mother and father, and six brothers and sisters, joined the Church. Before long, they turned their attention to gathering to Zion and in September 1842 embarked for America. These early experiences, coupled with loss of his mother—a virtual sacrifice of her life for the Church—strengthened his spiritual resolve and testimony.[7]

Although less than ten years of age, Angus was impressed by Nauvoo and by the Prophet Joseph Smith. Writing about the Prophet, he recalls, "He was one of the grandest examples of manhood that I ever saw walk or ride at the head of a legion of men."[8]

Both his baptism and rebaptism constitute impressive evidence of the spiritual stature of young Angus Cannon. Having lost both parents, Angus had not been baptized, even though he was ten years of age. Consequently, in the fall of 1844, Angus took it upon himself to request baptism and was baptized in the Mississippi River by Lyman O. Littlefield.[9] Some years later, after having emigrated to the Salt Lake Valley, Angus decided to request rebaptism, as was customary for early Church members.[10] Before applying for rebaptism, however, Angus believed it was both desirable and necessary to have his own testimony of the truthfulness of the gospel of Jesus Christ and of The Church of Jesus Christ of Latter-day

Saints. He perceived that it would no longer be possible to rely on the testimonies of others. Thus, he determined to fast and pray for his own witness. At the end of the third day of this fast, a Sunday, he decided to attend church with some friends and to break his fast, feeling that God would not answer him. During the sacrament meeting held in the Sixth Ward, he received his answer. As the patriarch, Jesse West, bore his testimony, young Angus felt a power take hold of him—a power which shook the bench and all those seated upon it. As he later recalled, "The heavenly power I experienced when under the influence of that occasion I can never forget."[11] Having received his answer and his own testimony, Angus was rebaptized, at age seventeen.

At age twenty he received a mission call to serve in the eastern United States. During his mission, lasting from September 1854 until June 1858, Angus served in Connecticut, New York, New Jersey, Pennsylvania, Delaware, and Maryland.[12] Part of his time as a missionary he spent in New York City, where he helped his uncle, Elder John Taylor, publish an important Church newspaper called *The Mormon*. After laboring in this capacity for one year, Angus had planned to enter West Point but was dissuaded from this goal by his uncle, who believed Angus should continue his missionary labors.[13]

An examination of his missionary journals suggests that Angus M. Cannon served effectively as a representative of the Church. This young elder was privileged to baptize several people during his mission. Even when he traveled by railroad, he seized every opportunity to preach the gospel. The favorable impression he made is evident in the following excerpt from the *Public Medium* of Wilamantic, Connecticut: "A young man all the way from Great Salt Lake City, seemingly not more than 20 years of age, preached in the Universalist Church last Sunday morning and afternoon. . . . He bears the appearance in his face of good moral character, and high tone of mind, accompanied with rather superior intelligence."[14] Parley P. Pratt, who worked for a time with Angus as his missionary companion, recorded this favorable observation in his autobiography: "We sang and prayed, feasted and rejoiced, and taught them as we were led by the Spirit. Elder Angus M. Cannon being with me in this and nearly all my visitings and meetings in this city [Philadelphia]. A happier companion is seldom found."[15]

As was typical of nineteenth-century missionary work, Angus encountered opposition. Once, while he was attempting to perform a baptism, a large crowd assembled and forced the elders to find another location where they could perform the ordinance.[16] His mission experiences also included spiritual experiences, both as an individual and as a member of a group. One such personal spiritual experience was a dream Angus had—a dream of the spirit world. He wrote that he learned from this experience that he should trust in God and do his bidding.[17]

During the excitement of the Utah War, the Church leaders called Angus home from his mission. He arrived in Salt Lake on 21 June 1858. Following his mission and, indeed, throughout his life, Angus Cannon held many positions of trust in the Church. In April 1876 President Brigham Young set him apart as president of the Salt Lake Stake, a position he held for twenty-eight years.[18] The Salt Lake Stake, at that time, included a very large territory. It encompassed not only Salt Lake County but also the counties of Tooele, Davis, Morgan, Summit, and Wasatch. One indication of the size of the stake is the number of patriarchs. In 1887 the Salt Lake Stake had twelve patriarchs. Ward membership figures ran from a low of 58 members at Mountain Dell in Parley's Canyon to a high of 1165 members in the Eleventh Ward in the City.[19]

His responsibilities as stake president included visiting wards, installing ward and stake officers, holding courts, conducting temple recommend interviews, holding stake meetings such as high council meetings, and conducting weekly meetings in the Salt Lake Tabernacle for the Saints throughout the Valley. Frequently these meetings featured General Authorities as speakers, even though they came under the jurisdiction of the Salt Lake Stake president, who presided at the meetings. In addition to those who spoke, others from among the General Authorities attended this meeting and other stake meetings. At the stake priesthood meeting, for example, held on 15 September 1877, John Taylor, Erastus Snow, George Q. Cannon, and Brigham Young, Jr., were in attendance.[20]

Sometimes the Brethren invited Angus to speak in general conference, even though he was not a General Authority. He spoke, for example, at April conference in 1903. In his remarks he reminisced about his long term as stake president, during which time five different men had presided over the Church— Brigham Young, John Taylor, Wilford Woodruff, Lorenzo Snow, and Joseph F. Smith. The fact that he participated in such meetings underscores the significance of his position as president of the Salt Lake Stake.[21]

When Angus M. Cannon visited the wards in his stake, he was not just a routine visitor. The members of the Herriman Ward found out that he meant business. Arthur W. Crane, a lifeong resident of that ward recalls one incident vividly. When President Cannon came to visit, he released the bishop and presented the name of James S. Crane as the new bishop. Because of factions in the ward, a majority voted against Brother Crane. Angus M. Cannon then disfellowshipped all who had so voted and set apart another man to act as presiding elder until such time as the majority of the ward should repent. Three months passed, the people repented, President Cannon returned, and the ward sustained James S. Crane as bishop. In time, most ward members thought Bishop Crane was one of the best bishops who ever served in Herriman.[22]

Stake presidents in nineteenth-century Utah had many responsibilities which would not be associated with stake presidencies of today. In his role as stake president, for example, Angus Cannon had major responsibilities for the education of his people. Early in his term of office he had responsibility for the Salt Lake Stake Academy. Later, this responsibility shifted to the LDS College. In this capacity President Cannon had responsibilities that would today be assumed by the board of trustees. Frequently Angus attended meetings with other Church leaders who had responsibility for education in the Salt

Lake Valley. Sometimes he met with the stake board of education. At other times he met as a member of the board of trustees. Most often their meetings were routine, as is the case of one meeting in which they ordered chairs for Barrett Hall at LDS College.[23] Sometimes, however, their meetings dealt with crises, such as the time when the entire business faculty at LDS College resigned in protest of administration policies. On that occasion, and in a number of subsequent meetings, the board worked closely with the president of the college, Joshua H. Paul, to hire the necessary replacements.[24]

An analysis of the extensive diaries of Angus M. Cannon indicates that much of his time as stake president was devoted to Church courts. Although Angus was careful not to recall the nature of the charges against the accused or the details of the court proceedings, his journals do contain frequent references to court sessions over which he presided.

Some of the court procedures were decidedly different than those of later periods. For example, today a stake presidency generally retires to an adjoining room and makes a decision which is announced to the court, after which a vote of the council is called for. This procedure usually takes place within hours or even minutes after the high council has finished its consideration of the case. In contrast, in the days when he presided over courts, Angus would take time to write a decision—somewhat in the fashion of today's United States Supreme Court. The written decision would then be considered by the council.[25] Another practice which seems foreign in the modern Church is the public confession of one's sins. In the case of the Second Counselor in the Presiding Bishopric, John Q. Cannon, son of George Q. Cannon and a nephew of Angus, John was called upon to make a public confession before the congregation in the Salt Lake Tabernacle. Following this public confession, Angus as stake president proposed that John be cut off from the Church. The vote was taken, and John Cannon was excommunicated.[26]

For his work in Church law, Angus M. Cannon has received ample praise. A grandson, Quayle Cannon, Jr., recalls hearing Elder Levi Edgar Young say that Angus was without equal in the field of Church law. According to Marion Bennion Cannon, Levi Edgar Young said Angus M. Cannon "was one of the most just men he had ever known, speaking of his administration as president of the Salt Lake Stake in the days when that meant being both civil and religious judge in the whole county."[27] Perhaps these feelings of praise came because of Angus's charity and compassion in Church courts. Angus writes: "Better let 99 guilty ones go uncondemned than condemn one innocent one."[28]

The Church courts over which he presided often dealt with matters of a purely secular nature—something rarely done in the Church in the twentieth century. One such court involved a case of a woman accused of stealing drugs from a hospital. After hearing the evidence President Cannon and the court decided that the charges against the woman could not be sustained.[29] Furthermore, the Salt Lake Stake high council frequently considered cases involving Gentiles. Thus, non-Mormons came by choice to a Church court to consider purely secular matters.

Studying his work as stake president, one quickly realizes that not only Church law but also customs in the nineteenth-century Church differed sharply with customs and practices of a later era. Even ordinances as basic as baptism assumed a different character in that time. Angus writes, for example, of baptizing his son Eugene in the Logan Temple for his health.[30] On another occasion Angus writes: "At 2 p.m. I baptized little Catherine Lynch Cannon in the bath tub, I getting into the tub with her. She is 8 years old today."[31] Obviously, baptisms were held wherever it was convenient, not just in places provided for that purpose.

Information from the diaries of Angus M. Cannon indicates that the Saints administered to the sick more often than is done today. Angus not only administered to his large family but also to members of the Church under his jurisdiction. An entry from his journal shows his faith in this practice: "I was called from my breakfast at 7 and went with George and Brother Jesse A. Fox and administered to the daughter of Brother Wm.

C. Morris—she is affected with heart disease. In administering to her I said she should live." Three days later, he writes cryptically that she was better.[32]

Angus M. Cannon sternly enforced provisions of the Word of Wisdom. When his son, Angus, Jr., developed a drinking habit, he came under severe condemnation from his father. His journals also show that Angus thoroughly disapproved of smoking. His belief in this important principle and practice surfaced often in his discourses and public testimonies. During one fast and testimony meeting Angus spoke on the Word of Wisdom "as a revelation of God to the people."[33]

While he energetically decried violations of the Word of Wisdom, Angus reserved his heaviest ammunition for the war against round dancing. By mid-nineteenth century, round dancing had nearly replaced square and line dancing in America. In round dancing the gentleman and his partner held each other in close proximity and circled together around the hall. Waltzes and foxtrots were among the most popular round dances.[34] Church leaders at all levels lost little time in vigorously condemning the sin of round dancing. At a stake leadership meeting, President Cannon said: "The young should be restrained in their excesses in round dancing." Excesses of round dancing should also be restricted so that "older persons may join in the dance with them, without having to sit and look on more than half the time or of being entrapped onto the floor by the evasive titles given to round dances." He further warned that the youth of Zion sought to evade justice and cloak their sins by using "evasive titles" for dances that were obviously round dances.[35] At a high priest quorum meeting held almost twenty years later, he was still preaching against round dancing.[36] President Cannon, however, was not alone in decrying this form of evil. In an official statement issued by the First Presidency in 1912, members were instructed "to avoid 'dances that require or permit the close embrace.' "[37]

President Cannon agreed with the General Authorities on such issues, and he supported them with complete energy and devotion. This agreement was facilitated and enhanced by his close personal relationship with the leaders of the Church. In part, this intimate association stemmed from his kinship with some of the Brethren. His older brother, George Q. Cannon, served as counselor in the First Presidency during most of Angus's twenty-eight years as stake president. During the 1880s his uncle, John Taylor, served as President of the Church. Thus, Angus M. Cannon had, by virtue of family ties, easy access to the highest councils of the Church. In fact, many of the General Authorities were blood relatives.[38]

The familial tie which created the most intimate bond to the Church hierarchy was his relationship with his renowned brother, George Q. Cannon. Their voluminous correspondence bears eloquent testimony to their firm personal relationship and to their common interest in Church affairs. While George represented Utah Territory in Washington, D.C., the brothers frequently exchanged letters. Writing, for example, in 1880, George Q. sent forty dollars for the building fund for the Assembly Hall on Temple Square, commenting: "I wish it was ten times the amount; but I am cramped, and it is all I can afford at present."[39] Always a careful and prescient observer of the political scene, the older brother commented during the explosive Congressional debates concerning polygamy: "Both sides are ready to join hands upon any measure which will be likely to strike down plural marriage."[40] When George was in Salt Lake City, of course, his position in the First Presidency provided Angus with ready access to the President of the Church.

At one point during his presidency, Angus was closely related to two of the three members of the First Presidency— John Taylor and George Q. Cannon. Angus felt a special affinity for his uncle, John Taylor, having served with him in the mission field in the 1850s. This affinity drew them into frequent contact during President Taylor's administration. Contact between Angus and President John Taylor occurred largely through correspondence since those years were marked by harassment over polygamy and the two were often forced into hiding. Angus wrote to and received advice from President

Taylor on such matters as Church court procedure,[41] temple recommend problems,[42] Church education,[43] stake office needs,[44] and organizational changes.[45] His respect and concern for President Taylor is evident. For example, he wrote: "Praying God to preserve you from all evil and endow you with strength to maintain his rule upon the earth."[46]

Although his association with Church leaders was facilitated by his kinship, Angus Cannon's relationship to Church leaders was not restricted to kinsmen. He enjoyed, for example, an intimate association with President Wilford Woodruff. In fact, his journals are replete with references to Wilford Woodruff. For example, he visited Wilford Woodruff and said he looked well;[47] he attended a special serenade by the Tabernacle Choir for President Woodruff;[48] he heard Wilford Woodruff bear testimony "of the Lord and the Keys of the Priesthood";[49] President Woodruff asked Angus to sell some of his property to the Church, and Angus replied, "I will do anything you wish with any of my property, that it may be of good to the Church";[50] he visited President Woodruff, who was ill, and gave him some medicine and advice on his health;[51] he asked President Woodruff if the veil should be up or down on a deceased woman, and the President responded, "put it down."[52] After attending the laying of the capstone on the Salt Lake Temple, Angus referred to Wilford W. Woodruff as "the greatest man living."[53] Obviously these men enjoyed a meaningful personal relationship.

With each of the Presidents of the Church from Brigham Young to Joseph F. Smith, President Cannon experienced a close personal association. In those relationships Angus respected both the office and the man who occupied it. Respect, however, did not mean bowing and scraping to please the Brethren. If he had a difference of opinion on an important issue, he freely and candidly expressed his point of view. As a consequence, there were some stormy moments. In conversation with President Lorenzo Snow, Angus stood his ground when President Snow reprimanded him for being too harsh with one of his members. Said Angus, "I believe you would be quite as impatient as I am." President Snow replied, "I might be worse than you."[54] Occasionally his frankness and tenacity caused some bitterness in his association with the Brethren. Such was the case in his relationship with one of the Apostles, Heber J. Grant. Following a meeting, he ran into Heber J. Grant, who said: "I do not think you are fit to preside over a stake until you make an apology." Angus replied, "I do not think you fit to be an Apostle to talk out as you do!"[55] To the credit of both men, they resolved their differences and enjoyed a cordial companionship in later years.

In the main, Angus's relationship with the General Authorities was close and friendly. He went to them with questions, conferred with them on policy, and enjoyed a pleasant social interaction with them and their wives and families. This close relationship stemmed in part from kinship, but also from the fact that the Church was much smaller and more intimate in the early days than it is now. From this condition Angus benefited, as did the members of the Salt Lake Stake.

One program which the General Authorities encouraged Angus to implement was the home missionary program. While some of its features are found among various twentieth-century Church programs, the home missionary program *per se* is not found in today's Church. In the nineteenth century, each stake in the Church had its own corps of home missionaries—missionaries used for a variety of purposes, as determined by each stake president. In general, home missionaries stressed temple building, repentance, and economic stability. According to a regularly scheduled plan, these home missionaries visited each of the wards in the stake. As envisaged by Church leaders, the home missionaries were to improve the quality of ward sacrament meetings by giving better than average talks. Indeed, instructions for home missionaries given in their home missionary meetings constantly stressed that they improve their speaking ability and strive to make their talks more stimulating and interesting.[56] The home missionaries were counseled on how to teach. They were instructed "to teach doctrines rather than incidents of their personal experience and to warn the people to repent and reform."[57]

President Cannon called several home missionaries in October 1877 and also inaugurated monthly home missionary meetings, held in the Council House. The home missionaries of the Salt Lake Stake visited the wards on a regular basis, carrying the messages which they had been assigned. Some home missionaries served for as long as twenty years, preaching sermons almost every week. Eventually, as many as one hundred fifty home missionaries served at one time in the Salt Lake Stake.[58]

In home missionary meetings, stake priesthood meetings, and other meetings, Angus M. Cannon gave hundreds of speeches during his lengthy term as stake president. The subjects of these talks give some insight into the matters which he considered important for the members of the Salt Lake Stake to hear. One of the subjects Angus most frequently spoke on was the responsibility of parents for their children. In home missionary meetings as well as at stake conferences, he urged parents to teach their children the gospel.[59]

Sometimes the pronouncements of President Cannon received quasi-General Authority status. His talks on women and the priesthood are a case in point. At the stake conference held in October 1878 he spoke on this subject, and his remarks were subsequently reported in the *Woman's Exponent.*[60] Other subjects frequently discussed by Angus included tithing, priesthood, Church courts, backbiting, and judging others.[61] Concerning the matter of judging others, Angus taught about "the danger of judging the actions of our brethren without understanding their motives."[62] In a word, an examination of his speeches convinces one that Angus M. Cannon cared deeply about teaching the Saints their duties.

The information presented thus far concerning Angus M. Cannon's experiences and activities as president of the Salt Lake Stake make it possible to draw certain conclusions. When this information is compared with research on the history of stakes in the Church even more meaningful conclusions may be reached. Although considerable work has been done on the organizational and institutional features of Mormonism in general, unfortunately this is not true of the stake.[63]

One conclusion which is quite apparent is that Angus M. Cannon served as stake president during a time of transition—transition not only for the Salt Lake Stake but also for all stakes in the Church. Prior to 1877 Salt Lake Stake had enjoyed a position of superiority in relation to other stakes. The stake presidency of the Salt Lake Stake even approved personnel called to serve in other stakes. In 1877 such a position of superiority came to an end as a part of the priesthood reorganization of 1877. Salt Lake Stake no longer held any authority over other stakes, and all stakes were declared equal and independent of each other.[64]

The size of the stake was changed during this transition period. As noted previously, when Brigham Young set Angus apart in 1876, Salt Lake Stake included not only all of Salt Lake County but also the counties of Tooele, Davis, Morgan, Summit, and Wasatch. One year later, it was reduced in size to include only Salt Lake County. Each of the other counties was organized as a separate stake. Even after losing such a huge amount of territory, Salt Lake Stake still had 19,798 members in 1877.[65]

The transition associated with the priesthood reorganization of 1877 introduced several changes in the priesthood quorums. High priests were to be organized in one stake quorum with unlimited numbers. Seventies were to meet together only for missionary purposes; their regular priesthood meetings would be held jointly with high priests or elders quorums. All priesthood quorums were to have minimum numbers of members established by modern revelation. Consequently, no less than ninety-six elders, forty-eight priests, twenty-four teachers, and twelve deacons were necessary.[66]

Significant changes also occurred in the relationship between the stake leaders and the General Authorities and in the role and jurisdiction of the stake presidency. Beginning in

1877 all stakes were to hold regular quarterly conferences at which General Authorities would visit. Stake presidencies and high councilors were to visit wards frequently and systematically. Furthermore, stakes were to hold monthly priesthood meetings. To accommodate these priesthood meetings and other meetings, stake tabernacles were to be built. Since the Salt Lake Stake could hold its conferences in the Tabernacle on Temple Square, they needed a smaller building for priesthood meetings. This requirement resulted in the construction of the Assembly Hall on Temple Square.[67]

Although one of the goals of Brigham Young's reorganization of 1877 was to standardize the stakes and make them equal and autonomous, as far as the Salt Lake Stake was concerned, this goal was only partially realized. In the minds of Angus M. Cannon and other leaders of the Salt Lake Stake, it remained "the stake." To make their point, these men could call attention to the weekly general sacrament meeting for all of Salt Lake Valley. This meeting, held in the Tabernacle and involving many General Authorities, was under the jurisdiction of the Salt Lake Stake. Furthermore, they could point out that Salt Lake Stake was by far the largest stake in the entire Church, even when five new stakes were created within its original boundaries.

Much of the time Angus served as stake president he shared an office with the Presidency of the Church. This sharing of physical facilities included not only the office space, desks, and other equipment, but it also included the use of the carriage and horses that were provided for the First Presidency.[68] This close proximity and identification with the top leaders of the Church made it possible for Angus M. Cannon and other leaders of the Salt Lake Stake to feel that their stake enjoyed a special status, a status apart from other stakes.

Another factor which might have influenced Angus and his associates to regard the Salt Lake Stake as paramount was the responsibility which they had for some Church matters outside the confines of their own stake. One such responsibility concerned temples and temple work. Angus M. Cannon had responsibility and authority for matters concerning the Logan Temple. He was directly and influentially involved in matters of policy concerning the operation of that temple. This role, of course, ceased once the Salt Lake Temple was completed in the 1890s. Clearly the role which Angus Cannon played concerning the Logan Temple made him feel that his position and his stake were in some ways superior to other stakes in the Church.[69] Although the general direction and tenor of the Church had changed, Angus M. Cannon continued to think this way about the Salt Lake Stake until he was released.

When Angus Cannon was replaced as Salt Lake Stake president, after serving for twenty-eight years, he found his release an unpleasant and trying experience. The circumstances of that release bear repeating. In the weeks and months immediately preceding his release, President Cannon had a premonition that a change was imminent. He wrote in his journal that the General Authorities had been heaping praise on him to make it "easier on me." As they consulted with him on the proposed division of the Salt Lake Stake, his feelings about being released became more intense. Feeling especially depressed, he wrote: "In these thoughts I find comfort, knowing He has always been my true friend."[70] Implicit in this statement is the belief that while the Savior had remained his true friend, the Church leaders had not. The experience of Angus shows not only the difficulty of being released after a long period of service but also the hurt which often results when leaders are seen as insensitive. By 1 April 1904, the Salt Lake Stake had been divided into four stakes—Salt Lake, Liberty, Pioneer, and Ensign—with four new presidents; Nephi L. Morris, Hugh J. Cannon, William McLachlin, and Richard W. Young. Angus was sustained as patriarch in the new Salt Lake Stake.[71] Angus felt like a man without a country. Some weeks later he told President Joseph F. Smith that he felt all used up and of no more value to the Church.[72] President Smith tried to console him, and eventually the wound healed and Angus M. Cannon's Church career took a new course.

In his later years Angus divided his Church-related activities between genealogical research, temple work, and his duties as patriarch. He made a lengthy trip to the Isle of Man in 1906 in search of his ancestors, successfully gathering many family records. He spent as much as four days a week in the performance of ordinances and as a temple worker at the Salt Lake Temple until his death in 1915. He also faithfully gave patriarchal blessings to members of the stake who had a desire to receive them.

In earlier years Angus had received four patriarchal blessings of his own: John Smith gave him a patriarchal blessing in 1853 and another in 1867; William G. Perkins gave him a blessing in 1874; and he received a blessing under the hands of Zebedee Coltrin in 1886. His blessings were beautiful and meaningful, and they reveal significant insights concerning his life and his relationship to the Church. One passage from the patriarchal blessing given by Zebedee Coltrin reads: "Thou wast called and chosen of the Lord before the foundations of the earth was laid to come forth in this dispensation to assist in building up an holy city unto the Lord."[73]

In discharging his duties as patriarch, Angus M. Cannon earnestly sought the Spirit of the Lord and hoped to be his mouthpiece. He also responded to the needs of the members. One journal entry reads: "I met brother Merlin Jones Bartholemew going on a mission to the Middle States, who desired a Patriarchal blessing, as he was going away this evening. I took him to my office and blessed him while Quayle wrote it."[74] His experiences as patriarch also indicate that Church customs regarding these blessings have changed over the years. Evidently the patriarch charged a small fee for his services and for the purpose of paying the recorder of the blessing. Thus, he writes: "Gave 7 Patriarchal blessings for which each gave $1. . . . Ann wrote them for me and I gave Ann $3.00 for writing them for us."[75] From the records available, it would seem that he gave most of his patriarchal blessings on Sunday. His journal entries indicate that he was conscientious in attending to his patriarchal duties, and he also derived a sense of spiritual satisfaction from this challenging and spiritually demanding activity.

One of the most important aspects of Angus M. Cannon's relationship to the Church is his practice of plural marriage. He entered voluntarily into ᴧne practice of polygamy because of his conviction that Church leaders represented the will of God when they instructed him to do so. Based on that conviction, he married and lived with six women: Sarah Maria Mousley, Ann Amanda Mousley, Clarissa Cordelia Moses Mason, Martha Hughes, Maria Bennion, and Johanna Cristina Danielson.

The story of his first marriage is a classic in the annals of Mormon polygamy. During his days as a missionary in Delaware, Angus had become acquainted with the Titus Mousley family of Wilmington, Delaware. He was especially fond of Amanda, one of the Mousley daughters, and after the family immigrated to Utah he continued this relationship by courting her. Desiring to marry her, he consulted with Church leaders, who recommended that he marry not only Ann Amanda but her sister Sarah Maria, as well. So it was, on the morning of 18 July 1858, Angus M. Cannon, Ann Amanda Mousley, and her sister Sarah Maria Mousley arrived at President Brigham Young's office in the Beehive House for the purpose of being united in marriage. Being the sweetheart of Angus, Amanda fully expected to become the first wife. Brigham Young, however, relying perhaps on biblical precedent, decided that Sarah, being the eldest, should become the first wife. Obviously upset by such a development, Amanda consented to become the second wife only upon Angus's solemn promise that he would honor her with the privileges normally reserved for the first wife in a polygamous marriage. Thus, they were married by President Brigham Young, and all three set out on their honeymoon.[76]

True to his promise, Angus treated Amanda as his first wife. While he carefully divided his time among his six wives, he spent more time with Amanda than any other of his wives. She served as hostess for most of his social functions as stake president. While she fulfilled her role as hostess with grace and dignity, she preferred the privacy of her home. Indeed, Amanda was an intensely private person, devoted to rearing her children and attending to her husband's needs. She bore Angus ten children, more than any other of his wives.[77]

According to his journal entries Angus enjoyed his best husband-wife relationship with Amanda. They had fewer quarrels and certainly fewer displays of anger. Because Amanda's health was somewhat frail, Angus conscientiously administered to her and purchased medicine for her.[78] His love and concern for Amanda are shown in this entry: "Arose at 6:45 and made a fire, fearful the room was too cold for Amanda. I prayed at Amanda's bed side, for the church Amanda and myself and all God has intrusted to me."[79] Each Monday he gave her the week's financial allowance, and his journals prove that he never missed this payment. Unlike some forgetful husbands, Angus always remembered Amanda's birthday.[80] She returned his thoughtfulness by keeping his clothing in good order and preparing delicious meals. When Angus was in prison as a convicted polygamist, she visited him regularly, thus easing the pain of that experience.[81] All in all, Angus and Amanda enjoyed an excellent relationship.

Amanda also enjoyed a harmonious relationship with her sister Sarah. Although technically the first wife, Sarah assumed a role similar to that of his other wives and seemed not to be offended by her secondary status. Whether homesteading at her Bluffdale farm or comfortably housed in Salt Lake, Sarah earned a reputation as an excellent homemaker. She always kept her home attractive and pleasant. Though only ninety pounds in weight, this diminutive woman never shirked hard work. Sarah Maria bore Angus six children.[82]

The marriage of Angus M. Cannon and Clarissa Cordelia Moses Mason Cannon on 16 June 1875 attests to the humanitarian nature of Mormon polygamy. Clara's husband had died, leaving her with five children. Clearly the welfare of her and her children was a major consideration when Angus decided to take her as his third wife. This gracious, bilingual woman had come around Cape Horn with Sam Brannan on the *Brooklyn*. Settling in San Francisco, she became fluent in Spanish through association with Spanish-speaking playmates. She brought five children into the marriage, and bore Angus three additional children.[83]

By far the most famous and unquestionably the most difficult of all of his wives, Martha Hughes Cannon became his fourth wife in a secret ceremony conducted in the Endowment House of 6 October 1884. While working as a medical doctor at Deseret Hospital, Mattie met and married Angus, who served as a member of the hospital board of directors. Although Mattie was twenty-three years younger than her husband, she felt herself drawn to his "deep spirituality"[84] and considered him "handsome and magnetic."[85]

During the 1890s she added political ambitions to her interest in medicine. In 1893 she spoke in Chicago on women's rights and in 1895 became involved in the Utah Constitutional Convention. In the 1896 election, Utah's first election as a state, she made history by being elected the first woman state senator in the United States and by defeating her husband in that political contest. Technically, Martha and Angus did not oppose each other directly. Each party nominated five candidates for a total slate of ten. Actually, both Angus and Mattie could have won or both could have lost the election, since she ran on the Democratic slate and he on the Republican slate. As it turned out, Mattie won and Angus lost. Mattie's victory and Angus's defeat, of course, caused the stake president considerable embarrassment. However, too much should not be made of his so-called humiliation. In a letter to a prominent acquaintance in New York, shortly after the election, Angus wrote: "My wife aspired to be a State Senator and it looks as if she will get there while I planned to get there but failed. Notwithstanding this I am not going to separate from my wife but will try and keep as near as I can and *be happy*.[86]

Obviously, Martha Hughes Cannon desired fulfillment through a dual career as homemaker and career woman. Her pursuit of fulfillment through a public career in medicine and politics made her the most challenging of Angus's wives. That Mattie and Angus loved each other is evident, but equally manifest were their disputes. Indeed, theirs was a bittersweet relationship. Love letters and valentines[87] were interspersed with complaints about neglect and threats of divorce.[88] Ultimately, Martha elected to separate, at least geographically, from Angus, living the last years of her life in Los Angeles near her three children. She outlived Angus by seventeen years, dying on 10 July 1932.[89]

Like Martha, Maria Bennion Cannon was twenty-three years younger than her husband. The daughter of John and Esther Bennion, she was born in Taylorsville, Utah, 5 August 1857. She married Angus on 11 March 1886, following his prison term for cohabitation. Her years in hiding because of persecution over polygamy were spent in Logan, Utah. After about 1910 she lived in Salt Lake County. Fond of music and talented, she served as ward organist in many places. She bore Angus four children.[90]

Angus married his sixth wife, Johanna Christine Danielson, 21 March 1887. She was born 2 October 1850, in Carlshaven, Sweden. She bore Angus one child.[91] According to his journal, she lived on a farm in Sandy, Utah. Although little information is available concerning Johanna, it is obvious from his personal records that he visited her frequently and cared for her when she was ill.[92]

Being the husband of six polygamous wives brought two penalties to Angus—harassment by federal officials and imprisonment in the state penitentiary. All during the 1880s Angus lived "on the underground" and suffered frequent harassment at the hands of federal marshals. On 26 August 1886, for example, he records: "Dep. Marshals surrounded my Bluff-Dale Farm house and searched it for Mr. Cannon."[93] The following day he learned that ten federal marshals had warrants for his arrest. In November he began carrying a pistol for protection. In fact, when marshals did try to arrest him, they were amused by his arsenal—one needle, gun, one Colt automatic, one Winchester rifle.[94] Feeling pressure as his hearing approached, he appealed to the Lord. "I went before the Lord in prayer and dedicated myself and all I had to Him and said I was ready to go to prison unto death if it was his will. . . . I was comforted of the Spirit."[95]

Angus's apprehension about going to prison was intensified, no doubt, by his earlier prison experience. He had already served a term in the Utah State prison for unlawful cohabitation. Indeed, Angus Cannon was one of the first to be tried and convicted of unlawful cohabitation when legal prosecutions began for violation of the Edmunds law. Seeking to conform to the letter of the law, Angus, by providing separate living quarters for each of his wives and by actually not living with them and avoiding normal husband-wife relationships, sought to avoid conviction for unlawful cohabitation. The judge, however, thought differently. Chief Justice Charles S. Zane convicted Angus and sentenced him to six months in prison and fined him three hundred dollars.[96]

Fortunately, Angus continued writing in his journal while he served his prison term. Consequently, we are in a better position to understand his experience there. On the eve of his imprisonment a "farewell testimonial" was held in the Fourteenth Ward assembly hall in his honor.[97] On 9 May 1885, his first day in prison, he writes: "I ate a little bread and water for supper and slept in a hammock placed in a small prison house, where there were between thirty and forty criminals, charged with every crime, and of every color."[98] Angus thought he received fair treatment and especially looked forward to regular visits from family members, who brought fruit, baked goods, and flowers. In order to pass the long, monotonous hours, he played croquet, pitched quoits, and read. Some of the books and newspapers he read include Parley P. Pratt, *Key to Theology; Highways to Literature;* Draper's *Intellectual Development of Europe; History and Philosophy of Marriage;* Herbert Spencer, *Education, Intellectual and Moral;* Leonard Schmitz, *A Manual of Ancient History; Harper's Weekly; Juvenile Instructor; St. Louis Globe Democrat; Provo Enquirer; Deseret News; Salt Lake Herald;* and *Salt Lake Tribune.*[99]

His spirits varied, but for the most part he remained optimistic about his prison experience. On at least one occasion the prisoners received a letter of encouragement from President Joseph F. Smith.[100] Sometimes Angus had to renew his determination and resolve to endure to the end. Once he wrote his resolve in capital letters: "I AM HAPPY AND CAN ENDURE WITH THE HELP OF GOD AS MANY YEAR'S IMPRISONMENT AS I HAVE DONE WEEKS."[101]

As it turned out, Angus remained in prison almost two months longer than his original sentence while his lawyers tested the constitutionality of the legal concept of unlawful cohabitation. Finally, the government decided that the concept was constitutional, but Angus was then released. Of his release, he writes:

> It is with anxiety I await news from Washington relating to my case of appeal. I was in line at 3 bells come into supper when I was called by Warden Dow and told to change my dress as I was to be discharged from prison. It was only the work of a few minutes and I bade a due to my brethren and fellow prisoners. All of whom gathered around me; the former reminding me of some little message to friends and all joining and wishing that I might not have to return to their midst.[102]

As one surveys his activities as a churchman, two areas, previously unmentioned, loom prominently on the horizon: First, his experience in 1888 with David Whitmer, and second, his visit with Joseph Smith III in 1905. In January 1888, while on a business trip to the East, Angus stopped in Richmond, Missouri, to pay a visit to David Whitmer, the last survivor of the three witnesses of the Book of Mormon. While in Richmond, Angus heard David Whitmer bear solemn testimony of Joseph Smith and the Book of Mormon. Within the month, David Whitmer died. Having a premonition that he would be the last of the Latter-day Saints to hear the testimony of David Whitmer, Angus had written: "I feel I should be the last stranger to hear it."[103]

A little more than a year after his release as stake president, Angus had a most interesting visit with Joseph Smith III, the son of the Prophet. Angus and Joseph III were nearly the same age and had attended school together in the Red Brick Store in Nauvoo. Thus, their relationship spanned a lifetime. While on a visit to Salt Lake in 1906, Joseph Smith III requested to see Angus, who gladly consented to spend some time with his friend. During the course of their visit, they both addressed each other as "Brother" and had a lively discussion about their respective churches, and especially about polygamy. Interestingly, Angus also told Joseph about his being the last elder of the Church to hear the testimony of David Whitmer. Throughout their lengthy conversation, Angus M. Cannon vigorously defended the position of The Church of Jesus Christ of Latter-day Saints and frequently bore testimony of the truth.[104]

Much of his life, Angus bore witness of the truth as he understood it, in word and deed. His testimony he regarded as a sacred possession, and he had received many remarkable spiritual manifestations which definitely strengthened his personal conviction of the truthfulness of the gospel of Jesus Christ. During his first mission in the 1850s he had a special manifestation which fortified his nascent testimony. Later in life he experienced a truly astonishing vision which put the finishing touches on his now mature testimony. While visiting in the British Isles in 1906, Angus responded to a request by President Heber J. Grant to bear his testimony by relating the following experience:

> I have been introduced as having seen the Prophet Joseph Smith, but I now wish to say I not only have seen him but I have seen the Lord, Jesus, himself.
>
> As near as I can tell it was in the days of President Taylor's Presidency and after I came out of prison. Brother Abraham Hatch said to me one day: I hear you have seen the Lord, why do you not publish it? I replied—I have seen him but not to be glorified in doing so. I took it to be rather a rebuke. I did hear a voice which said—Angus, it is your privilege to appear before the Lord and I immediately looked and beheld him, apparently about 30 rods distant. I was crouching down at the time but was as wide awake as it was possible for me to be, but I saw his profile down to his waist.

He looked to me more like James Townsend, whom I worked with, in St. Joseph than any man I remember seeing, before Brother Townsend turned grey. I undertook to arise and go to him but dared not approach him, and said: 'My God! Who can appear before Him.' I imagined he would say: How have you used my name and what use have you made of my Priesthood? When I thought of my many light speeches and the manner in which I had striven to embelish my remarks, in addressing people as His servant, circumlocuting around the truths given of Him, as witness his sermon on the mount, I was unable to go to him.[105]

Such experiences are witnessed by relatively few people. Certainly such a vision must have caused Angus to feel that he had indeed been "called and chosen" before the foundations of the world. One thing is certain: whatever else this pioneer, president, and patriarch did, whatever else he aspired to, Angus M. Cannon was first and foremost a churchman.

Notes

1. Interview with T. Quentin Cannon, 12 November 1980, Salt Lake City, Utah.

2. Interview with Quayle Cannon, Jr., 10 September 1980, Bountiful, Utah.

3. Sources constitute the building blocks of history. In the case of Angus M. Cannon more than sufficient building blocks are available. Major sources on Angus include primarily the Angus Munn Cannon Papers located at the Library-Archives, Historical Department, The Church of Jesus Christ of Latter-day Saints, Salt Lake City, Utah; hereafter cited as LDS Church Archives. This massive collection contains such items as seventy-two volumes of his journals, letterbooks, business papers, and miscellaneous items. The material in the LDS Church Archives fills twelve reels of microfilm. In addition to the collection held by the Church, family members still have some journals and letters. Seven volumes in the possession of T. Quentin Cannon were recently loaned to the Church Historical Department for microfilming. Brigham Young University has three volumes of his journals—essentially his prison diaries, written while he served a term for polygamy. From this wealth of material one can gain insight into many facets of nineteenth-century Utah. The Angus M. Cannon Papers reveal much about the Church, polygamy, agriculture, business,

politics, and human relations. In a real sense, the source material almost demands a topical approach to the life of Angus M. Cannon.

4. The other children, named in order of age, were George Q., Mary Alice, Ann, John Q., David H., and Leonora.

5. There are several good biographical sketches of Angus M. Cannon. My biographical essay has been drawn essentially from the following: Andrew Jenson, *Latter-day Saint Biographical Encyclopedia,* 4 vols. (Salt Lake City: Andrew Jenson Historical Co., 1901–1936), 1:292–95; Orson F. Whitney, *History of Utah,* 4 vols. (Salt Lake City: George Q. Cannon & Sons, Publications, 1892–1904), 4:373–76; Edward W. Tullidge, *The History of Salt Lake City and Its Founders* (Salt Lake City: Edward Tullidge, 1886), pp. 107–110; Frank Esshom, *Pioneers and Prominent Men of Utah* (Salt Lake City: Utah Pioneers Book Publishing Company, 1913), p. 188, 793; Thomas C. Romney, *The Gospel in Action* (Salt Lake City: Deseret Sunday School Union Board, 1949), pp. 30–34; Beatrice Cannon Evans, "Angus Munn Cannon," *Cannon Family Historical Treasury,* eds. Beatrice Cannon Evans and Janath Russell Cannon (Salt Lake City: George Cannon Family Association, 1967), pp. 189–216 (hereafter cited as *Treasury*). Inasmuch as the remainder of my biographical sketch has been drawn from a composite of the above-mentioned sources, no further footnote citations will be made for the sketch.

6. *Deseret News,* 7 June 1915, p. 4.

7. *Treasury,* pp. 34–50.

8. *Young Woman's Journal* 17 (Dec. 1906): 546.

9. Jenson, *LDS Biographical Encyclopedia,* p. 292.

10. For a meaningful account of the practice of rebaptism, see D. Michael Quinn, "The Practice of Rebaptism at Nauvoo," *BYU Studies* 18 (Winter 1978): 226–32.

11. *Treasury,* p. 194.

12. Whitney, *History of Utah,* 4:374.

13. Romney, *Gospel in Action,* p. 32.

14. "The Public Medium," 5 May 1855, in ibid.

15. Parley P. Pratt, *Autobiography of Parley Parker Pratt,* ed. Parley P. Pratt Jr., reprint, (Salt Lake City: Deseret Book Company, 1976), p. 439.

16. Journal of Angus M. Cannon, 16 June 1856, Angus Munn Cannon Papers, LDS Church Archives; the Angus M. Cannon Journals at the LDS Church Archives will be cited hereafter as Journal, with a date for each entry. Journals in other locations will be duly cited with reference to their exact location.

17. Journal, 25 November 1855.

18. The newspapers and biographies make such a fuss over Angus M. Cannon's twenty-eight-year term as stake president that I assumed he must

have served longer than any other stake president. My research assistant, Steven P. Knowles, determined, however, that Angus did not hold the record. Lewis W. Shurtliff served as president of the Weber Stake from 21 January 1883 until his death 2 May 1922, a total of thirty-nine years.

19. Andrew Jenson, *Historical Record, Church Encyclopedia,* Book 1 (Salt Lake City: Andrew Jenson, 1886), pp. 273–74. Note that the Salt Lake Stake was reduced in size in 1877, when Tooele, Davis, Morgan, Summit, and Wasatch stakes were created (ibid., p. 281).

20. Salt Lake Stake Minutes, Historical Record Book, 15 September 1877, LDS Church Archives.

21. *Conference Report* (Salt Lake City: The Deseret News, 1903), pp. 58–60. See article by Kenneth W. Godfrey, "150 years of General Conference," *Ensign,* 1981, pp. 66–74. See also, Jay R. Lowe, "A Study of the General Conferences of The Church of Jesus Christ of Latter-day Saints, 1830–1901" (Ph.D. diss., Brigham Young University, 1972).

22. Taped interview with Arthur W. Crane, 10 April 1980, Herriman, Utah. See also Journal, 8 August 1897.

23. Journal, 3 March 1902.

24. Journal, 2 February 1900. See also *The Deseret Evening News,* 3 February 1900, p. 11. For additional information concerning the formation and early history of LDS College, see Ernest L. Wilkinson, ed., *Brigham Young University: The First One Hundred Years,* 4 vols. (Provo, Utah: BYU Press, 1975), 1:222–25.

25. See, for example, Journal, 11–12 August 1886.

26. Journal, 5 September 1886. John Q. Cannon was serving as a General Authority at the time of his excommunication. He was second counselor in the Presiding Bishopric.

27. Marion Cannon Bennion, "Where the Cannon Family Came From," talk given at the Angus M. Cannon Family Reunion, Salt Lake City, 12 July 1957.

28. Angus M. Cannon to Orin P. Miller, 4 April 1895, Letterbooks, Angus M. Cannon Papers, LDS Church Archives; hereafter cited as Letterbooks.

29. John Taylor, 20 February 1884, *Journal of Discourses,* 26 vols. (London: Latter-day Saints Book Depot, 1854–1886): 26:361–63.

30. Journal, 10 July 1892. On baptism for health, see Quinn, "Rebaptism," pp. 229–31.

31. Journal, 17 July 1901. That such a practice was not unusual is evident from the fact that Spencer W. Kimball was baptized in a washtub and later in a canal (see Edward L. Kimball and Andrew E. Kimball, Jr., *Spencer W. Kimball* [Salt Lake City: Bookcraft, 1977], p. 33).

32. Journal, 10 January 1889 and 13 January 1889. That they also tried to teach priesthood order in administering to the sick is shown in Angus's

refusal to ask President Lorenzo Snow to administer to someone; he told those making the request that President Snow should not indulge in an activity that "thousands of strong Elders are able to do" (Journal, 25 November 1900).

33. Journal, 2 June 1892. For information on changing attitudes toward the Word of Wisdom, see Paul H. Peterson, "An Historical Analysis of the Word of Wisdom" (Master's thesis, Brigham Young University, 1972).

34. Davis Bitton, "These Licentious Days: Dancing among the Mormons," *Sunstone* 2 (Spring 1977): 18–19.

35. Salt Lake Historical Record Book, 1876–1880, 26 March, 1879, p. 240. LDS Church Archives.

36. Journal, 24 February 1894.

37. Bitton, "Licentious Days," p. 17.

38. For excellent information on kinship in the Church, see D. Michael Quinn, "The Mormon Hierarchy, 1832–1932: An American Elite" (Ph.D. diss., Yale University, 1976).

39. George Q. Cannon to Angus M. Cannon, 15 December 1880, Letterbooks.

40. George Q. Cannon to Angus M. Cannon, 21 January 1882, Letterbooks.

41. Journal, 10 July 1886.

42. Angus M. Cannon to John Taylor, 25 May 1887, Letterbooks.

43. Cannon to Taylor, 17 February 1887, Letterbooks.

44. Cannon to Taylor, 29 March 1887, Letterbooks.

45. Cannon to Taylor, 3 May 1887, Letterbooks.

46. Cannon to Taylor, 3 June 1887, Letterbooks.

47. Journal, 21 February 1889.

48. Journal, 22 February 1889.

49. Journal, 2 June 1889.

50. Journal, 17 April 1890.

51. Journal, 11 May 1891.

52. Journal, 1 October 1891.

53. Journal, 6 April 1892.

54. Journal, 15 February 1899.

55. Journal, 19 February 1899.

56. A. Glen Humphreys, "Missionaries to the Saints," *BYU Studies* 17 (Autumn 1976): 88–100.

57. Home Missionary Meeting, 28 August 1878, p. 189.

58. Humphreys, "Missionaries to the Saints," pp. 88–100. Salt Lake Stake Minutes, 1876–1880, 8 October 1877, p. 88, LDS Church Archives; hereafter referred to as SLS Minutes, 1876–1880.

59. SLS Minutes, 1876–1880, pp. 92, 181, 226, 232.

60. *Woman's Exponent*, 1 November 1878. For more information on women and the priesthood as well as administering to the sick, see Linda K. Newell, "A Gift Given, A Gift Taken: Washing, Anointing and Blessing the Sick among Mormon Women," *Sunstone* 6 (Sept.–Oct. 1981): 16–25.

61. SLS Minutes, 1876–1880, pp. 138, 181, 194, 202, 263, 282.

62. Ibid.; Home Missionary Meeting, 29 October 1879.

63. Several members of the Joseph Fielding Smith Institute for Church History at Brigham Young University have completed excellent studies on various aspects of LDS institutional history. Under the skilled direction of Leonard J. Arrington, many fine studies on priesthood quorums, the office of bishop, etc., have been completed. Most useful in connection with this study is the work of William G. Hartley. Although his work today has been only indirectly related to the stake in the Church, much of his work is of value on this subject. Of special worth are the following studies by Hartley:

"An Historical Look at the Relationship between Melchizedek Priesthood Quorums and Wards and Stakes," unpublished paper.

"The Priesthood Reorganization of 1877: Brigham Young's Last Achievement," *BYU Studies* 20 (Fall 1979): 3–36.

William Hartley is currently engaged in a study of stakes in the period of Angus Cannon's administration. His projected title is "When Stakes Reached Their Full Flower, 1877–1904."

64. Hartley, "Priesthood Reorganization," p. 5.

65. Ibid., p. 27.

66. Ibid., pp. 20–21.

67. Ibid., pp. 21–22.

68. Angus M. Cannon to John Taylor, 29 March 1887, Letterbooks.

69. Cannon to Taylor, 31 May 1887; Angus M. Cannon to George Q. Cannon, 15 July 1887, Letterbooks.

70. Journal, 8 February 1904.

71. Journal History of The Church of Jesus Christ of Latter-day Saints, LDS Church Archives, 2 April 1904, pp. 10–11; Joseph Fielding Smith, *Essentials in Church History* (Salt Lake City: Deseret Book Company, 1963), p. 713; *Salt Lake Herald,* 29 March 1904.

72. Journal, 19 May 1904.

73. Copy of patriarchal blessing in possession of author. Original is in LDS Church Archives.

74. Journal, 5 December 1906.

75. Journal, 14 August 1910.

76. *Treasury,* pp. 224–25. While it was not unusual to marry sisters, marrying two at once, the first time around was indeed unusual.

77. Ibid., p. 226.

78. Journal, 6 December 1901.

79. Journal, 1 November 1903.

80. Journal, 10 June 1904.

81. Journal, 4 June 1885. His "prison" journals are located in Special Collection, Harold B. Lee Library, Brigham Young University, Provo, Utah. Hereafter such journals will be referred to as Journal, BYU.

82. *Treasury,* pp. 220–23.

83. *Treasury,* pp. 227–29.

84. Barbara Hayward, "The Election of Martha Hughes Cannon," paper submitted to Dr. Eugene E. Campbell, November 1977, Brigham Young University, p. 4. Copy in possession of author.

85. The statement that Mattie considered Angus as "handsome, magnetic, with a gift for language," was made by their daughter Jean Bickmore White, "Martha H. Cannon," *Sister Saints,* ed. Vicki Burgess-Olson, (Provo: BYU Press, 1978), pp. 293–388. It should be noted that Martha was one of the first LDS women medical doctors. For additional information on early LDS women in medicine, see also articles in *Sister Saints* on Dr. Romania Pratt Penrose and Dr. Ellis Reynolds Shipp.

86. Angus M. Cannon to Judge H. McNalley, 19 December 1896, Letterbooks.

87. Journal, 14 February 1889.

88. Journal, 7 February 1902.

89. White, "Martha Cannon," pp. 392–95.

90. *Treasury,* pp. 234–36.

91. Ibid., p. 237.

92. Journal, 23 February 1907.

93. Journal, 26 August 1886.

94. Journal, 24 November 1886.

95. Journal, 11 December 1886.

96. *Treasury,* pp. 210–11. For a more complete account of the trials, see Whitney, *History of Utah,* 3:334–39, 357–58, 363–72. For an insightful account of Mormons who chose not to go to prison, see James B. Allen, "Good Guys vs. Good Guys: Rudger Clawson, John Sharp, and Civil Disobedience in Nineteenth-century Utah," *Utah Historical Quarterly* (Spring

1980), pp. 148–74. For an interesting study of prison experiences of Mormon polygamists, see Melvin L. Bashore, "Life behind Bars: Mormon Cohabs of the 1880's," *Utah Historical Quarterly* (Winter 1979), pp. 22–41.

97. Journal, 8 May 1885, BYU.

98. Journal, 9 May 1885, BYU.

99. This list of items read by Angus during his prison term was compiled from a survey of journal entries made while he was in prison.

100. Journal, 12 August 1885, BYU.

101. Journal, 6 August 1885, BYU.

102. Journal, 14 December 1885, BYU.

103. Journal, 7 January 1888. For more information on this incident, see Donald Q. Cannon, "Angus M. Cannon and David Whitmer: A Comment on History and Historical Method," *BYU Studies* 20 (Spring 1980): 297–99.

104. Journal, 12 October 1905, Angus M. Cannon Papers. Biographical and autobiographical notes, reel 12, box 11, folder 6, LDS Church Archives.

105. Journal, 16 April 1906.

Index